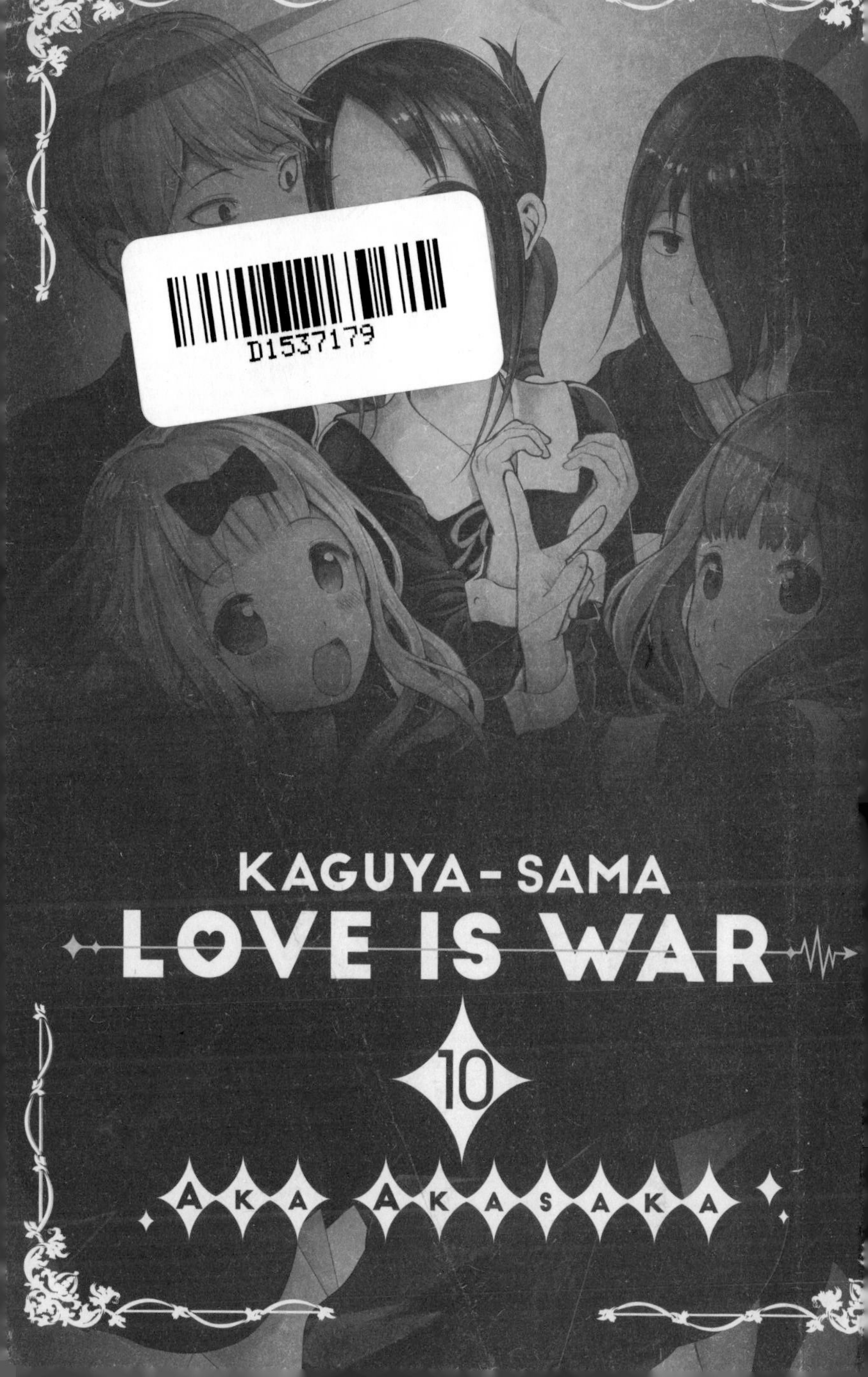

KAGUYA-SAMA
LOVE IS WAR

10

AKA AKASAKA

Meet the Characters!

Kaguya Shinomiya

★ Shuchiin Academy High School Second-Year
★ Student Council Vice President
★ Notable characteristics: stunning beauty
★ Main character

Miyuki Shirogane

★ Shuchiin Academy High School Second-Year
★ Student Council President
★ Notable characteristics: penetrating eyes
★ Main character

Yu Ishigami

★ Shuchiin Academy High School First-Year
★ Student Council Treasurer
★ Notable characteristics: emo bangs
★ Background character

Chika Fujiwara

★ Shuchiin Academy High School Second-Year
★ Student Council Secretary
★ Notable characteristics: soft, poofy, large boobs
★ Supporting character

Ai Hayasaka

★ Shuchiin Academy High School Second-Year
★ Notable characteristics: one-quarter Irish
★ Profession: Kaguya Shinomiya's personal assistant

Miko Ino

★ Shuchiin Academy High School First-Year
★ Student Council Financial Auditor
★ Notable characteristics: short
★ Background character

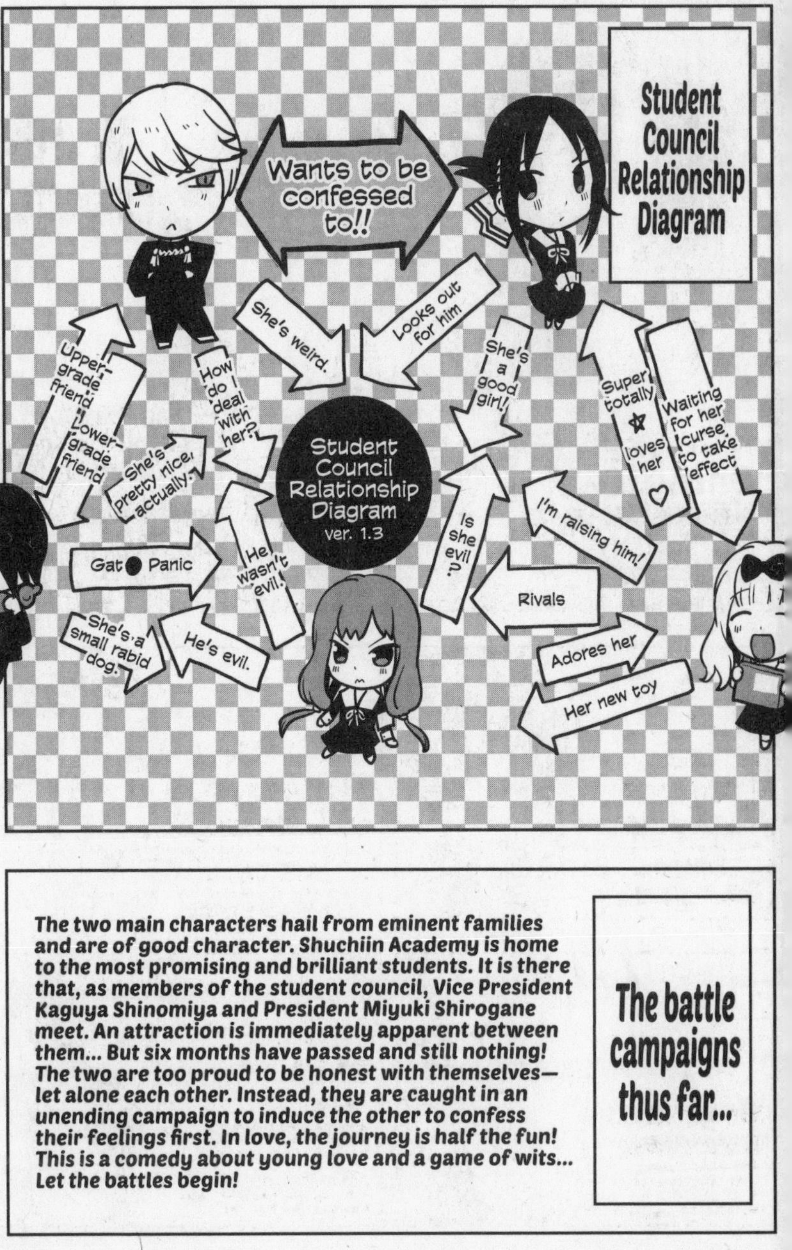
Student Council Relationship Diagram
Wants to be confessed to!!
She's weird.
Looks out for him
Upper-grade friend
Lower-grade friend
How do I deal with her?
She's pretty nice, actually.
Student Council Relationship Diagram
ver. 1.3
She's a good girl!
Super totally ☆ loves her ♡
Waiting for her curse to take effect
I'm raising him!
Is she evil?
Gat● Panic
He wasn't evil.
Rivals
She's a small rabid dog.
He's evil.
Adores her
Her new toy

The battle campaigns thus far...

The two main characters hail from eminent families and are of good character. Shuchiin Academy is home to the most promising and brilliant students. It is there that, as members of the student council, Vice President Kaguya Shinomiya and President Miyuki Shirogane meet. An attraction is immediately apparent between them... But six months have passed and still nothing! The two are too proud to be honest with themselves—let alone each other. Instead, they are caught in an unending campaign to induce the other to confess their feelings first. In love, the journey is half the fun! This is a comedy about young love and a game of wits... Let the battles begin!

KAGUYA-SAMA LOVE IS WAR

BATTLE CAMPAIGNS 10

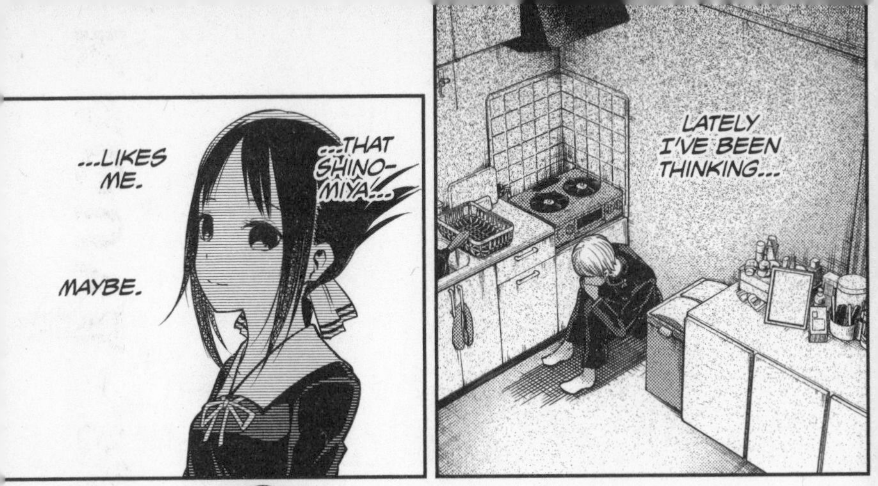
LATELY I'VE BEEN THINKING...
...THAT SHINOMIYA...
...LIKES ME.
MAYBE.

Battle 92
Someone Wants Kaguya to Be Shy

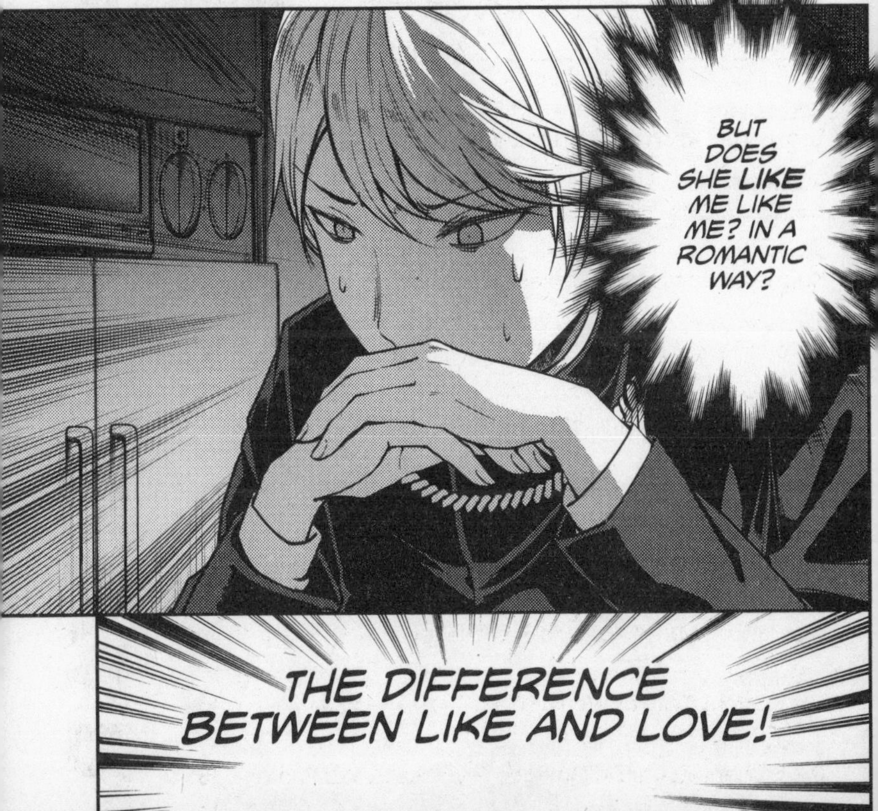
BUT DOES SHE LIKE ME LIKE ME? IN A ROMANTIC WAY?
THE DIFFERENCE BETWEEN LIKE AND LOVE!

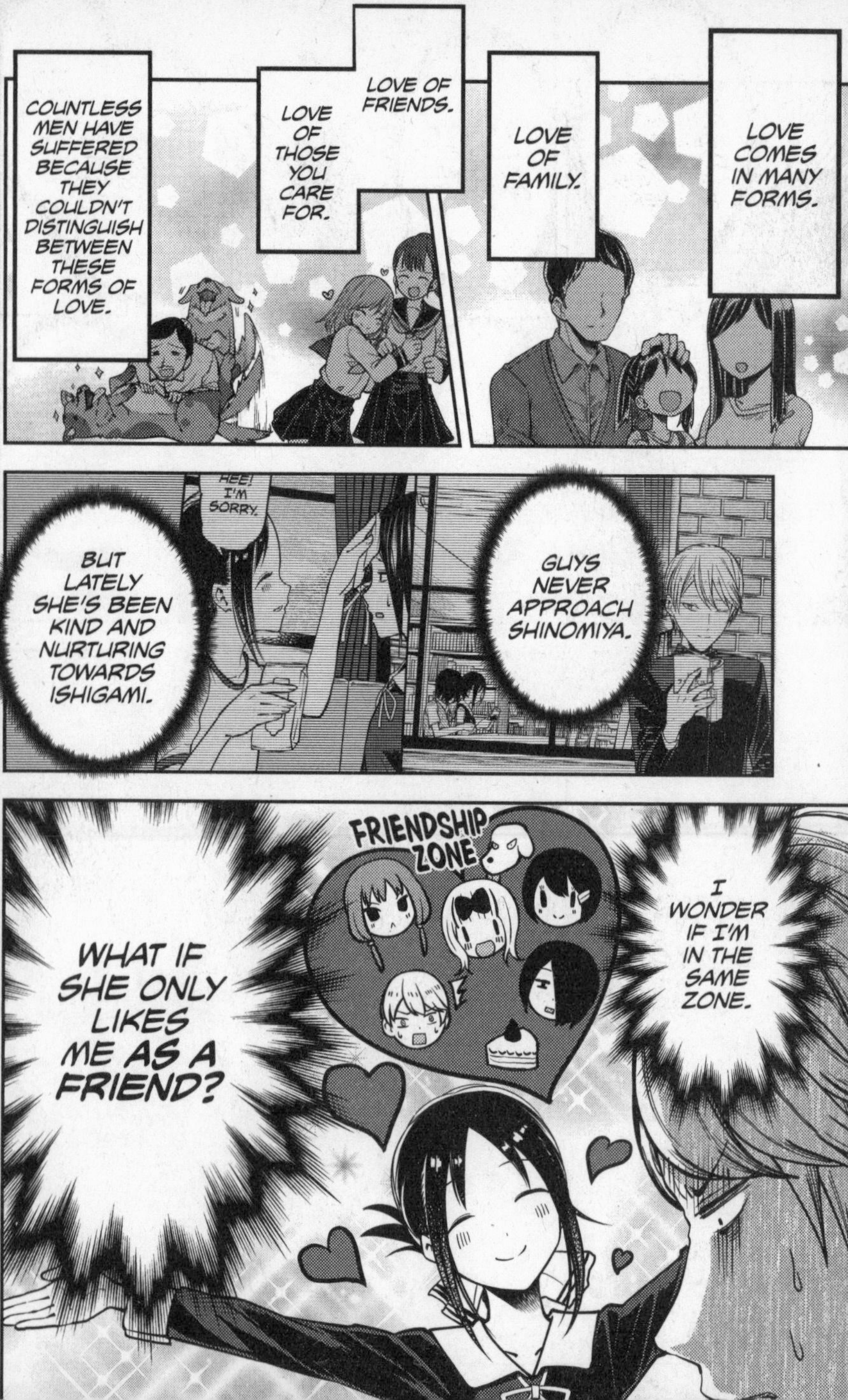
LOVE COMES IN MANY FORMS.
LOVE OF FAMILY.
LOVE OF FRIENDS.
LOVE OF THOSE YOU CARE FOR.
COUNTLESS MEN HAVE SUFFERED BECAUSE THEY COULDN'T DISTINGUISH BETWEEN THESE FORMS OF LOVE.
GUYS NEVER APPROACH SHINOMIYA.
HEE! I'M SORRY.
BUT LATELY SHE'S BEEN KIND AND NURTURING TOWARDS ISHIGAMI.
I WONDER IF I'M IN THE SAME ZONE.
FRIENDSHIP ZONE
WHAT IF SHE ONLY LIKES ME AS A FRIEND?

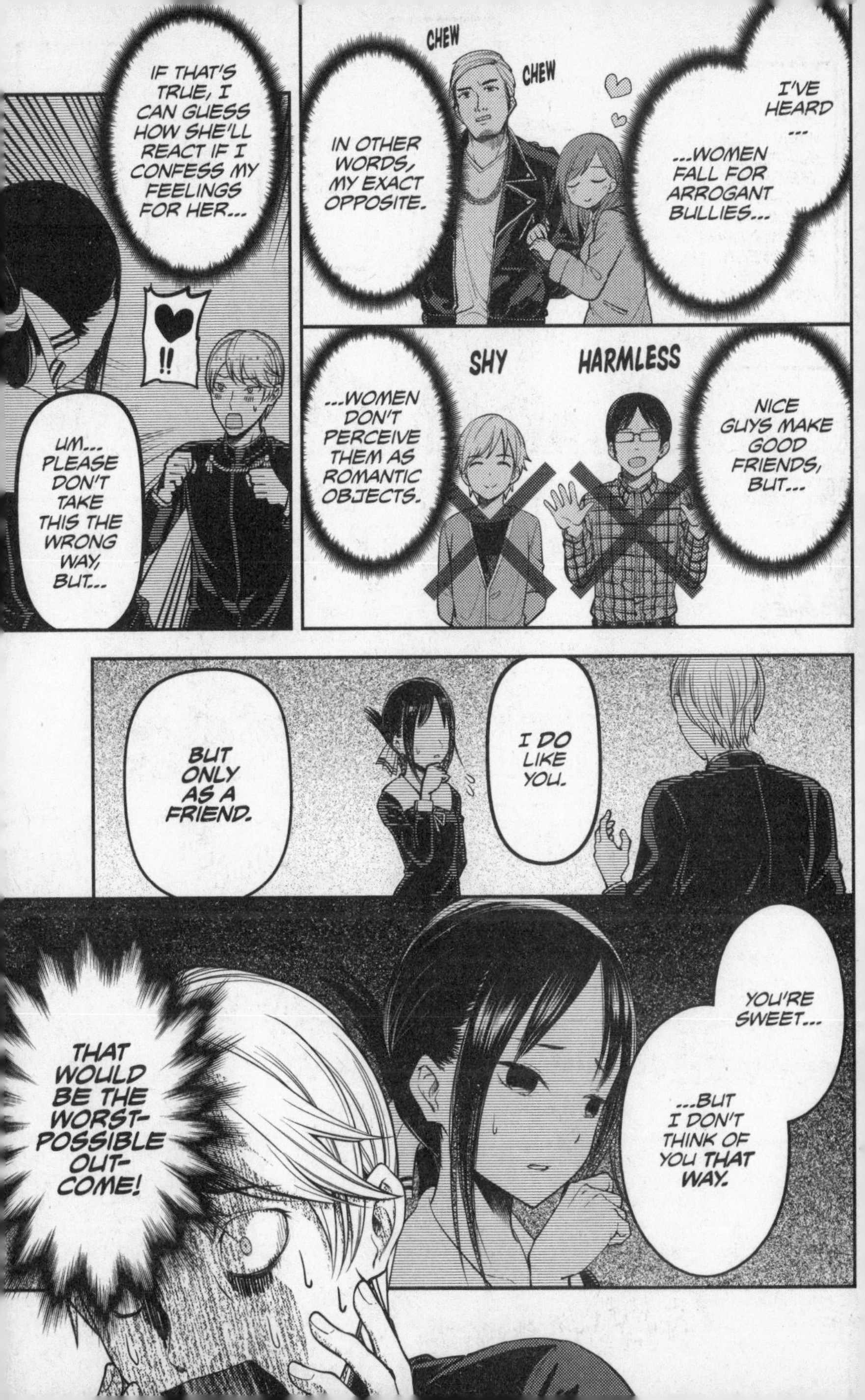
I'VE HEARD ...
...WOMEN FALL FOR ARROGANT BULLIES...
CHEW
CHEW
IN OTHER WORDS, MY EXACT OPPOSITE.
NICE GUYS MAKE GOOD FRIENDS, BUT...
HARMLESS
SHY
...WOMEN DON'T PERCEIVE THEM AS ROMANTIC OBJECTS.
IF THAT'S TRUE, I CAN GUESS HOW SHE'LL REACT IF I CONFESS MY FEELINGS FOR HER...
!!
UM... PLEASE DON'T TAKE THIS THE WRONG WAY, BUT...
I DO LIKE YOU.
BUT ONLY AS A FRIEND.
YOU'RE SWEET...
...BUT I DON'T THINK OF YOU THAT WAY.
THAT WOULD BE THE WORST-POSSIBLE OUT-COME!

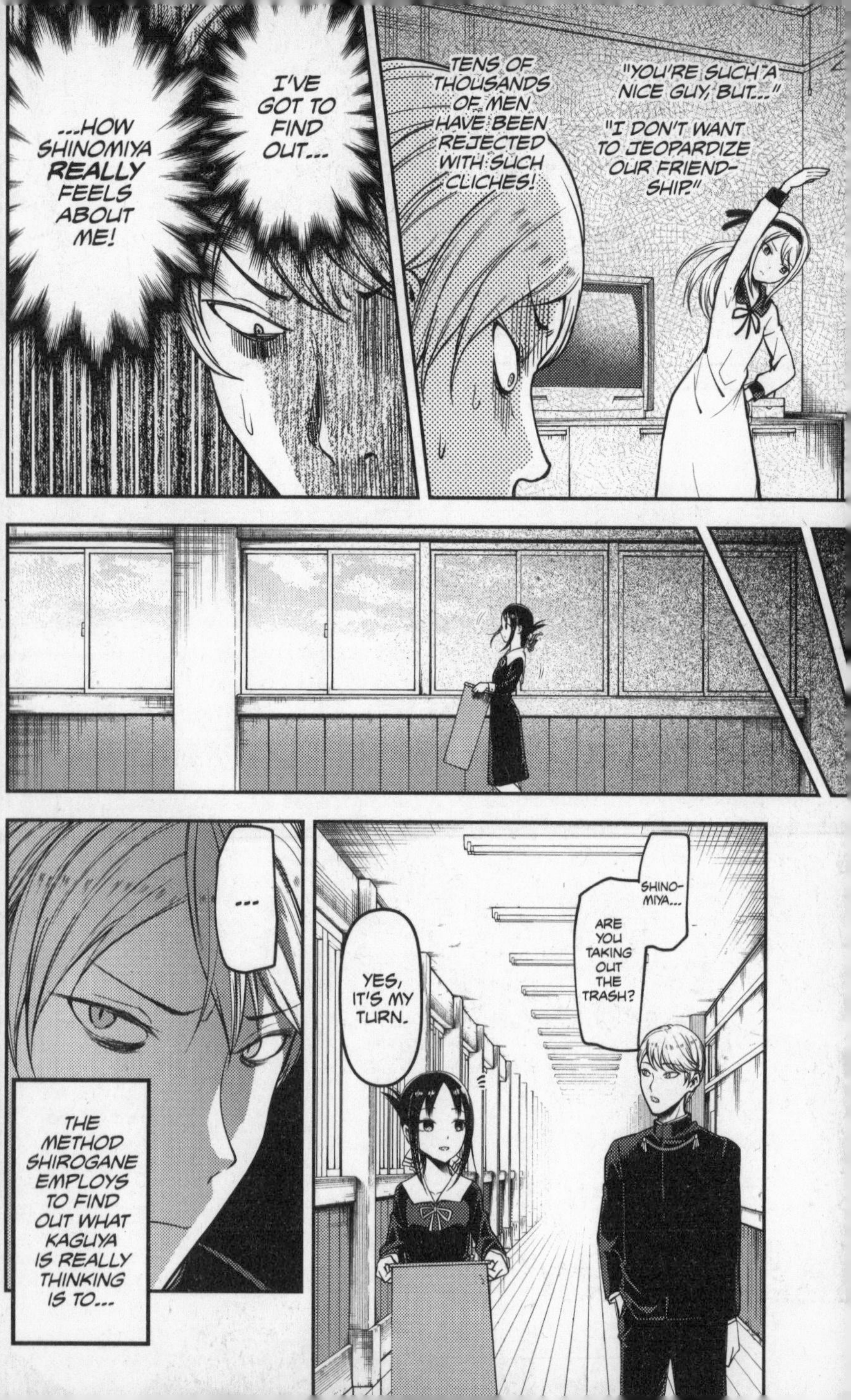
"YOU'RE SUCH A NICE GUY, BUT..."
"I DON'T WANT TO JEOPARDIZE OUR FRIENDSHIP."
TENS OF THOUSANDS OF MEN HAVE BEEN REJECTED WITH SUCH CLICHES!
I'VE GOT TO FIND OUT...
...HOW SHINOMIYA **REALLY** FEELS ABOUT ME!
SHINOMIYA...
ARE YOU TAKING OUT THE TRASH?
YES, IT'S MY TURN.
...
THE METHOD SHIROGANE EMPLOYS TO FIND OUT WHAT KAGUYA IS REALLY THINKING IS TO...

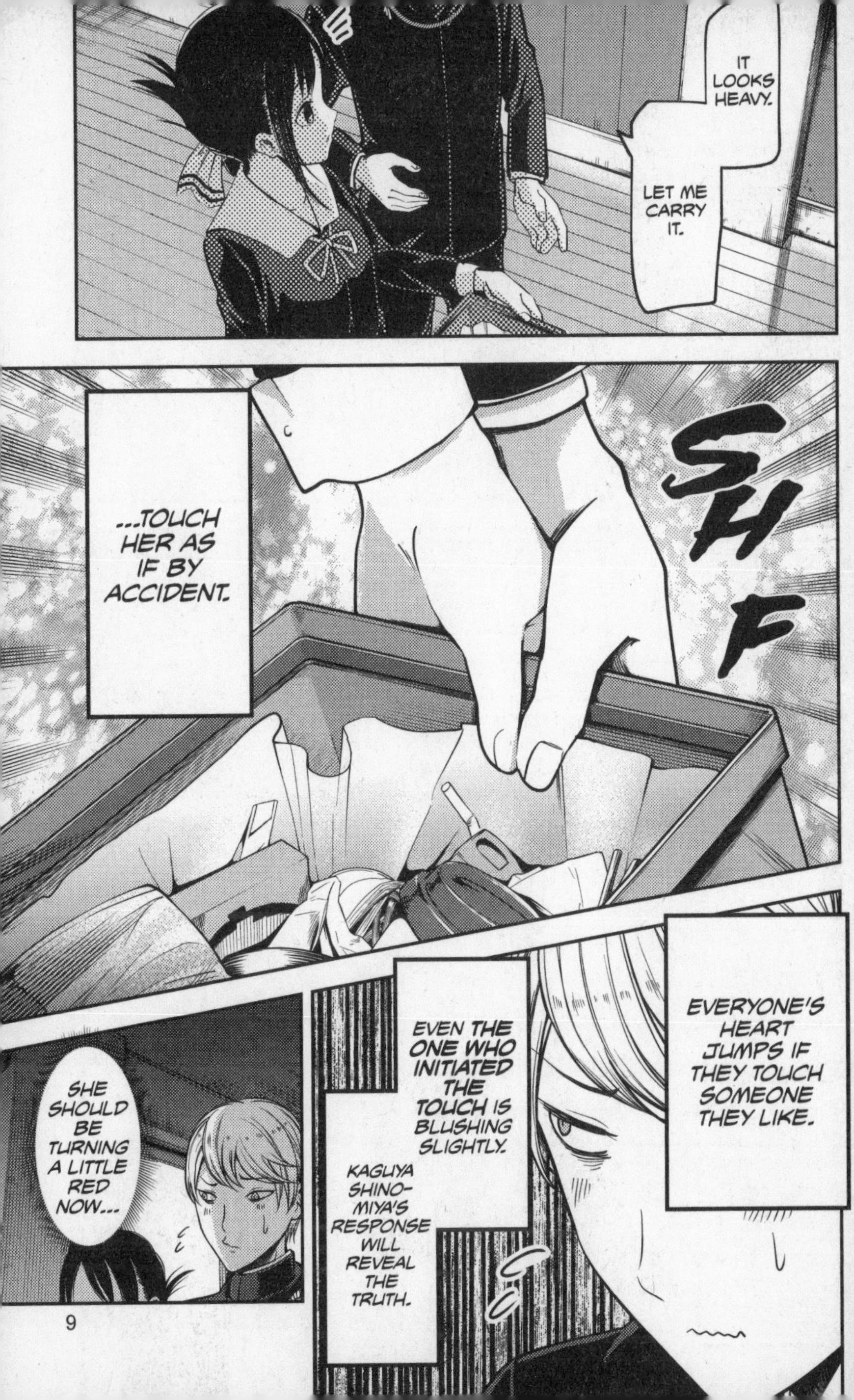
IT LOOKS HEAVY.
LET ME CARRY IT.
SHF
...TOUCH HER AS IF BY ACCIDENT.
EVERYONE'S HEART JUMPS IF THEY TOUCH SOMEONE THEY LIKE.
EVEN THE ONE WHO INITIATED THE TOUCH IS BLUSHING SLIGHTLY.
KAGUYA SHINOMIYA'S RESPONSE WILL REVEAL THE TRUTH.
SHE SHOULD BE TURNING A LITTLE RED NOW...

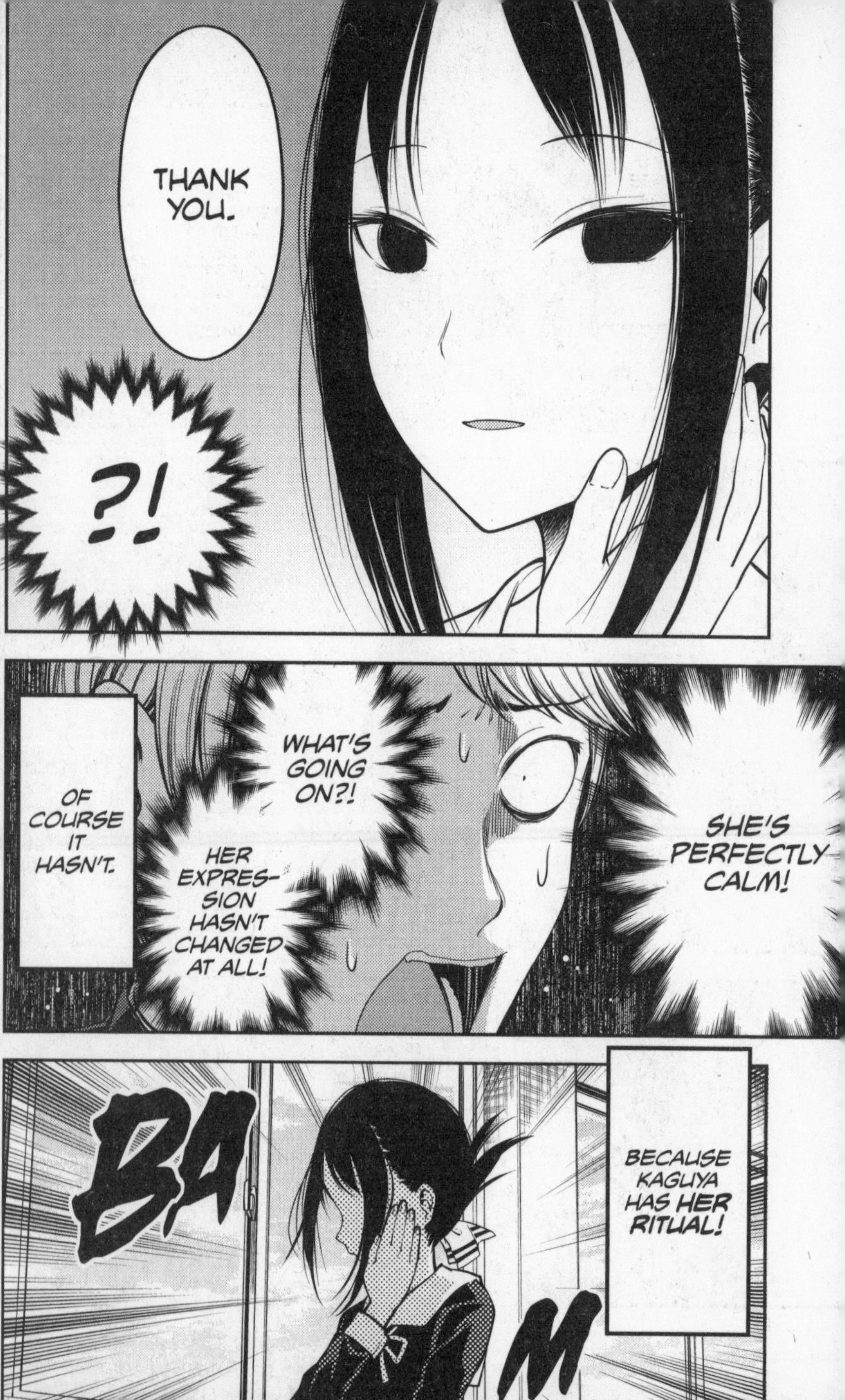
THANK YOU.
?!
SHE'S PERFECTLY CALM!
WHAT'S GOING ON?!
HER EXPRESSION HASN'T CHANGED AT ALL!
OF COURSE IT HASN'T.
BECAUSE KAGUYA HAS HER RITUAL!
BAM

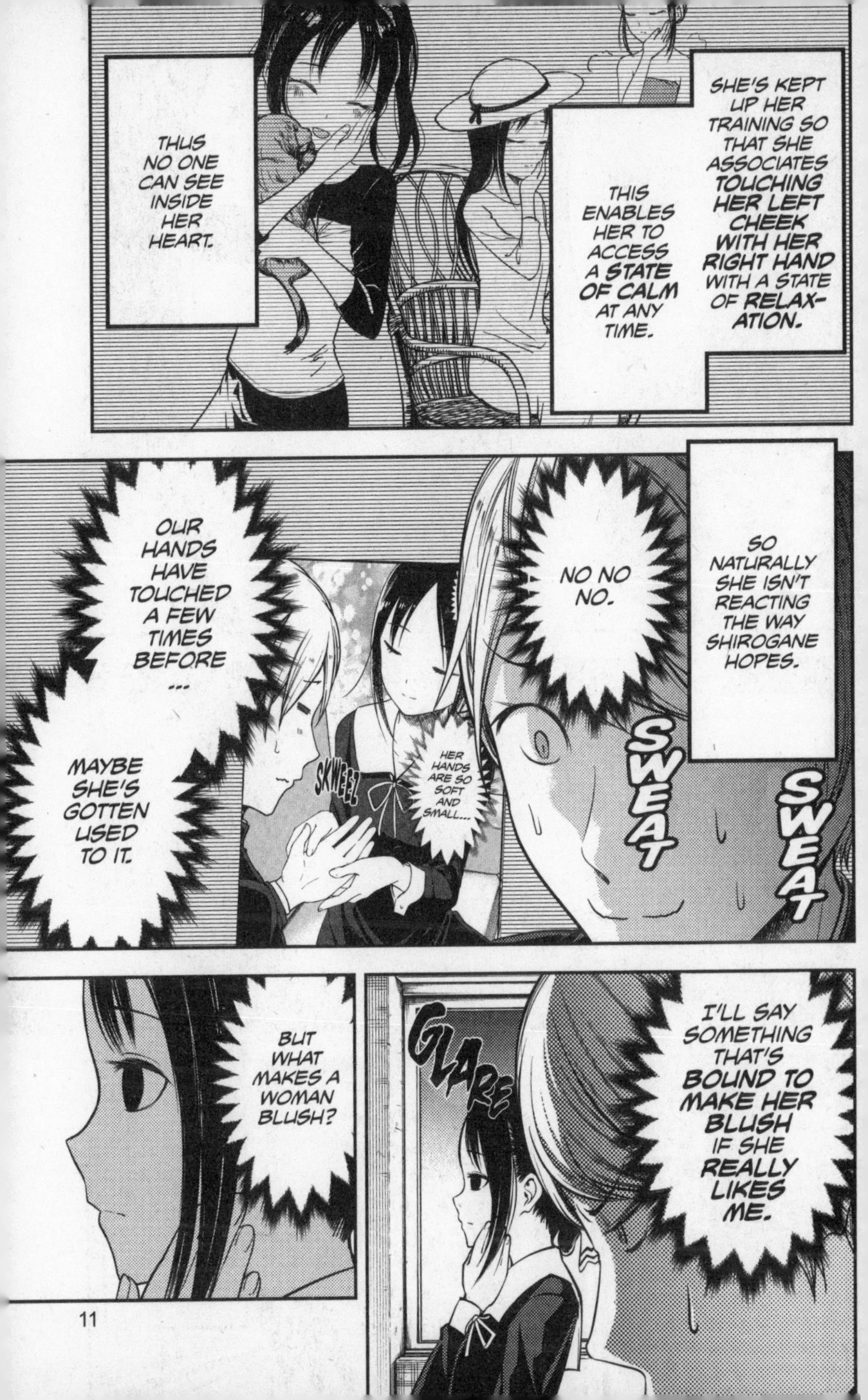
SHE'S KEPT UP HER TRAINING SO THAT SHE ASSOCIATES TOUCHING HER LEFT CHEEK WITH HER RIGHT HAND WITH A STATE OF RELAXATION.
THIS ENABLES HER TO ACCESS A STATE OF CALM AT ANY TIME.
THUS NO ONE CAN SEE INSIDE HER HEART.
SO NATURALLY SHE ISN'T REACTING THE WAY SHIROGANE HOPES.
NO NO NO.
SWEAT
SWEAT
HER HANDS ARE SO SOFT AND SMALL...
SKWEEL
OUR HANDS HAVE TOUCHED A FEW TIMES BEFORE...
MAYBE SHE'S GOTTEN USED TO IT.
I'LL SAY SOMETHING THAT'S BOUND TO MAKE HER BLUSH IF SHE REALLY LIKES ME.
GLARE
BUT WHAT MAKES A WOMAN BLUSH?

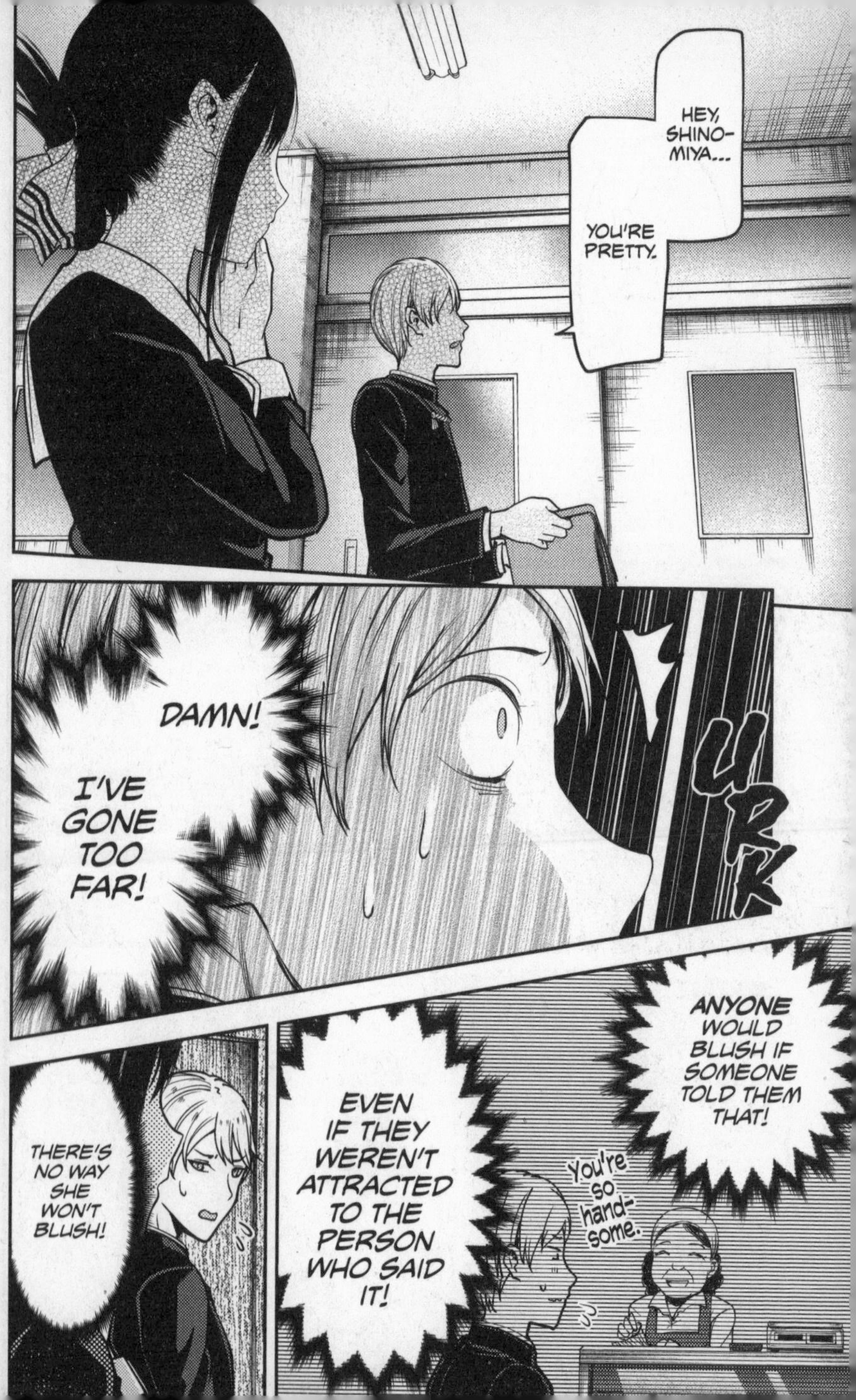
HEY, SHINO-MIYA...
YOU'RE PRETTY.
URK
DAMN!
I'VE GONE TOO FAR!
ANYONE WOULD BLUSH IF SOMEONE TOLD THEM THAT!
You're so hand-some.
EVEN IF THEY WEREN'T ATTRACTED TO THE PERSON WHO SAID IT!
THERE'S NO WAY SHE WON'T BLUSH!

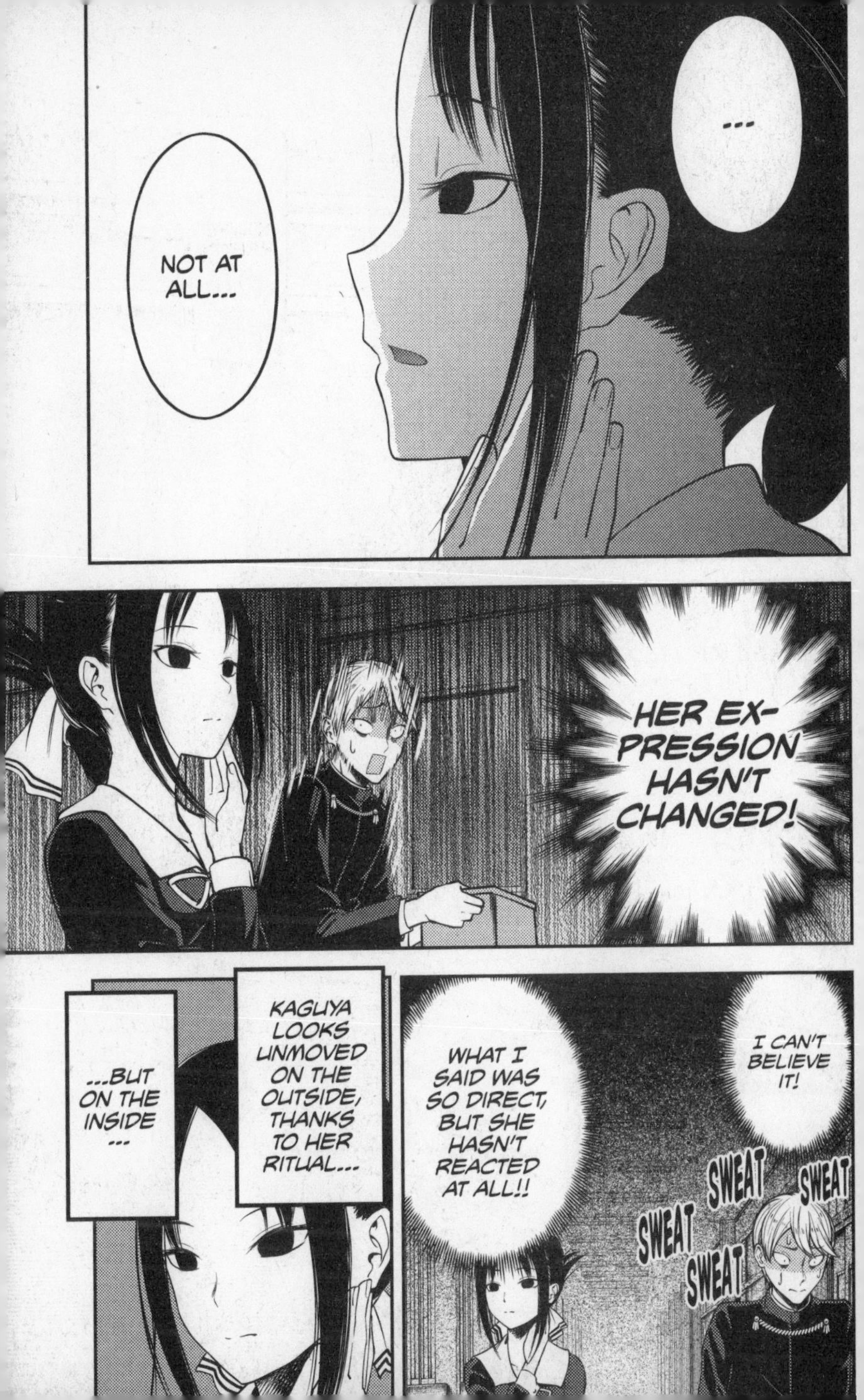
...
NOT AT ALL...
HER EX-PRESSION HASN'T CHANGED!
I CAN'T BELIEVE IT!
WHAT I SAID WAS SO DIRECT, BUT SHE HASN'T REACTED AT ALL!!
SWEAT
SWEAT
SWEAT
SWEAT
KAGUYA LOOKS UNMOVED ON THE OUTSIDE, THANKS TO HER RITUAL...
...BUT ON THE INSIDE...

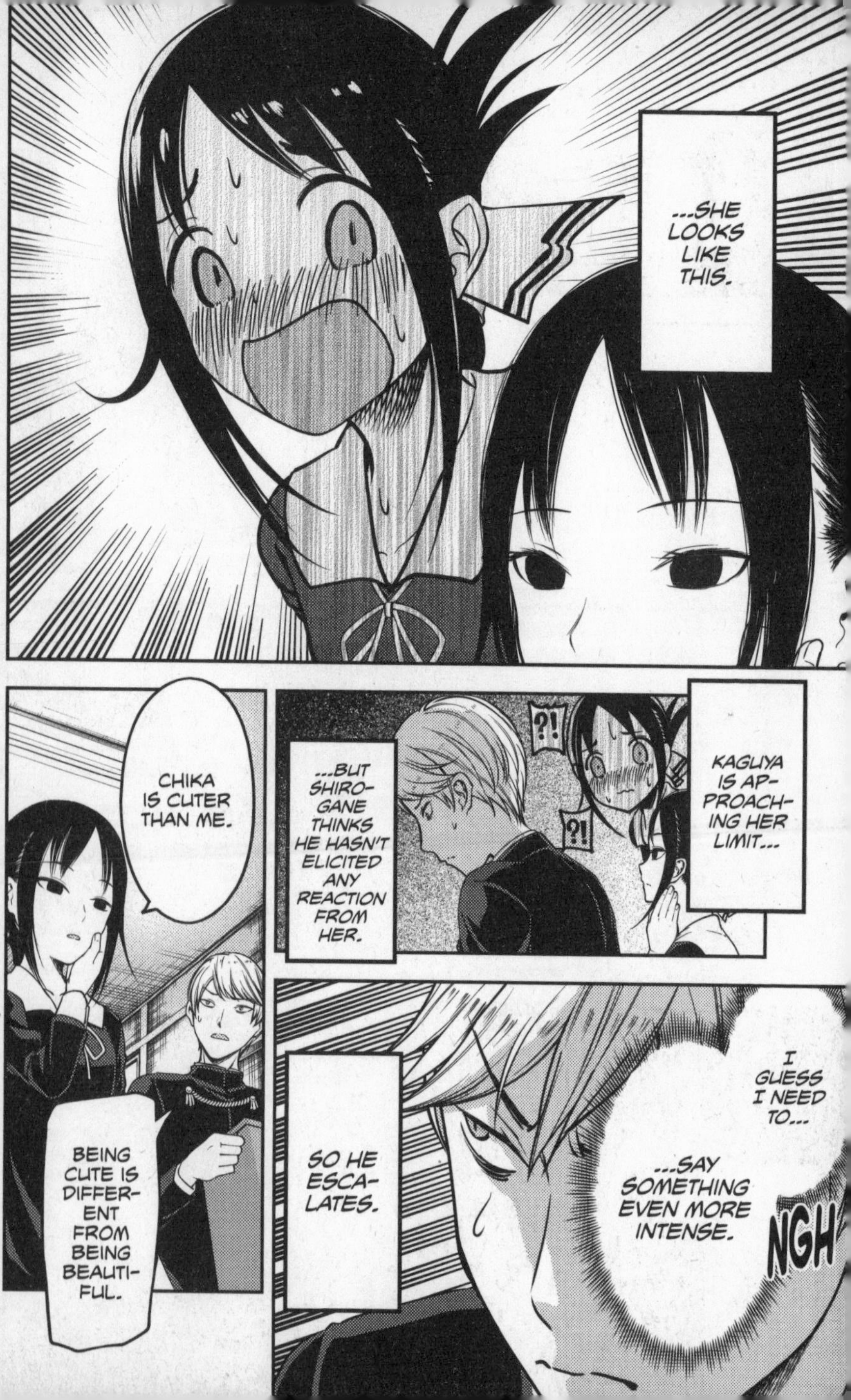
...SHE LOOKS LIKE THIS.
KAGUYA IS APPROACHING HER LIMIT...
?!
?!
...BUT SHIROGANE THINKS HE HASN'T ELICITED ANY REACTION FROM HER.
I GUESS I NEED TO...
...SAY SOMETHING EVEN MORE INTENSE.
NGH
SO HE ESCALATES.
CHIKA IS CUTER THAN ME.
BEING CUTE IS DIFFERENT FROM BEING BEAUTIFUL.

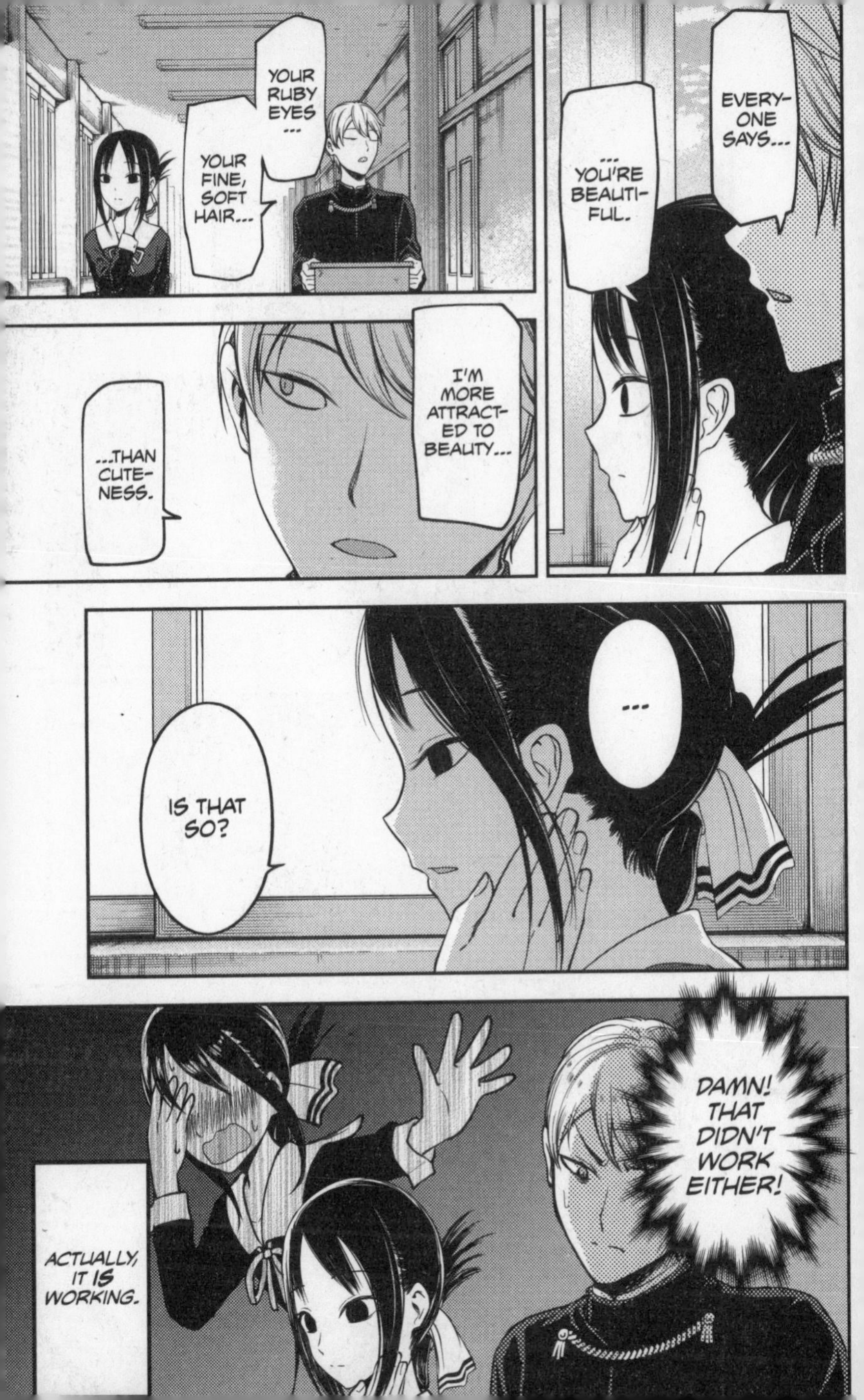
EVERYONE SAYS...
...YOU'RE BEAUTIFUL.
YOUR RUBY EYES...
YOUR FINE, SOFT HAIR...
I'M MORE ATTRACTED TO BEAUTY...
...THAN CUTENESS.
...
IS THAT SO?
DAMN! THAT DIDN'T WORK EITHER!
ACTUALLY, IT IS WORKING.

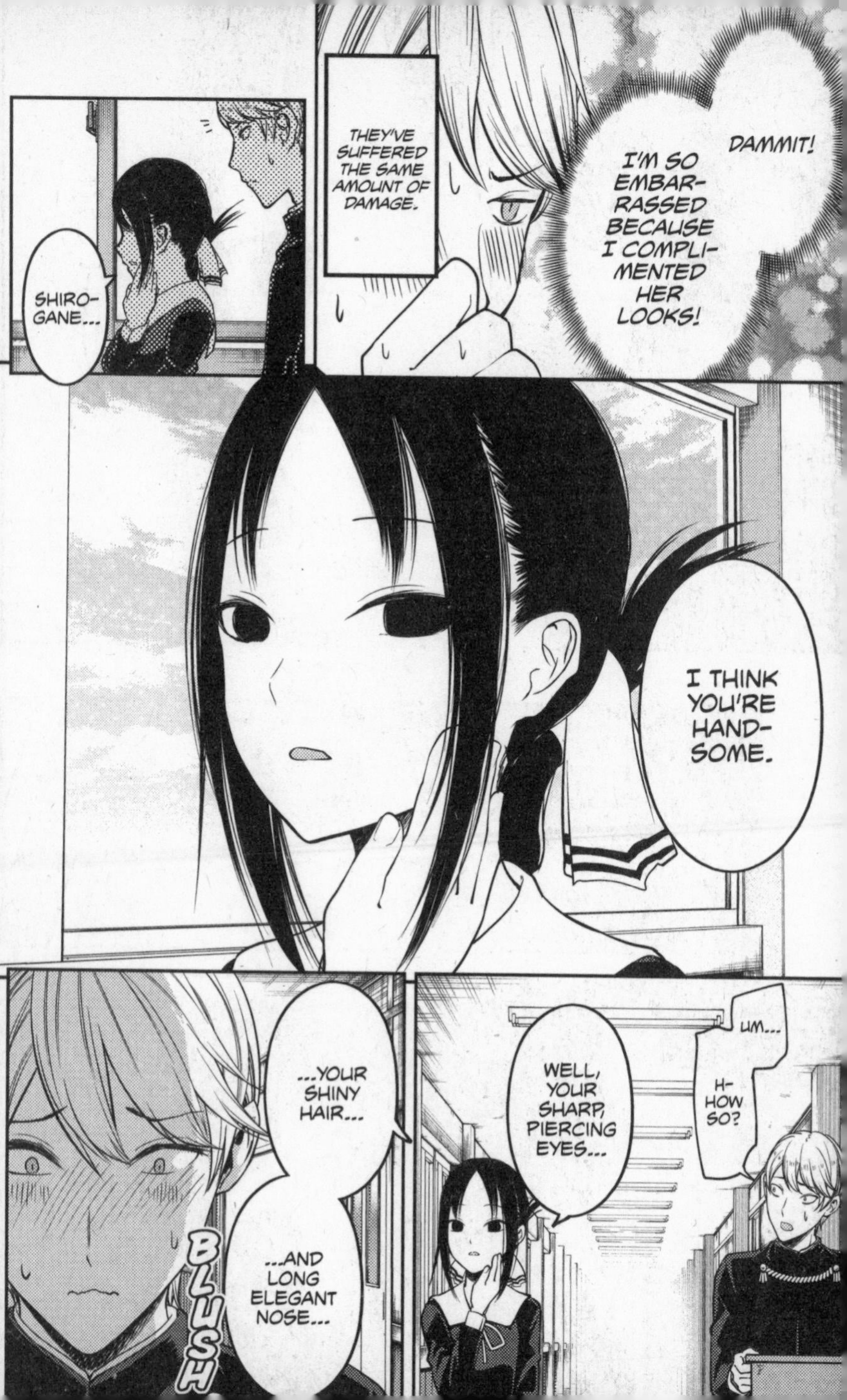
DAMMIT!
I'M SO EMBAR-RASSED BECAUSE I COMPLI-MENTED HER LOOKS!
THEY'VE SUFFERED THE SAME AMOUNT OF DAMAGE.
SHIRO-GANE...
I THINK YOU'RE HAND-SOME.
UM...
H-HOW SO?
WELL, YOUR SHARP, PIERCING EYES...
...YOUR SHINY HAIR...
...AND LONG ELEGANT NOSE...
BLUSH

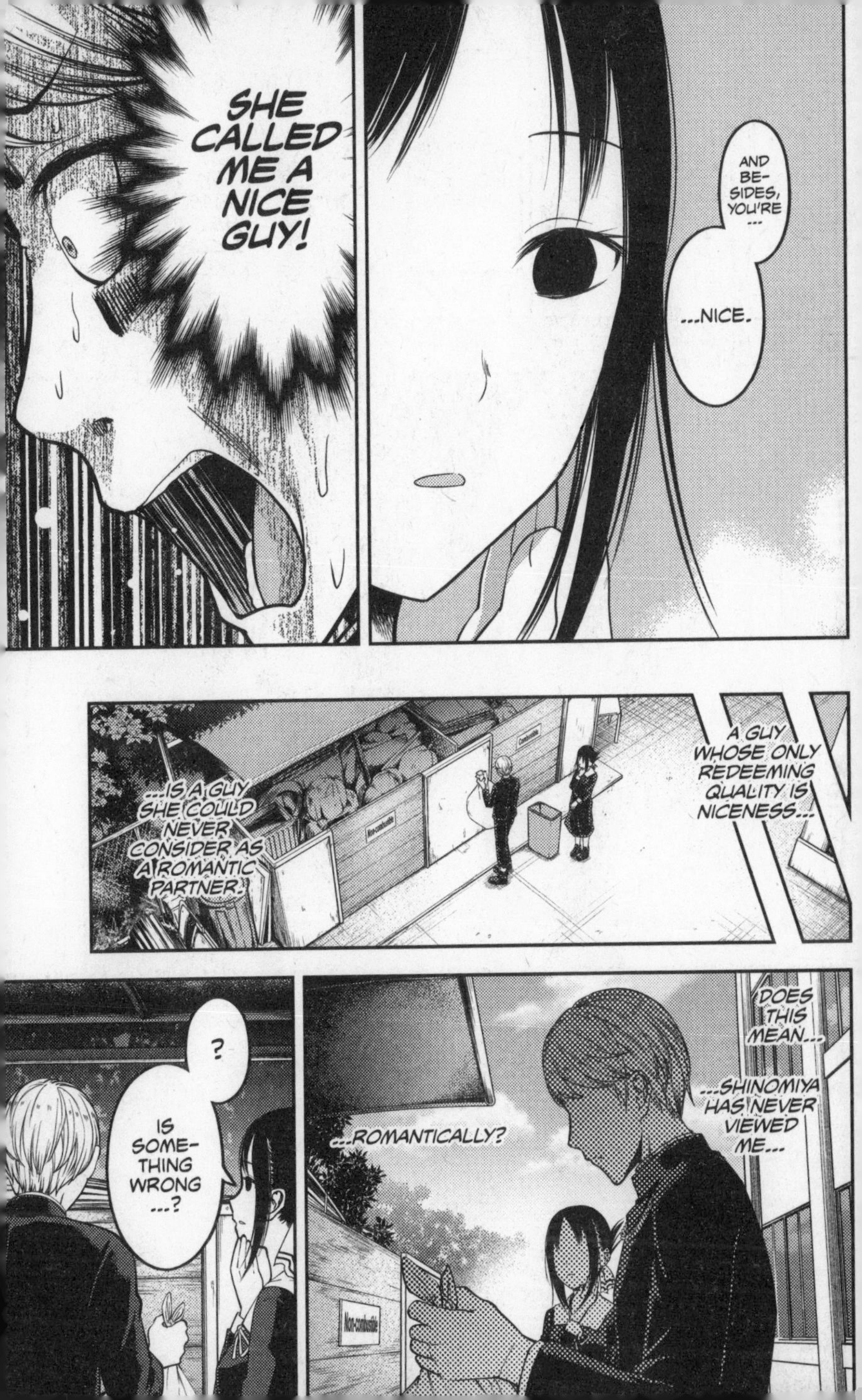
AND BE- SIDES, YOU'RE ...
...NICE.
SHE CALLED ME A NICE GUY!
A GUY WHOSE ONLY REDEEMING QUALITY IS NICENESS...
...IS A GUY SHE COULD NEVER CONSIDER AS A ROMANTIC PARTNER.
DOES THIS MEAN...
...SHINOMIYA HAS NEVER VIEWED ME...
...ROMANTICALLY?
Non-combustible
?
IS SOME- THING WRONG ...?

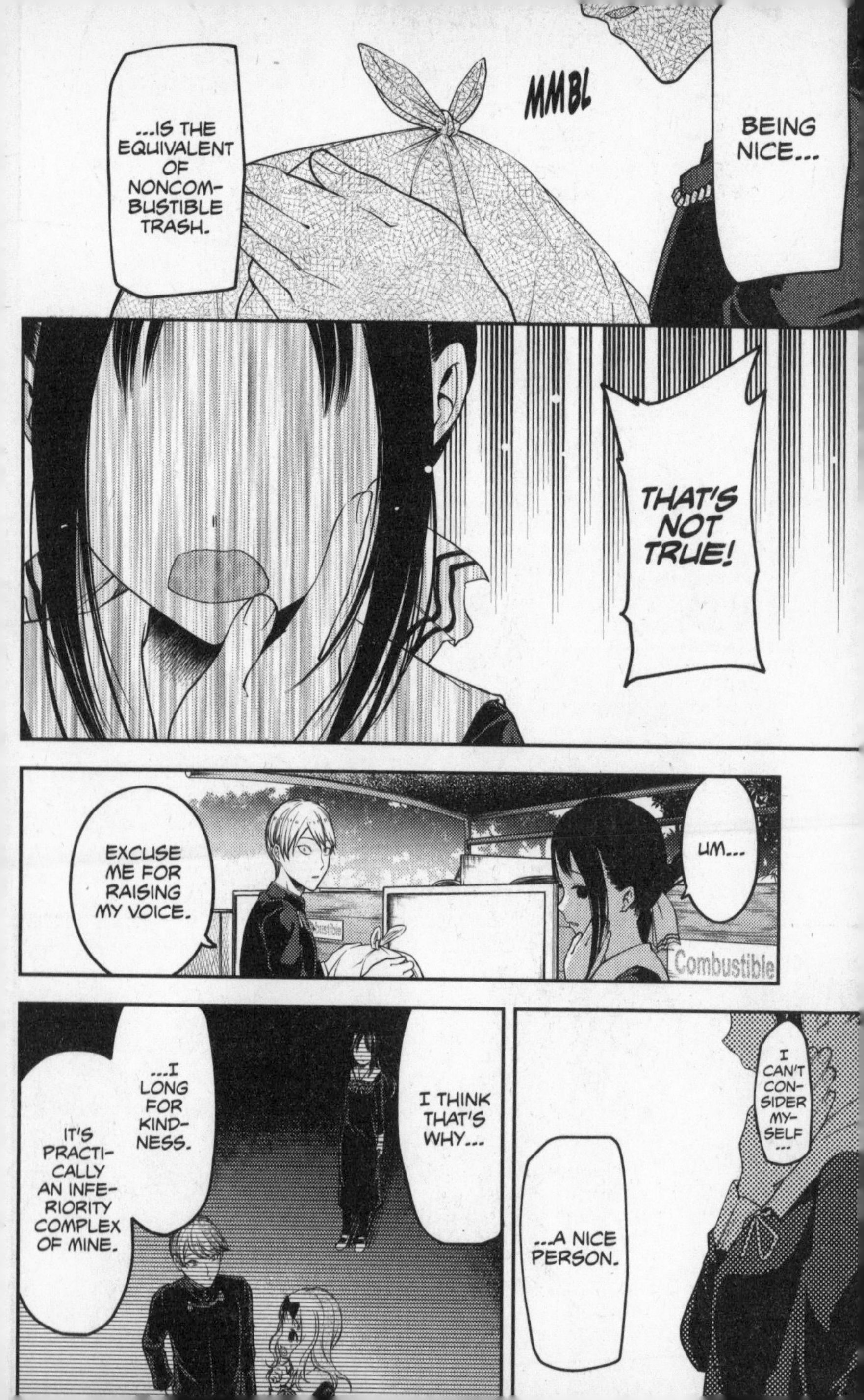
BEING NICE...
MMBL
...IS THE EQUIVALENT OF NONCOMBUSTIBLE TRASH.
THAT'S NOT TRUE!
UM...
EXCUSE ME FOR RAISING MY VOICE.
Combustible
I CAN'T CONSIDER MYSELF...
...A NICE PERSON.
I THINK THAT'S WHY...
...I LONG FOR KINDNESS.
IT'S PRACTICALLY AN INFERIORITY COMPLEX OF MINE.

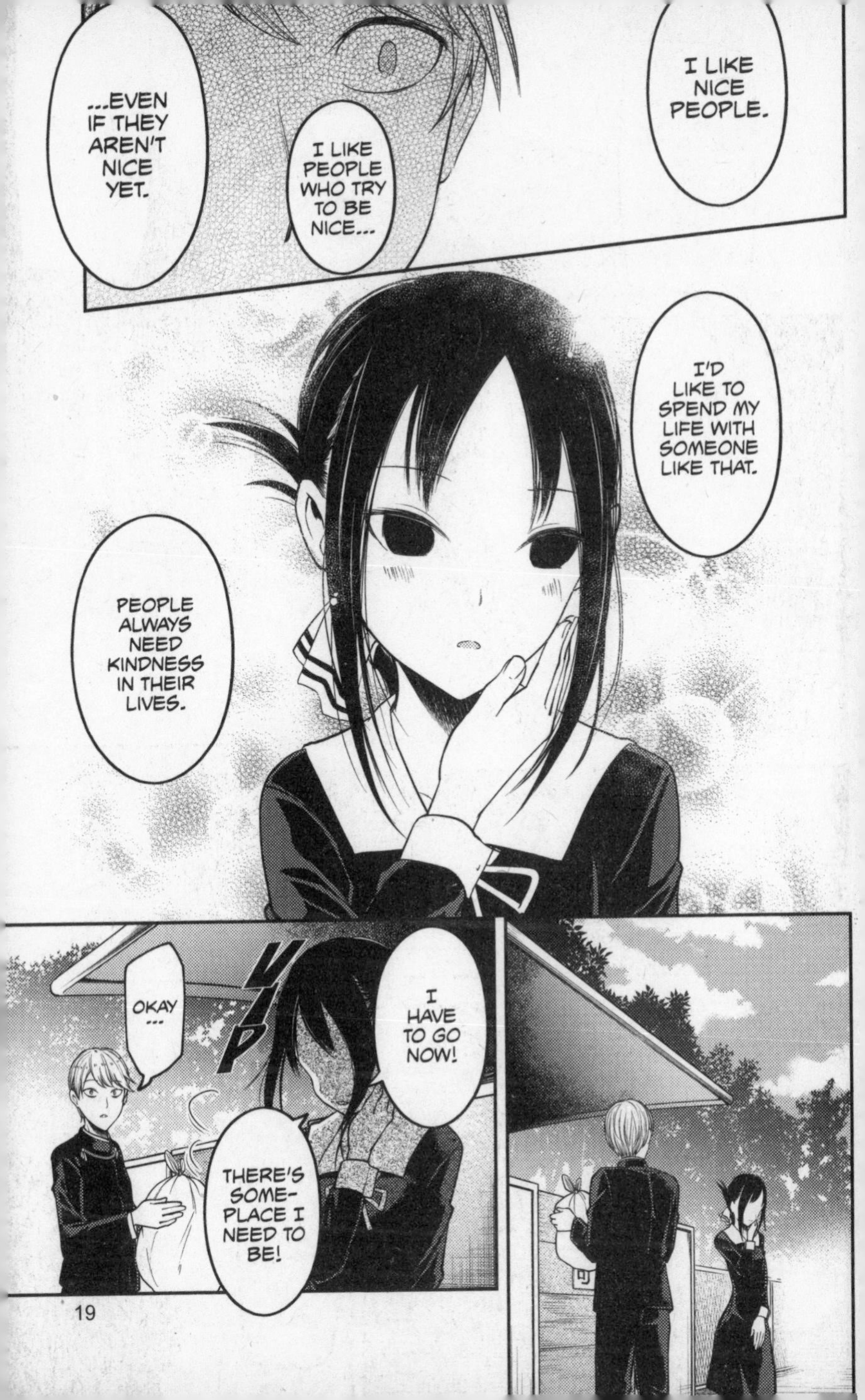
I LIKE NICE PEOPLE.
I LIKE PEOPLE WHO TRY TO BE NICE...
...EVEN IF THEY AREN'T NICE YET.
I'D LIKE TO SPEND MY LIFE WITH SOMEONE LIKE THAT.
PEOPLE ALWAYS NEED KINDNESS IN THEIR LIVES.
I HAVE TO GO NOW!
THERE'S SOME-PLACE I NEED TO BE!
OKAY...

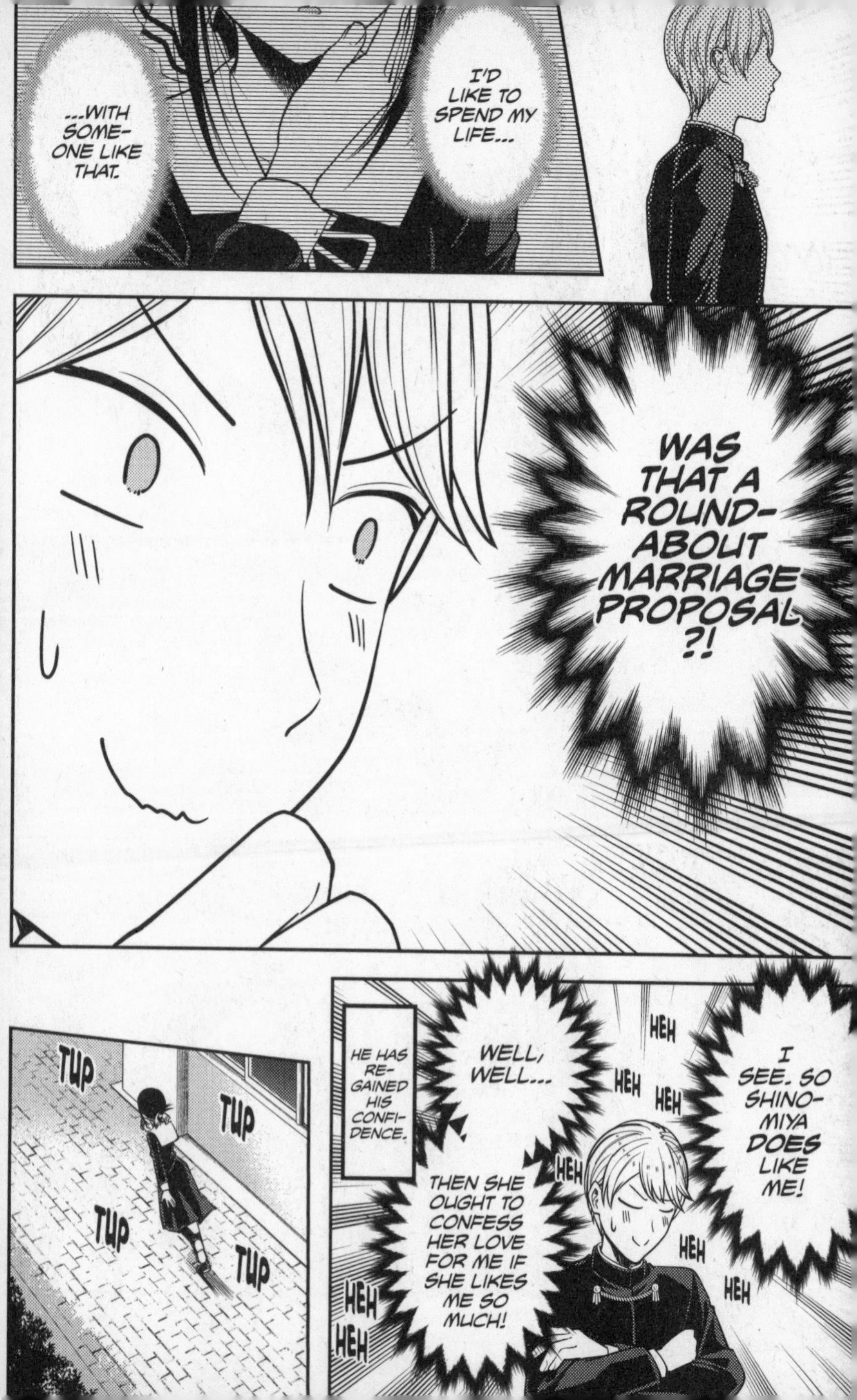
I'D LIKE TO SPEND MY LIFE...
...WITH SOME-ONE LIKE THAT.
WAS THAT A ROUND-ABOUT MARRIAGE PROPOSAL ?!
I SEE. SO SHINO-MIYA DOES LIKE ME!
HEH
HEH
HEH
HEH
HEH
HEH
WELL, WELL...
HE HAS RE-GAINED HIS CONFI-DENCE.
THEN SHE OUGHT TO CONFESS HER LOVE FOR ME IF SHE LIKES ME SO MUCH!
HEH
HEH
TUP
TUP
TUP
TUP

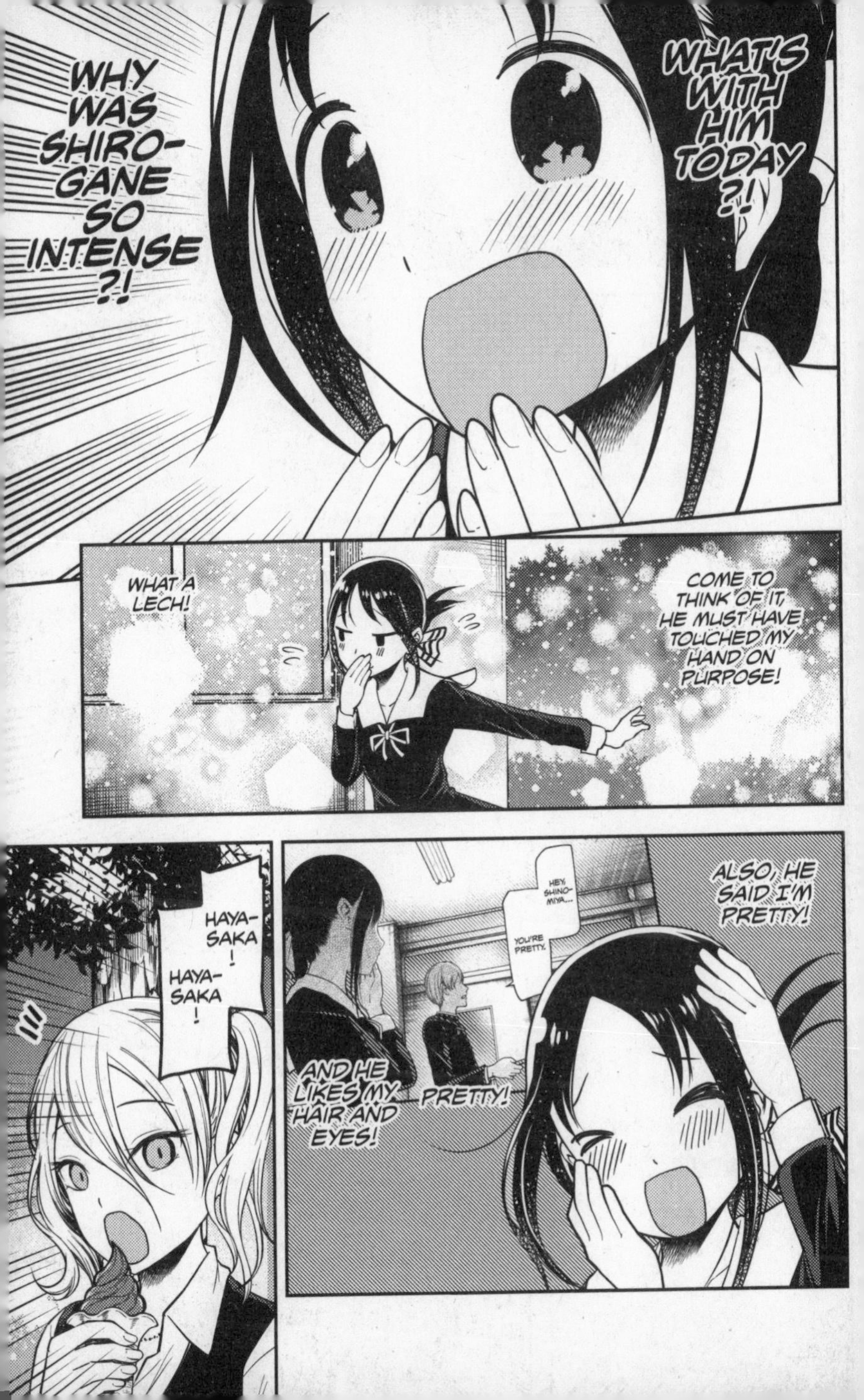

WHAT'S WITH HIM TODAY?!
WHY WAS SHIRO-GANE SO INTENSE?!
COME TO THINK OF IT, HE MUST HAVE TOUCHED MY HAND ON PURPOSE!
WHAT A LECH!
ALSO, HE SAID I'M PRETTY!
HEY, SHINO-MIYA...
YOU'RE PRETTY.
PRETTY!
AND HE LIKES MY HAIR AND EYES!
HAYA-SAKA! HAYA-SAKA!
!!!

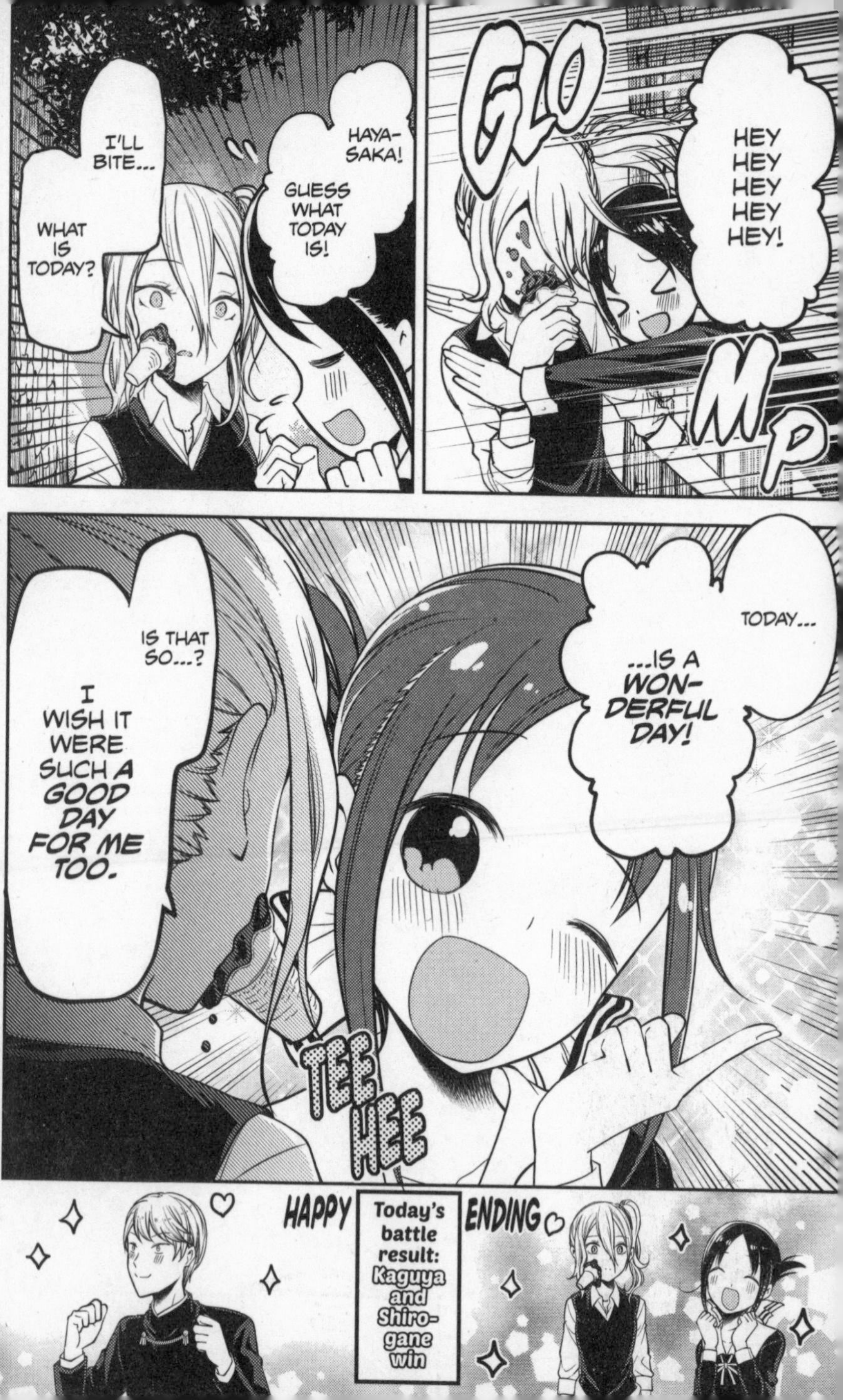
GLO
HEY HEY HEY HEY HEY!
MP
HAYA-SAKA!
GUESS WHAT TODAY IS!
I'LL BITE...
WHAT IS TODAY?
TODAY...
...IS A WON-DERFUL DAY!
TEE HEE
IS THAT SO...?
I WISH IT WERE SUCH A GOOD DAY FOR ME TOO.
HAPPY ENDING
Today's battle result: Kaguya and Shiro-gane win

I've gotta take this back too?!

Hey!

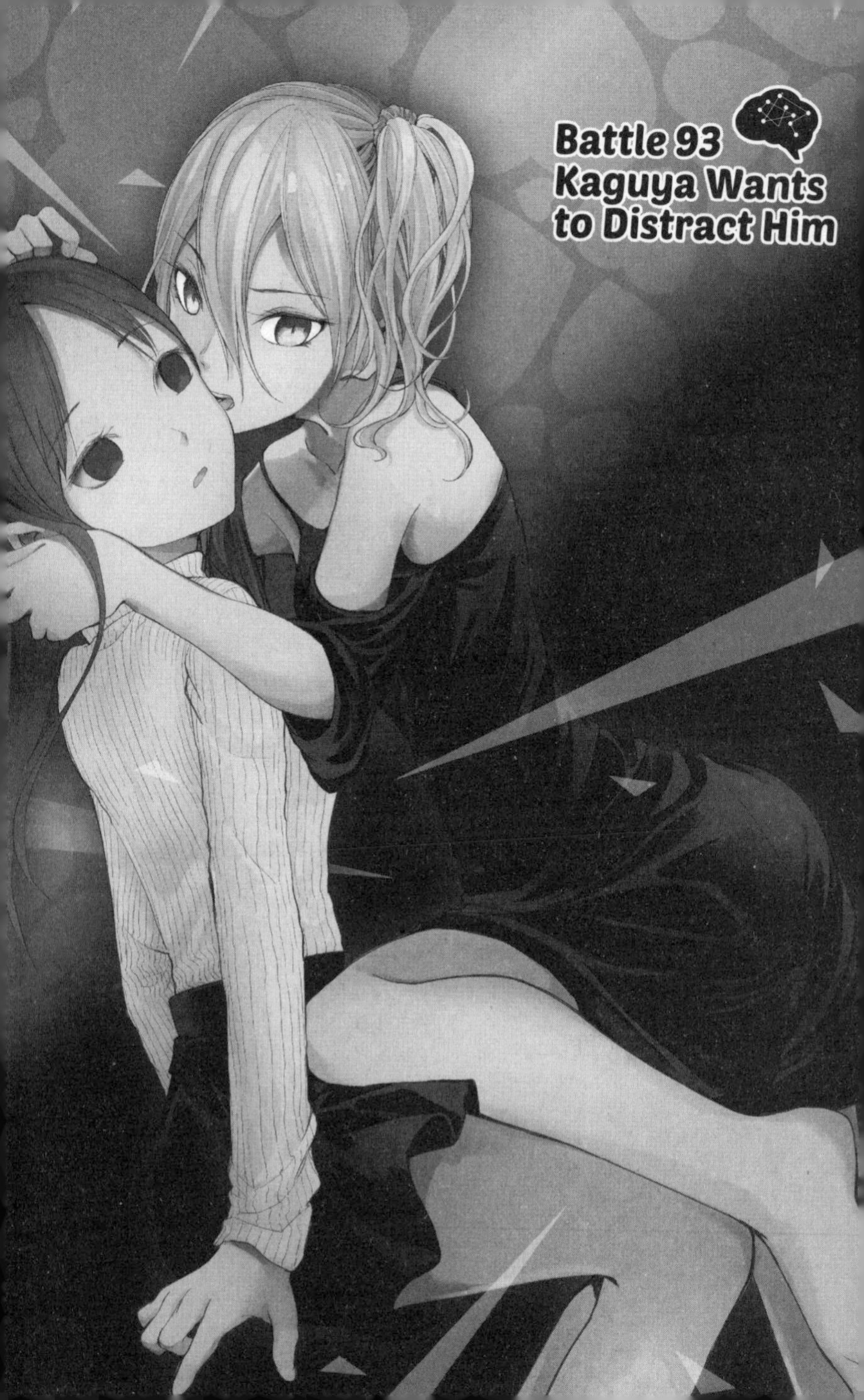
Battle 93
Kaguya Wants to Distract Him

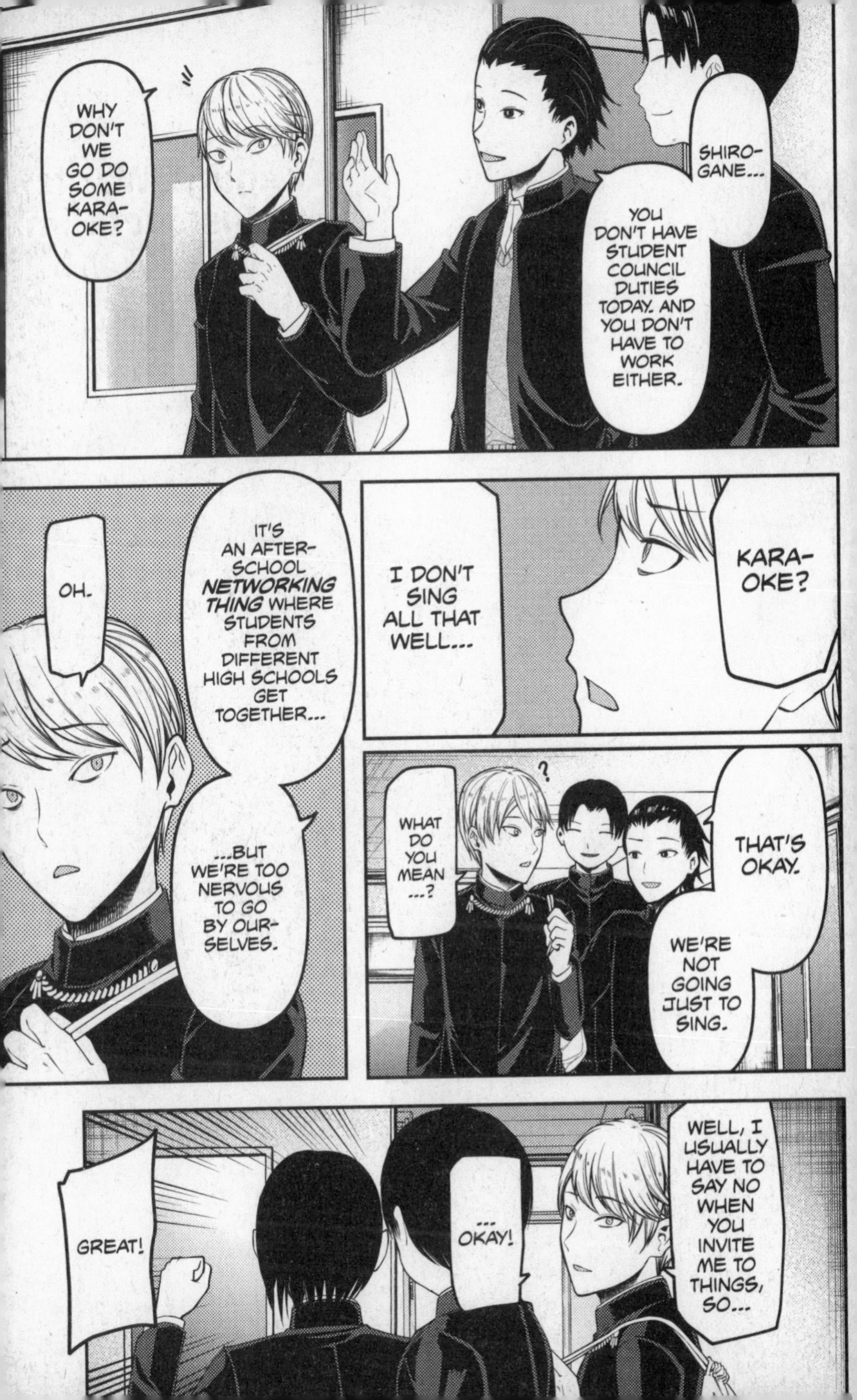
SHIRO-GANE...
YOU DON'T HAVE STUDENT COUNCIL DUTIES TODAY. AND YOU DON'T HAVE TO WORK EITHER.
WHY DON'T WE GO DO SOME KARA-OKE?
KARA-OKE?
I DON'T SING ALL THAT WELL...
THAT'S OKAY.
WE'RE NOT GOING JUST TO SING.
WHAT DO YOU MEAN...?
IT'S AN AFTER-SCHOOL NETWORKING THING WHERE STUDENTS FROM DIFFERENT HIGH SCHOOLS GET TOGETHER...
...BUT WE'RE TOO NERVOUS TO GO BY OUR-SELVES.
OH.
WELL, I USUALLY HAVE TO SAY NO WHEN YOU INVITE ME TO THINGS, SO...
...OKAY!
GREAT!

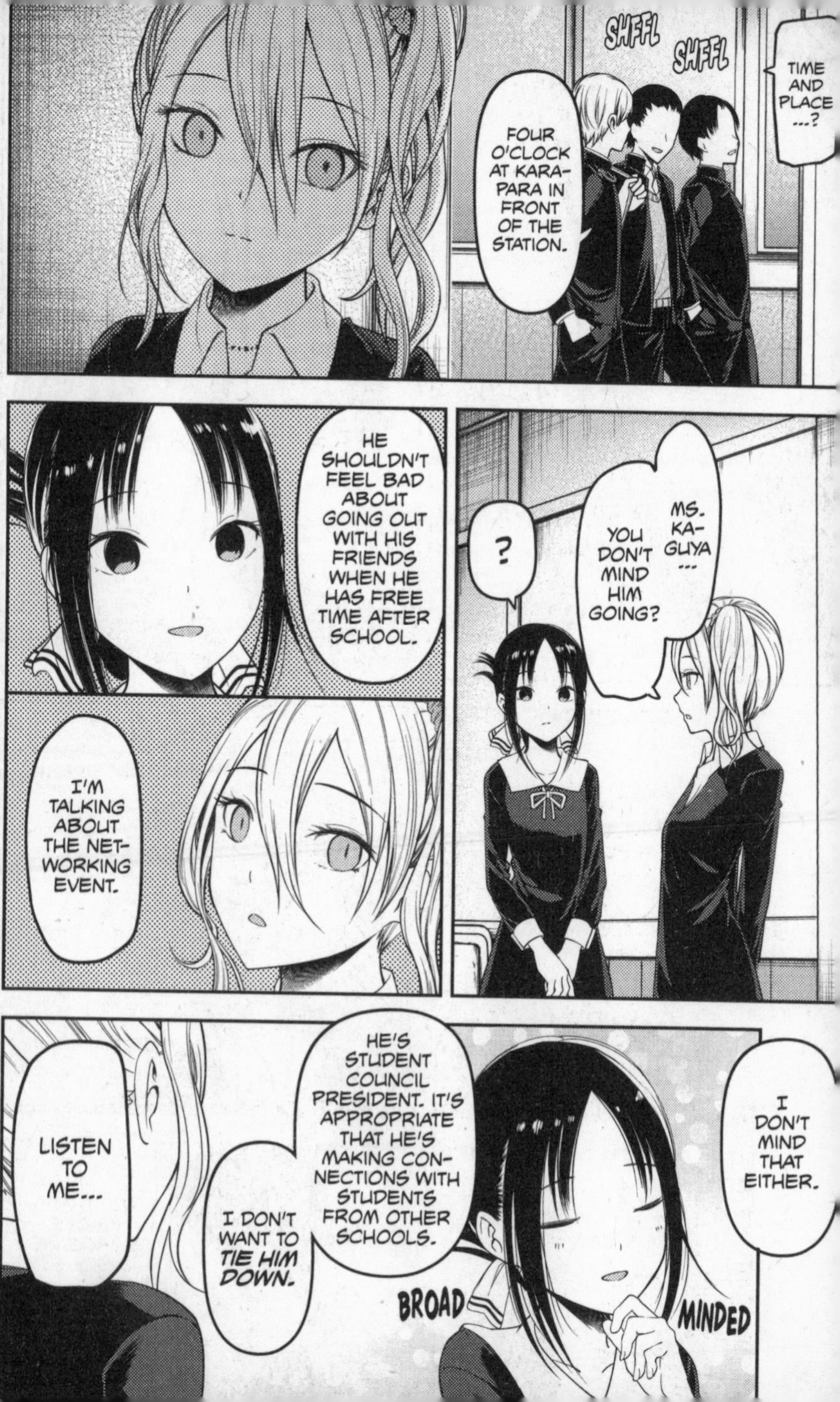
SHFFL
SHFFL
TIME AND PLACE...?
FOUR O'CLOCK AT KARA-PARA IN FRONT OF THE STATION.
MS. KAGUYA... YOU DON'T MIND HIM GOING?
?
HE SHOULDN'T FEEL BAD ABOUT GOING OUT WITH HIS FRIENDS WHEN HE HAS FREE TIME AFTER SCHOOL.
I'M TALKING ABOUT THE NET-WORKING EVENT.
I DON'T MIND THAT EITHER.
HE'S STUDENT COUNCIL PRESIDENT. IT'S APPROPRIATE THAT HE'S MAKING CON-NECTIONS WITH STUDENTS FROM OTHER SCHOOLS.
I DON'T WANT TO *TIE HIM DOWN*.
BROAD
MINDED
LISTEN TO ME...

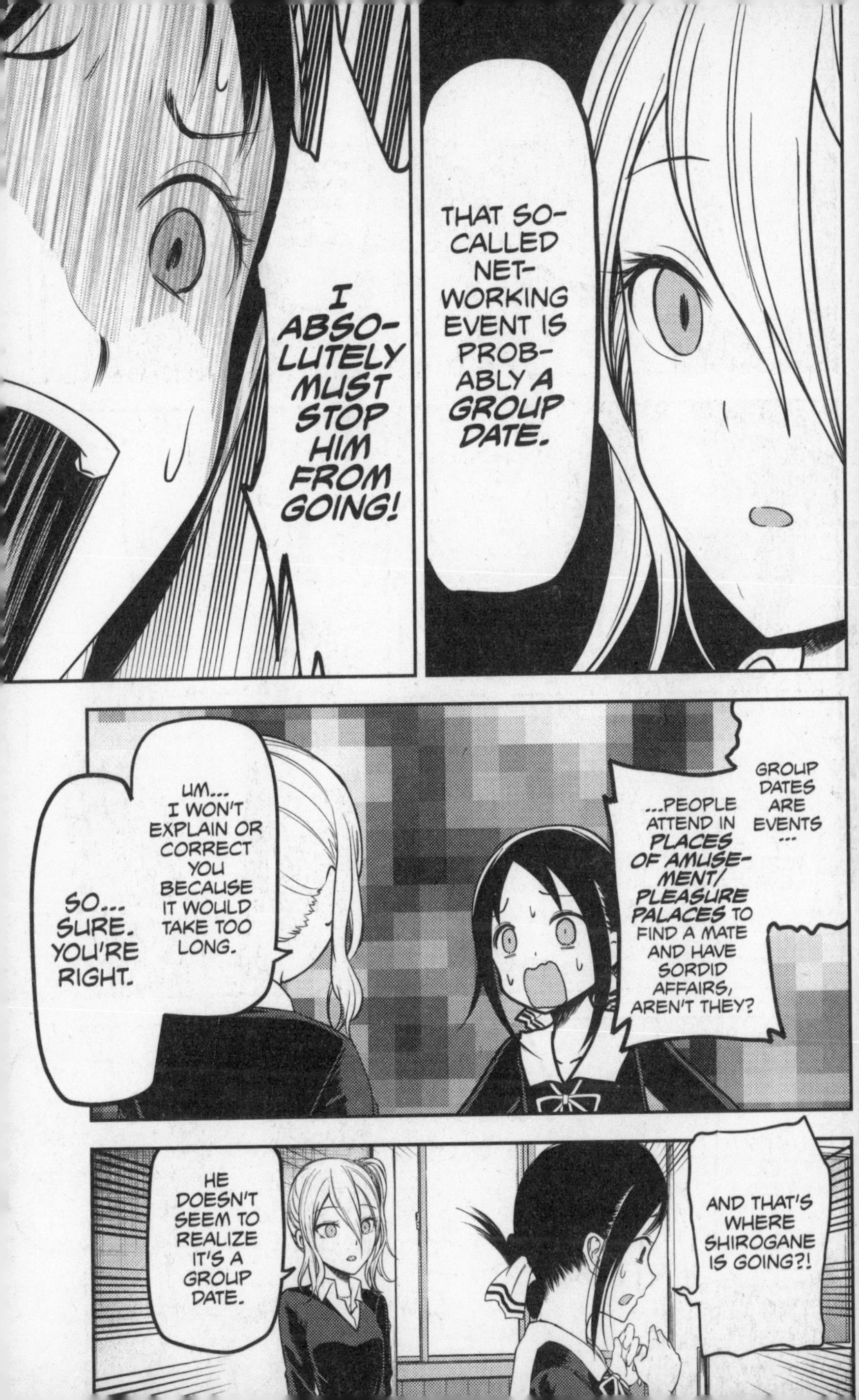
THAT SO-CALLED NETWORKING EVENT IS PROBABLY A GROUP DATE.
I ABSOLUTELY MUST STOP HIM FROM GOING!
GROUP DATES ARE EVENTS...
...PEOPLE ATTEND IN *PLACES OF AMUSEMENT/PLEASURE PALACES* TO FIND A MATE AND HAVE SORDID AFFAIRS, AREN'T THEY?
UM... I WON'T EXPLAIN OR CORRECT YOU BECAUSE IT WOULD TAKE TOO LONG.
SO... SURE. YOU'RE RIGHT.
AND THAT'S WHERE SHIROGANE IS GOING?!
HE DOESN'T SEEM TO REALIZE IT'S A GROUP DATE.

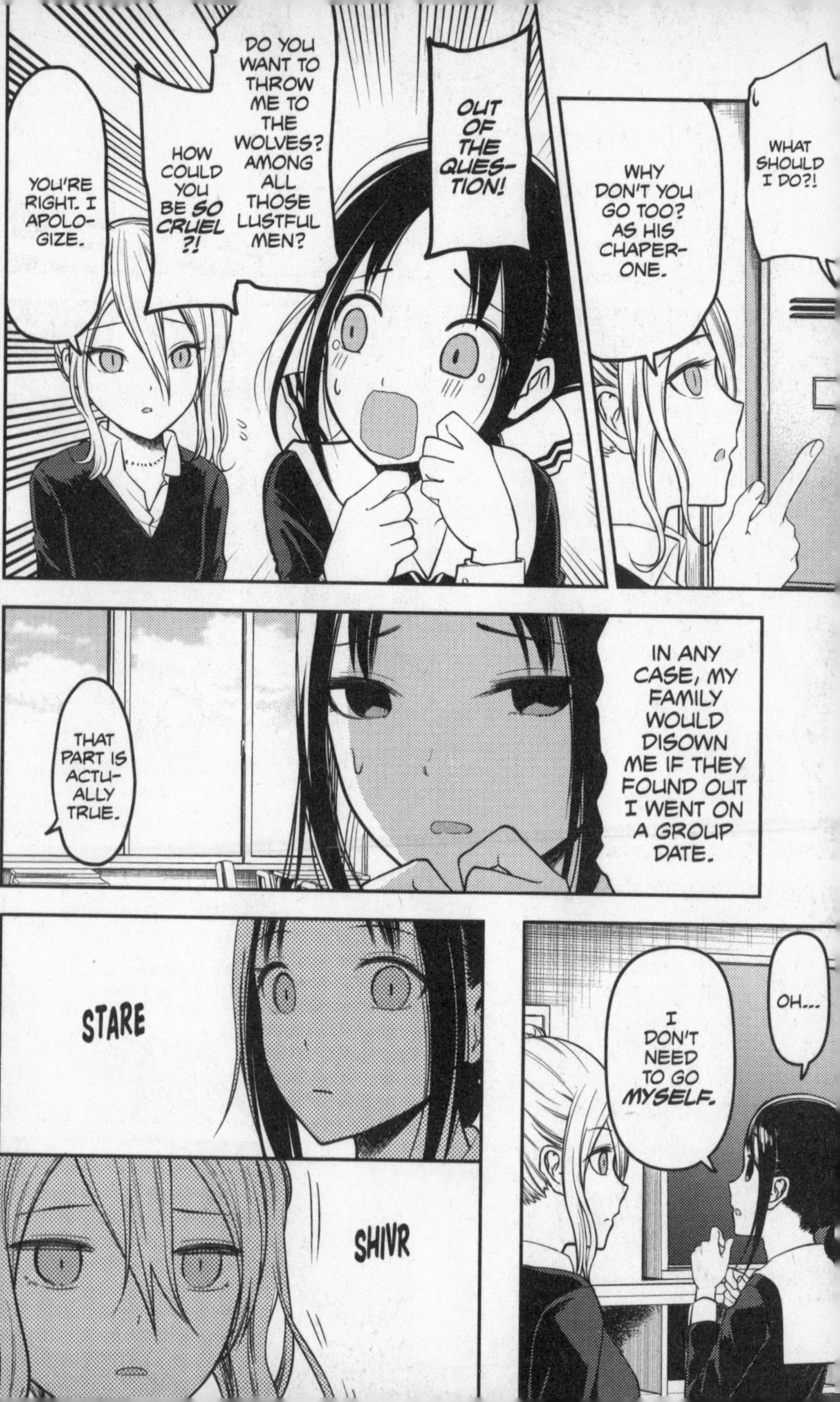
WHAT SHOULD I DO?!
WHY DON'T YOU GO TOO? AS HIS CHAPER-ONE.
OUT OF THE QUES-TION!
DO YOU WANT TO THROW ME TO THE WOLVES? AMONG ALL THOSE LUSTFUL MEN?
HOW COULD YOU BE SO CRUEL?!
YOU'RE RIGHT. I APOLO-GIZE.
IN ANY CASE, MY FAMILY WOULD DISOWN ME IF THEY FOUND OUT I WENT ON A GROUP DATE.
THAT PART IS ACTU-ALLY TRUE.
OH...
I DON'T NEED TO GO MYSELF.
STARE
SHIVR

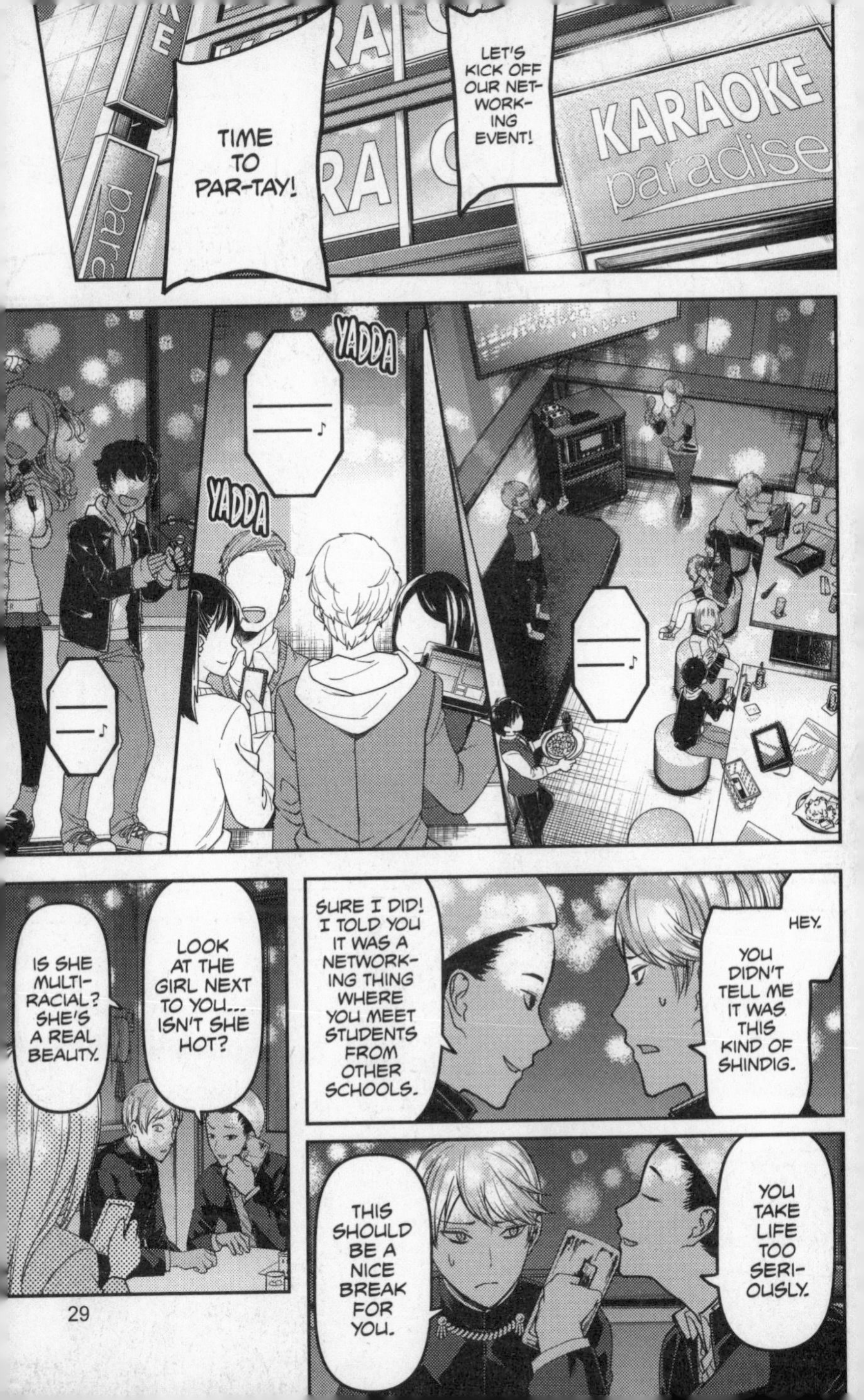
LET'S KICK OFF OUR NETWORKING EVENT!
KARAOKE paradise
TIME TO PAR-TAY!
YADDA
YADDA
HEY.
YOU DIDN'T TELL ME IT WAS THIS KIND OF SHINDIG.
SURE I DID! I TOLD YOU IT WAS A NETWORKING THING WHERE YOU MEET STUDENTS FROM OTHER SCHOOLS.
YOU TAKE LIFE TOO SERIOUSLY.
THIS SHOULD BE A NICE BREAK FOR YOU.
LOOK AT THE GIRL NEXT TO YOU... ISN'T SHE HOT?
IS SHE MULTI-RACIAL? SHE'S A REAL BEAUTY.

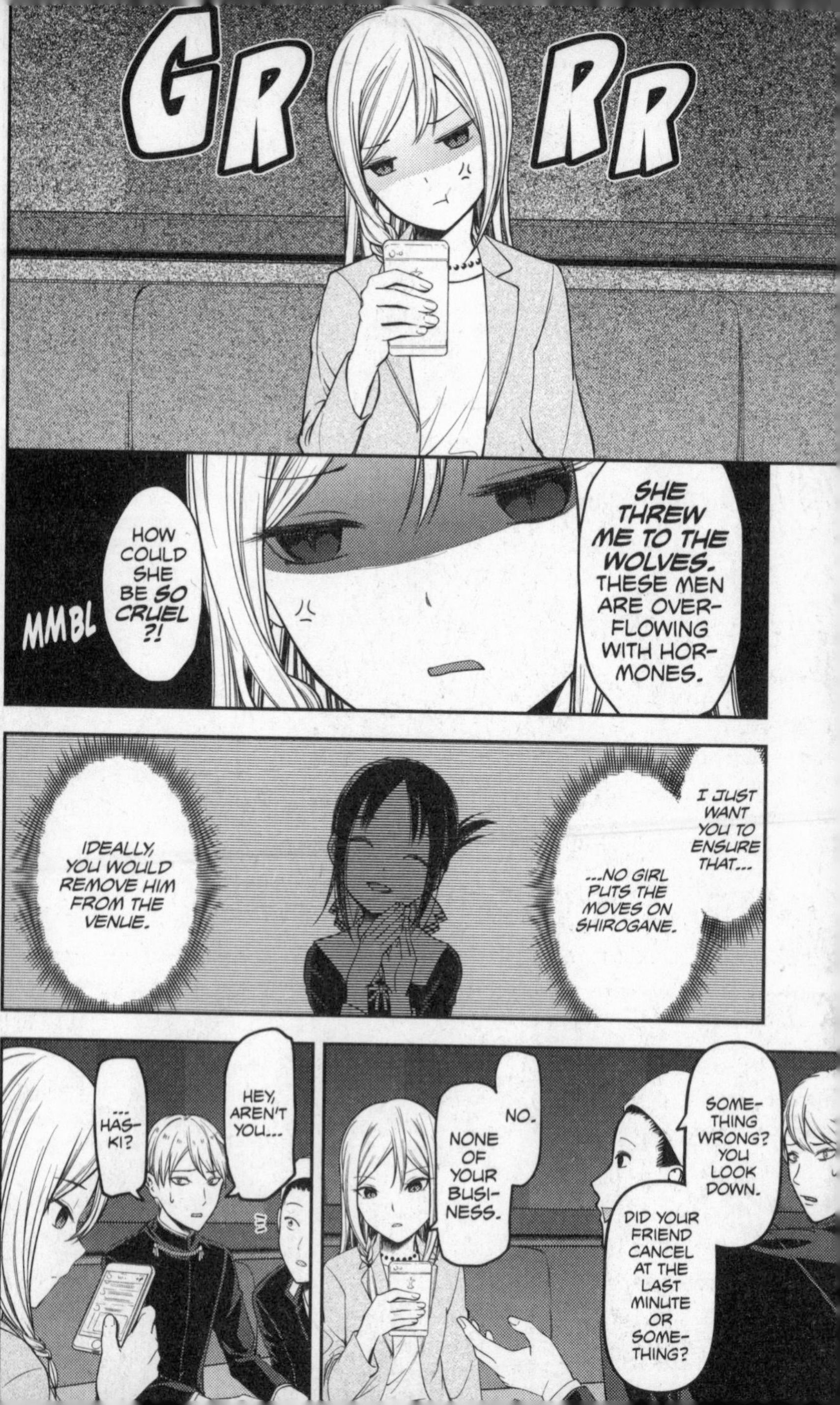
GRRR
SHE THREW ME TO THE WOLVES. THESE MEN ARE OVERFLOWING WITH HORMONES.
HOW COULD SHE BE SO CRUEL?!
MMBL
I JUST WANT YOU TO ENSURE THAT...
...NO GIRL PUTS THE MOVES ON SHIROGANE.
IDEALLY, YOU WOULD REMOVE HIM FROM THE VENUE.
SOMETHING WRONG? YOU LOOK DOWN.
DID YOUR FRIEND CANCEL AT THE LAST MINUTE OR SOMETHING?
NO.
NONE OF YOUR BUSINESS.
HEY, AREN'T YOU...
...HASKI?

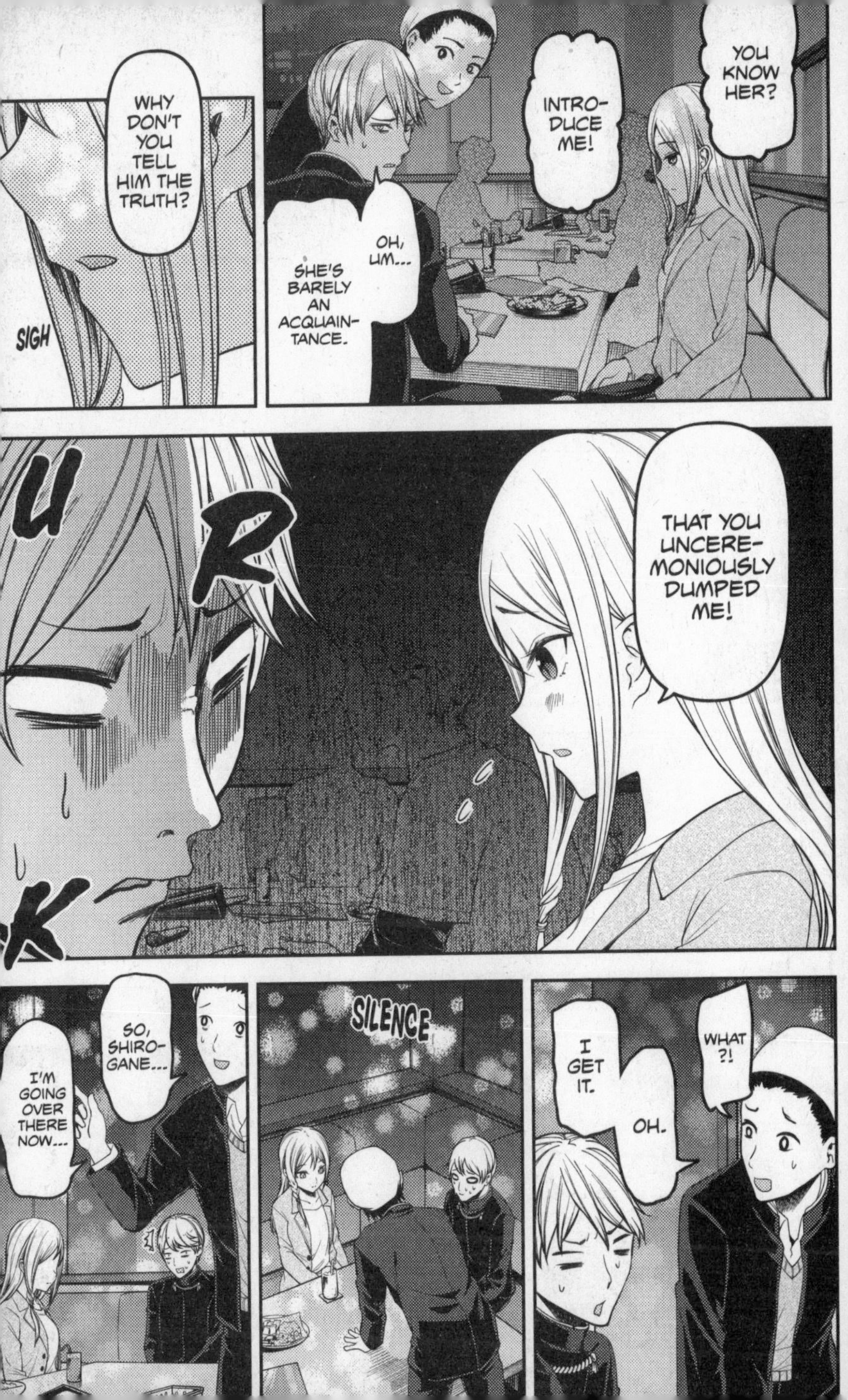
YOU KNOW HER?
INTRO-DUCE ME!
OH, UM...
SHE'S BARELY AN ACQUAIN-TANCE.
WHY DON'T YOU TELL HIM THE TRUTH?
SIGH
THAT YOU UNCERE-MONIOUSLY DUMPED ME!
URK
WHAT?!
I GET IT.
OH.
SILENCE
SO, SHIRO-GANE...
I'M GOING OVER THERE NOW...

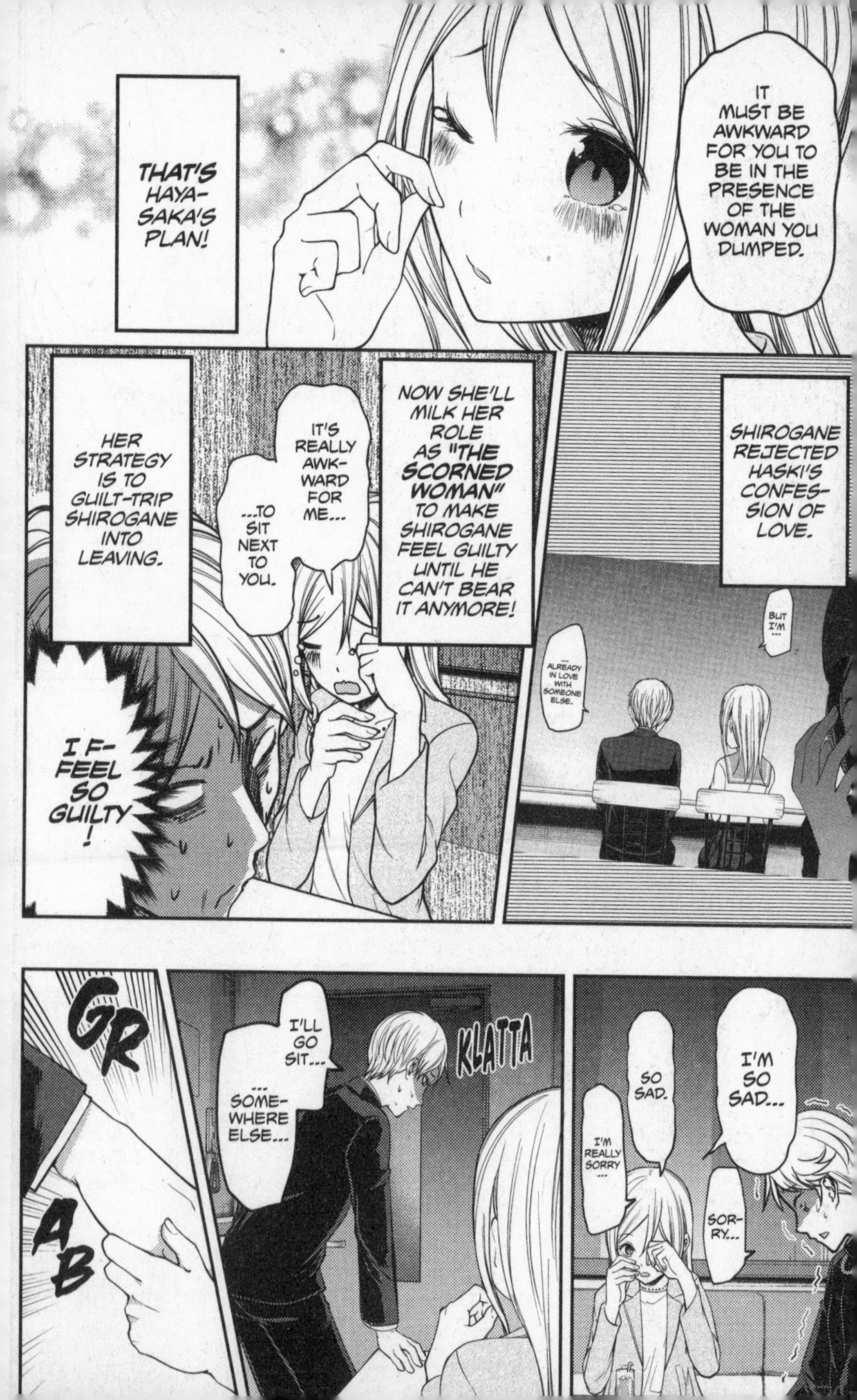

IT MUST BE AWKWARD FOR YOU TO BE IN THE PRESENCE OF THE WOMAN YOU DUMPED.
THAT'S HAYA-SAKA'S PLAN!
SHIROGANE REJECTED HASKI'S CONFES-SION OF LOVE.
BUT I'M...
...ALREADY IN LOVE WITH SOMEONE ELSE.
NOW SHE'LL MILK HER ROLE AS "THE SCORNED WOMAN" TO MAKE SHIROGANE FEEL GUILTY UNTIL HE CAN'T BEAR IT ANYMORE!
IT'S REALLY AWK-WARD FOR ME...
...TO SIT NEXT TO YOU.
HER STRATEGY IS TO GUILT-TRIP SHIROGANE INTO LEAVING.
I F-FEEL SO GUILTY!
I'M SO SAD...
SO SAD.
SOR-RY...
I'M REALLY SORRY...
KLATTA
I'LL GO SIT...
...SOME-WHERE ELSE...
GR
AB

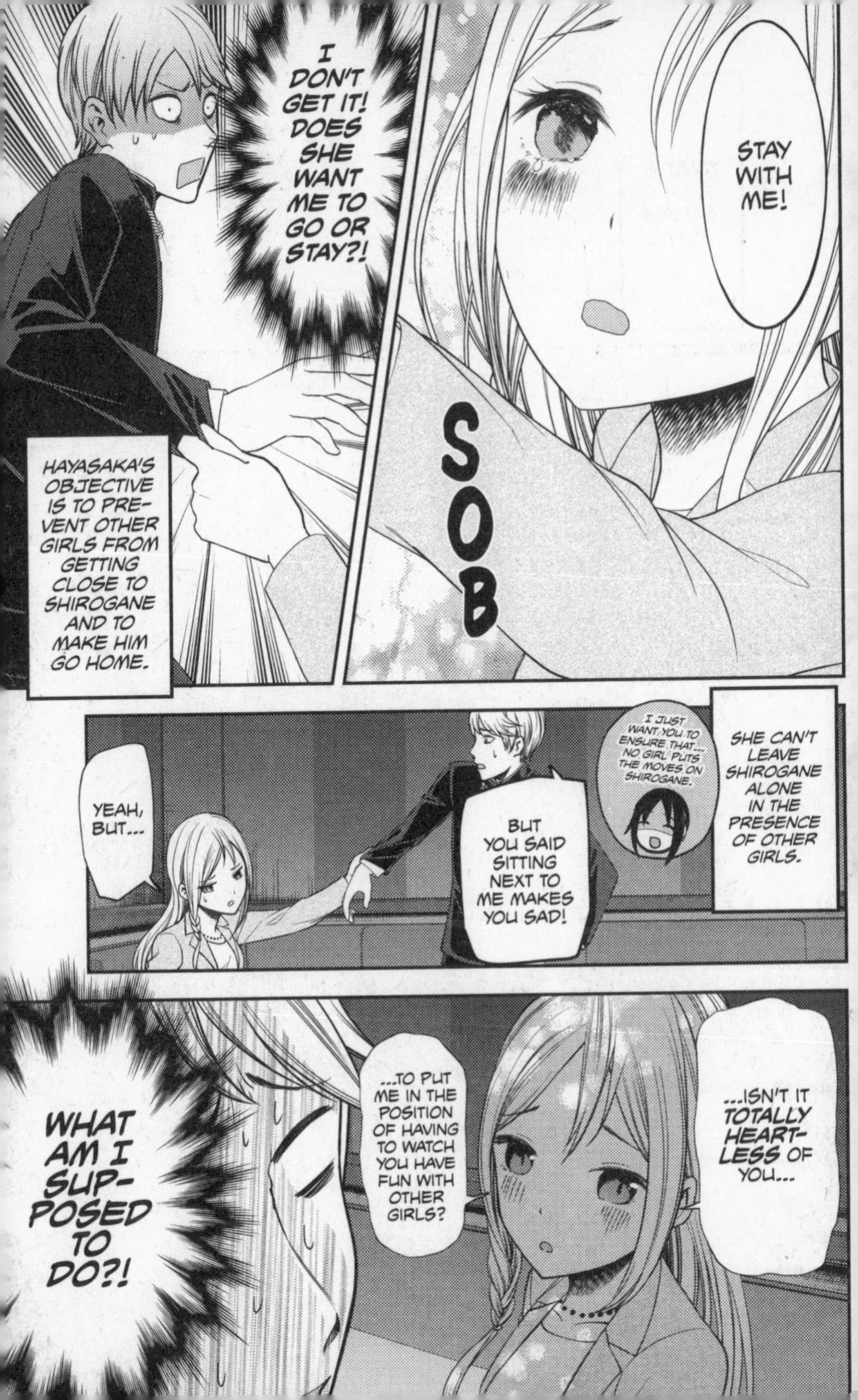
STAY WITH ME!
SOB
I DON'T GET IT! DOES SHE WANT ME TO GO OR STAY?!
HAYASAKA'S OBJECTIVE IS TO PREVENT OTHER GIRLS FROM GETTING CLOSE TO SHIROGANE AND TO MAKE HIM GO HOME.
SHE CAN'T LEAVE SHIROGANE ALONE IN THE PRESENCE OF OTHER GIRLS.
I JUST WANT YOU TO ENSURE THAT... NO GIRL PUTS THE MOVES ON SHIROGANE.
BUT YOU SAID SITTING NEXT TO ME MAKES YOU SAD!
YEAH, BUT...
...ISN'T IT TOTALLY HEARTLESS OF YOU...
...TO PUT ME IN THE POSITION OF HAVING TO WATCH YOU HAVE FUN WITH OTHER GIRLS?
WHAT AM I SUPPOSED TO DO?!

I'LL EXPRESS MY EMOTIONS THROUGH SONG.

OH!

IT'S MY TURN TO SING.

WHAT THE HELL AM I SUPPOSED TO DO?!

I WISH I'D NEVER FALLEN IN LOVE WITH YOU.♪

I'M SAD. SO SAD I'M TREMBLING.♪

WHY CAN'T I BE YOUR NUMBER ONE?

THEN WHY ARE YOU—?!

I'M NOT COMFORTABLE SURROUNDED BY BOYS.

NO.

DO YOU COME TO EVENTS LIKE THIS OFTEN?

YOU...

...SING WELL.

very moving...

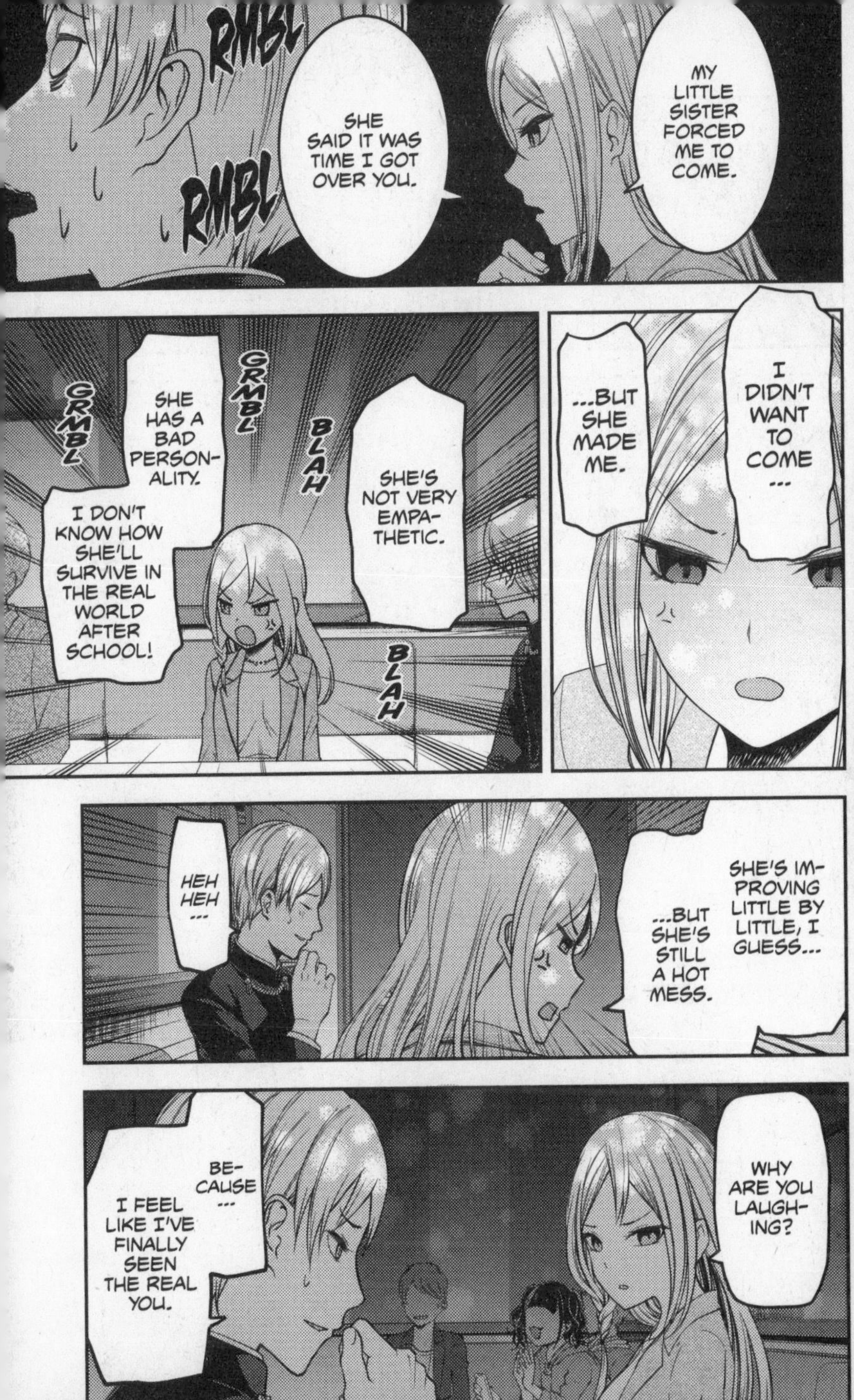
MY LITTLE SISTER FORCED ME TO COME.
SHE SAID IT WAS TIME I GOT OVER YOU.
RMBL
RMBL
I DIDN'T WANT TO COME...
...BUT SHE MADE ME.
SHE'S NOT VERY EMPA-THETIC.
BLAH
BLAH
SHE HAS A BAD PERSON-ALITY.
GRMBL
GRMBL
I DON'T KNOW HOW SHE'LL SURVIVE IN THE REAL WORLD AFTER SCHOOL!
SHE'S IM-PROVING LITTLE BY LITTLE, I GUESS...
...BUT SHE'S STILL A HOT MESS.
HEH HEH...
WHY ARE YOU LAUGH-ING?
BE-CAUSE...
I FEEL LIKE I'VE FINALLY SEEN THE REAL YOU.

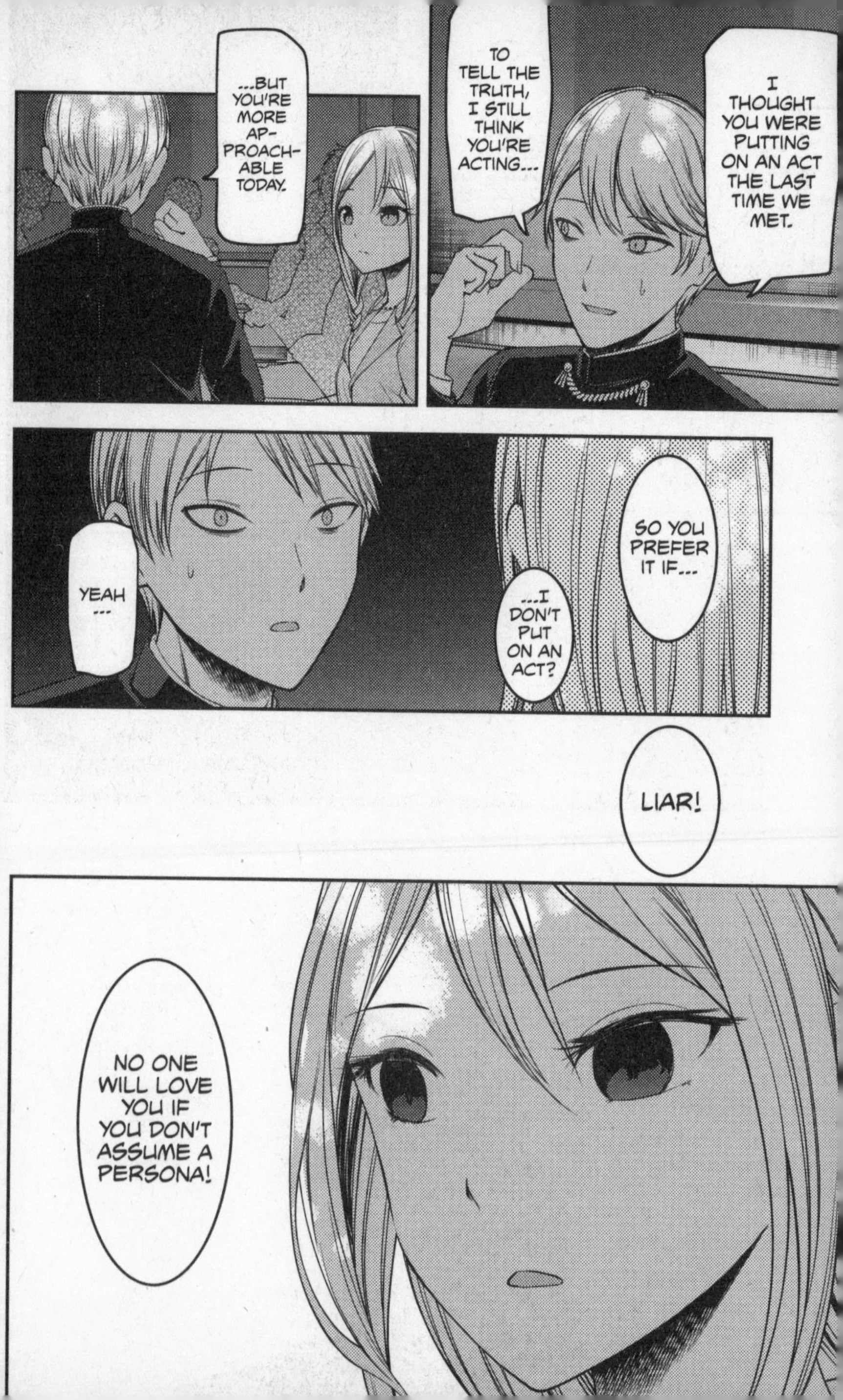
I THOUGHT YOU WERE PUTTING ON AN ACT THE LAST TIME WE MET.
TO TELL THE TRUTH, I STILL THINK YOU'RE ACTING...
...BUT YOU'RE MORE AP-PROACH-ABLE TODAY.
SO YOU PREFER IT IF...
...I DON'T PUT ON AN ACT?
YEAH...
LIAR!
NO ONE WILL LOVE YOU IF YOU DON'T ASSUME A PERSONA!

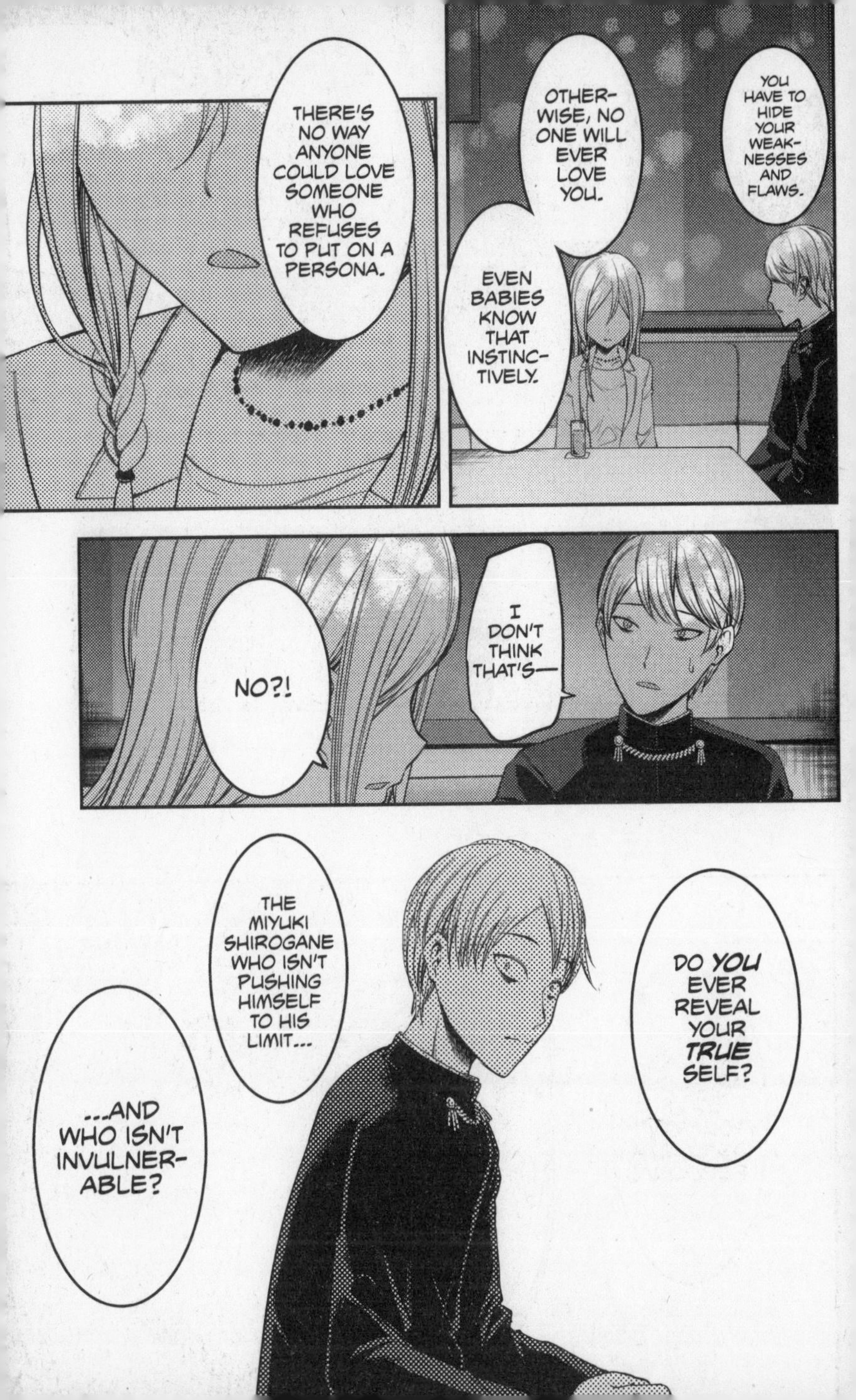
YOU HAVE TO HIDE YOUR WEAKNESSES AND FLAWS.
OTHERWISE, NO ONE WILL EVER LOVE YOU.
EVEN BABIES KNOW THAT INSTINCTIVELY.
THERE'S NO WAY ANYONE COULD LOVE SOMEONE WHO REFUSES TO PUT ON A PERSONA.
I DON'T THINK THAT'S—
NO?!
DO *YOU* EVER REVEAL YOUR *TRUE* SELF?
THE MIYUKI SHIROGANE WHO ISN'T PUSHING HIMSELF TO HIS LIMIT...
...AND WHO ISN'T INVULNERABLE?

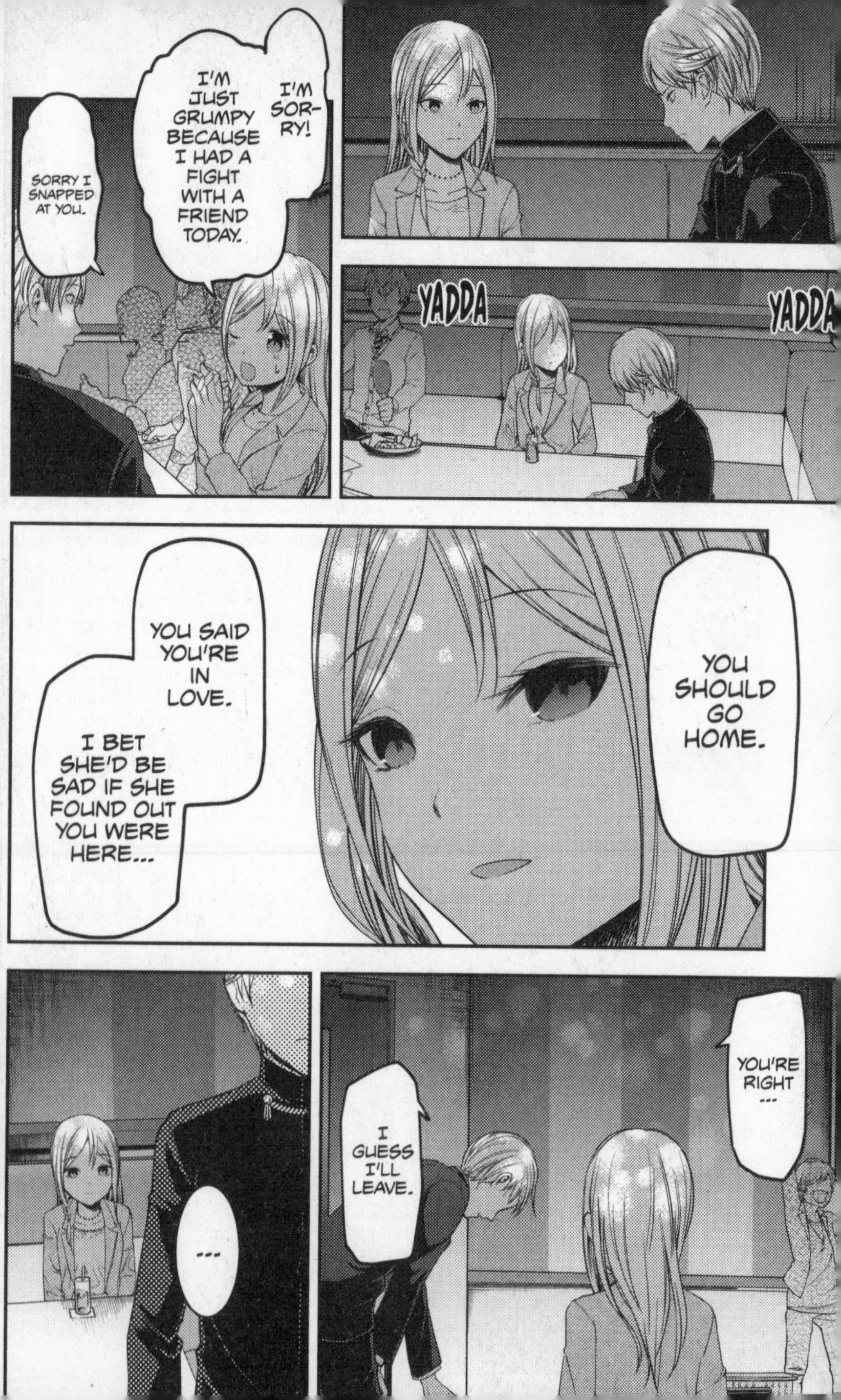
YADDA
YADDA
I'M SOR-RY!
I'M JUST GRUMPY BECAUSE I HAD A FIGHT WITH A FRIEND TODAY.
SORRY I SNAPPED AT YOU.
YOU SHOULD GO HOME.
YOU SAID YOU'RE IN LOVE.
I BET SHE'D BE SAD IF SHE FOUND OUT YOU WERE HERE...
YOU'RE RIGHT...
I GUESS I'LL LEAVE.
...

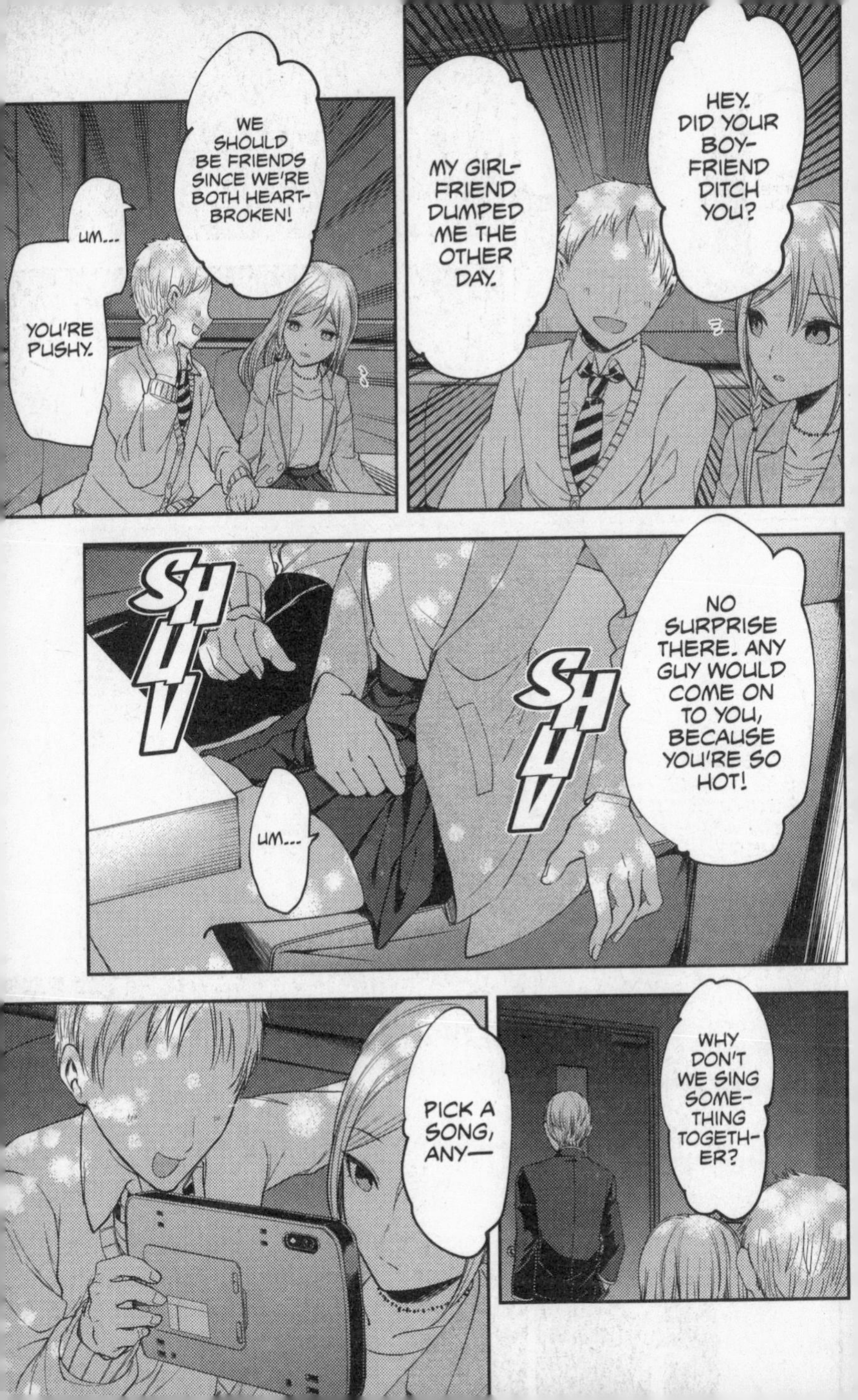
HEY. DID YOUR BOY-FRIEND DITCH YOU?
MY GIRL-FRIEND DUMPED ME THE OTHER DAY.
WE SHOULD BE FRIENDS SINCE WE'RE BOTH HEART-BROKEN!
UM... YOU'RE PUSHY.
NO SURPRISE THERE. ANY GUY WOULD COME ON TO YOU, BECAUSE YOU'RE SO HOT!
SHUV
SHUV
UM...
WHY DON'T WE SING SOME-THING TOGETH-ER?
PICK A SONG, ANY—

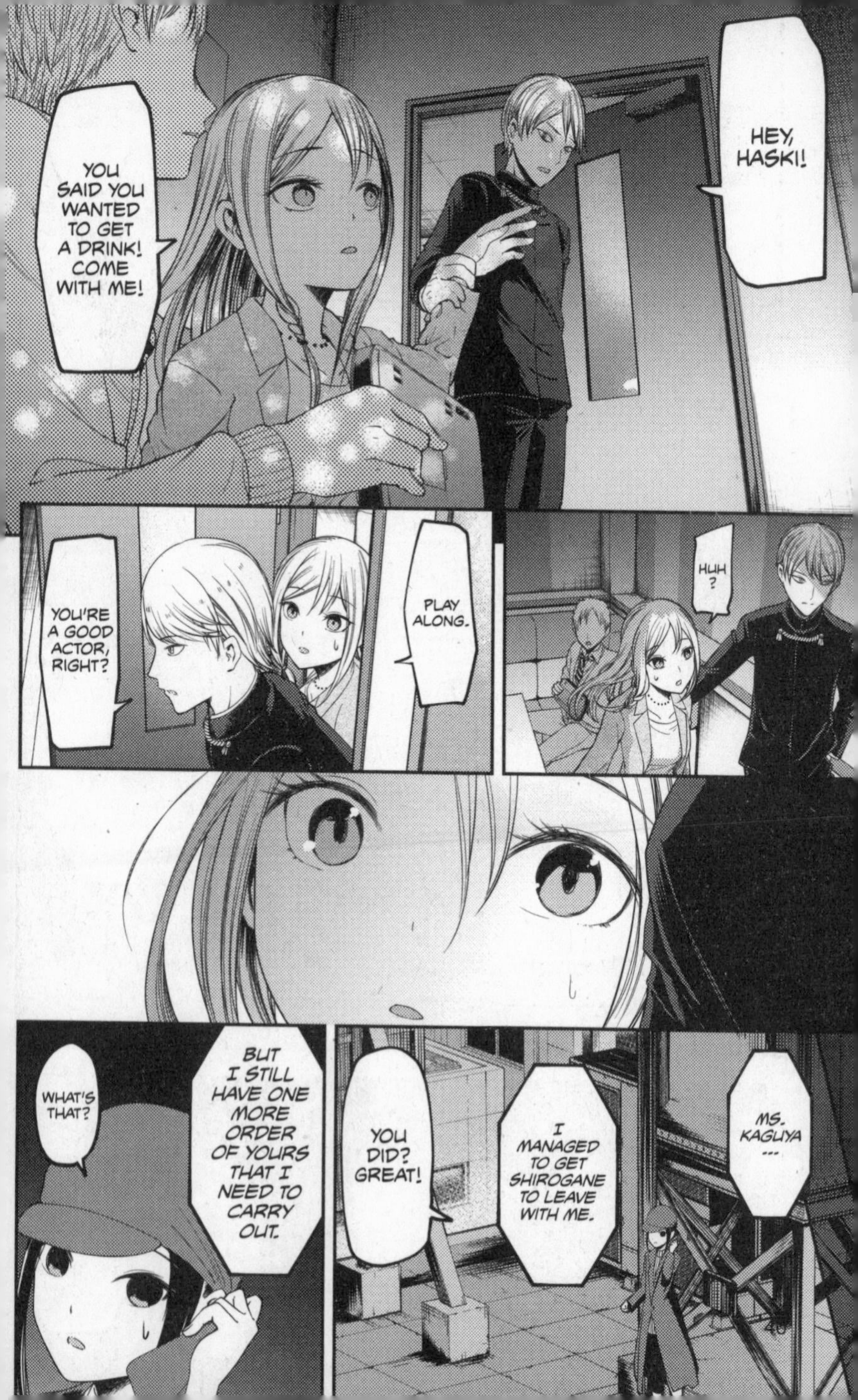
HEY, HASKI!
YOU SAID YOU WANTED TO GET A DRINK! COME WITH ME!
HUH?
PLAY ALONG.
YOU'RE A GOOD ACTOR, RIGHT?
MS. KAGUYA...
I MANAGED TO GET SHIROGANE TO LEAVE WITH ME.
YOU DID? GREAT!
BUT I STILL HAVE ONE MORE ORDER OF YOURS THAT I NEED TO CARRY OUT.
WHAT'S THAT?

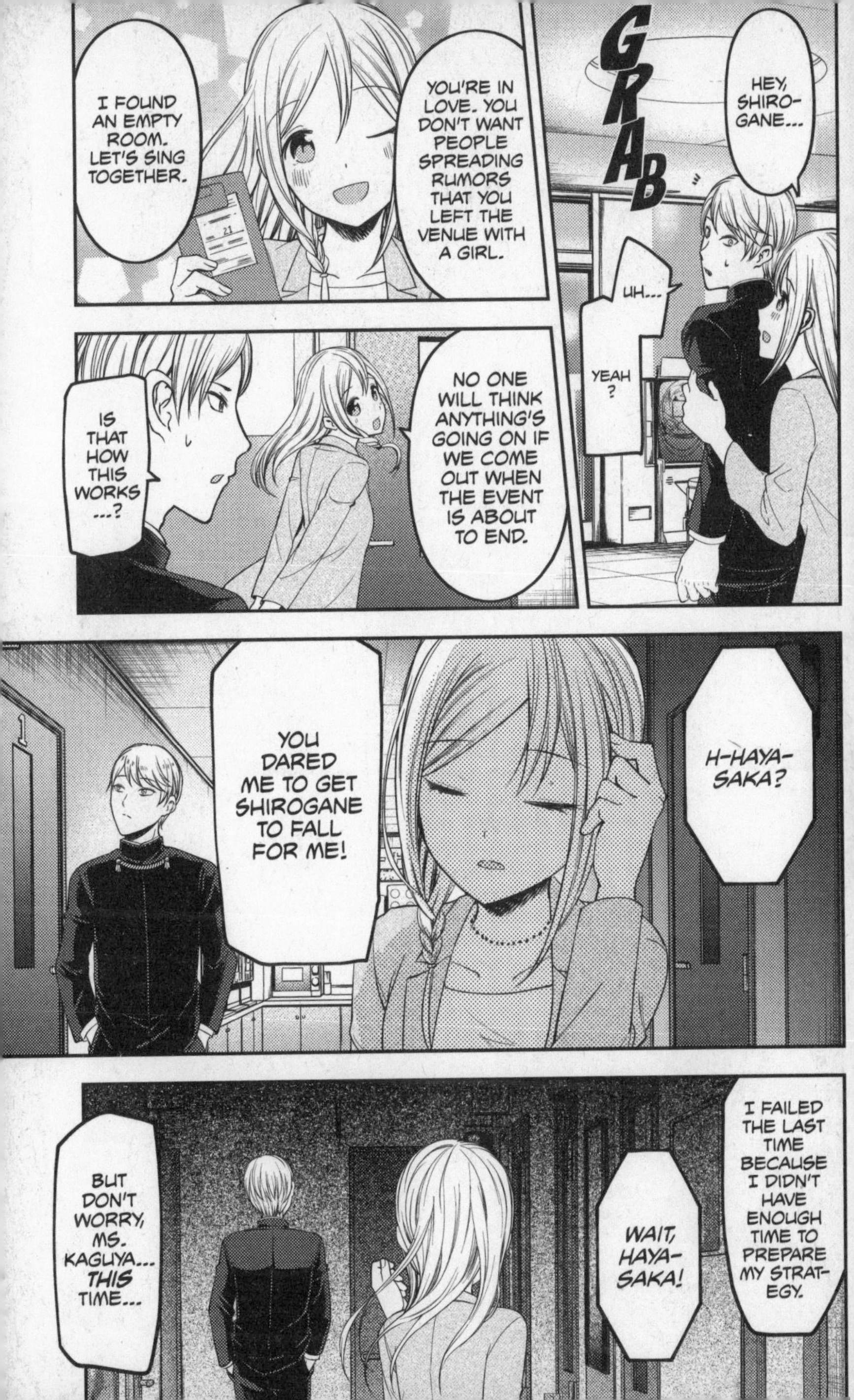
GRAB
HEY, SHIRO-GANE...
UH... YEAH?
YOU'RE IN LOVE. YOU DON'T WANT PEOPLE SPREADING RUMORS THAT YOU LEFT THE VENUE WITH A GIRL.
I FOUND AN EMPTY ROOM. LET'S SING TOGETHER.
NO ONE WILL THINK ANYTHING'S GOING ON IF WE COME OUT WHEN THE EVENT IS ABOUT TO END.
IS THAT HOW THIS WORKS...?
H-HAYA-SAKA?
YOU DARED ME TO GET SHIROGANE TO FALL FOR ME!
I FAILED THE LAST TIME BECAUSE I DIDN'T HAVE ENOUGH TIME TO PREPARE MY STRAT-EGY.
WAIT, HAYA-SAKA!
BUT DON'T WORRY, MS. KAGUYA... THIS TIME...

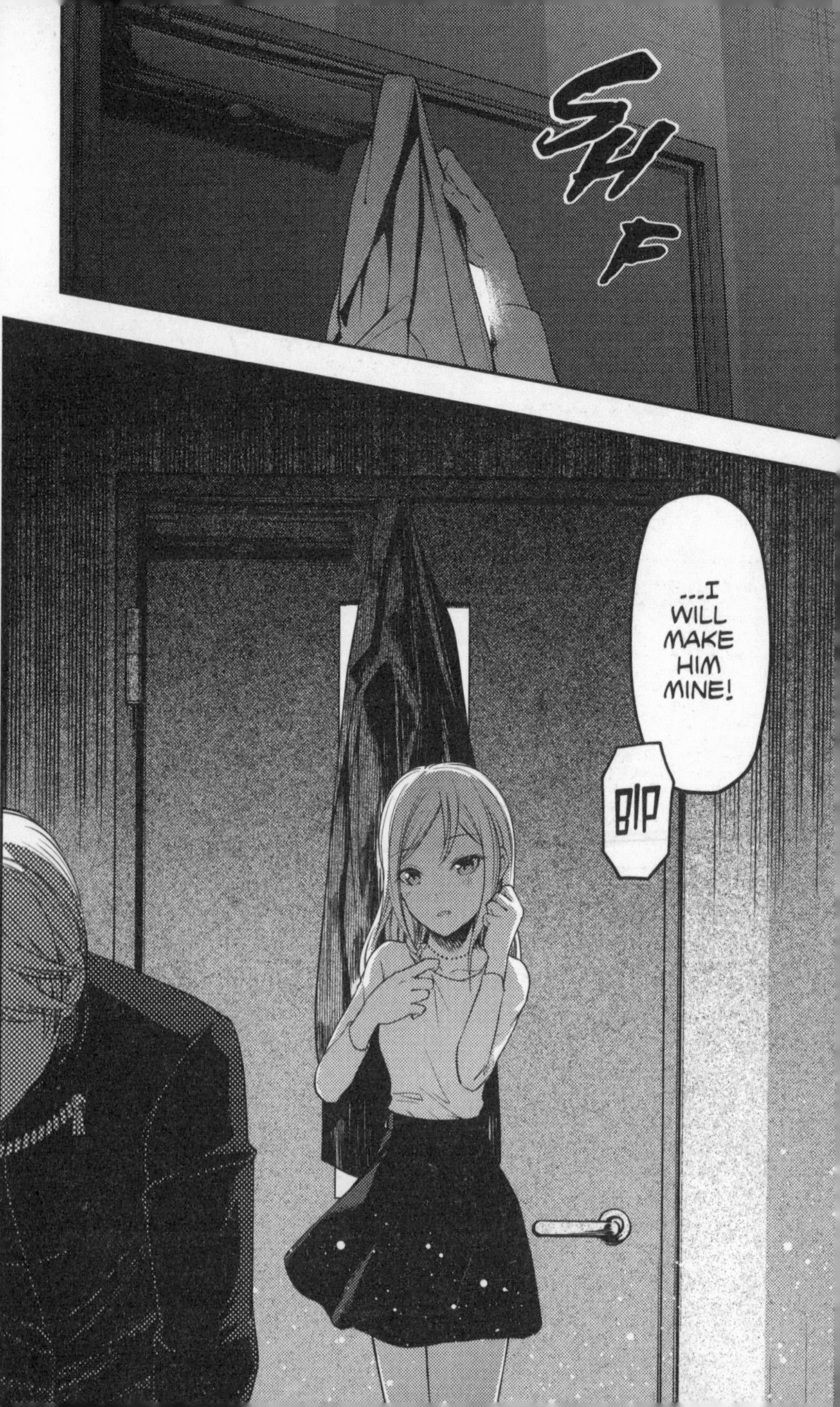
SHFF
...I WILL MAKE HIM MINE!
BIP

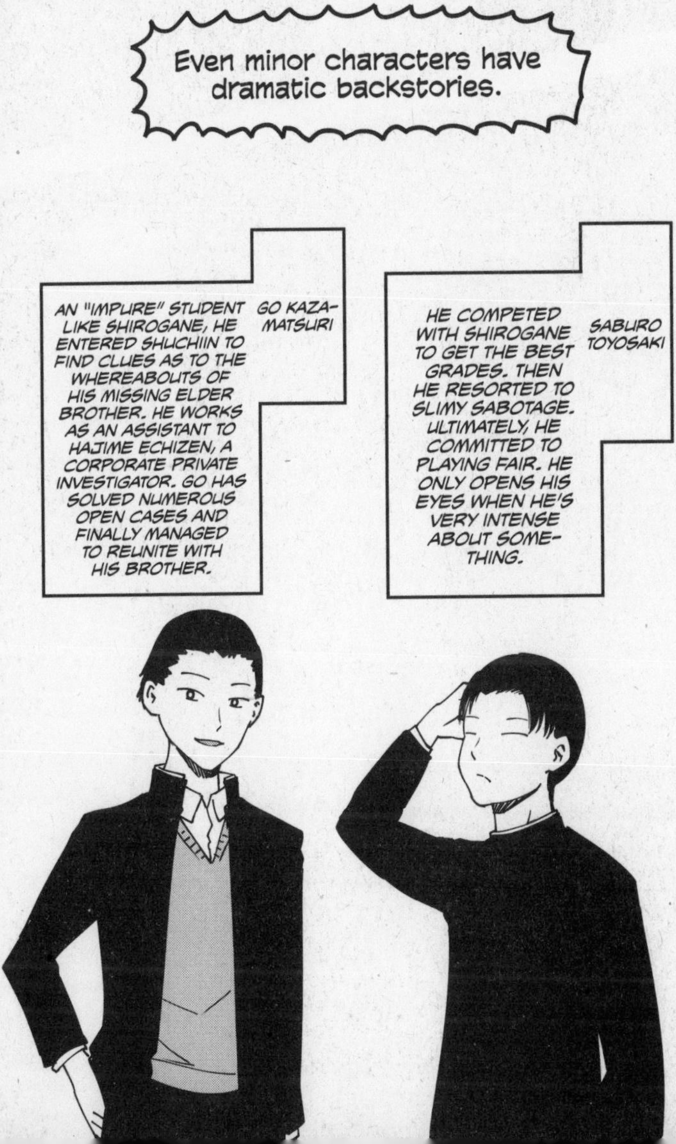
Even minor characters have dramatic backstories.
SABURO TOYOSAKI
HE COMPETED WITH SHIROGANE TO GET THE BEST GRADES. THEN HE RESORTED TO SLIMY SABOTAGE. ULTIMATELY, HE COMMITTED TO PLAYING FAIR. HE ONLY OPENS HIS EYES WHEN HE'S VERY INTENSE ABOUT SOME-THING.
GO KAZA-MATSURI
AN "IMPURE" STUDENT LIKE SHIROGANE, HE ENTERED SHUCHIIN TO FIND CLUES AS TO THE WHEREABOUTS OF HIS MISSING ELDER BROTHER. HE WORKS AS AN ASSISTANT TO HAJIME ECHIZEN, A CORPORATE PRIVATE INVESTIGATOR. GO HAS SOLVED NUMEROUS OPEN CASES AND FINALLY MANAGED TO REUNITE WITH HIS BROTHER.

KAGUYA-SAMA

LOVE IS WAR

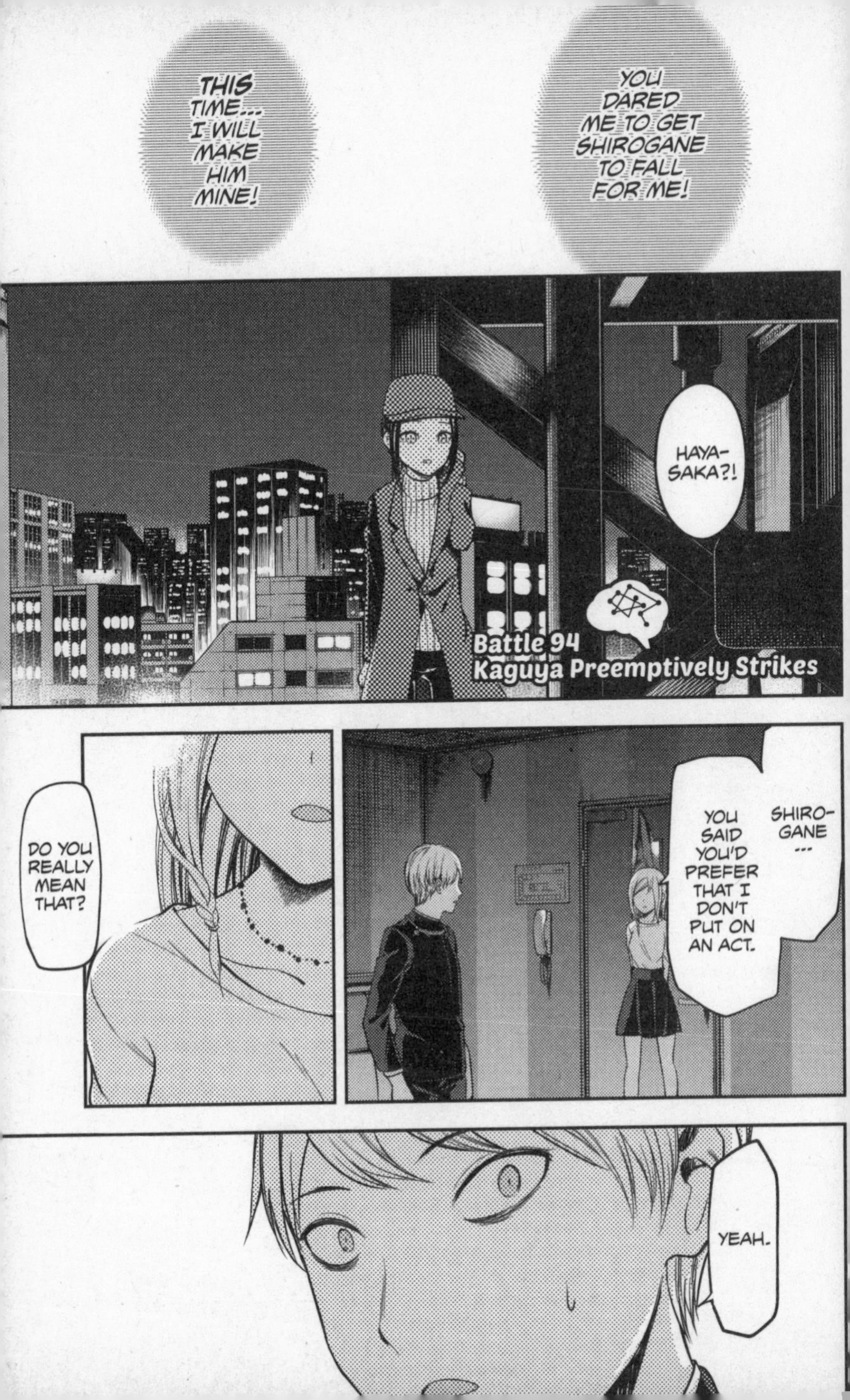
YOU DARED ME TO GET SHIROGANE TO FALL FOR ME!
THIS TIME... I WILL MAKE HIM MINE!
HAYA-SAKA?!
Battle 94
Kaguya Preemptively Strikes
SHIRO-GANE...
YOU SAID YOU'D PREFER THAT I DON'T PUT ON AN ACT.
DO YOU REALLY MEAN THAT?
YEAH.

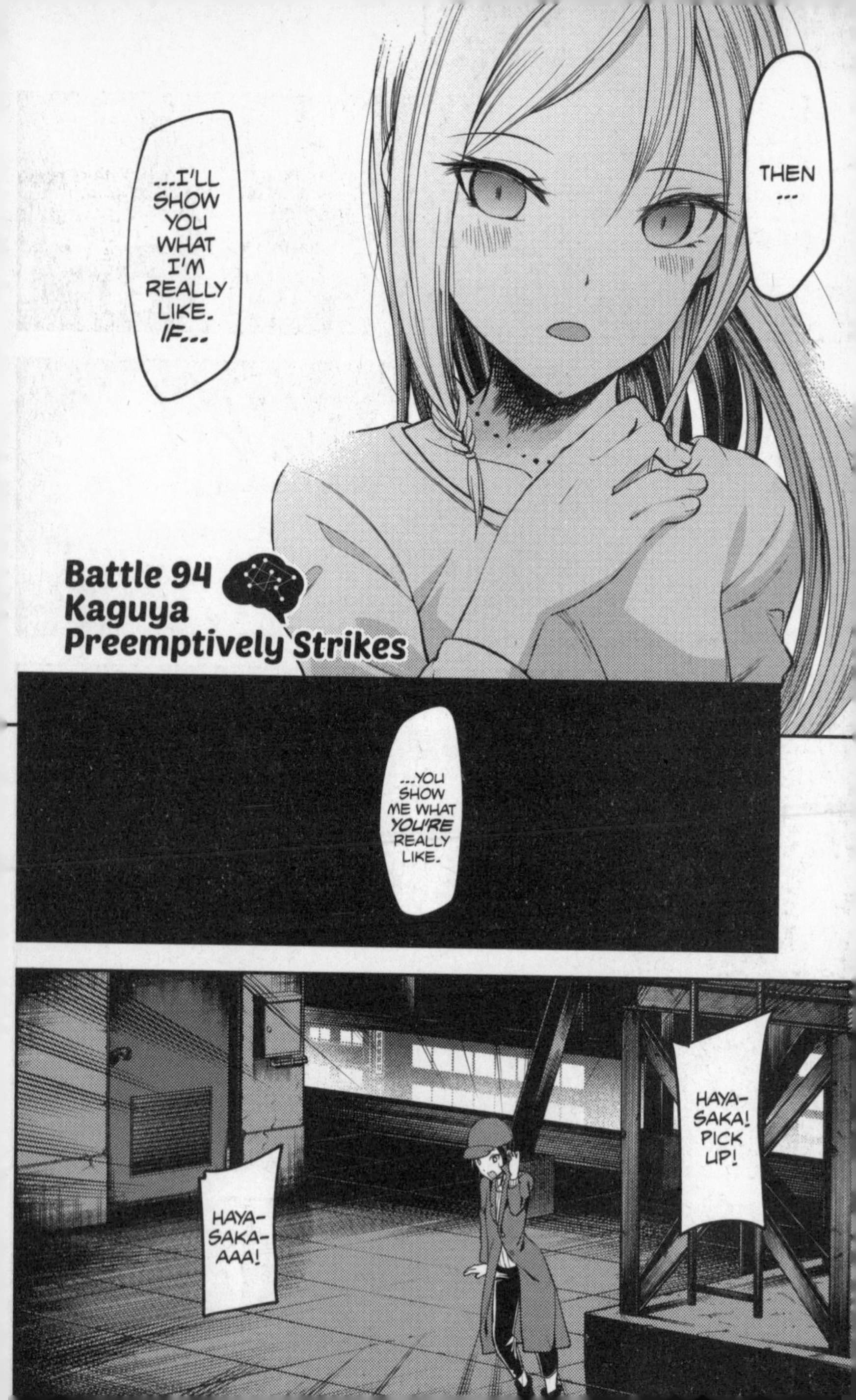
THEN ---
...I'LL SHOW YOU WHAT I'M REALLY LIKE. *IF...*
Battle 94 Kaguya Preemptively Strikes
...YOU SHOW ME WHAT *YOU'RE* REALLY LIKE.
HAYA-SAKA! PICK UP!
HAYA-SAKA-AAA!

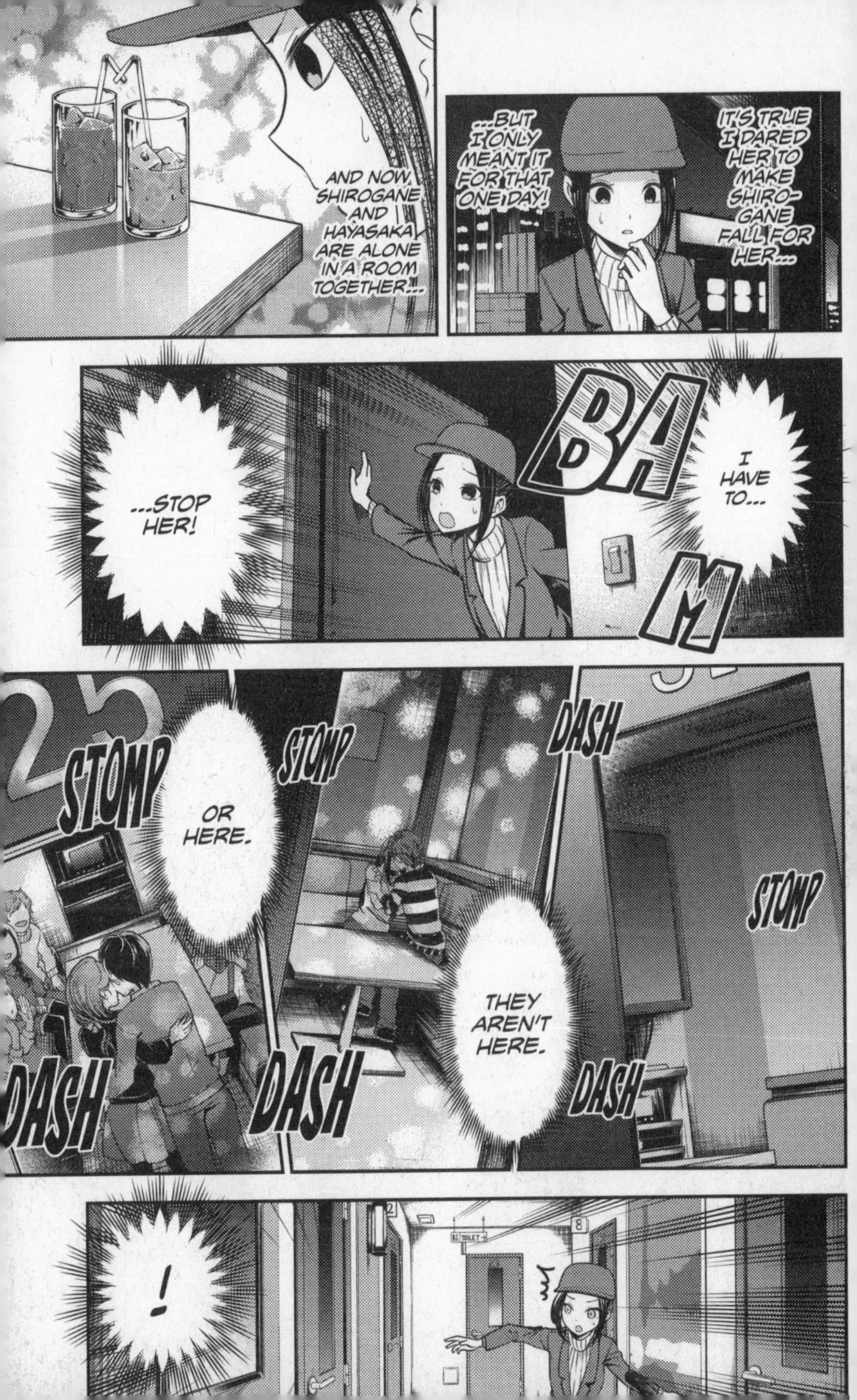
IT'S TRUE I DARED HER TO MAKE SHIROGANE FALL FOR HER...
...BUT I ONLY MEANT IT FOR THAT ONE DAY!
AND NOW, SHIROGANE AND HAYASAKA ARE ALONE IN A ROOM TOGETHER...
I HAVE TO...
BAM
...STOP HER!
DASH
STOMP
DASH
STOMP
THEY AREN'T HERE.
DASH
STOMP
OR HERE.
DASH
TOILET
!

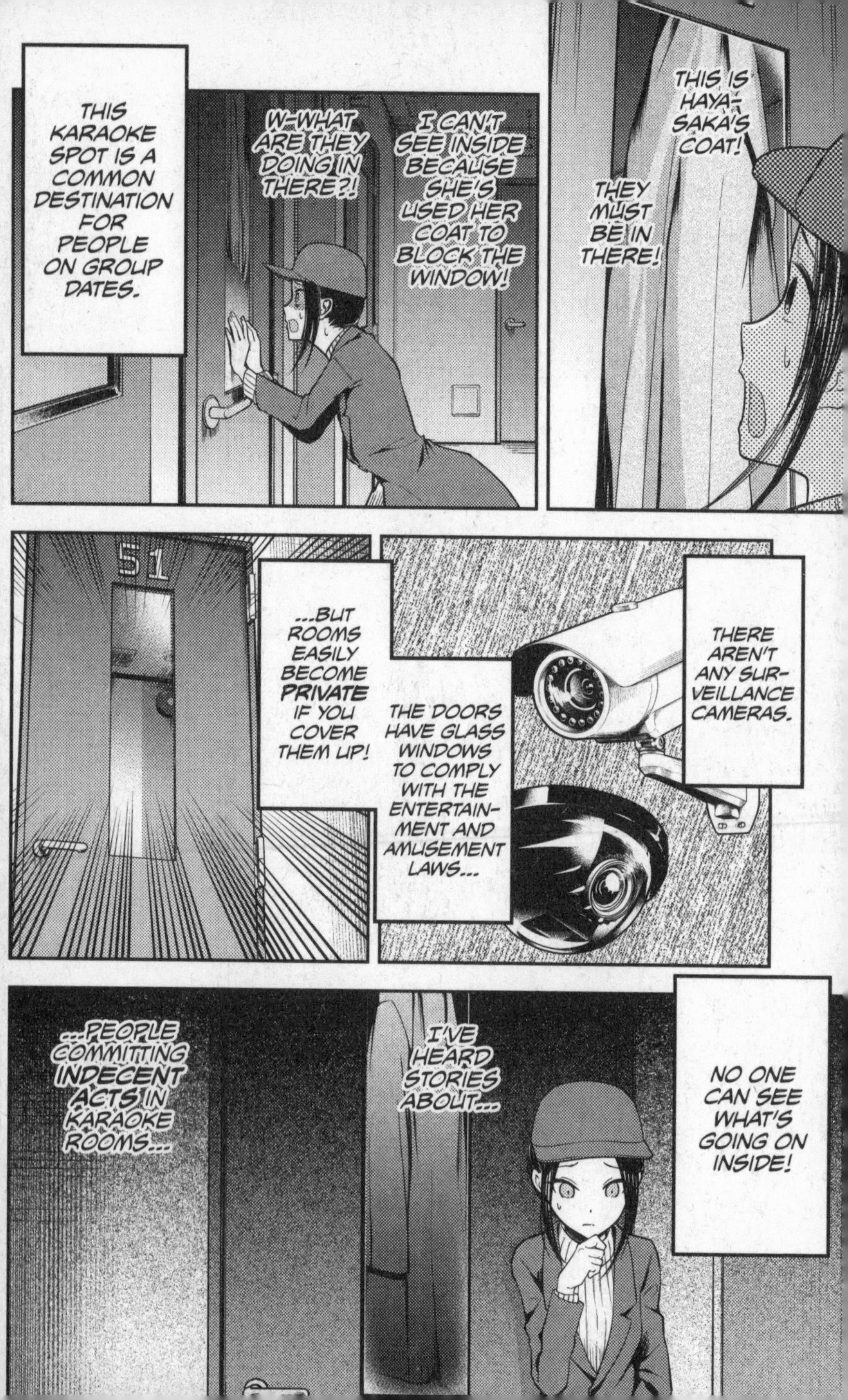
THIS IS HAYA-SAKA'S COAT!
THEY MUST BE IN THERE!
I CAN'T SEE INSIDE BECAUSE SHE'S USED HER COAT TO BLOCK THE WINDOW!
W-WHAT ARE THEY DOING IN THERE?!
THIS KARAOKE SPOT IS A COMMON DESTINATION FOR PEOPLE ON GROUP DATES.
THERE AREN'T ANY SURVEILLANCE CAMERAS.
THE DOORS HAVE GLASS WINDOWS TO COMPLY WITH THE ENTERTAINMENT AND AMUSEMENT LAWS...
...BUT ROOMS EASILY BECOME **PRIVATE** IF YOU COVER THEM UP!
51
NO ONE CAN SEE WHAT'S GOING ON INSIDE!
I'VE HEARD STORIES ABOUT...
...PEOPLE COMMITTING **INDECENT ACTS** IN KARAOKE ROOMS...

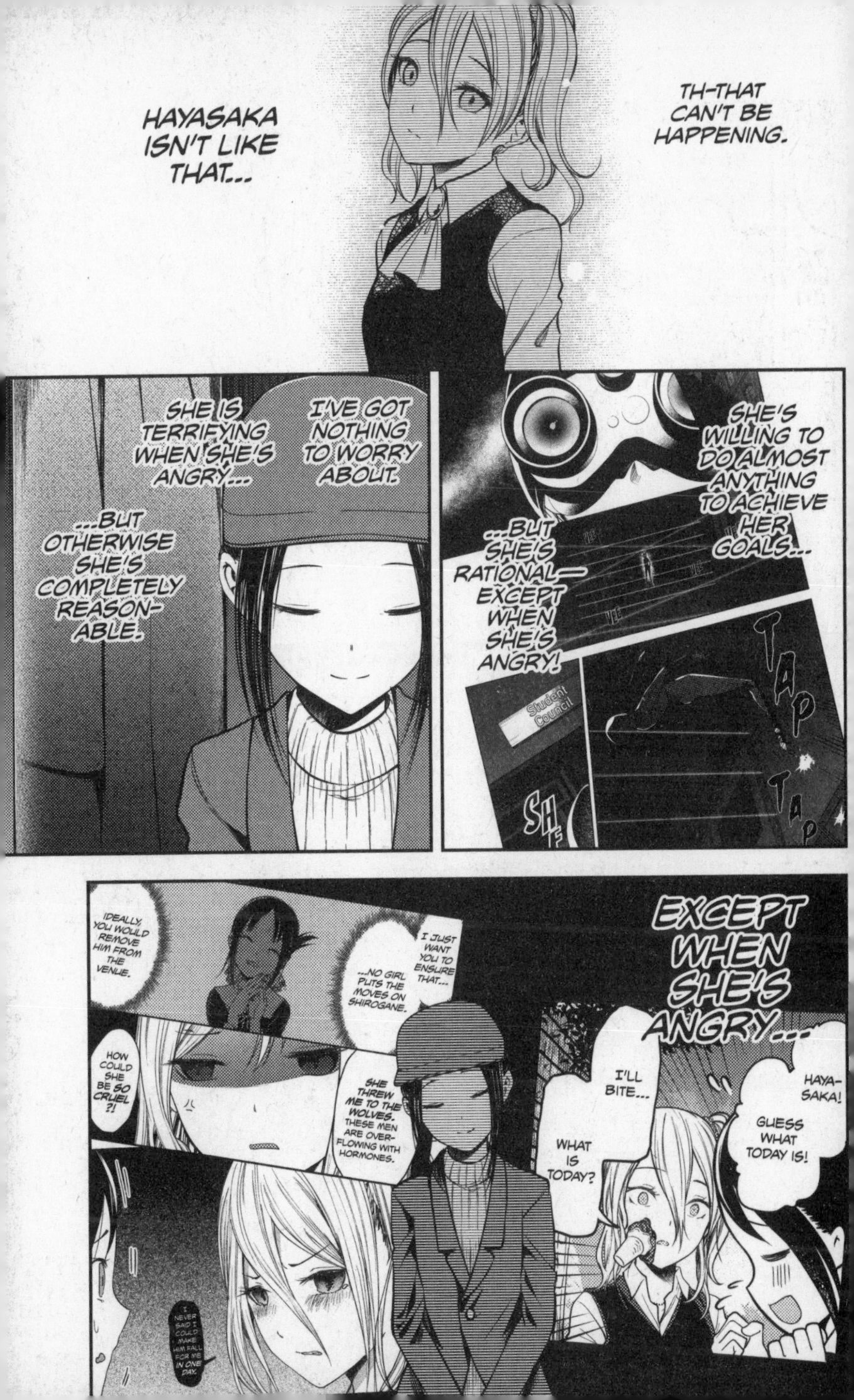

TH-THAT CAN'T BE HAPPENING.
HAYASAKA ISN'T LIKE THAT...
SHE'S WILLING TO DO ALMOST ANYTHING TO ACHIEVE HER GOALS...
...BUT SHE'S RATIONAL—EXCEPT WHEN SHE'S ANGRY!
Student Council
TAP TAP
I'VE GOT NOTHING TO WORRY ABOUT.
SHE IS TERRIFYING WHEN SHE'S ANGRY...
...BUT OTHERWISE SHE'S COMPLETELY REASON-ABLE.
EXCEPT WHEN SHE'S ANGRY...
HAYA-SAKA!
GUESS WHAT TODAY IS!
I'LL BITE...
WHAT IS TODAY?
I JUST WANT YOU TO ENSURE THAT...
...NO GIRL PUTS THE MOVES ON SHIROGANE.
IDEALLY, YOU WOULD REMOVE HIM FROM THE VENUE.
HOW COULD SHE BE SO CRUEL?!
SHE THREW ME TO THE WOLVES. THESE MEN ARE OVER-FLOWING WITH HORMONES.
I NEVER SAID I COULD MAKE HIM FALL FOR ME IN ONE DAY.

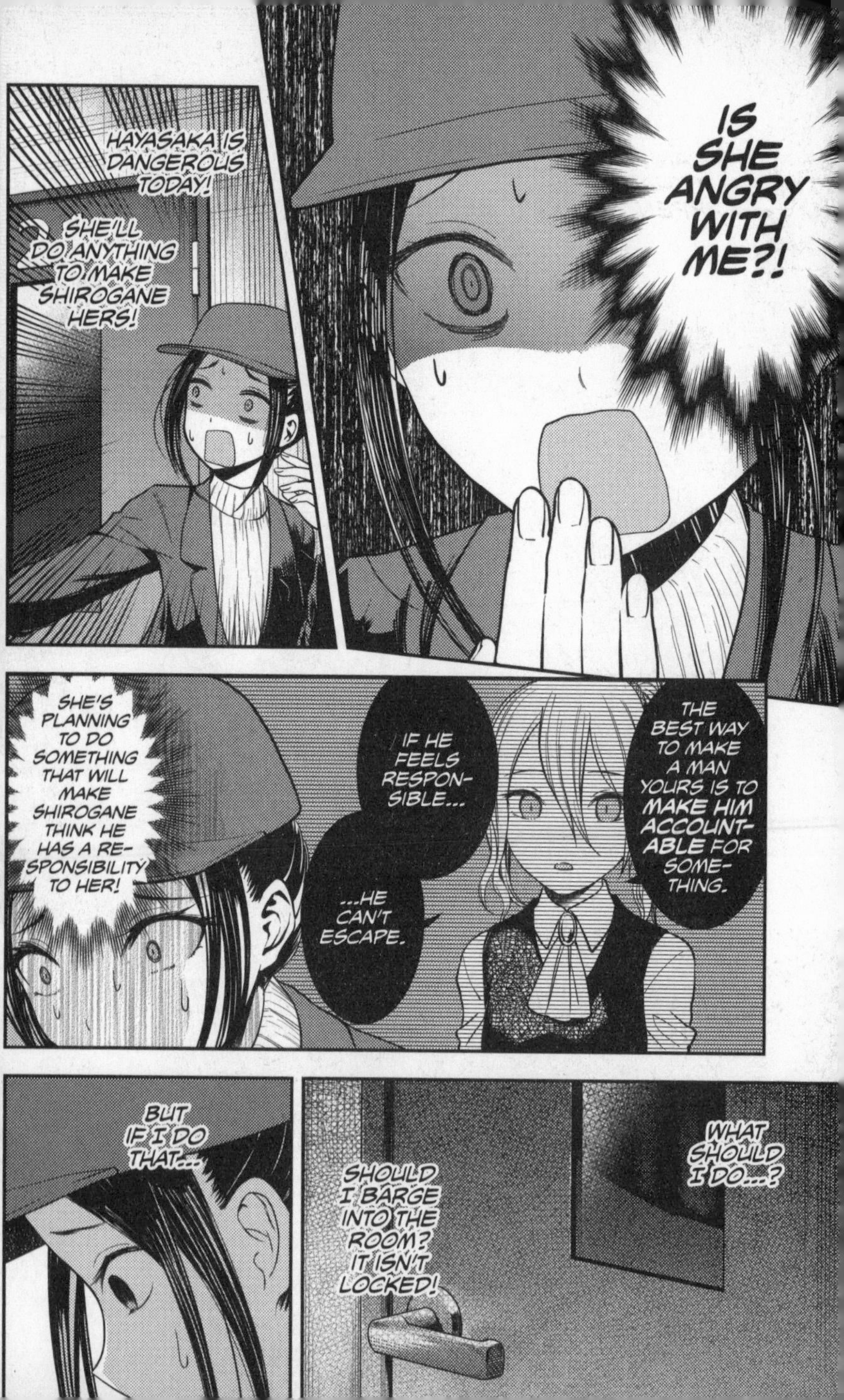
IS SHE ANGRY WITH ME?!
HAYASAKA IS DANGEROUS TODAY!
SHE'LL DO ANYTHING TO MAKE SHIROGANE HERS!
THE BEST WAY TO MAKE A MAN YOURS IS TO MAKE HIM ACCOUNTABLE FOR SOMETHING.
IF HE FEELS RESPONSIBLE...
...HE CAN'T ESCAPE.
SHE'S PLANNING TO DO SOMETHING THAT WILL MAKE SHIROGANE THINK HE HAS A RESPONSIBILITY TO HER!
WHAT SHOULD I DO...?
SHOULD I BARGE INTO THE ROOM? IT ISN'T LOCKED!
BUT IF I DO THAT...

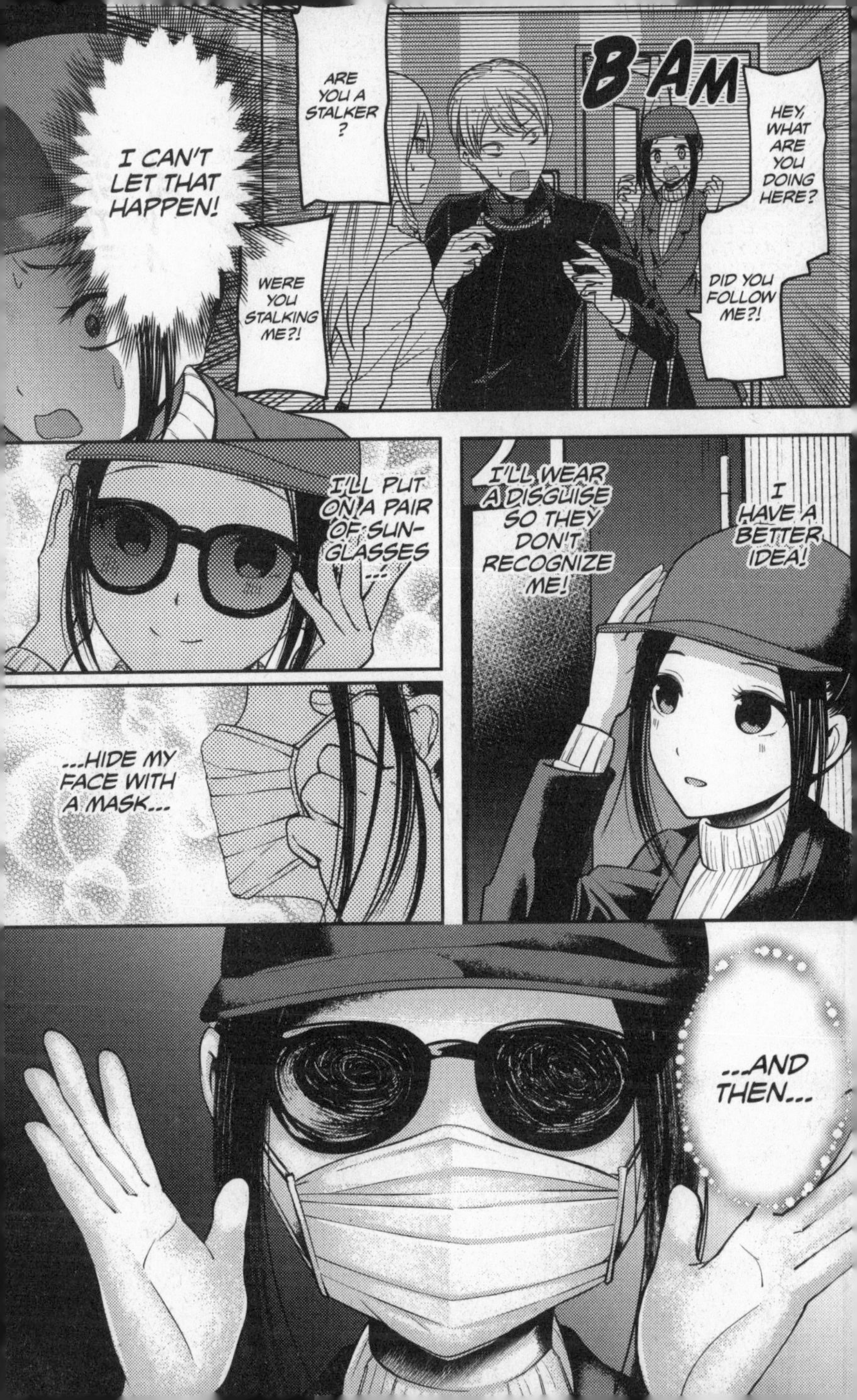
BAM
HEY, WHAT ARE YOU DOING HERE?
DID YOU FOLLOW ME?!
ARE YOU A STALKER?
WERE YOU STALKING ME?!
I CAN'T LET THAT HAPPEN!
I HAVE A BETTER IDEA!
I'LL WEAR A DISGUISE SO THEY DON'T RECOGNIZE ME!
I'LL PUT ON A PAIR OF SUN-GLASSES...
...HIDE MY FACE WITH A MASK...
...AND THEN...

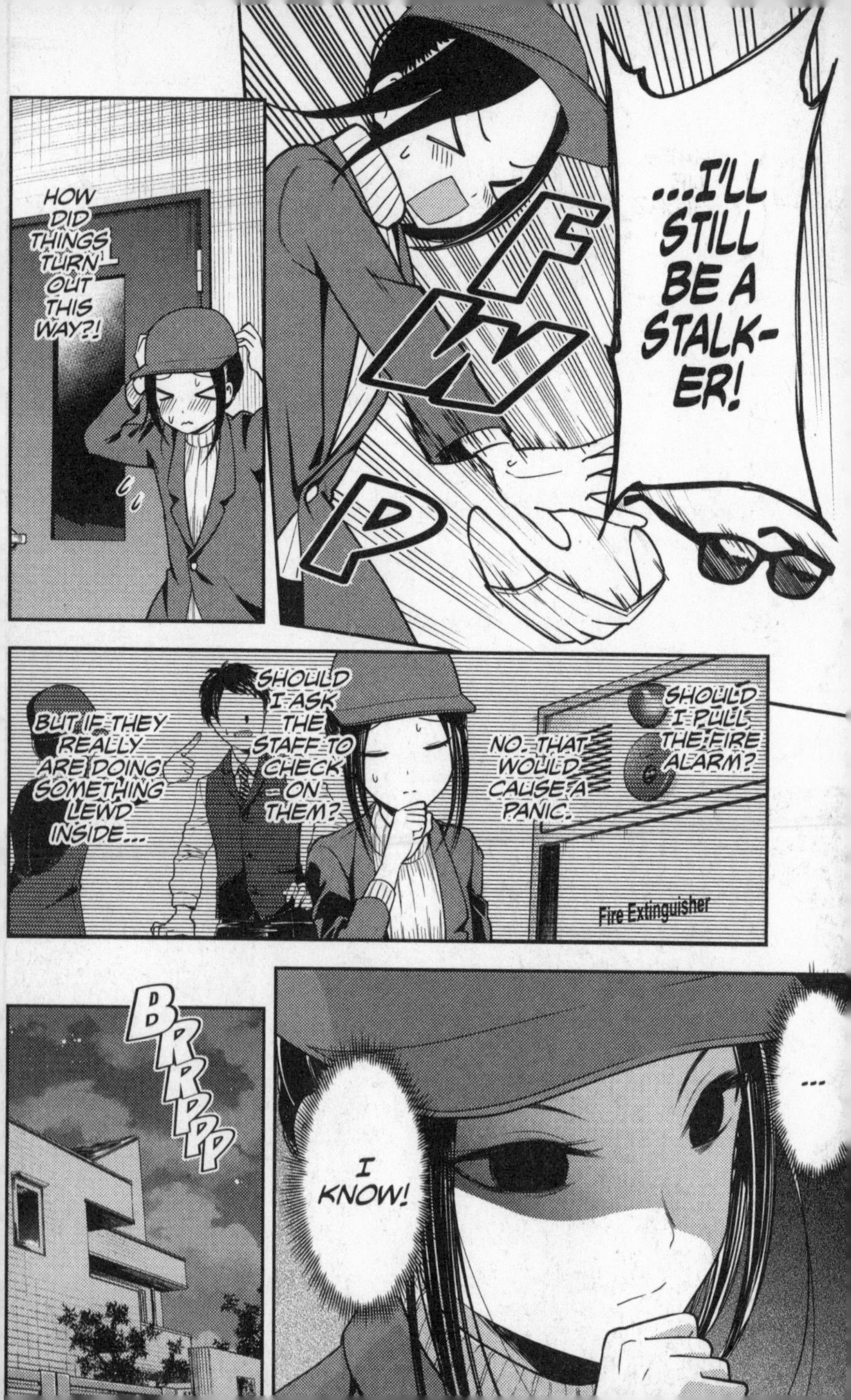
...I'LL STILL BE A STALKER!
FWP
HOW DID THINGS TURN OUT THIS WAY?!
SHOULD I PULL THE FIRE ALARM?
NO. THAT WOULD CAUSE A PANIC.
SHOULD I ASK THE STAFF TO CHECK ON THEM?
BUT IF THEY REALLY ARE DOING SOMETHING LEWD INSIDE...
Fire Extinguisher
...
I KNOW!
BRRPPP

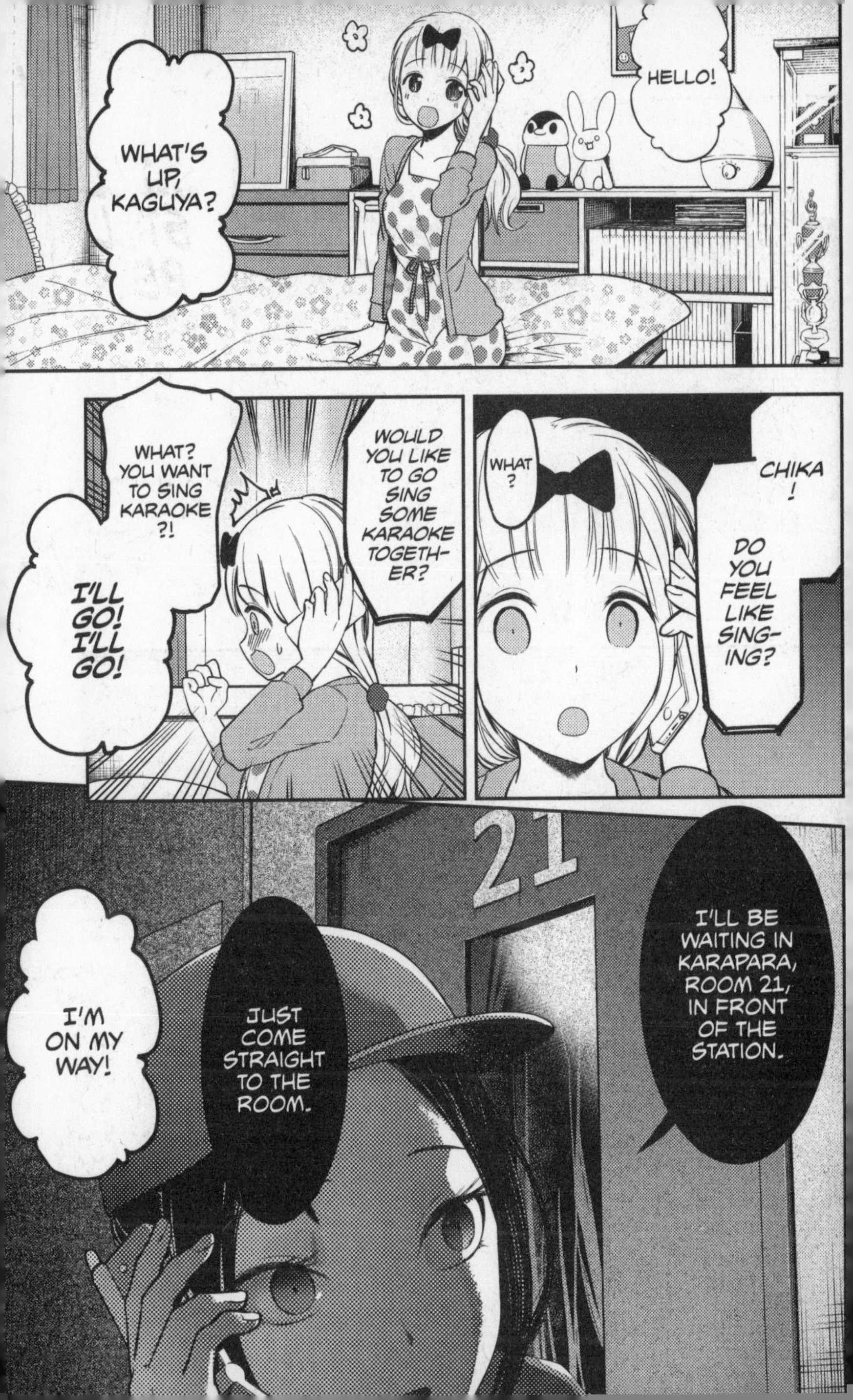
HELLO!
WHAT'S UP, KAGUYA?
CHIKA!
DO YOU FEEL LIKE SINGING?
WHAT?
WOULD YOU LIKE TO GO SING SOME KARAOKE TOGETHER?
WHAT? YOU WANT TO SING KARAOKE?!
I'LL GO! I'LL GO!
21
I'LL BE WAITING IN KARAPARA, ROOM 21, IN FRONT OF THE STATION.
JUST COME STRAIGHT TO THE ROOM.
I'M ON MY WAY!

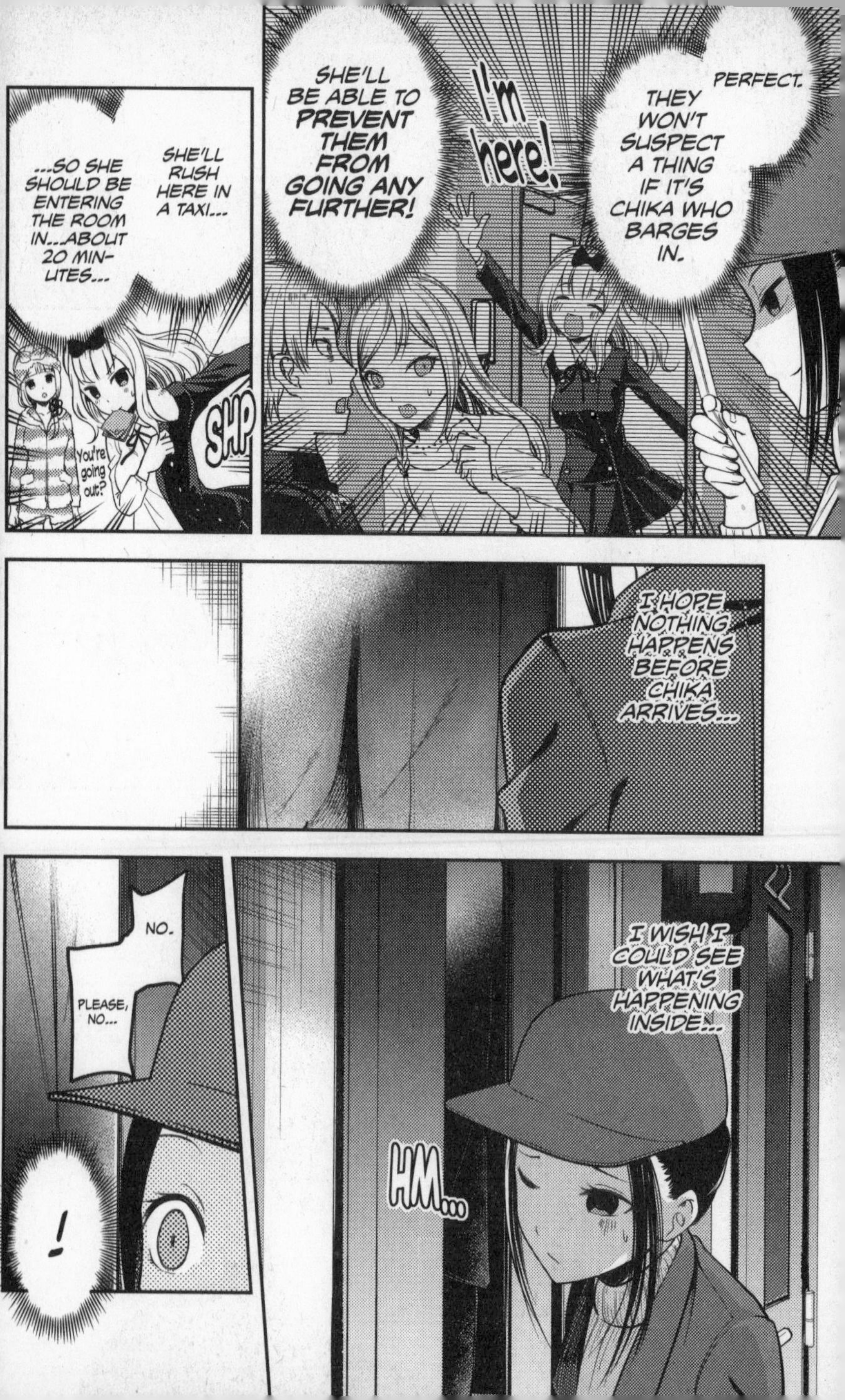
PERFECT.
THEY WON'T SUSPECT A THING IF IT'S CHIKA WHO BARGES IN.
I'm here!
SHE'LL BE ABLE TO PREVENT THEM FROM GOING ANY FURTHER!
SHE'LL RUSH HERE IN A TAXI...
...SO SHE SHOULD BE ENTERING THE ROOM IN...ABOUT 20 MIN-UTES...
SHP
You're going out?
I HOPE NOTHING HAPPENS BEFORE CHIKA ARRIVES...
I WISH I COULD SEE WHAT'S HAPPENING INSIDE...
HM...
NO.
PLEASE, NO...
!

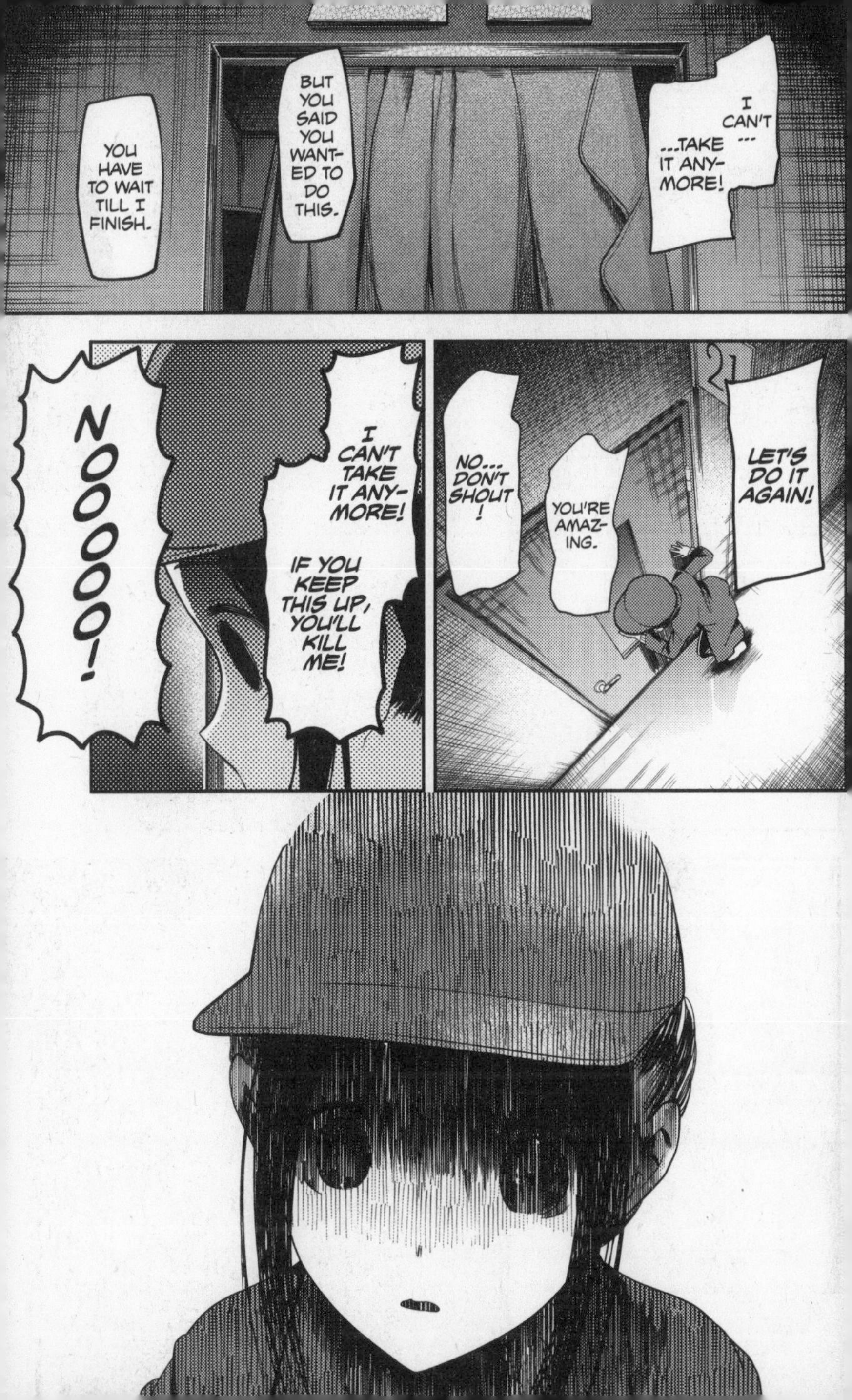
I CAN'T...
...TAKE IT ANYMORE!
BUT YOU SAID YOU WANTED TO DO THIS.
YOU HAVE TO WAIT TILL I FINISH.
LET'S DO IT AGAIN!
YOU'RE AMAZING.
NO... DON'T SHOUT!
I CAN'T TAKE IT ANYMORE!
IF YOU KEEP THIS UP, YOU'LL KILL ME!
NOOOOOO!

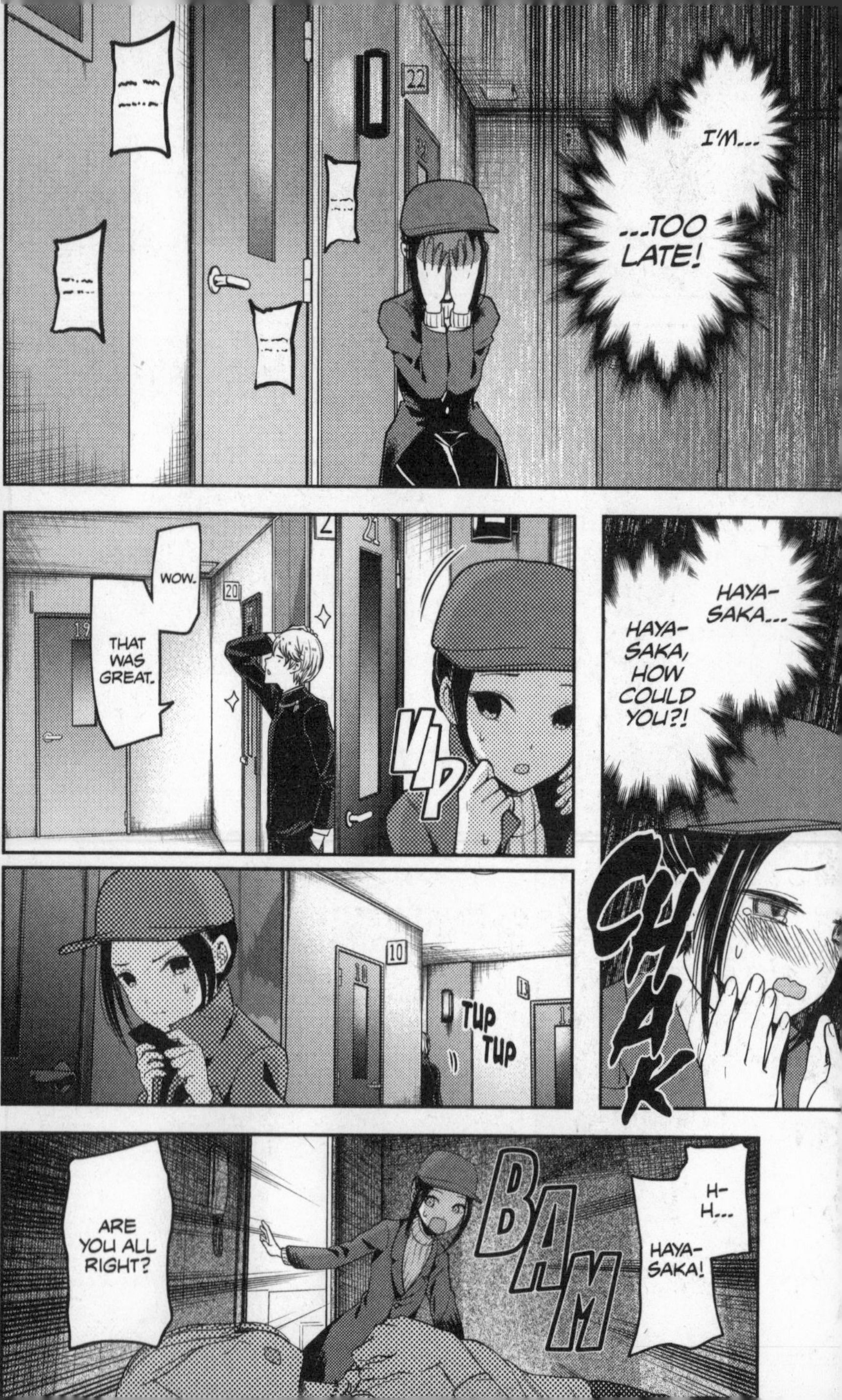
I'M...
...TOO LATE!
HAYA-SAKA...
HAYA-SAKA, HOW COULD YOU?!
CHAK
WOW.
THAT WAS GREAT.
VIP
TUP TUP
H-H...
HAYA-SAKA!
BAM
ARE YOU ALL RIGHT?

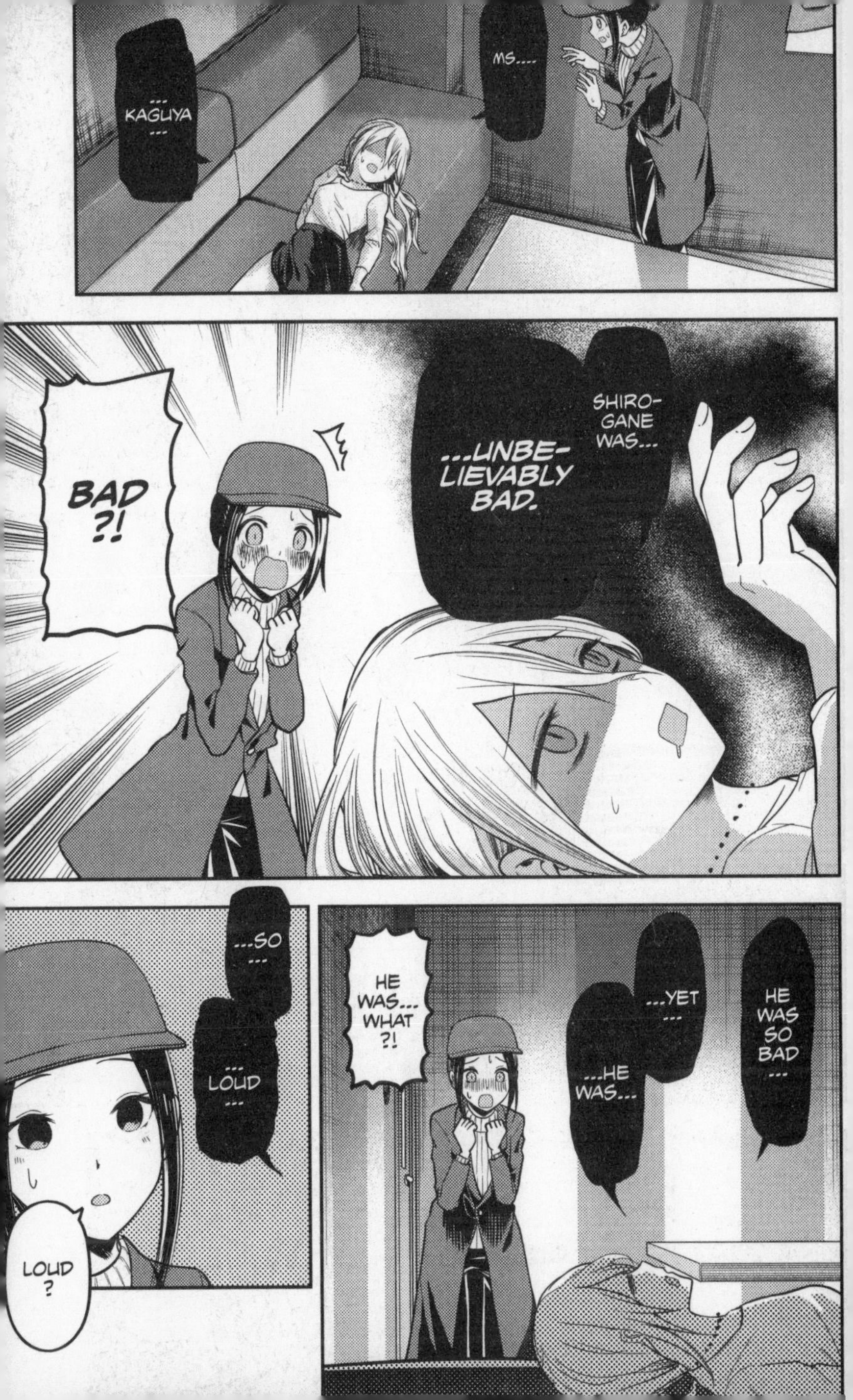
MS....
...KAGUYA...
SHIRO-GANE WAS...
...UNBE-LIEVABLY BAD.
BAD?!
HE WAS SO BAD...
...YET...
...HE WAS...
HE WAS... WHAT?!
...SO...
...LOUD...
LOUD?

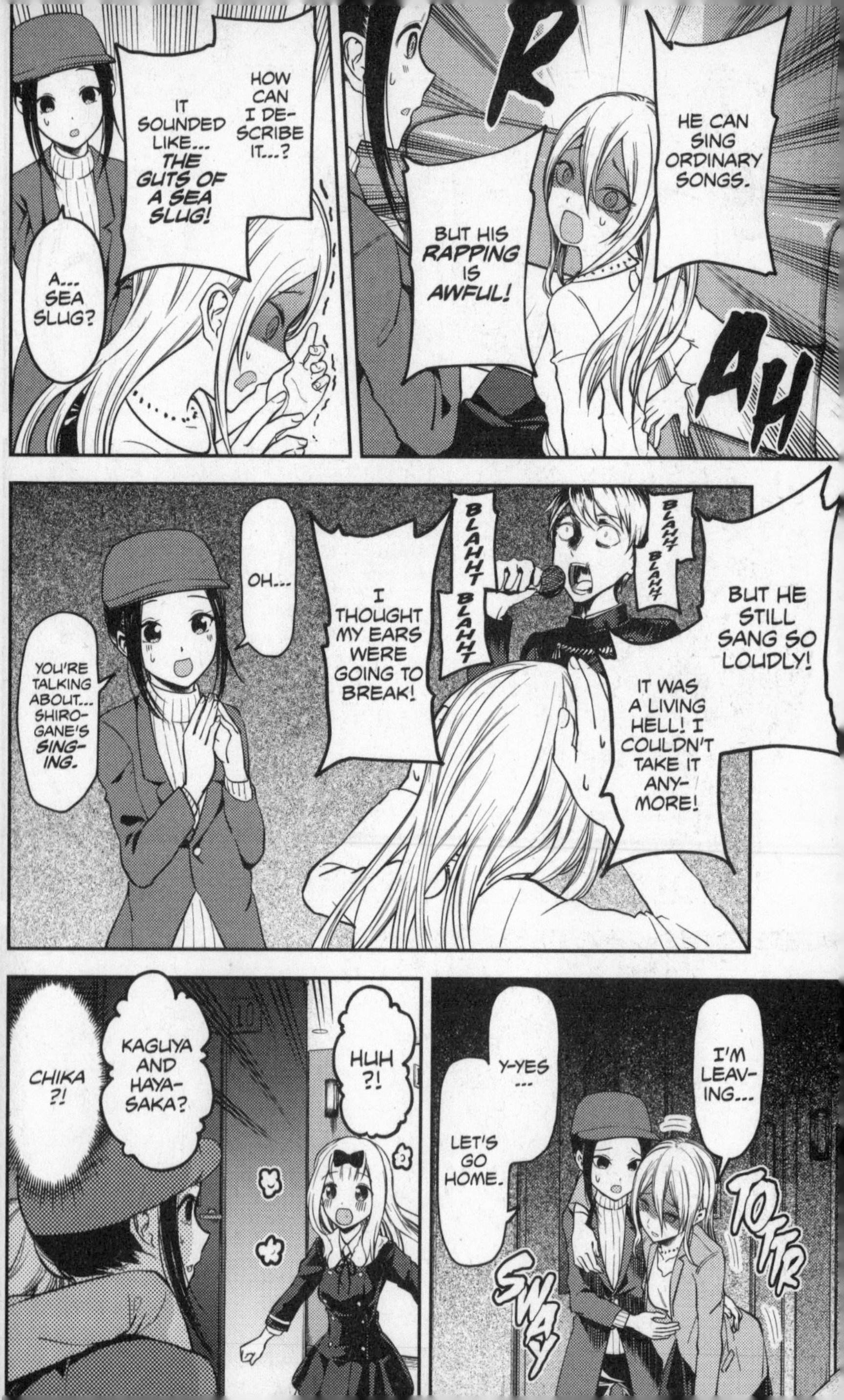

R
HE CAN SING ORDINARY SONGS.
BUT HIS RAPPING IS AWFUL!
AH
HOW CAN I DE-SCRIBE IT...?
IT SOUNDED LIKE... THE GUTS OF A SEA SLUG!
A... SEA SLUG?
BUT HE STILL SANG SO LOUDLY!
IT WAS A LIVING HELL! I COULDN'T TAKE IT ANY-MORE!
BLAHHT BLAHHT
BLAHHT BLAHHT
I THOUGHT MY EARS WERE GOING TO BREAK!
OH...
YOU'RE TALKING ABOUT... SHIRO-GANE'S SING-ING.
I'M LEAV-ING...
Y-YES...
LET'S GO HOME.
TOTTR
SWAY
HUH?!
KAGUYA AND HAYA-SAKA?
CHIKA?!

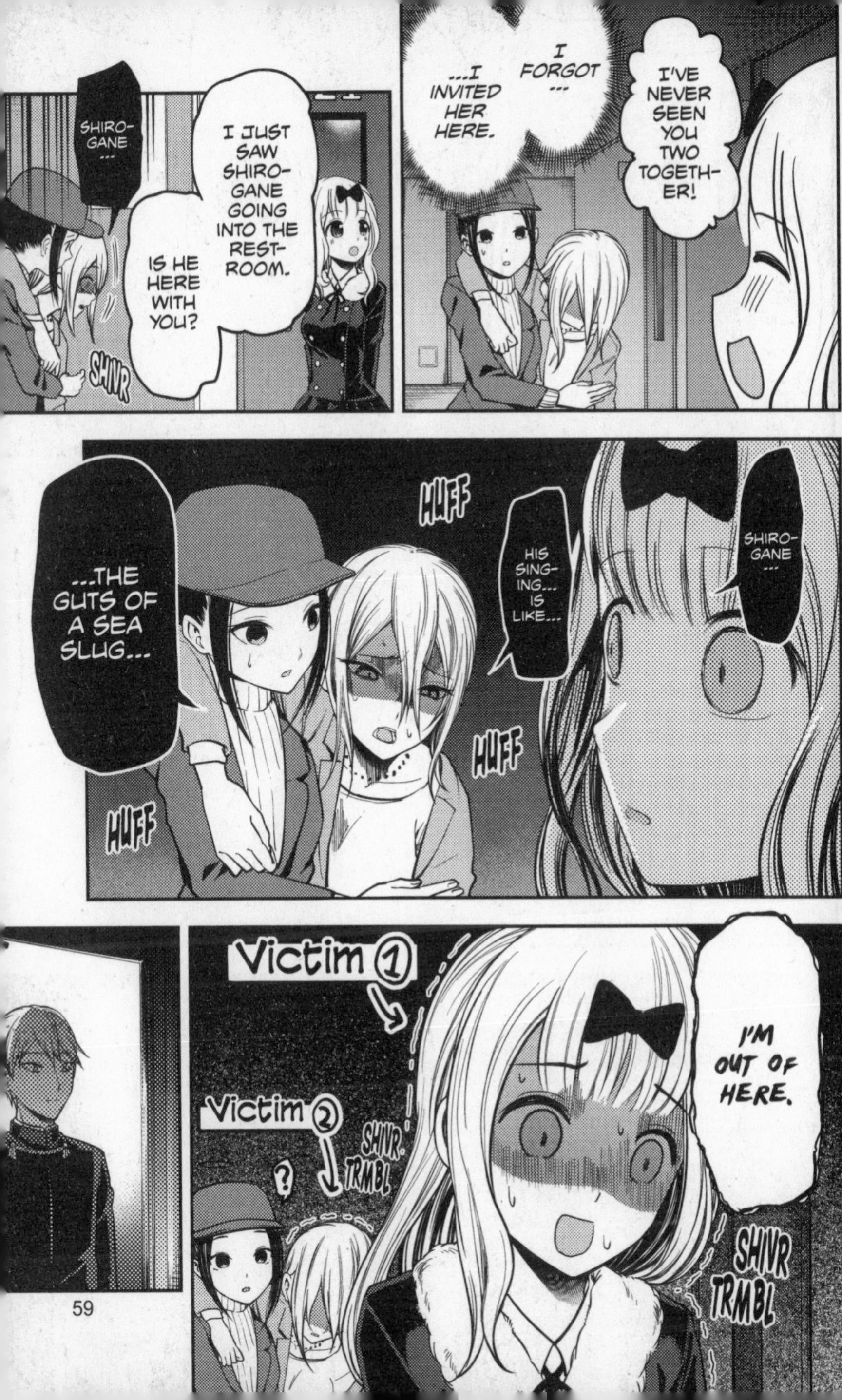
I'VE NEVER SEEN YOU TWO TOGETHER!
I FORGOT...
...I INVITED HER HERE.
I JUST SAW SHIROGANE GOING INTO THE RESTROOM.
IS HE HERE WITH YOU?
SHIROGANE...
SHIVR
SHIROGANE...
HIS SINGING... IS LIKE...
HUFF
...THE GUTS OF A SEA SLUG...
HUFF
HUFF
I'M OUT OF HERE.
SHIVR TRMBL
Victim 1
Victim 2
SHIVR. TRMBL
?

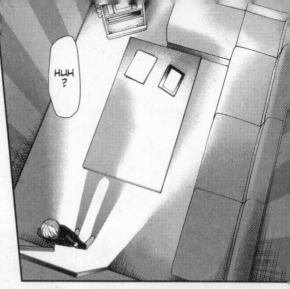

HUH
?

WHY
DID
YOU DO
THIS?

NGH

WORN
OUT

YOU
SEEMED
HAPPY
LATELY.

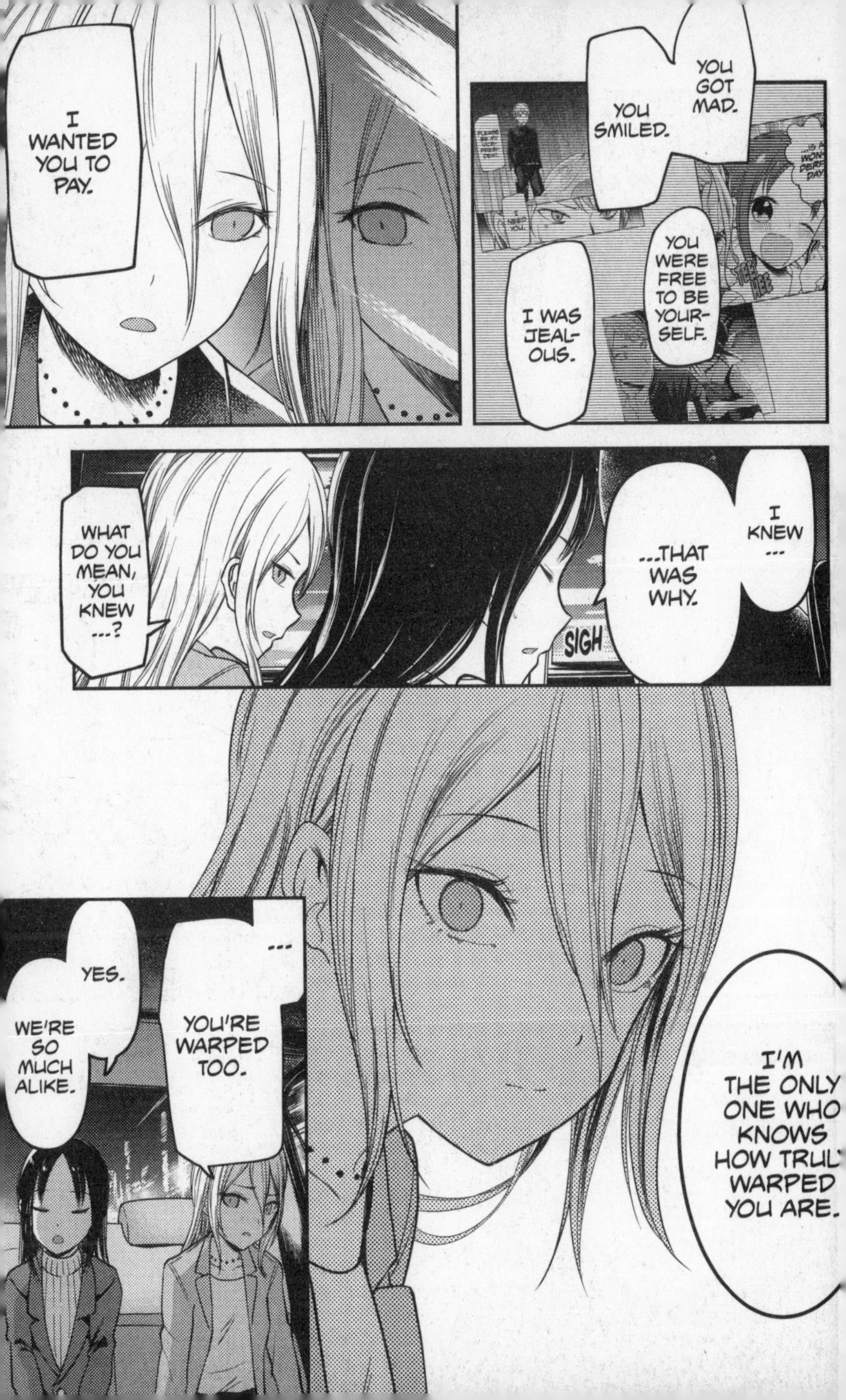
YOU GOT MAD.
YOU SMILED.
TEE HEE
YOU WERE FREE TO BE YOUR-SELF.
I WAS JEAL-OUS.
I WANTED YOU TO PAY.
I KNEW...
...THAT WAS WHY.
SIGH
WHAT DO YOU MEAN, YOU KNEW...?
I'M THE ONLY ONE WHO KNOWS HOW TRULY WARPED YOU ARE.
...
YOU'RE WARPED TOO.
YES.
WE'RE SO MUCH ALIKE.

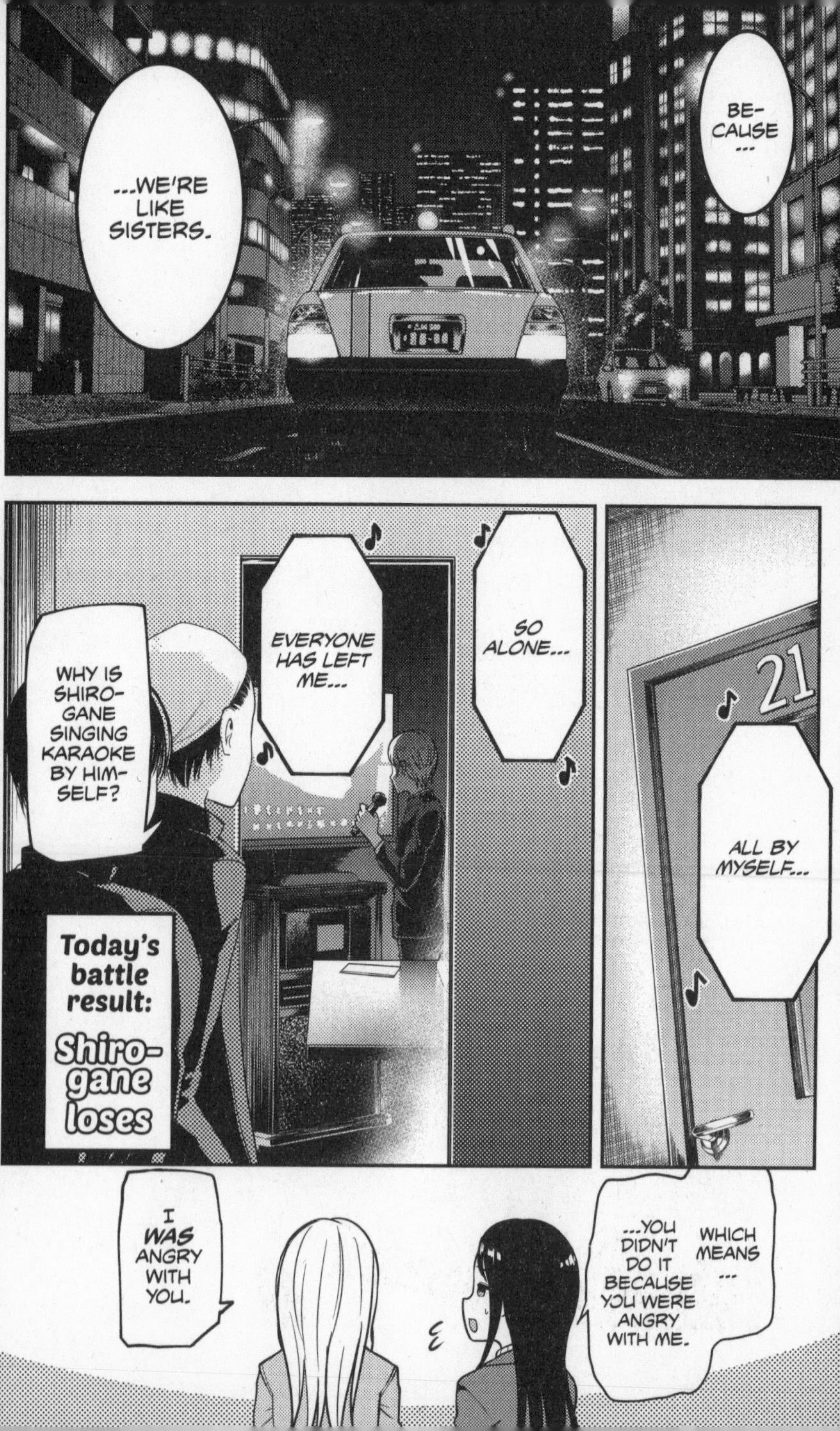
BE-CAUSE...
...WE'RE LIKE SISTERS.
ALL BY MYSELF...
SO ALONE...
EVERYONE HAS LEFT ME...
WHY IS SHIROGANE SINGING KARAOKE BY HIMSELF?
Today's battle result: Shirogane loses
WHICH MEANS...
...YOU DIDN'T DO IT BECAUSE YOU WERE ANGRY WITH ME.
I *WAS* ANGRY WITH YOU.

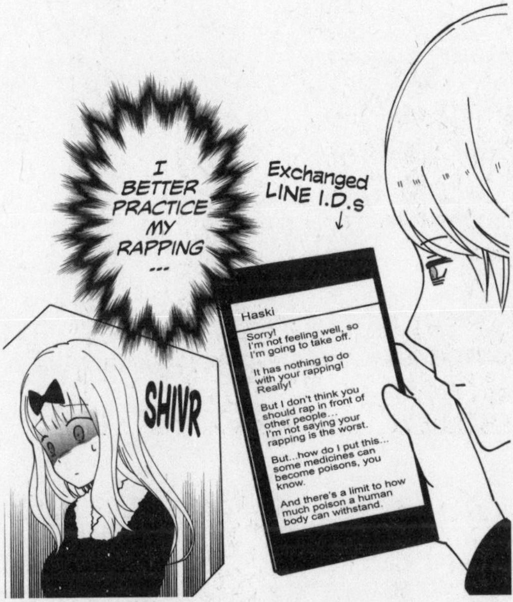
Exchanged LINE I.D.s
Haski
Sorry! I'm not feeling well, so I'm going to take off.
It has nothing to do with your rapping! Really!
But I don't think you should rap in front of other people... I'm not saying your rapping is the worst.
But...how do I put this... some medicines can become poisons, you know.
And there's a limit to how much poison a human body can withstand.
I BETTER PRACTICE MY RAPPING ...
SHIVR

KAGUYA-SAMA

LOVE IS WAR

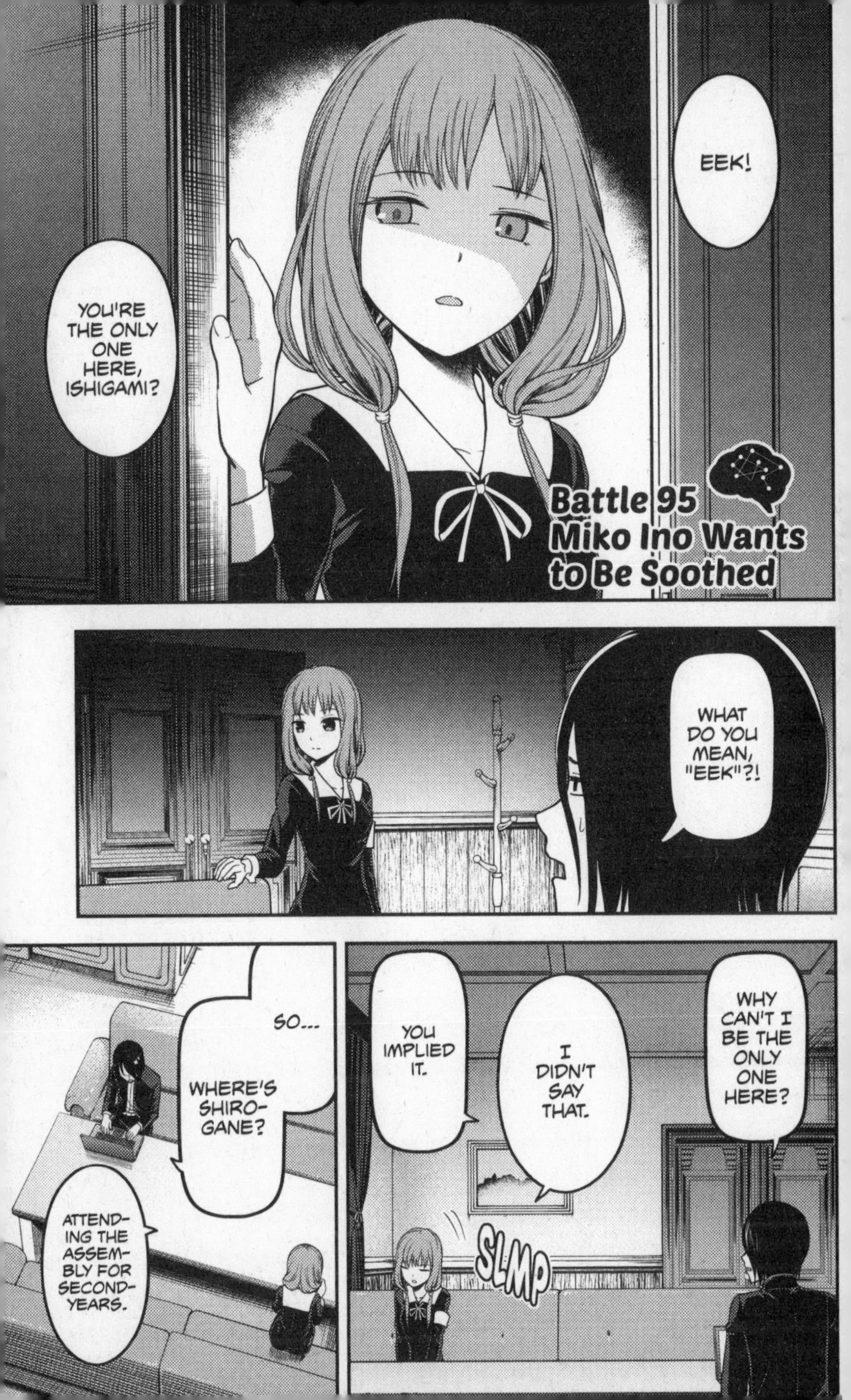
EEK!
YOU'RE THE ONLY ONE HERE, ISHIGAMI?
Battle 95
Miko Ino Wants to Be Soothed
WHAT DO YOU MEAN, "EEK"?!
WHY CAN'T I BE THE ONLY ONE HERE?
I DIDN'T SAY THAT.
YOU IMPLIED IT.
SLMP
SO...
WHERE'S SHIRO-GANE?
ATTEND-ING THE ASSEM-BLY FOR SECOND-YEARS.

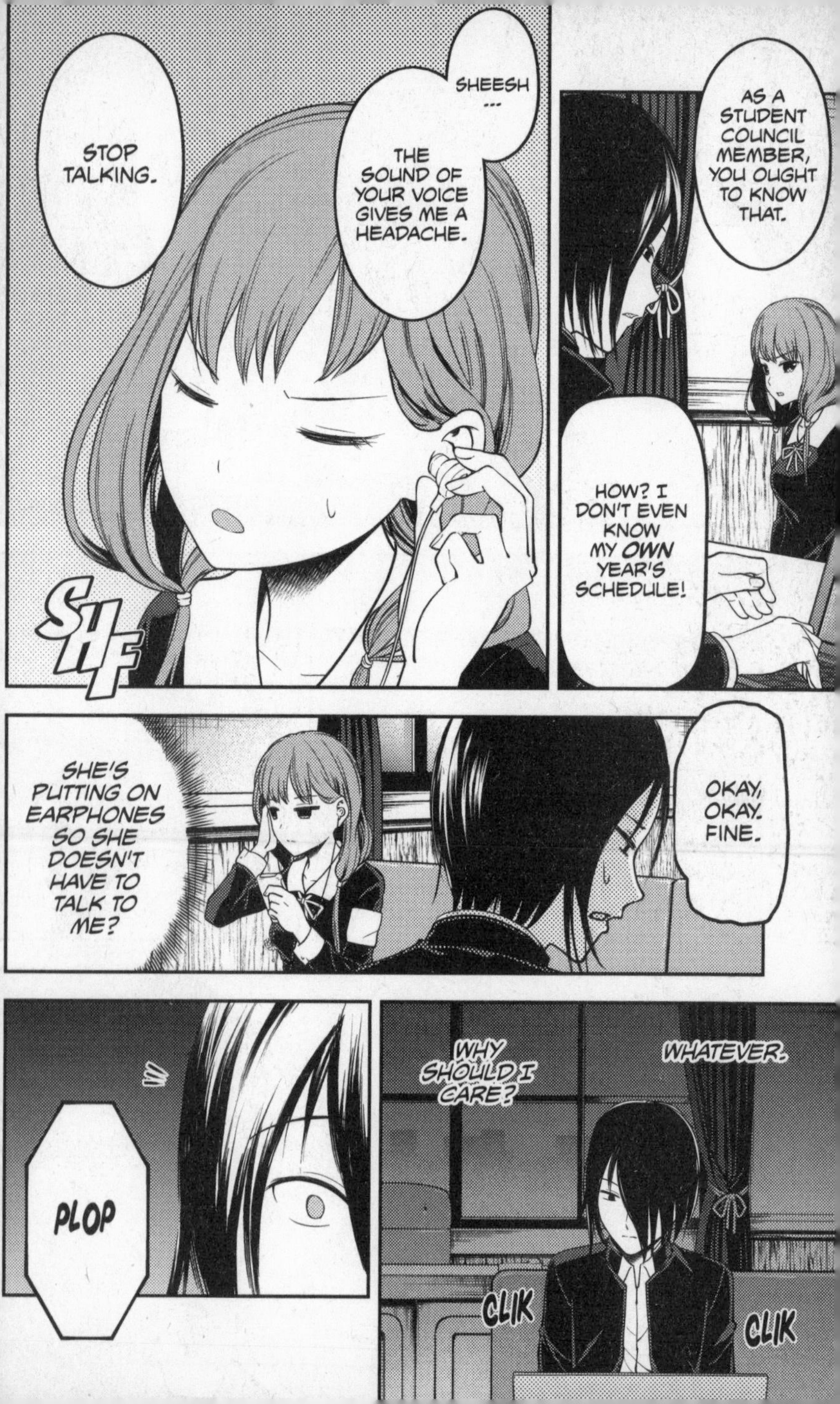
AS A STUDENT COUNCIL MEMBER, YOU OUGHT TO KNOW THAT.
HOW? I DON'T EVEN KNOW MY *OWN* YEAR'S SCHEDULE!
SHEESH...
THE SOUND OF YOUR VOICE GIVES ME A HEADACHE.
STOP TALKING.
SHF
OKAY, OKAY. FINE.
SHE'S PUTTING ON EARPHONES SO SHE DOESN'T HAVE TO TALK TO ME?
WHATEVER.
WHY SHOULD I CARE?
CLIK
CLIK
PLOP

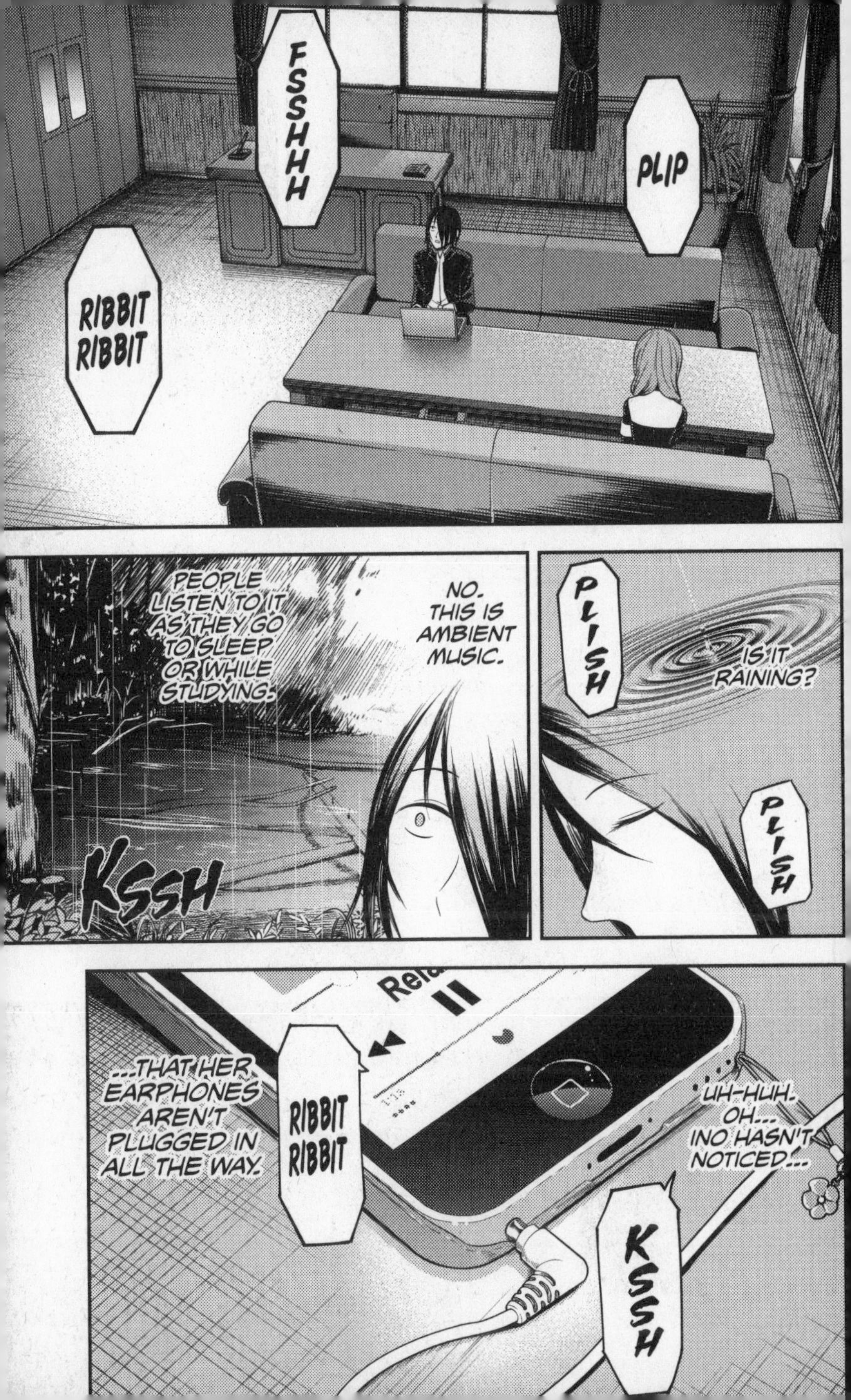
PLIP
FSSHHH
RIBBIT RIBBIT
PLISH
IS IT RAINING?
PLISH
NO. THIS IS AMBIENT MUSIC.
PEOPLE LISTEN TO IT AS THEY GO TO SLEEP OR WHILE STUDYING.
KSSH
UH-HUH. OH... INO HASN'T NOTICED...
...THAT HER EARPHONES AREN'T PLUGGED IN ALL THE WAY.
RIBBIT RIBBIT
KSSH

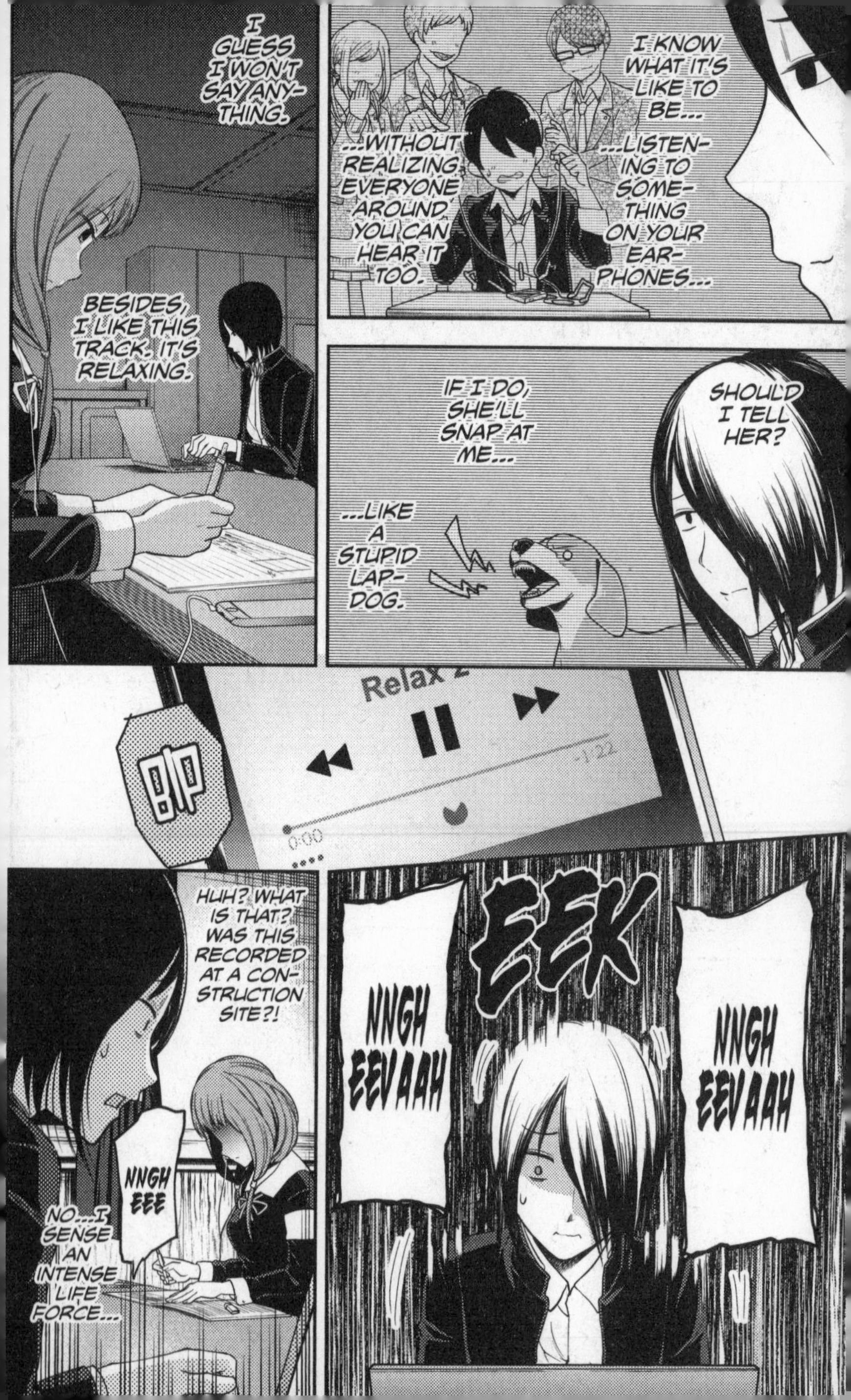
I KNOW WHAT IT'S LIKE TO BE...
...LISTENING TO SOMETHING ON YOUR EARPHONES...
...WITHOUT REALIZING EVERYONE AROUND YOU CAN HEAR IT TOO.
SHOULD I TELL HER?
IF I DO, SHE'LL SNAP AT ME...
...LIKE A STUPID LAPDOG.
I GUESS I WON'T SAY ANYTHING.
BESIDES, I LIKE THIS TRACK. IT'S RELAXING.
Relax 2
-1:22
0:00
BIP
EEK
NNGH EEVAAH
NNGH EEVAAH
HUH? WHAT IS THAT? WAS THIS RECORDED AT A CONSTRUCTION SITE?!
NNGH EEE
NO...I SENSE AN INTENSE LIFE FORCE...

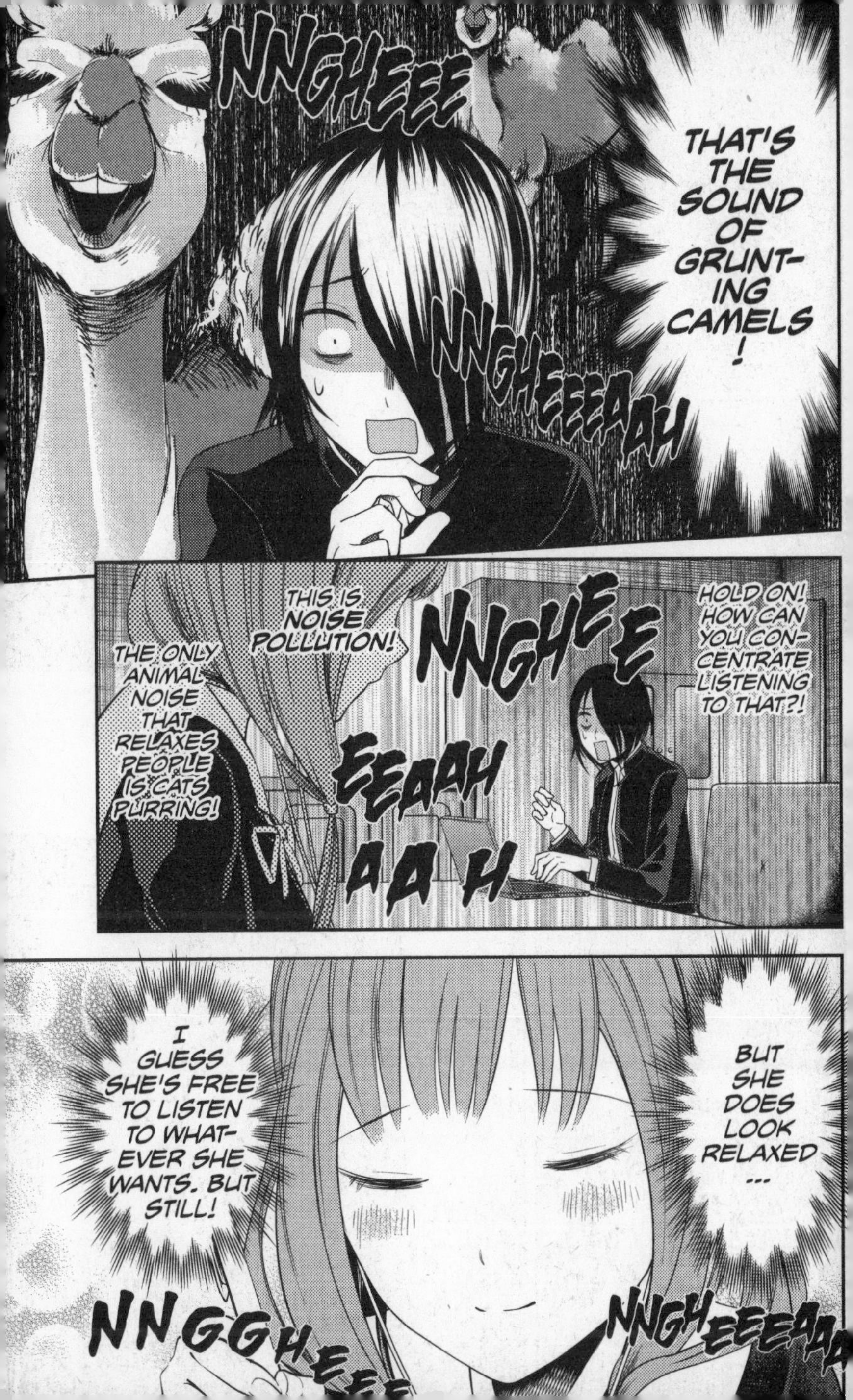
NNGHEEE
THAT'S THE SOUND OF GRUNTING CAMELS!
NNGHEEEAAH
HOLD ON! HOW CAN YOU CONCENTRATE LISTENING TO THAT?!
NNGHEE
THIS IS NOISE POLLUTION!
EEAAH AAH
THE ONLY ANIMAL NOISE THAT RELAXES PEOPLE IS CATS PURRING!
BUT SHE DOES LOOK RELAXED...
I GUESS SHE'S FREE TO LISTEN TO WHATEVER SHE WANTS. BUT STILL!
NNGHEEEAAA
NNGGHEEE

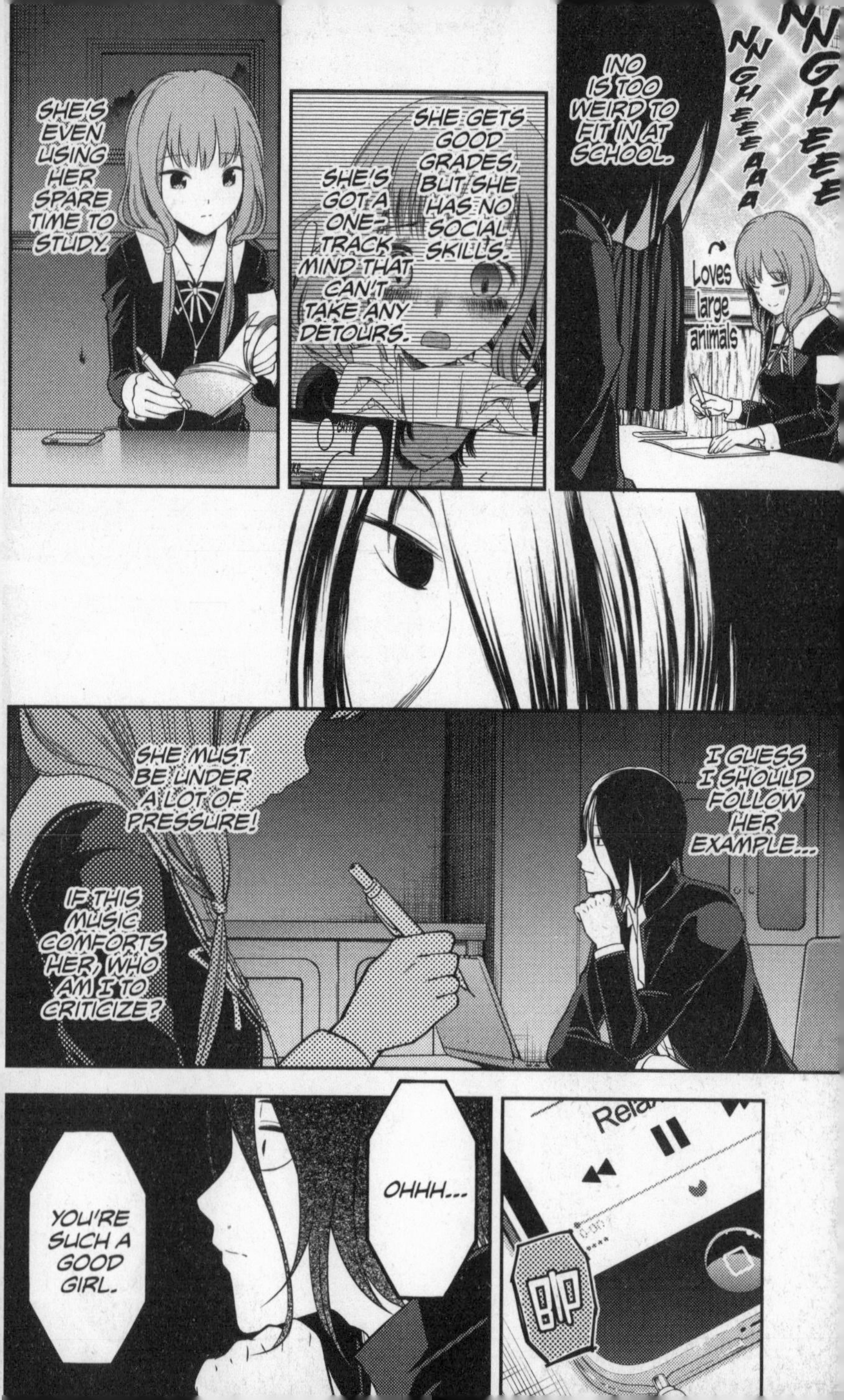
NNGHEEE
NNGHEEEAAA
INO IS TOO WEIRD TO FIT IN AT SCHOOL.
Loves large animals
SHE GETS GOOD GRADES, BUT SHE HAS NO SOCIAL SKILLS.
SHE'S GOT A ONE-TRACK MIND THAT CAN'T TAKE ANY DETOURS.
SHE'S EVEN USING HER SPARE TIME TO STUDY.
I GUESS I SHOULD FOLLOW HER EXAMPLE...
SHE MUST BE UNDER A LOT OF PRESSURE!
IF THIS MUSIC COMFORTS HER, WHO AM I TO CRITICIZE?
BIP
OHHH...
YOU'RE SUCH A GOOD GIRL.

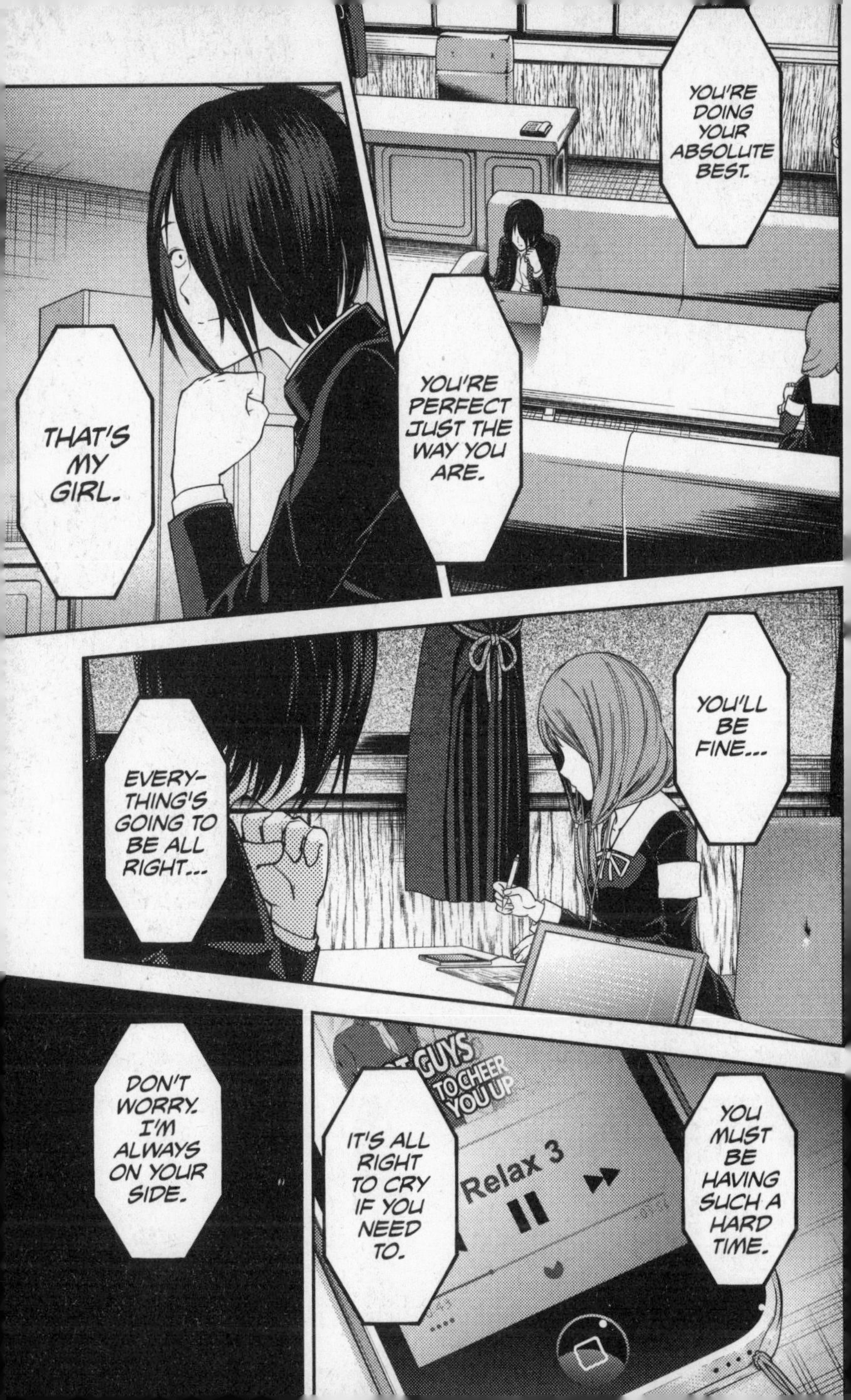
YOU'RE DOING YOUR ABSOLUTE BEST.
YOU'RE PERFECT JUST THE WAY YOU ARE.
THAT'S MY GIRL.
YOU'LL BE FINE...
EVERY-THING'S GOING TO BE ALL RIGHT...
GUYS TO CHEER YOU UP
Relax 3
YOU MUST BE HAVING SUCH A HARD TIME.
IT'S ALL RIGHT TO CRY IF YOU NEED TO.
DON'T WORRY. I'M ALWAYS ON YOUR SIDE.

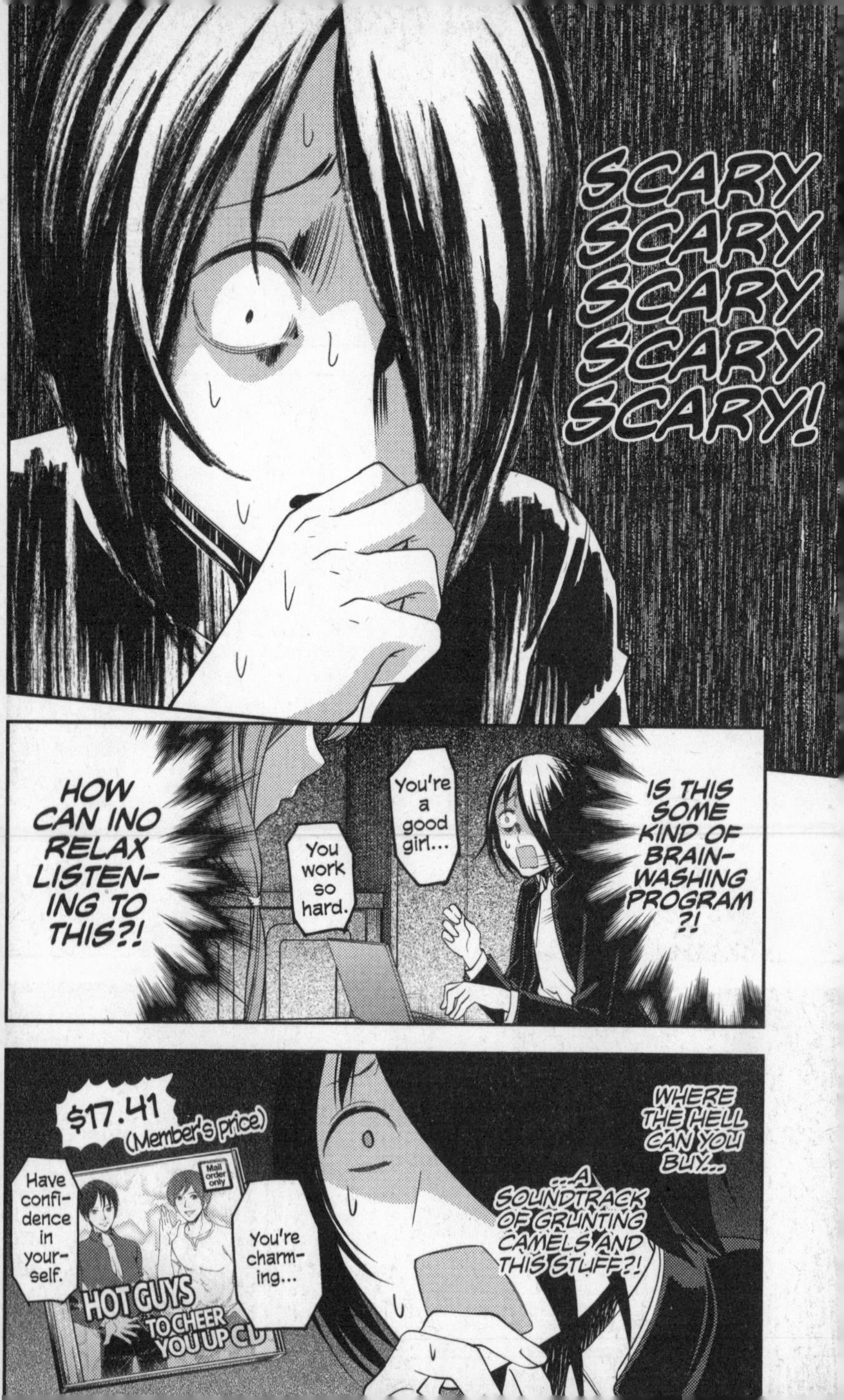
SCARY SCARY SCARY SCARY SCARY!
IS THIS SOME KIND OF BRAIN-WASHING PROGRAM?!
You're a good girl...
You work so hard.
HOW CAN INO RELAX LISTEN-ING TO THIS?!
WHERE THE HELL CAN YOU BUY...
...A SOUNDTRACK OF GRUNTING CAMELS AND THIS STUFF?!
You're charm-ing...
Have confi-dence in your-self.
$17.41 (Member's price)
Mail order only
HOT GUYS TO CHEER YOU UP CD

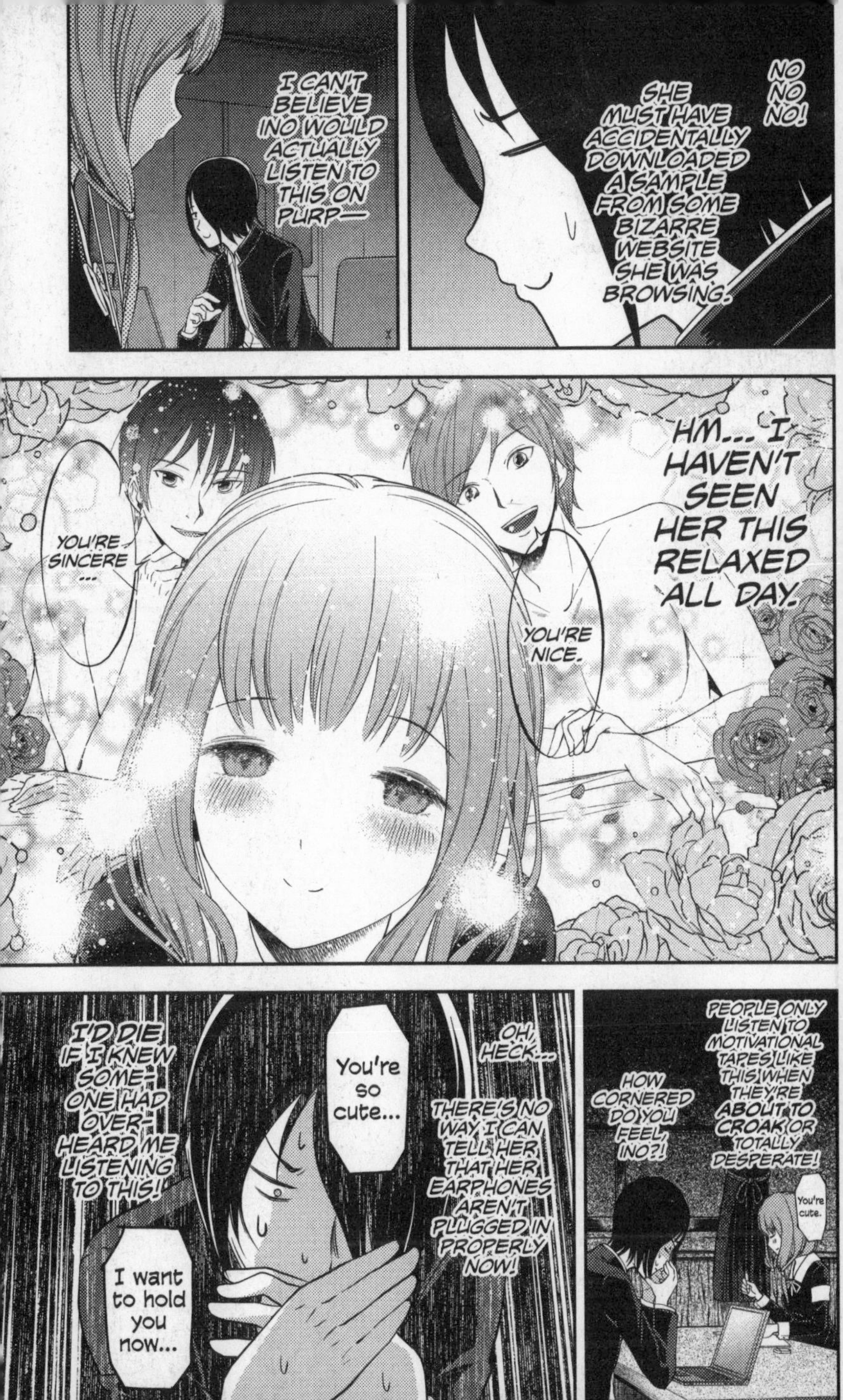
NO NO NO!
SHE MUST HAVE ACCIDENTALLY DOWNLOADED A SAMPLE FROM SOME BIZARRE WEBSITE SHE WAS BROWSING.
I CAN'T BELIEVE INO WOULD ACTUALLY LISTEN TO THIS ON PURP—
HM... I HAVEN'T SEEN HER THIS RELAXED ALL DAY.
YOU'RE NICE.
YOU'RE SINCERE...
PEOPLE ONLY LISTEN TO MOTIVATIONAL TAPES LIKE THIS WHEN THEY'RE ABOUT TO CROAK OR TOTALLY DESPERATE!
HOW CORNERED DO YOU FEEL, INO?!
You're cute.
OH, HECK...
THERE'S NO WAY I CAN TELL HER THAT HER EARPHONES AREN'T PLUGGED IN PROPERLY NOW!
You're so cute...
I'D DIE IF I KNEW SOME-ONE HAD OVER-HEARD ME LISTENING TO THIS!
I want to hold you now...

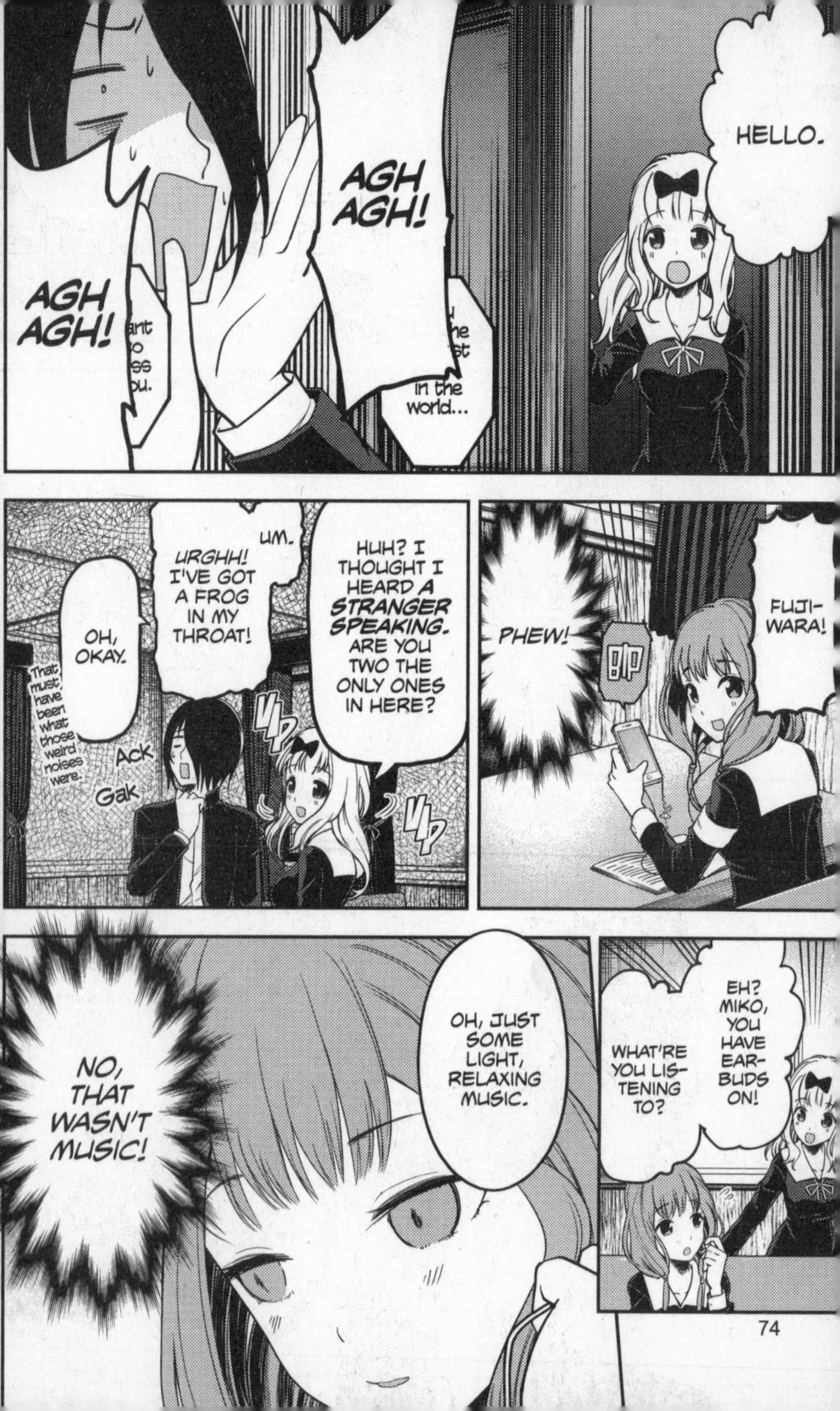
HELLO.
AGH AGH!
in the world...
AGH AGH!
FUJI-WARA!
BIP
PHEW!
HUH? I THOUGHT I HEARD A STRANGER SPEAKING. ARE YOU TWO THE ONLY ONES IN HERE?
UM.
URGHH! I'VE GOT A FROG IN MY THROAT!
OH, OKAY.
That must have been what those weird noises were.
Ack
Gak
EH? MIKO, YOU HAVE EAR-BUDS ON!
WHAT'RE YOU LIS-TENING TO?
OH, JUST SOME LIGHT, RELAXING MUSIC.
NO, THAT WASN'T MUSIC!

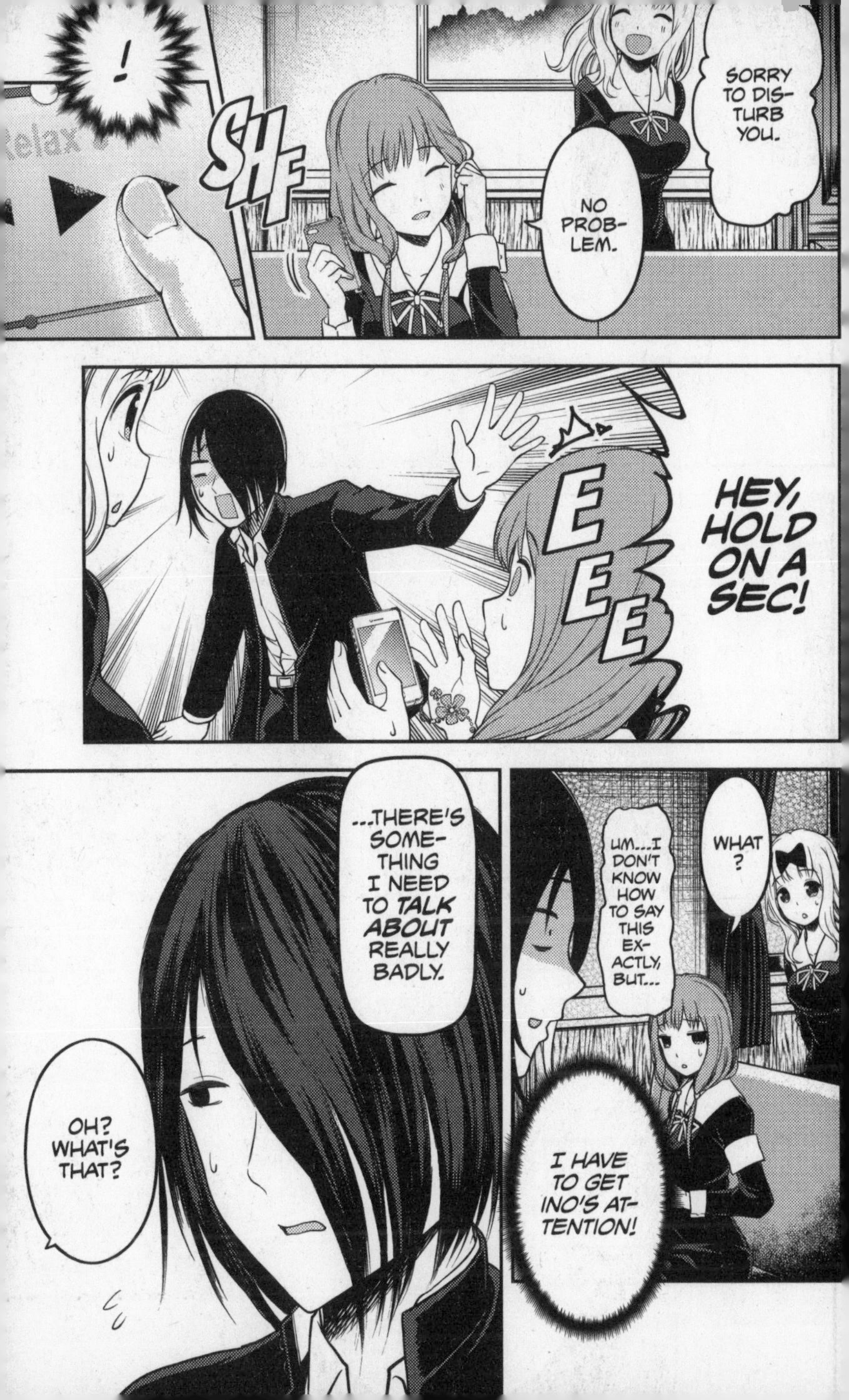
SORRY TO DIS-TURB YOU.
NO PROB-LEM.
SHF
!
Relax
HEY, HOLD ON A SEC!
EEE
WHAT?
UM...I DON'T KNOW HOW TO SAY THIS EX-ACTLY, BUT...
I HAVE TO GET INO'S AT-TENTION!
...THERE'S SOME-THING I NEED TO *TALK ABOUT* REALLY BADLY.
OH? WHAT'S THAT?

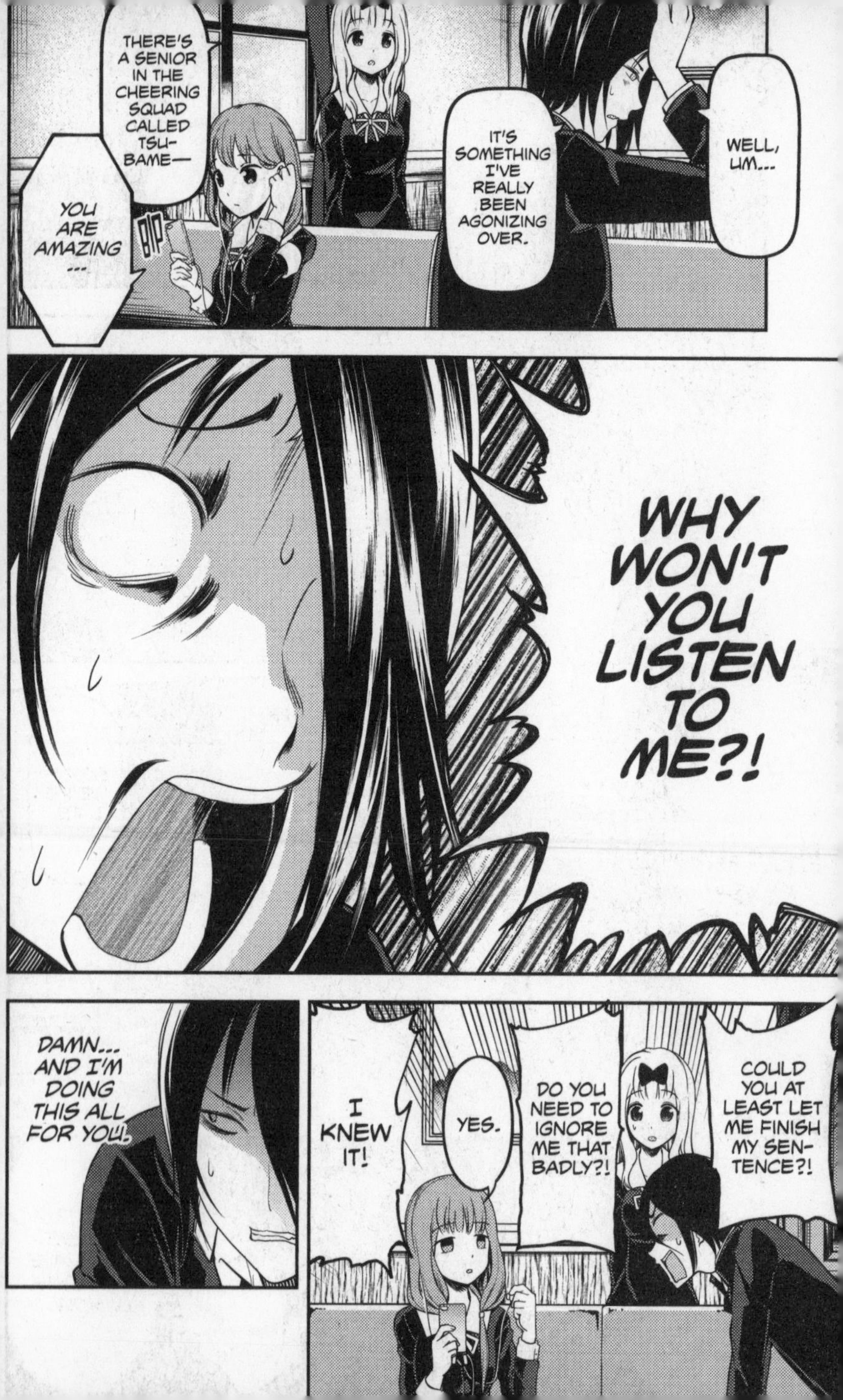
WELL, UM...
IT'S SOMETHING I'VE REALLY BEEN AGONIZING OVER.
THERE'S A SENIOR IN THE CHEERING SQUAD CALLED TSU-BAME—
BIP
YOU ARE AMAZING...
WHY WON'T YOU LISTEN TO ME?!
COULD YOU AT LEAST LET ME FINISH MY SEN-TENCE?!
DO YOU NEED TO IGNORE ME THAT BADLY?!
YES.
I KNEW IT!
DAMN... AND I'M DOING THIS ALL FOR YOU.

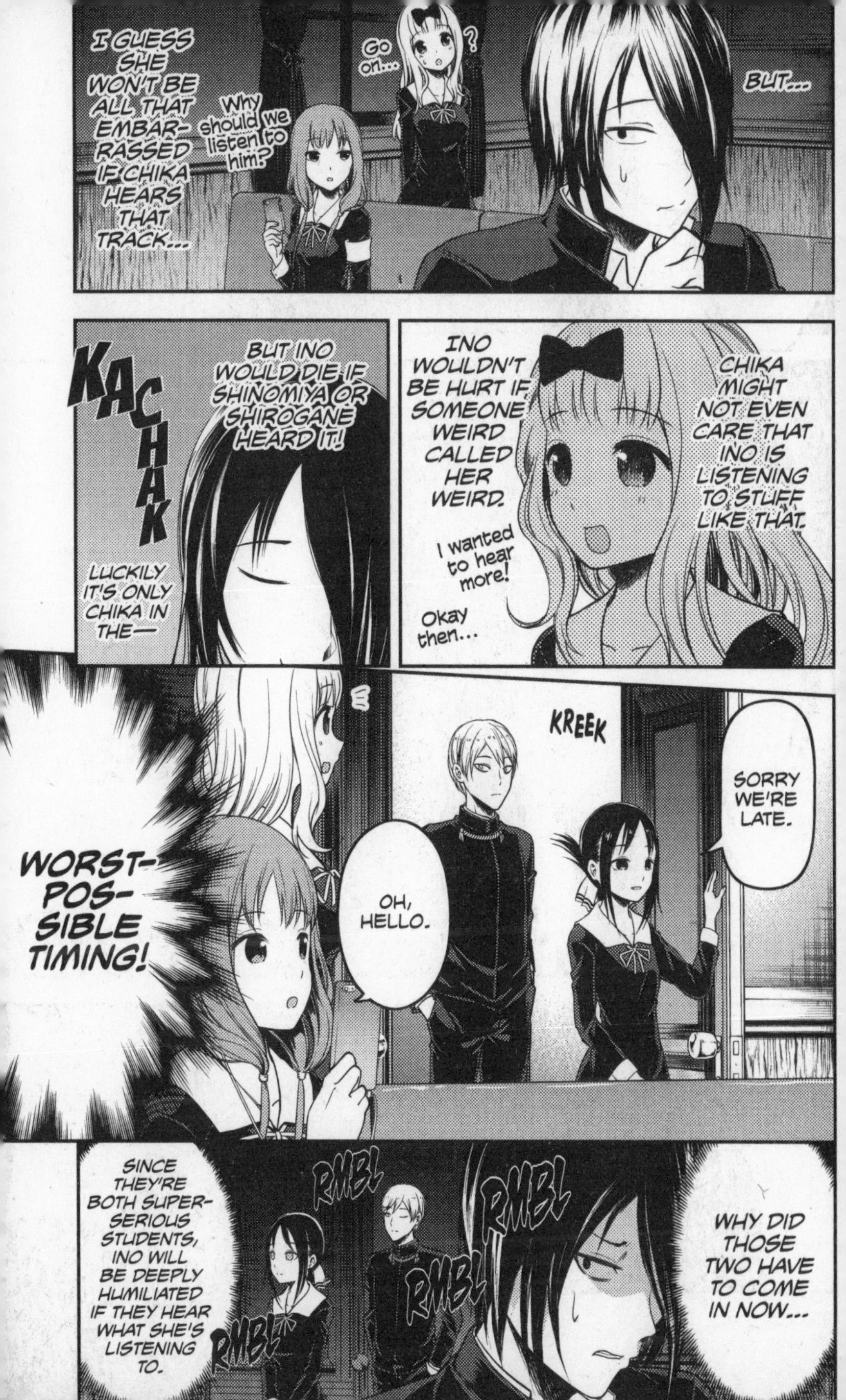
BUT...
Go on...
?
Why should we listen to him?
I GUESS SHE WON'T BE ALL THAT EMBARRASSED IF CHIKA HEARS THAT TRACK...
CHIKA MIGHT NOT EVEN CARE THAT INO IS LISTENING TO STUFF LIKE THAT.
INO WOULDN'T BE HURT IF SOMEONE WEIRD CALLED HER WEIRD.
I wanted to hear more!
Okay then...
BUT INO WOULD DIE IF SHINOMIYA OR SHIROGANE HEARD IT!
KACHAK
LUCKILY IT'S ONLY CHIKA IN THE—
KREEK
SORRY WE'RE LATE.
OH, HELLO.
WORST-POSSIBLE TIMING!
WHY DID THOSE TWO HAVE TO COME IN NOW...
RMBL
RMBL
RMBL
RMBL
SINCE THEY'RE BOTH SUPER-SERIOUS STUDENTS, INO WILL BE DEEPLY HUMILIATED IF THEY HEAR WHAT SHE'S LISTENING TO.

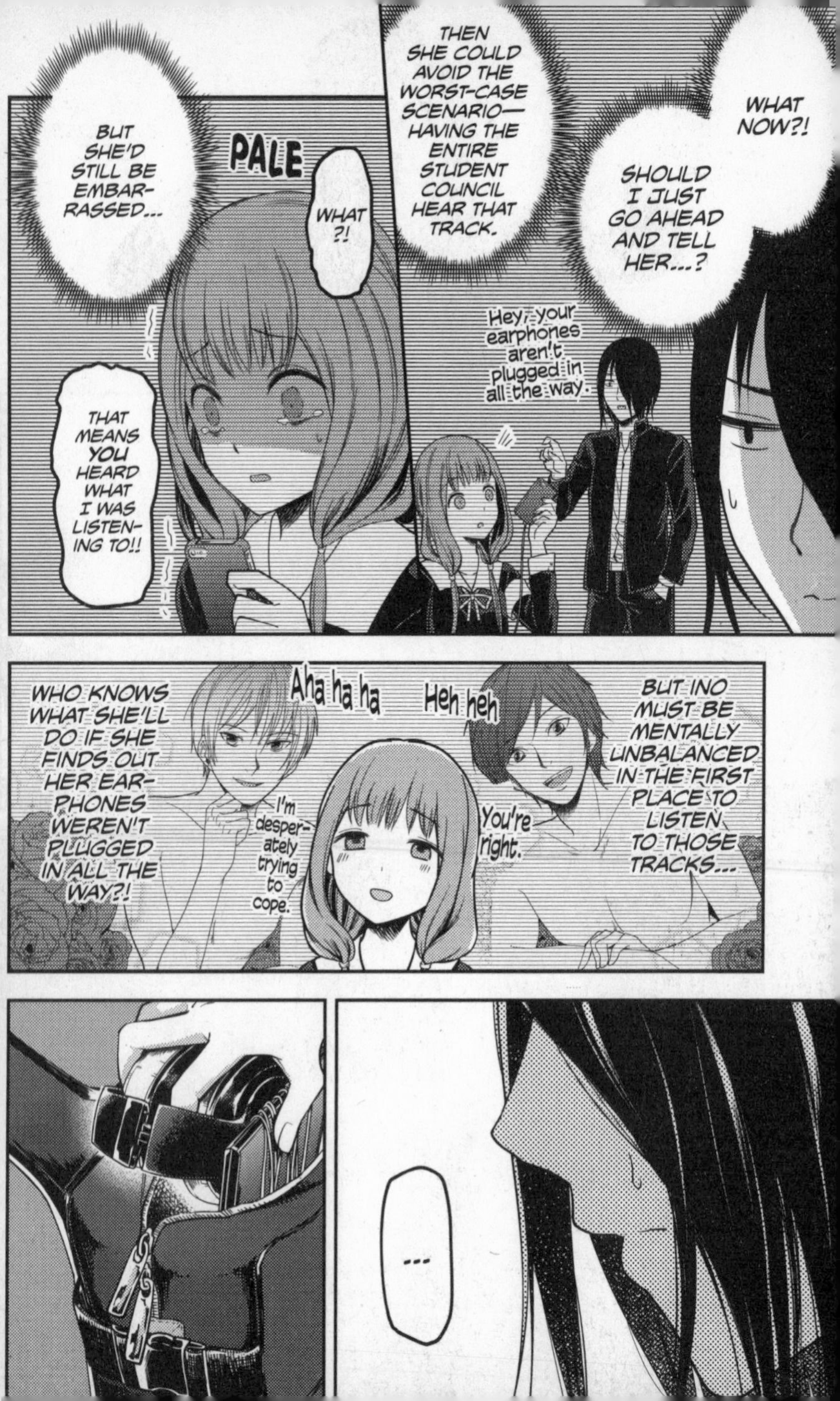
WHAT NOW?!
SHOULD I JUST GO AHEAD AND TELL HER...?
THEN SHE COULD AVOID THE WORST-CASE SCENARIO—HAVING THE ENTIRE STUDENT COUNCIL HEAR THAT TRACK.
Hey, your earphones aren't plugged in all the way.
WHAT?!
PALE
BUT SHE'D STILL BE EMBARRASSED...
THAT MEANS YOU HEARD WHAT I WAS LISTENING TO!!
BUT INO MUST BE MENTALLY UNBALANCED IN THE FIRST PLACE TO LISTEN TO THOSE TRACKS...
Heh heh
You're right.
I'm desperately trying to cope.
Aha ha ha
WHO KNOWS WHAT SHE'LL DO IF SHE FINDS OUT HER EARPHONES WEREN'T PLUGGED IN ALL THE WAY?!
...

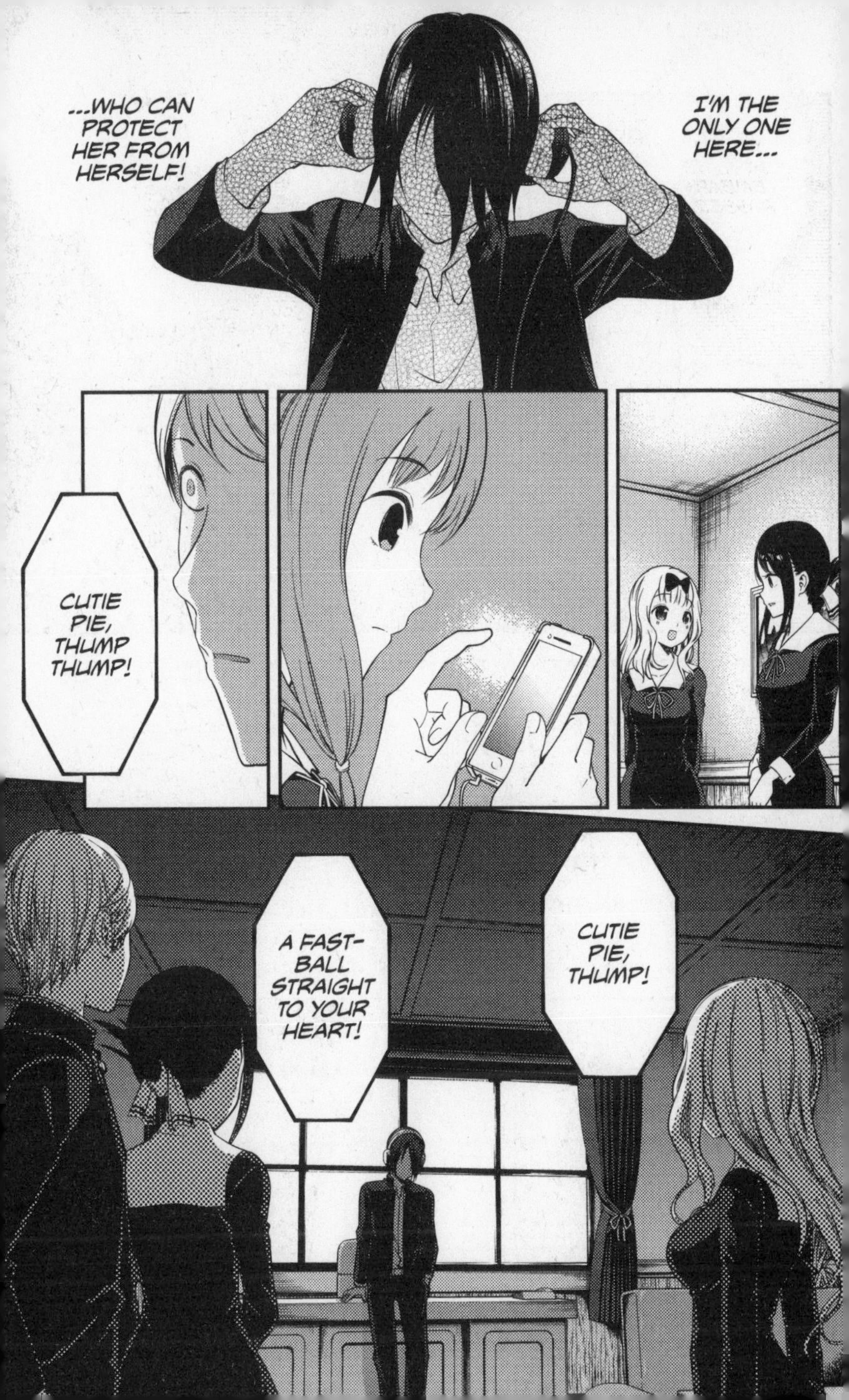
I'M THE ONLY ONE HERE...
...WHO CAN PROTECT HER FROM HERSELF!
CUTIE PIE, THUMP THUMP!
CUTIE PIE, THUMP!
A FAST-BALL STRAIGHT TO YOUR HEART!

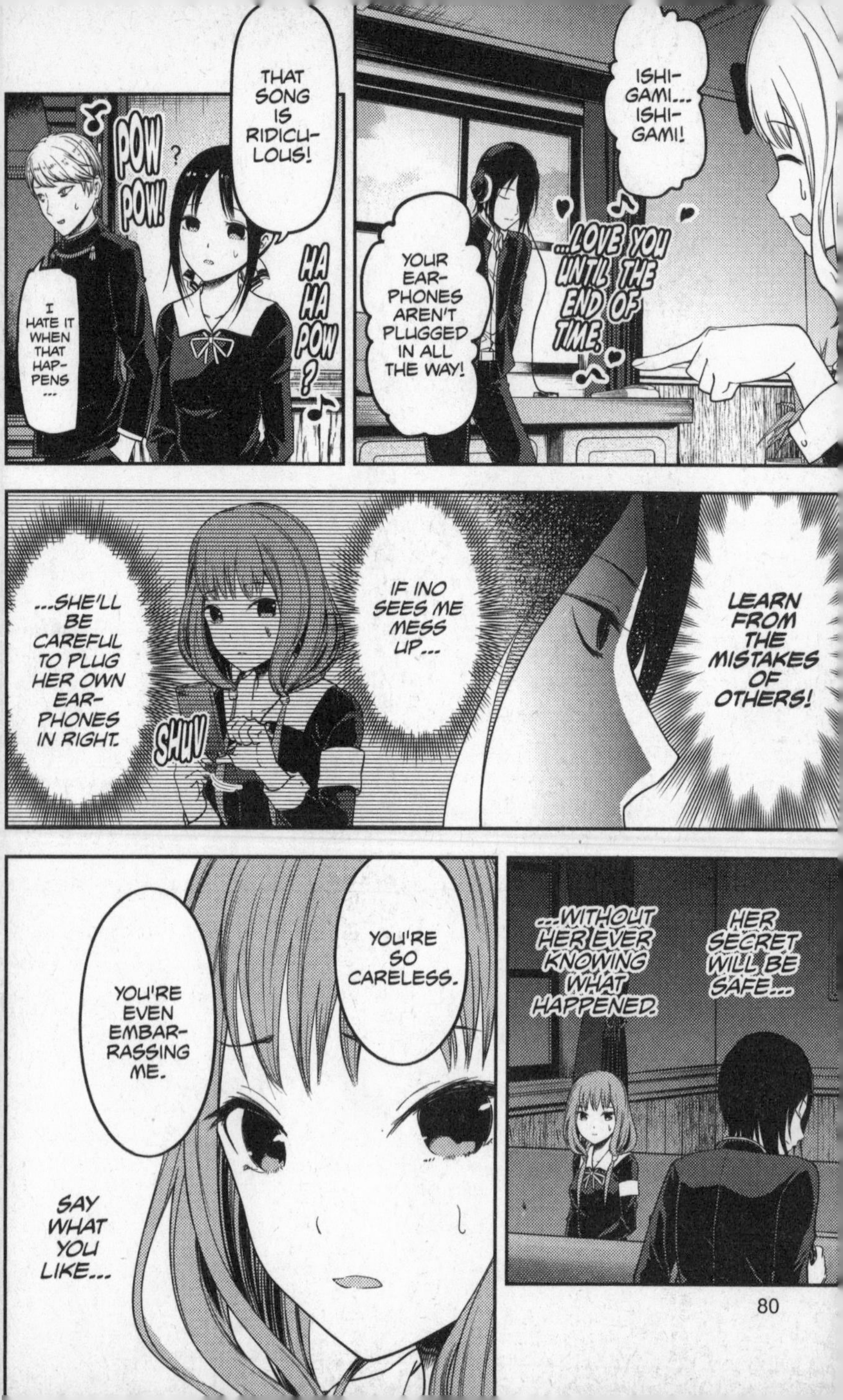

ISHI-GAMI... ISHI-GAMI!
...LOVE YOU UNTIL THE END OF TIME.
YOUR EAR-PHONES AREN'T PLUGGED IN ALL THE WAY!
THAT SONG IS RIDICU-LOUS!
POW POW!
?
HA HA POW?
I HATE IT WHEN THAT HAP-PENS...
LEARN FROM THE MISTAKES OF OTHERS!
IF INO SEES ME MESS UP...
...SHE'LL BE CAREFUL TO PLUG HER OWN EAR-PHONES IN RIGHT.
SHUV
HER SECRET WILL BE SAFE...
...WITHOUT HER EVER KNOWING WHAT HAPPENED.
YOU'RE SO CARELESS.
YOU'RE EVEN EMBAR-RASSING ME.
...
SAY WHAT YOU LIKE...

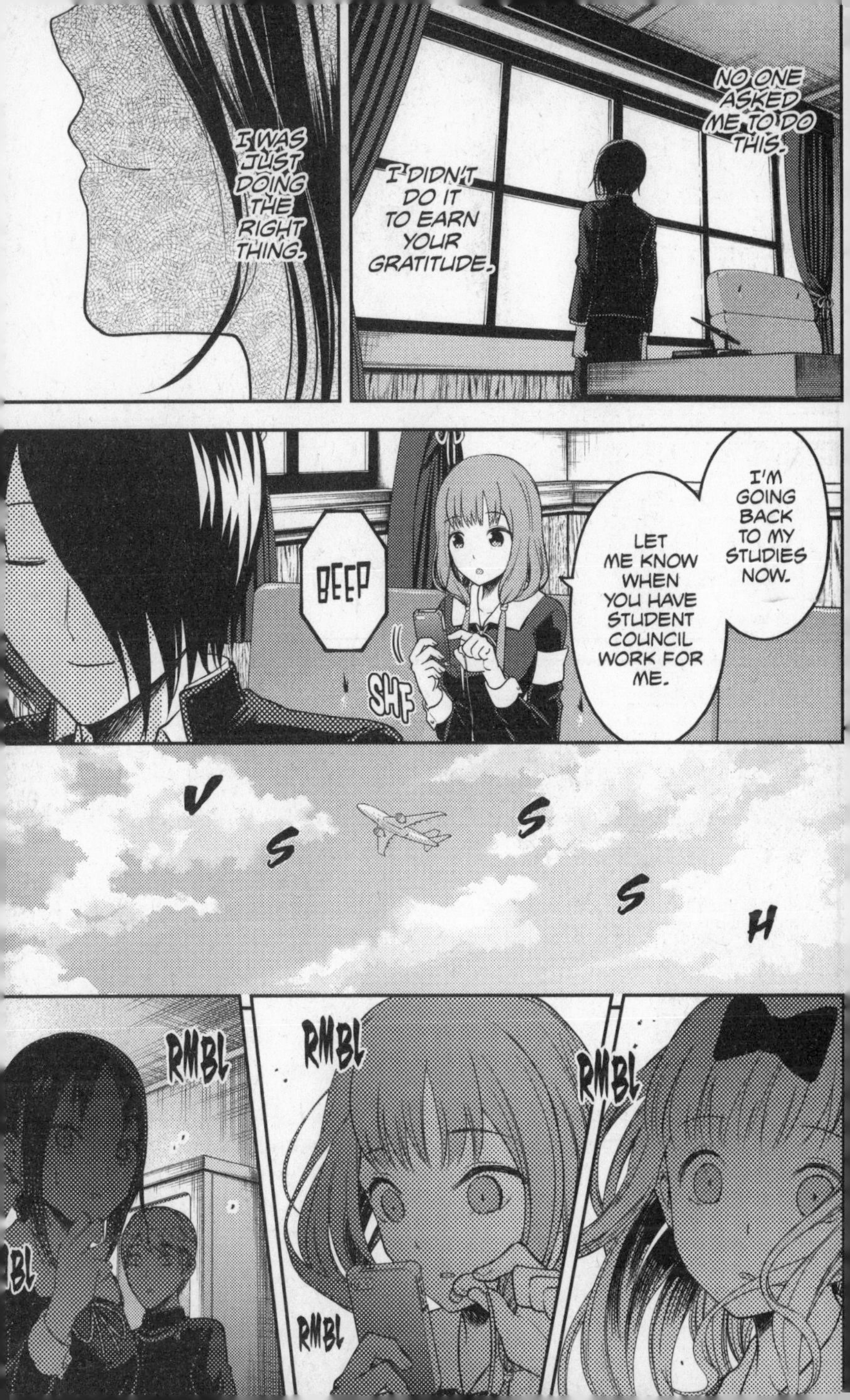
NO ONE ASKED ME TO DO THIS.
I DIDN'T DO IT TO EARN YOUR GRATITUDE.
I WAS JUST DOING THE RIGHT THING.
I'M GOING BACK TO MY STUDIES NOW.
LET ME KNOW WHEN YOU HAVE STUDENT COUNCIL WORK FOR ME.
BEEP
SHF
VSSSH
RMBL
RMBL
RMBL
RMBL

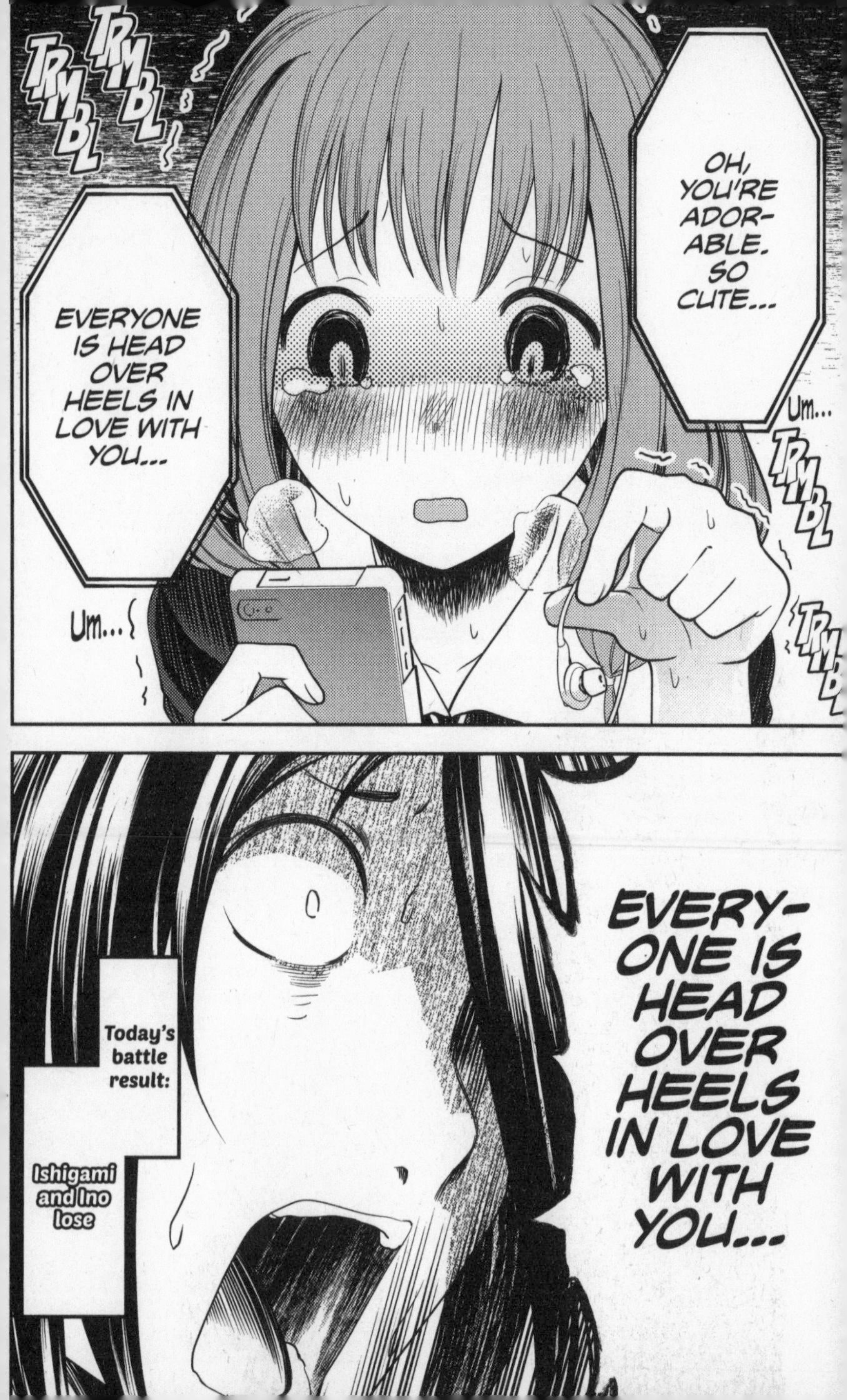
OH, YOU'RE ADORABLE. SO CUTE...
Um...
TRMBL
TRMBL
TRMBL
TRMBL
EVERYONE IS HEAD OVER HEELS IN LOVE WITH YOU...
Um...
EVERYONE IS HEAD OVER HEELS IN LOVE WITH YOU...
Today's battle result:
Ishigami and Ino lose

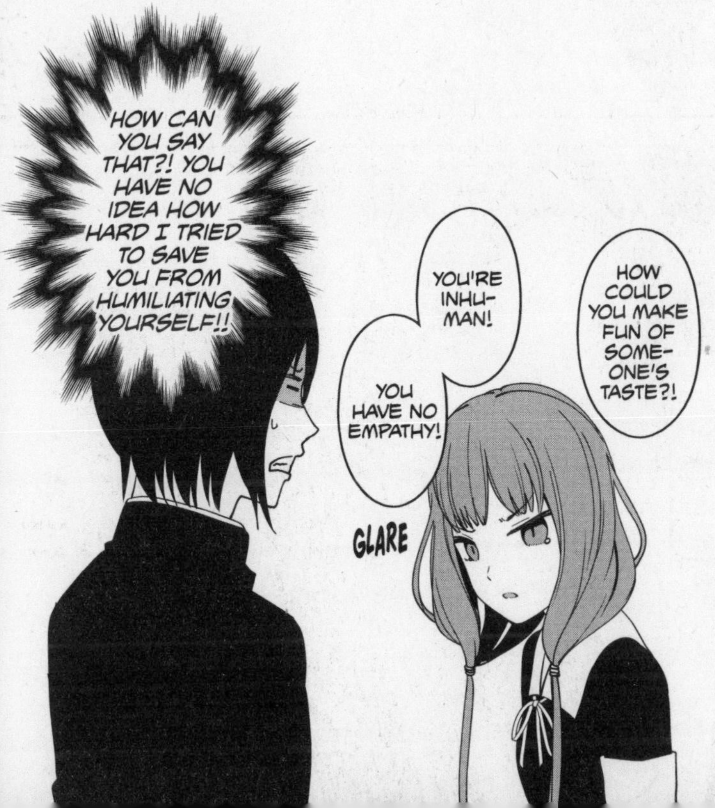
HOW COULD YOU MAKE FUN OF SOME-ONE'S TASTE?!
YOU'RE INHU-MAN!
YOU HAVE NO EMPATHY!
GLARE
HOW CAN YOU SAY THAT?! YOU HAVE NO IDEA HOW HARD I TRIED TO SAVE YOU FROM HUMILIATING YOURSELF!!

KAGUYA-SAMA
LOVE IS WAR

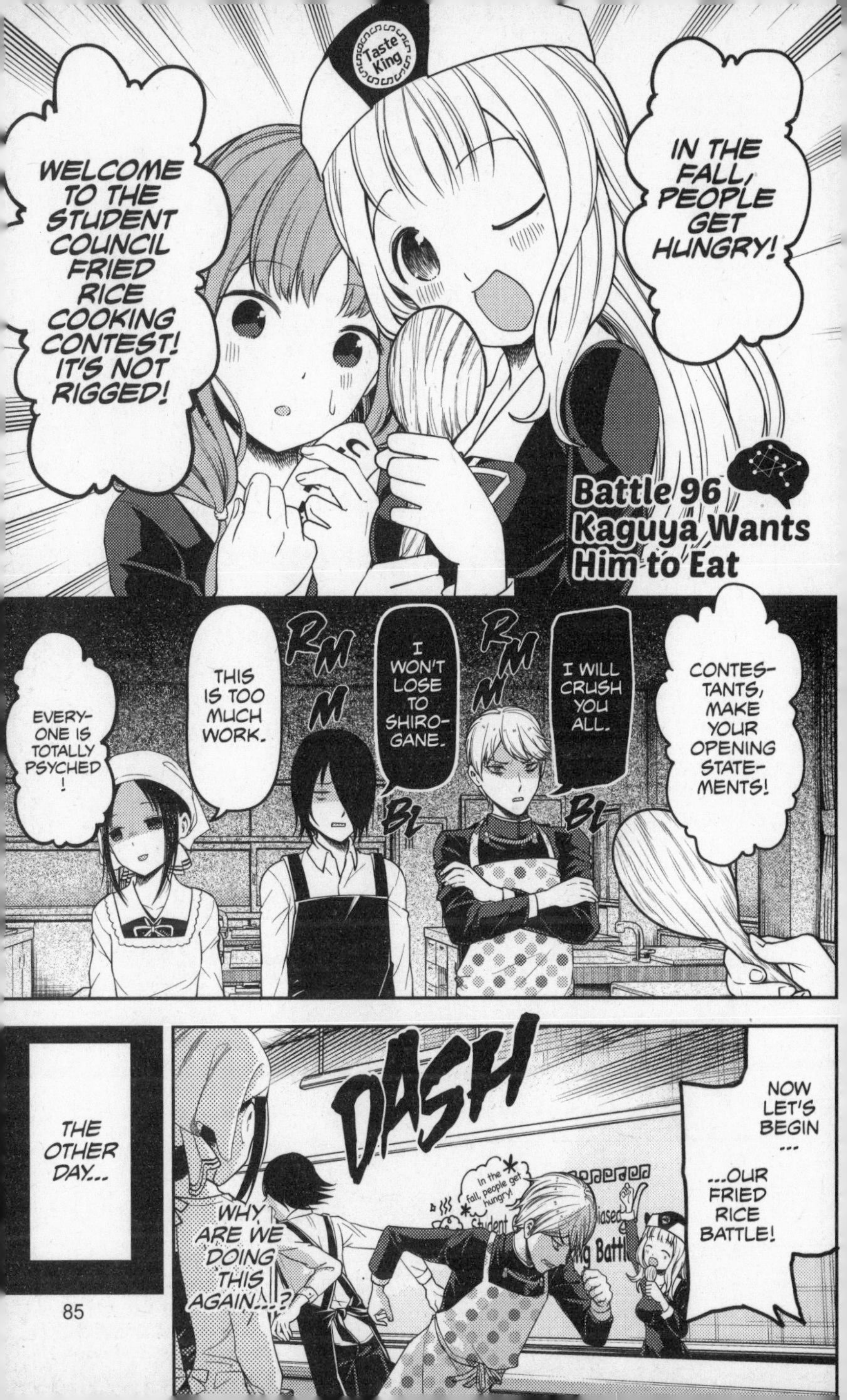
Taste King
IN THE FALL, PEOPLE GET HUNGRY!
WELCOME TO THE STUDENT COUNCIL FRIED RICE COOKING CONTEST! IT'S NOT RIGGED!
Battle 96 Kaguya Wants Him to Eat
CONTESTANTS, MAKE YOUR OPENING STATEMENTS!
I WILL CRUSH YOU ALL.
RMM
BL
I WON'T LOSE TO SHIROGANE.
RMM
BL
THIS IS TOO MUCH WORK.
EVERYONE IS TOTALLY PSYCHED!
NOW LET'S BEGIN...
...OUR FRIED RICE BATTLE!
DASH
*In the fall, people get hungry!
WHY ARE WE DOING THIS AGAIN...!?
THE OTHER DAY...

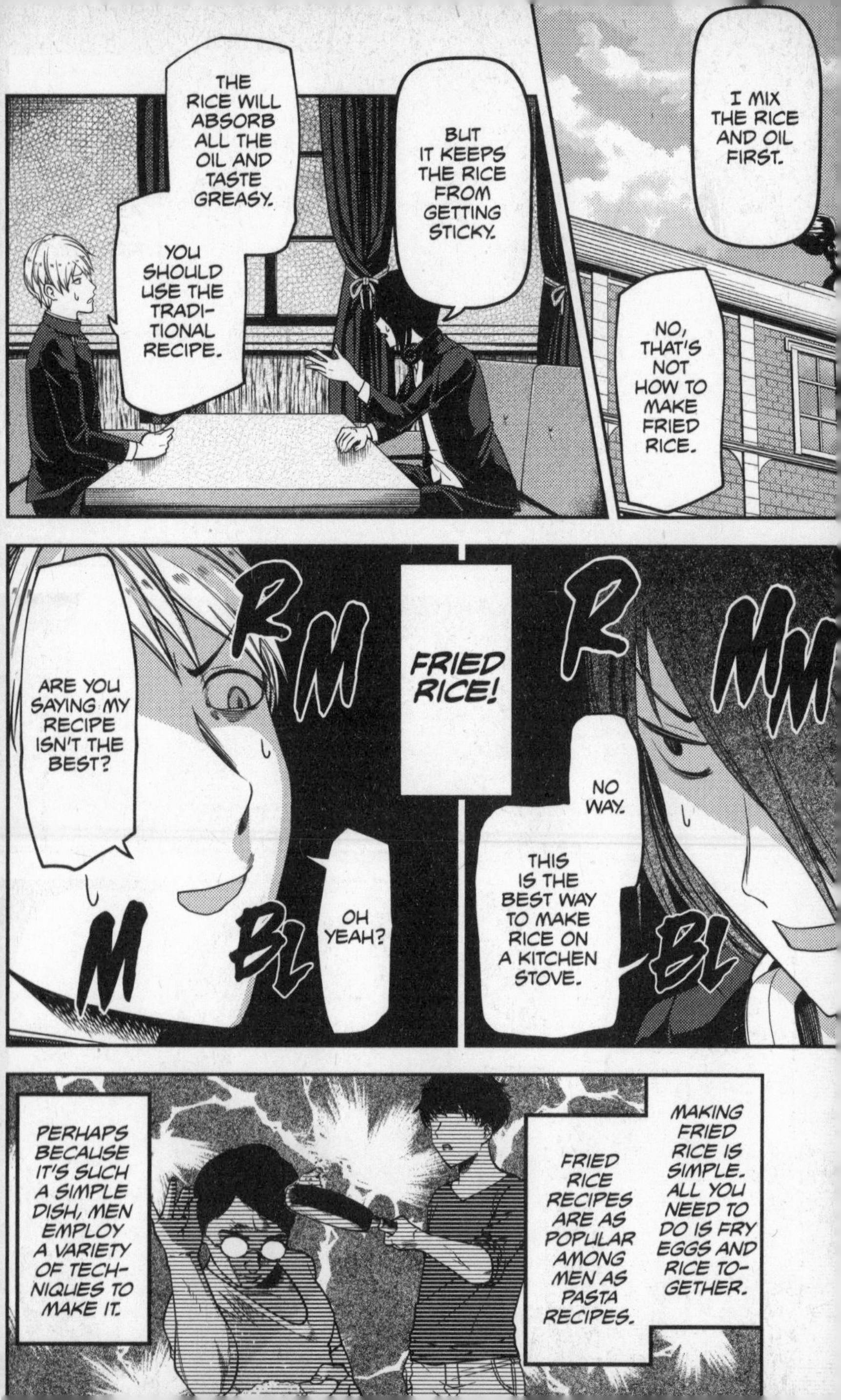
I MIX THE RICE AND OIL FIRST.
NO, THAT'S NOT HOW TO MAKE FRIED RICE.
BUT IT KEEPS THE RICE FROM GETTING STICKY.
THE RICE WILL ABSORB ALL THE OIL AND TASTE GREASY.
YOU SHOULD USE THE TRADITIONAL RECIPE.
R
MM
NO WAY.
THIS IS THE BEST WAY TO MAKE RICE ON A KITCHEN STOVE.
BL
FRIED RICE!
RM
ARE YOU SAYING MY RECIPE ISN'T THE BEST?
OH YEAH?
M
BL
MAKING FRIED RICE IS SIMPLE. ALL YOU NEED TO DO IS FRY EGGS AND RICE TOGETHER.
FRIED RICE RECIPES ARE AS POPULAR AMONG MEN AS PASTA RECIPES.
PERHAPS BECAUSE IT'S SUCH A SIMPLE DISH, MEN EMPLOY A VARIETY OF TECHNIQUES TO MAKE IT.

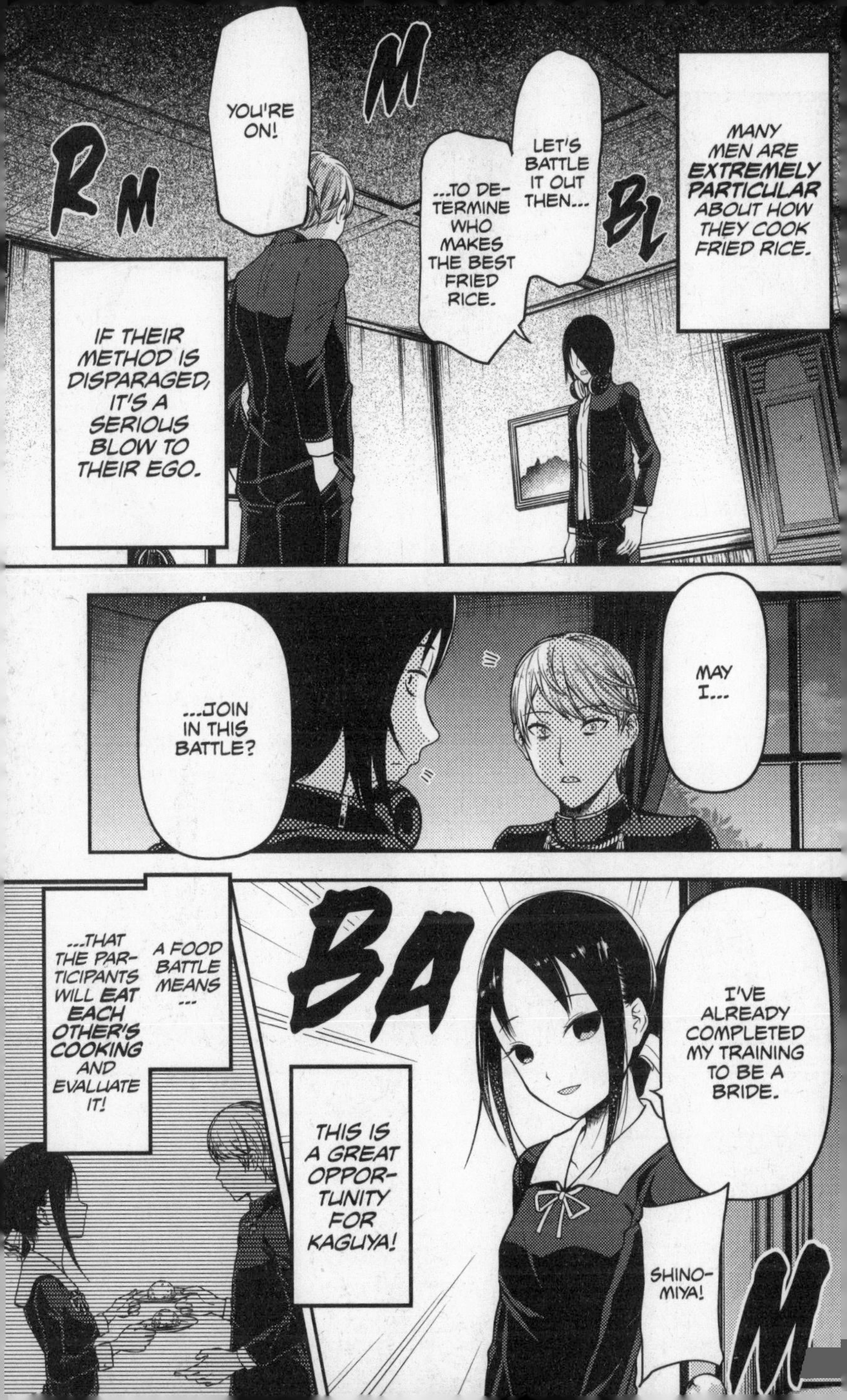
MANY MEN ARE EXTREMELY PARTICULAR ABOUT HOW THEY COOK FRIED RICE.
BL
LET'S BATTLE IT OUT THEN...
...TO DETERMINE WHO MAKES THE BEST FRIED RICE.
M
YOU'RE ON!
RM
IF THEIR METHOD IS DISPARAGED, IT'S A SERIOUS BLOW TO THEIR EGO.
MAY I...
...JOIN IN THIS BATTLE?
I'VE ALREADY COMPLETED MY TRAINING TO BE A BRIDE.
SHINOMIYA!
M
BA
THIS IS A GREAT OPPORTUNITY FOR KAGUYA!
A FOOD BATTLE MEANS...
...THAT THE PARTICIPANTS WILL EAT EACH OTHER'S COOKING AND EVALUATE IT!

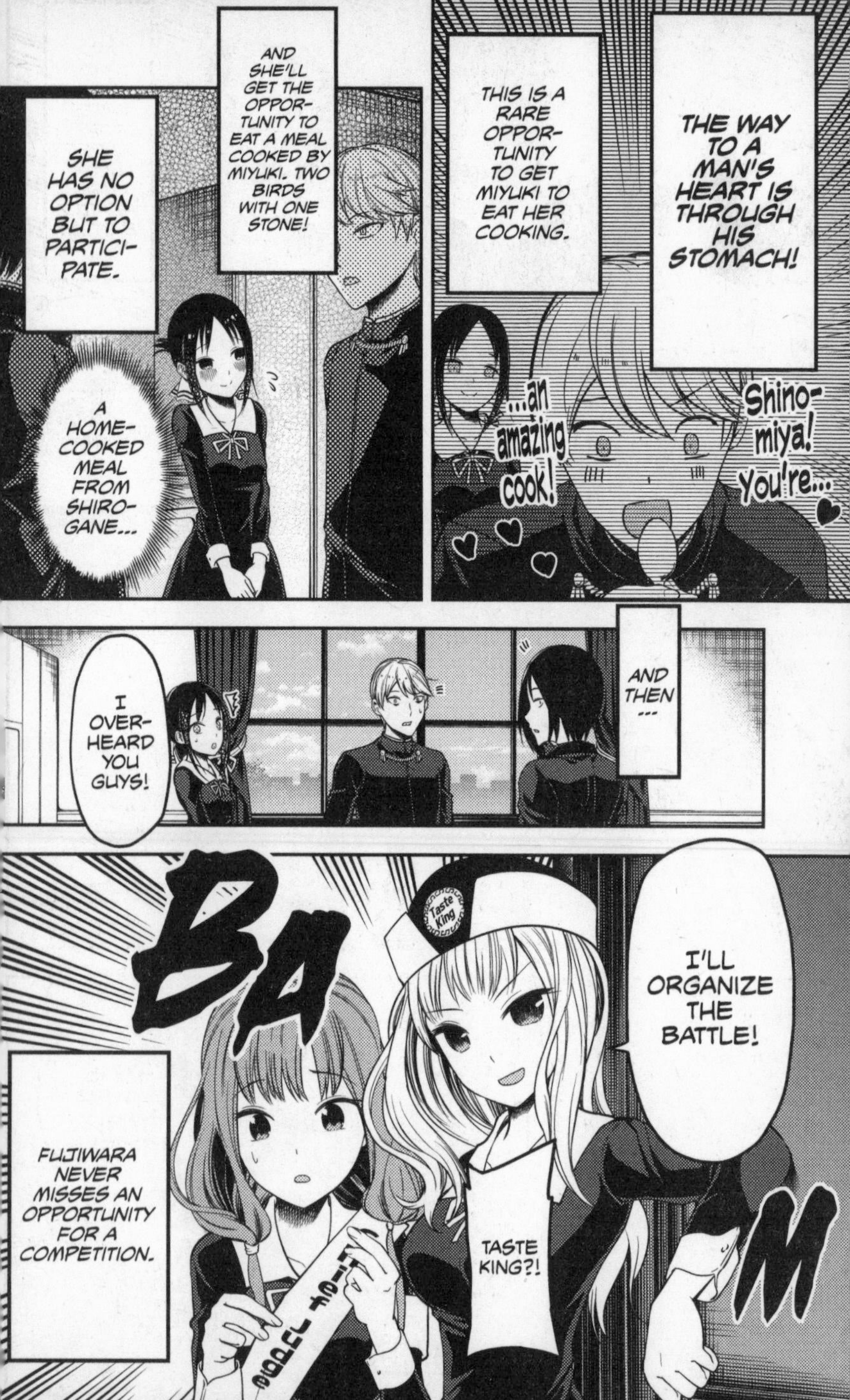
THE WAY TO A MAN'S HEART IS THROUGH HIS STOMACH!
THIS IS A RARE OPPORTUNITY TO GET MIYUKI TO EAT HER COOKING.
Shinomiya! You're...
...an amazing cook!
AND SHE'LL GET THE OPPORTUNITY TO EAT A MEAL COOKED BY MIYUKI. TWO BIRDS WITH ONE STONE!
SHE HAS NO OPTION BUT TO PARTICIPATE.
A HOME-COOKED MEAL FROM SHIROGANE...
AND THEN...
I OVERHEARD YOU GUYS!
I'LL ORGANIZE THE BATTLE!
BAM
Taste King
TASTE KING?!
FUJIWARA NEVER MISSES AN OPPORTUNITY FOR A COMPETITION.

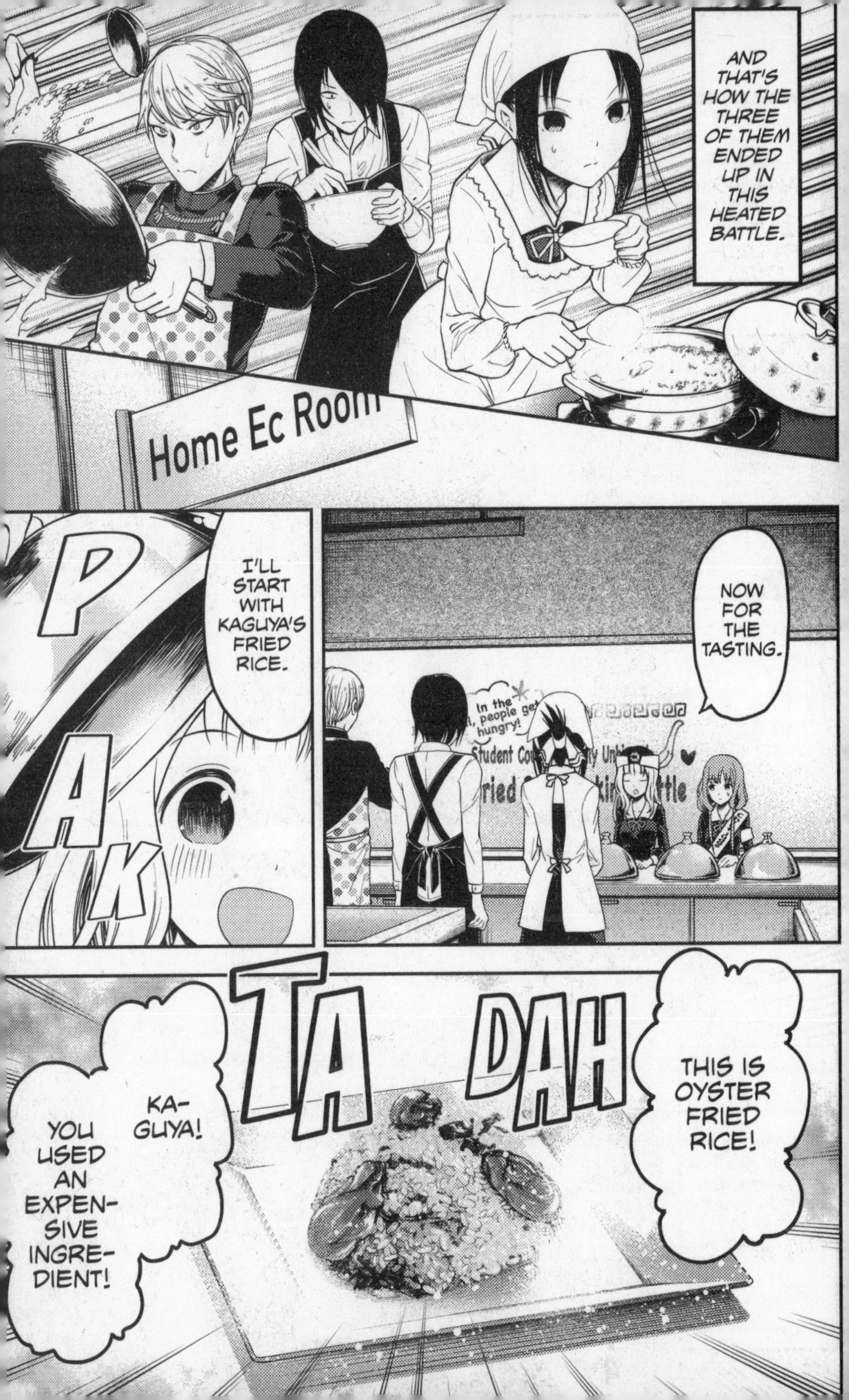
AND THAT'S HOW THE THREE OF THEM ENDED UP IN THIS HEATED BATTLE.
Home Ec Room
NOW FOR THE TASTING.
I'LL START WITH KAGUYA'S FRIED RICE.
PAK
TA DAH
THIS IS OYSTER FRIED RICE!
KA-GUYA!
YOU USED AN EXPENSIVE INGREDIENT!

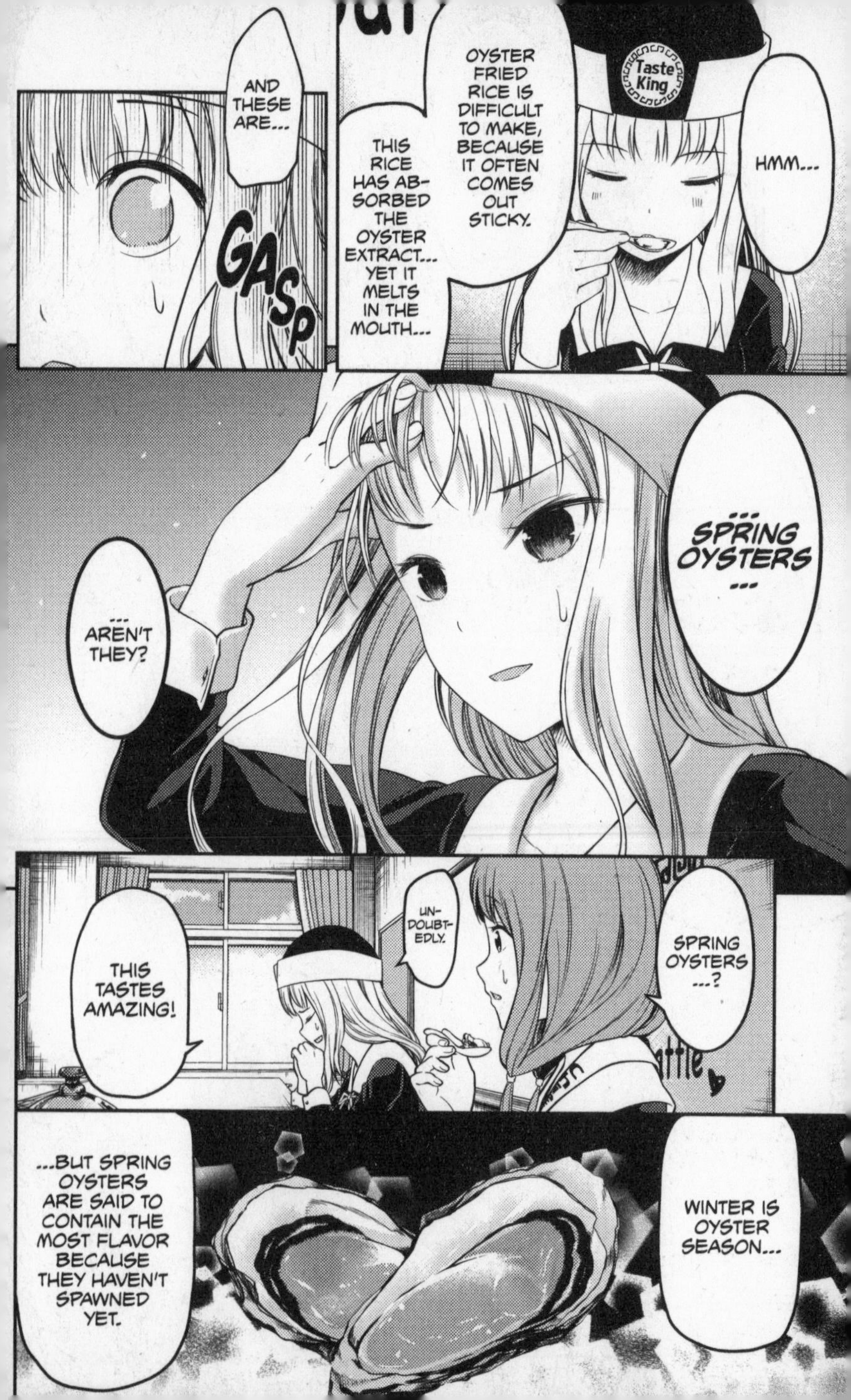

HMM...
OYSTER FRIED RICE IS DIFFICULT TO MAKE, BECAUSE IT OFTEN COMES OUT STICKY.
THIS RICE HAS ABSORBED THE OYSTER EXTRACT... YET IT MELTS IN THE MOUTH...
Taste King
AND THESE ARE...
GASP
...SPRING OYSTERS...
...AREN'T THEY?
SPRING OYSTERS...?
UN-DOUBT-EDLY.
THIS TASTES AMAZING!
WINTER IS OYSTER SEASON...
...BUT SPRING OYSTERS ARE SAID TO CONTAIN THE MOST FLAVOR BECAUSE THEY HAVEN'T SPAWNED YET.

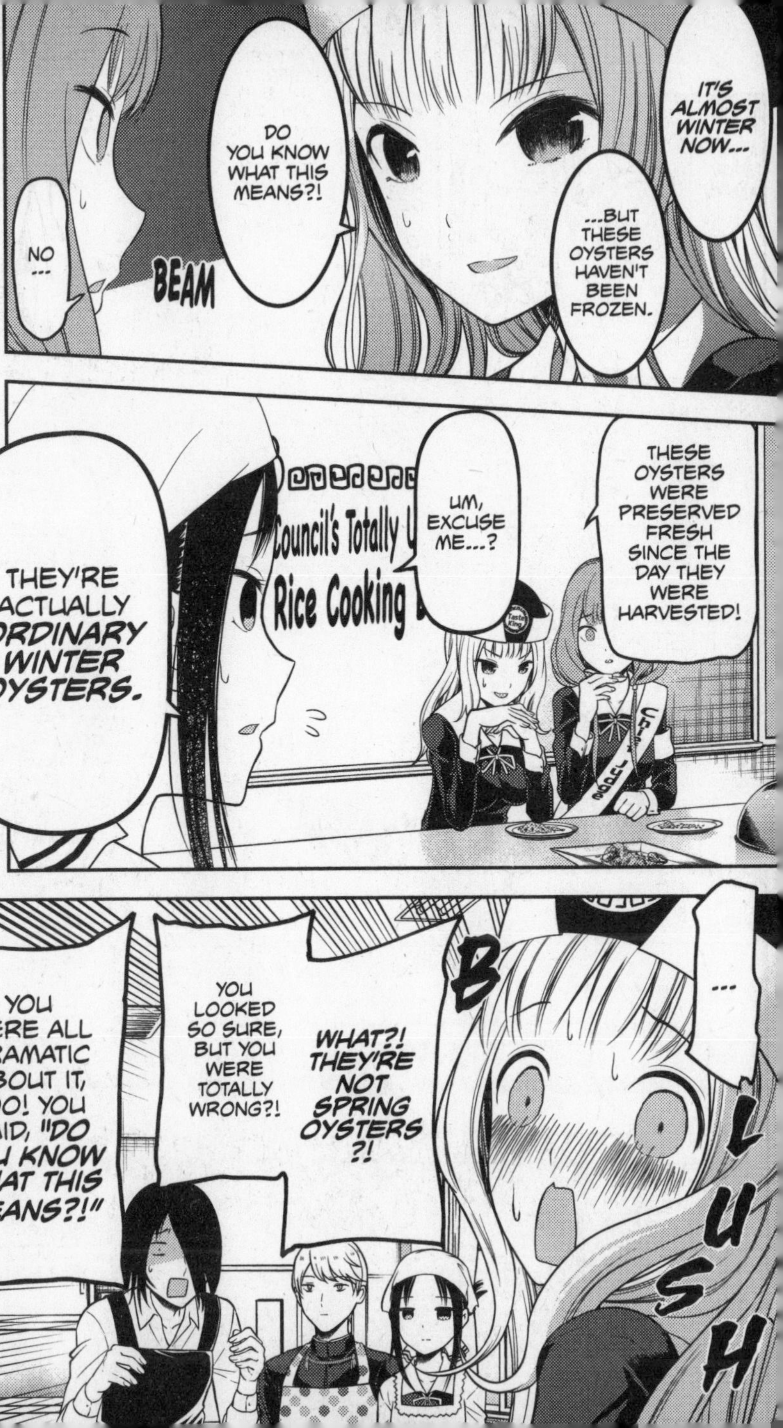

IT'S ALMOST WINTER NOW...
...BUT THESE OYSTERS HAVEN'T BEEN FROZEN.
DO YOU KNOW WHAT THIS MEANS?!
BEAM
NO...
THESE OYSTERS WERE PRESERVED FRESH SINCE THE DAY THEY WERE HARVESTED!
UM, EXCUSE ME...?
Council's Totally
Rice Cooking
THEY'RE ACTUALLY *ORDINARY WINTER OYSTERS.*
...
BLUSH
WHAT?! THEY'RE NOT SPRING OYSTERS?!
YOU LOOKED SO SURE, BUT YOU WERE TOTALLY WRONG?!
YOU WERE ALL DRAMATIC ABOUT IT, TOO! YOU SAID, *"DO YOU KNOW WHAT THIS MEANS?!"*

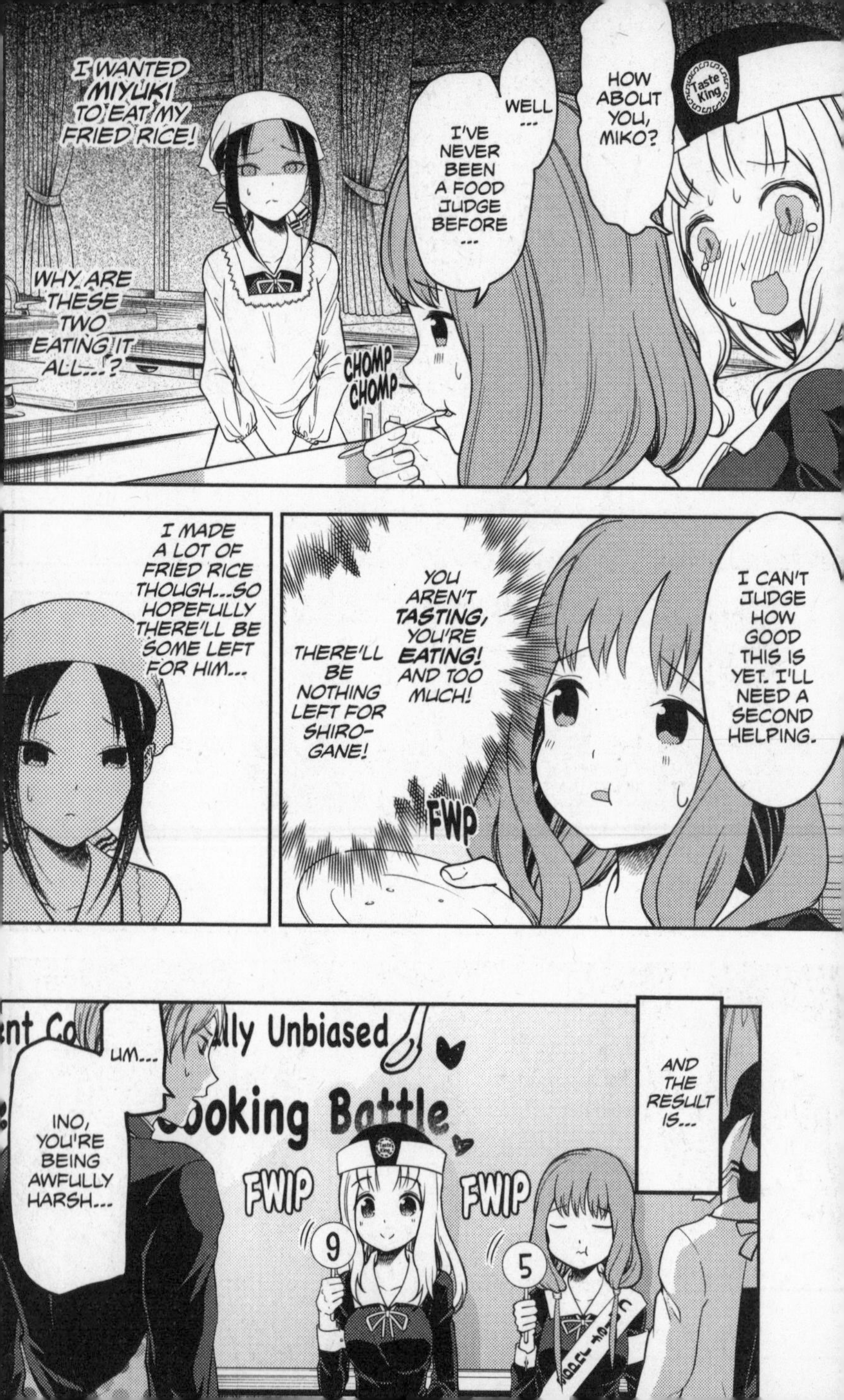
HOW ABOUT YOU, MIKO?
WELL...
I'VE NEVER BEEN A FOOD JUDGE BEFORE...
CHOMP CHOMP
I WANTED MIYUKI TO EAT MY FRIED RICE!
WHY ARE THESE TWO EATING IT ALL...?
I CAN'T JUDGE HOW GOOD THIS IS YET. I'LL NEED A SECOND HELPING.
FWP
YOU AREN'T TASTING, YOU'RE EATING! AND TOO MUCH!
THERE'LL BE NOTHING LEFT FOR SHIRO-GANE!
I MADE A LOT OF FRIED RICE THOUGH...SO HOPEFULLY THERE'LL BE SOME LEFT FOR HIM...
AND THE RESULT IS...
ally Unbiased
ooking Battle
FWIP
FWIP
5
9
UM...
INO, YOU'RE BEING AWFULLY HARSH...

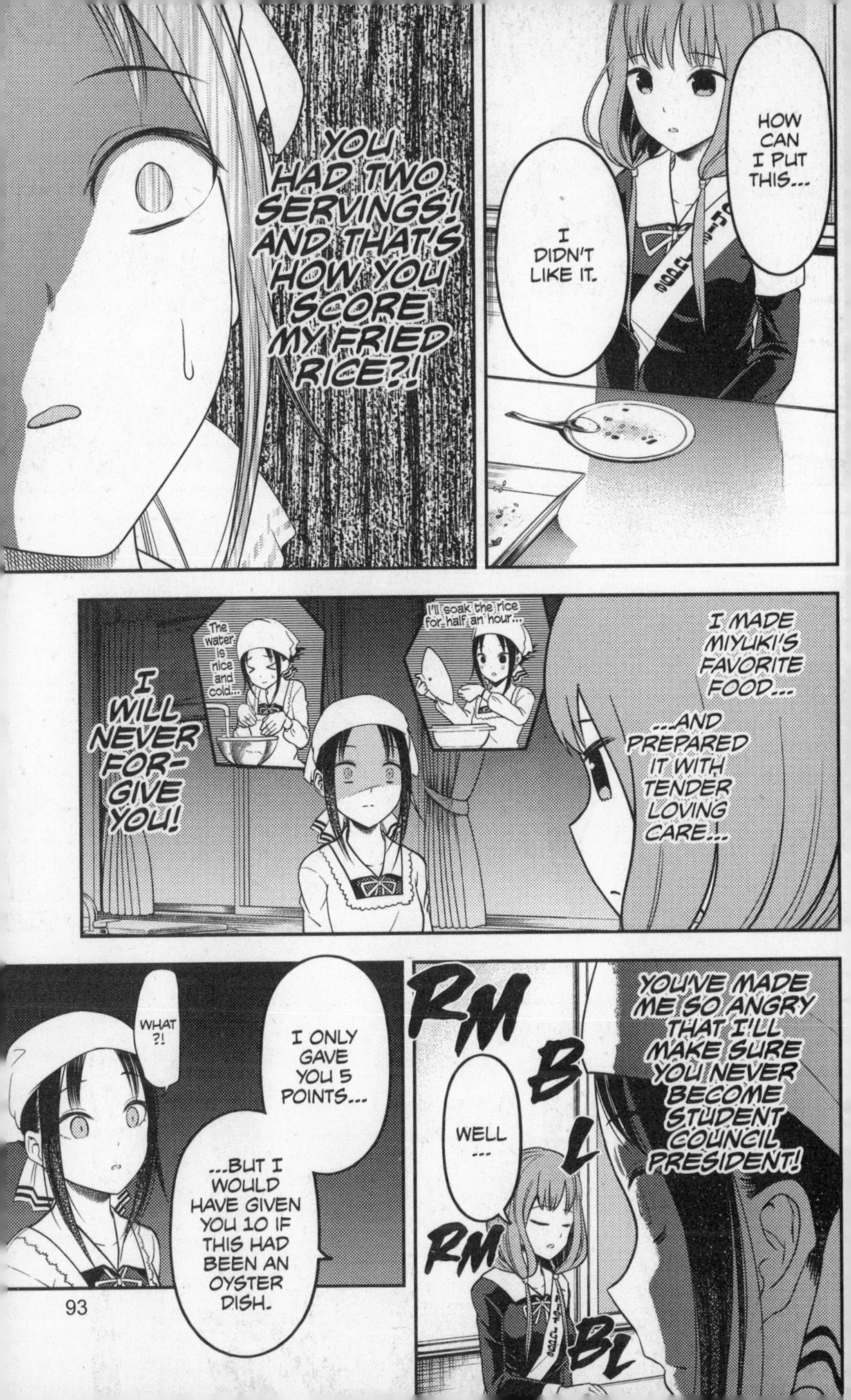

HOW CAN I PUT THIS...
I DIDN'T LIKE IT.
YOU HAD TWO SERVINGS! AND THAT'S HOW YOU SCORE MY FRIED RICE?!
I MADE MIYUKI'S FAVORITE FOOD...
...AND PREPARED IT WITH TENDER LOVING CARE...
I'll soak the rice for half an hour...
The water is nice and cold...
I WILL NEVER FOR-GIVE YOU!
YOU'VE MADE ME SO ANGRY THAT I'LL MAKE SURE YOU NEVER BECOME STUDENT COUNCIL PRESIDENT!
RMBL
RMBL
WELL...
I ONLY GAVE YOU 5 POINTS...
...BUT I WOULD HAVE GIVEN YOU 10 IF THIS HAD BEEN AN OYSTER DISH.
WHAT?!

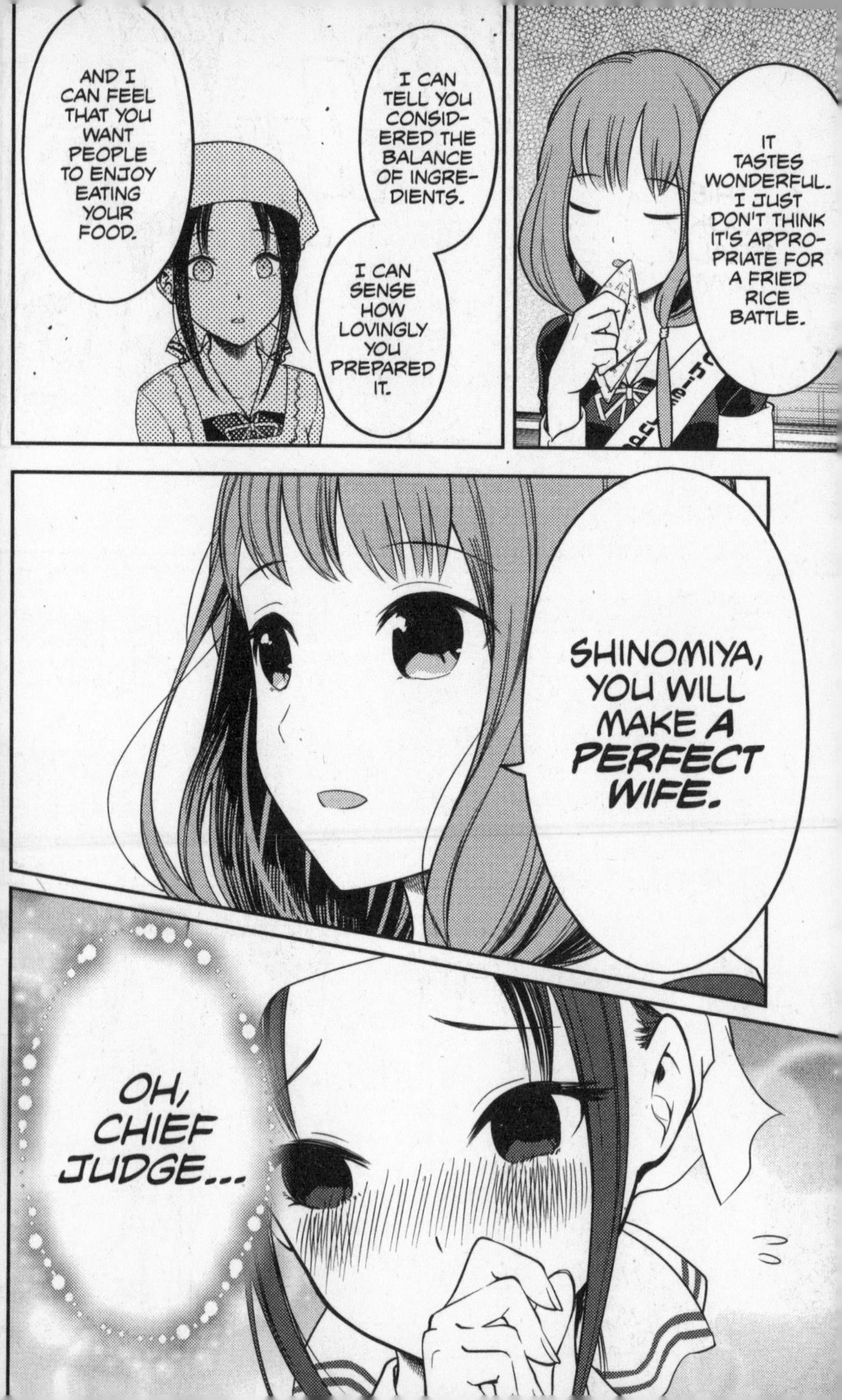
IT TASTES WONDERFUL. I JUST DON'T THINK IT'S APPROPRIATE FOR A FRIED RICE BATTLE.
I CAN TELL YOU CONSIDERED THE BALANCE OF INGREDIENTS.
I CAN SENSE HOW LOVINGLY YOU PREPARED IT.
AND I CAN FEEL THAT YOU WANT PEOPLE TO ENJOY EATING YOUR FOOD.
SHINOMIYA, YOU WILL MAKE A PERFECT WIFE.
OH, CHIEF JUDGE...

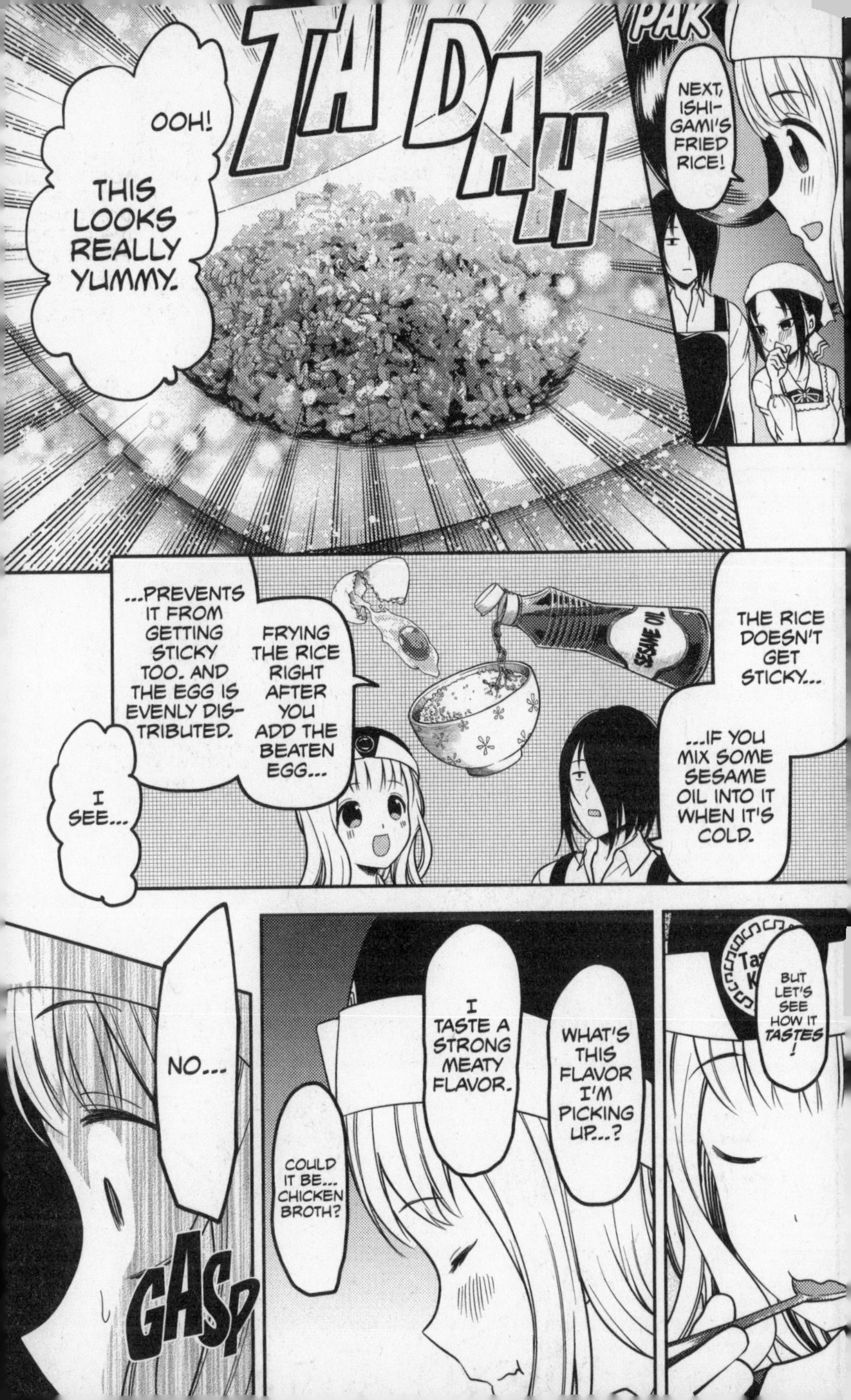
PAK
NEXT, ISHI-GAMI'S FRIED RICE!
TA DAH
OOH!
THIS LOOKS REALLY YUMMY.
THE RICE DOESN'T GET STICKY...
...IF YOU MIX SOME SESAME OIL INTO IT WHEN IT'S COLD.
SESAME OIL
FRYING THE RICE RIGHT AFTER YOU ADD THE BEATEN EGG...
...PREVENTS IT FROM GETTING STICKY TOO. AND THE EGG IS EVENLY DIS-TRIBUTED.
I SEE...
BUT LET'S SEE HOW IT TASTES!
WHAT'S THIS FLAVOR I'M PICKING UP...?
I TASTE A STRONG MEATY FLAVOR.
COULD IT BE... CHICKEN BROTH?
NO...
GASP

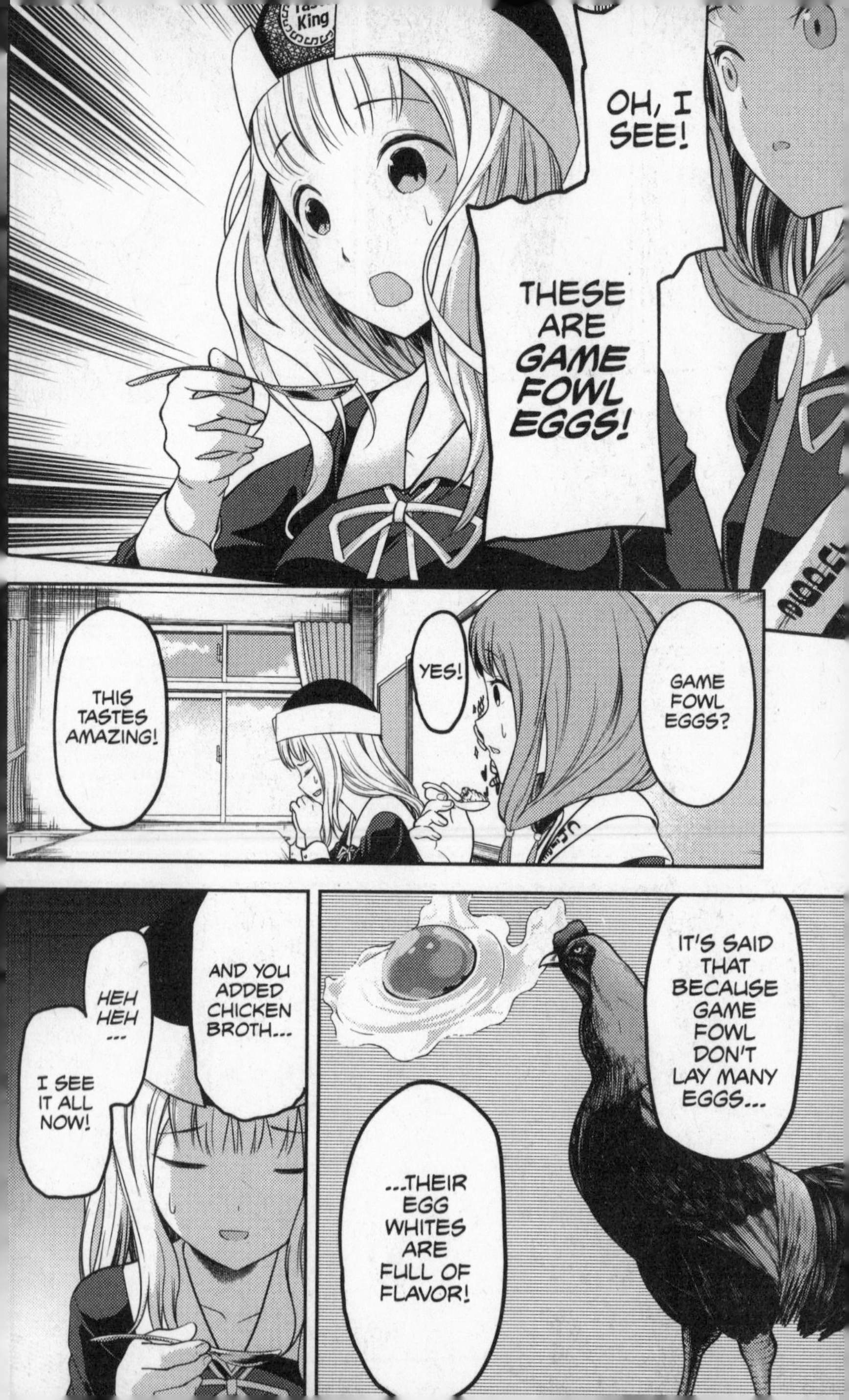
OH, I SEE!
THESE ARE GAME FOWL EGGS!
GAME FOWL EGGS?
YES!
THIS TASTES AMAZING!
IT'S SAID THAT BECAUSE GAME FOWL DON'T LAY MANY EGGS...
...THEIR EGG WHITES ARE FULL OF FLAVOR!
AND YOU ADDED CHICKEN BROTH...
HEH HEH...
I SEE IT ALL NOW!

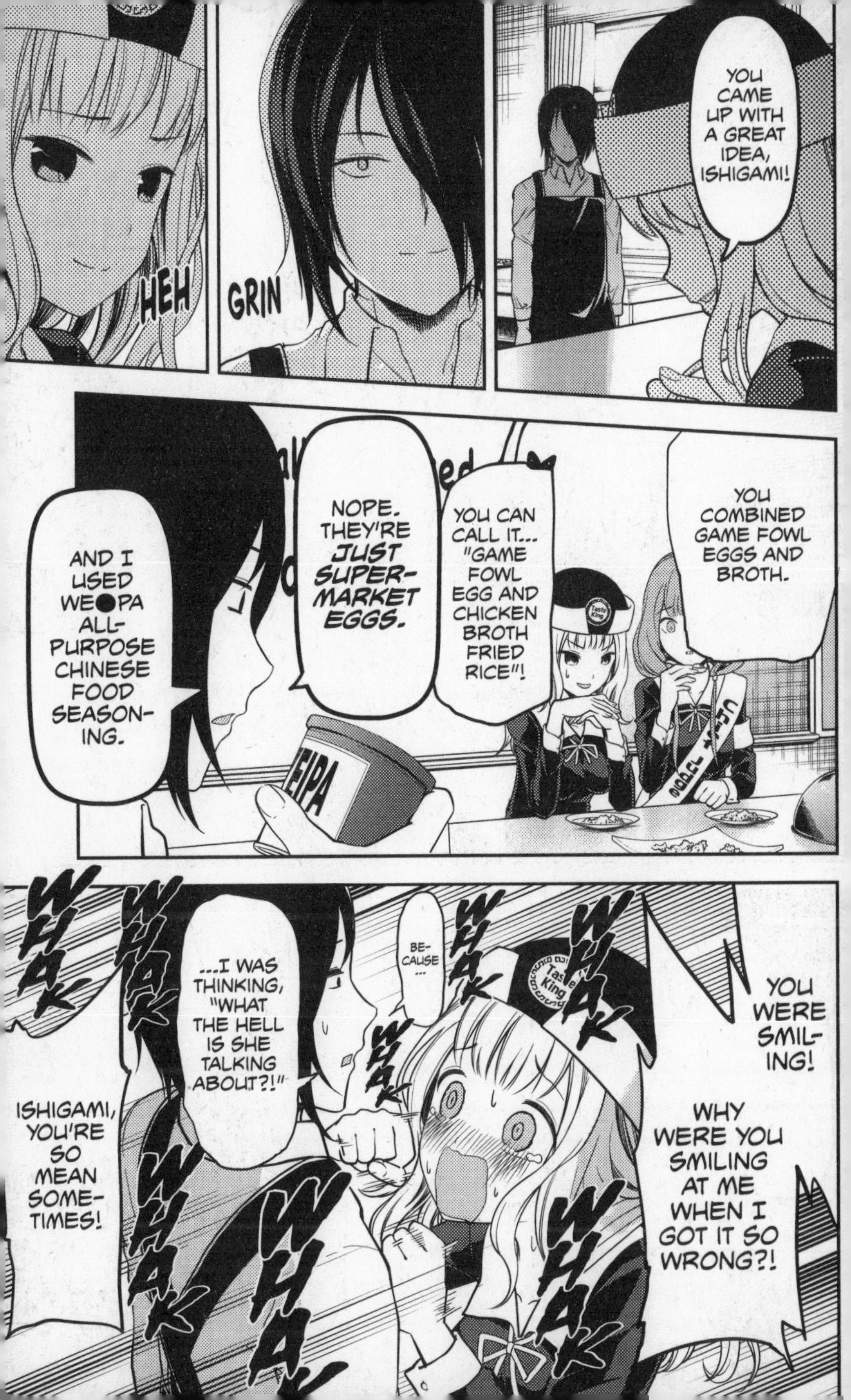
YOU CAME UP WITH A GREAT IDEA, ISHIGAMI!
GRIN
HEH
YOU COMBINED GAME FOWL EGGS AND BROTH.
Taste King
YOU CAN CALL IT... "GAME FOWL EGG AND CHICKEN BROTH FRIED RICE"!
NOPE. THEY'RE *JUST SUPERMARKET EGGS.*
AND I USED WE●PA ALL-PURPOSE CHINESE FOOD SEASONING.
YOU WERE SMILING!
WHY WERE YOU SMILING AT ME WHEN I GOT IT SO WRONG?!
WHAK WHAK WHAK
Taste King
BECAUSE...
...I WAS THINKING, "WHAT THE HELL IS SHE TALKING ABOUT?!"
ISHIGAMI, YOU'RE SO MEAN SOMETIMES!
WHAK WHAK WHAK WHAK WHAK

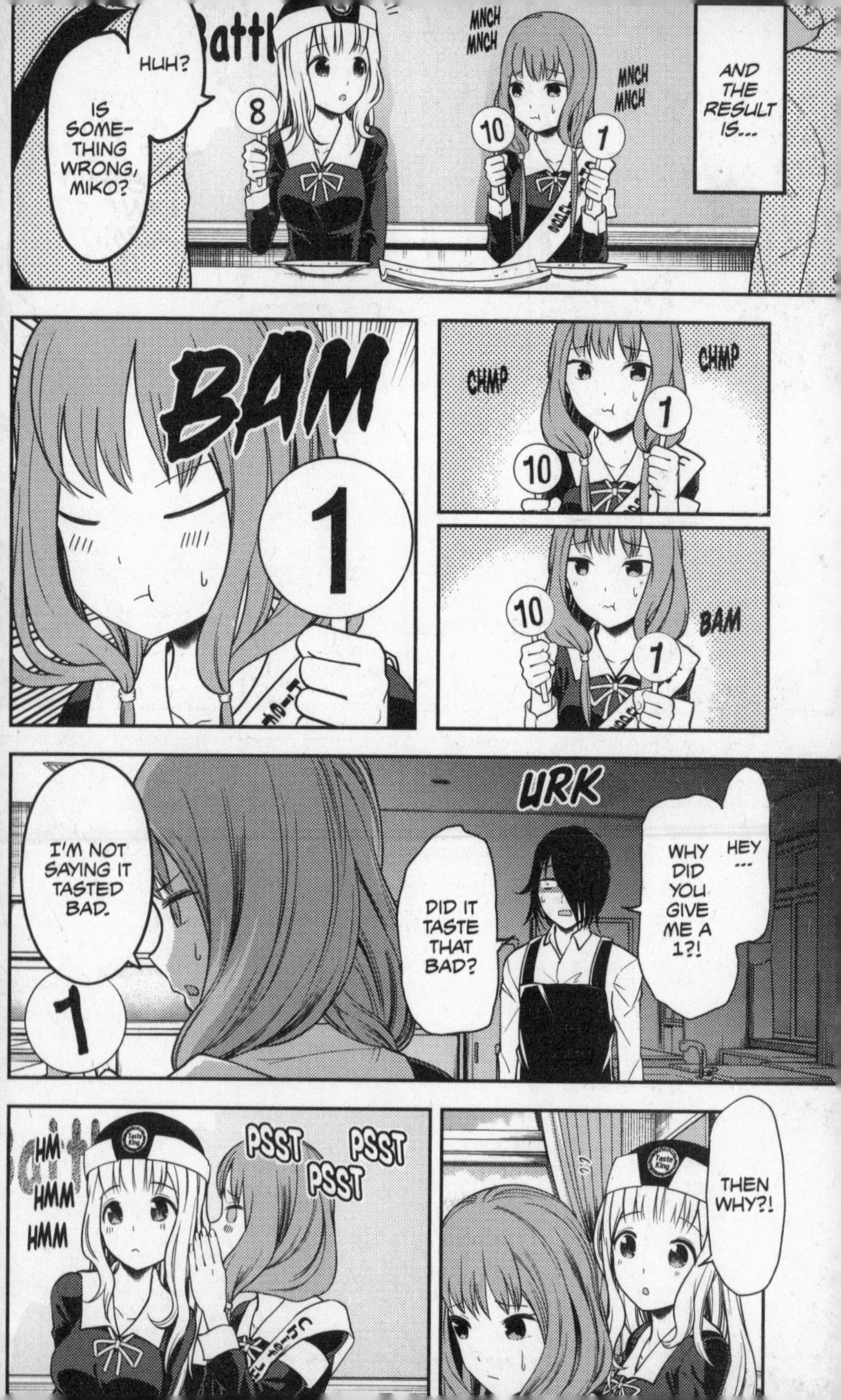
AND THE RESULT IS...
MNCH MNCH
MNCH MNCH
10
1
8
HUH?
IS SOMETHING WRONG, MIKO?
CHMP
CHMP
1
10
BAM
10
1
BAM
1
HEY... WHY DID YOU GIVE ME A 1?!
URK
DID IT TASTE THAT BAD?
I'M NOT SAYING IT TASTED BAD.
1
THEN WHY?!
PSST PSST
PSST
HM HMM HMM

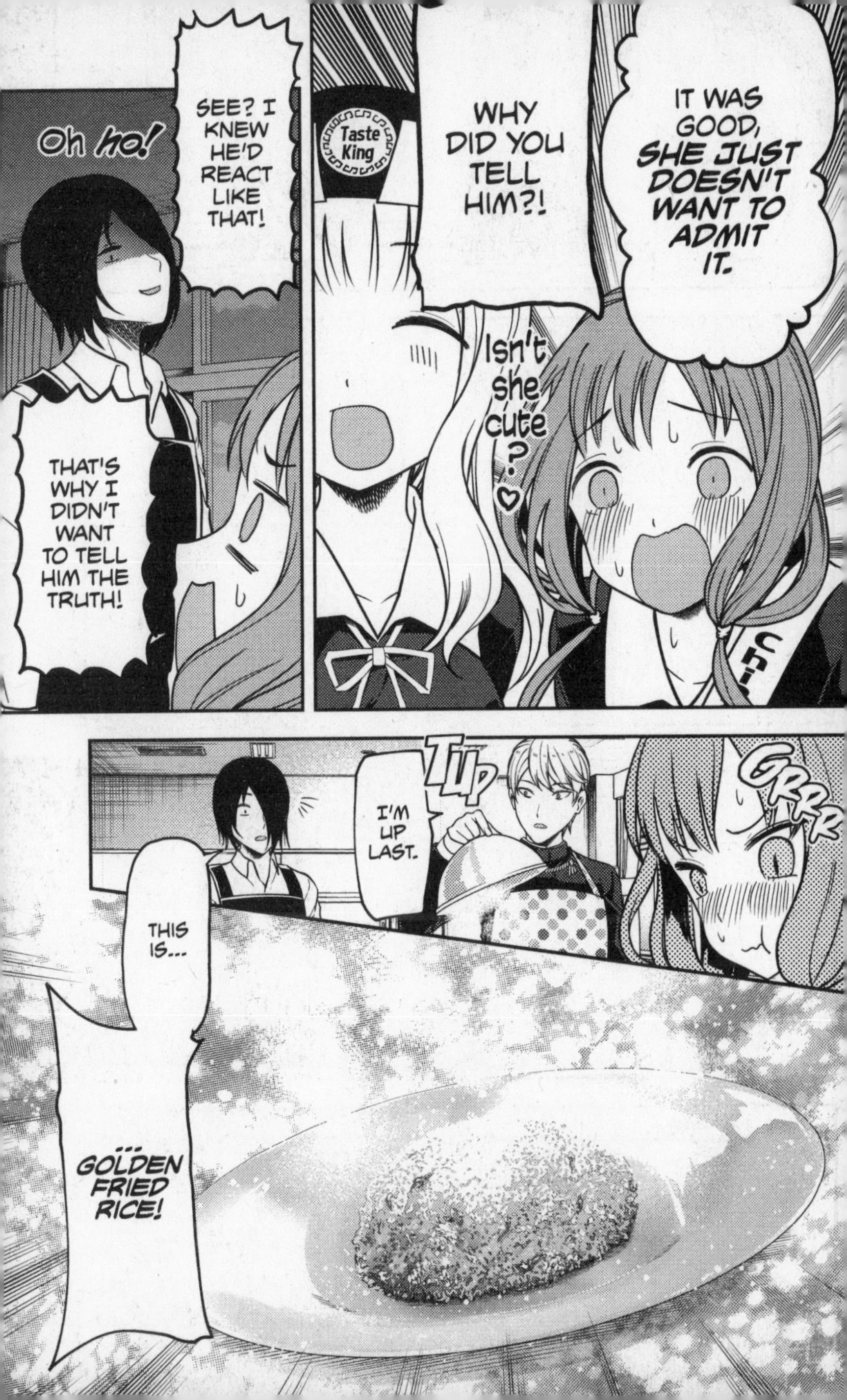
IT WAS GOOD, SHE JUST DOESN'T WANT TO ADMIT IT.
Isn't she cute?♡
Taste King
WHY DID YOU TELL HIM?!
SEE? I KNEW HE'D REACT LIKE THAT!
Oh ho!
THAT'S WHY I DIDN'T WANT TO TELL HIM THE TRUTH!
GRRR
TUP
I'M UP LAST.
THIS IS...
...GOLDEN FRIED RICE!

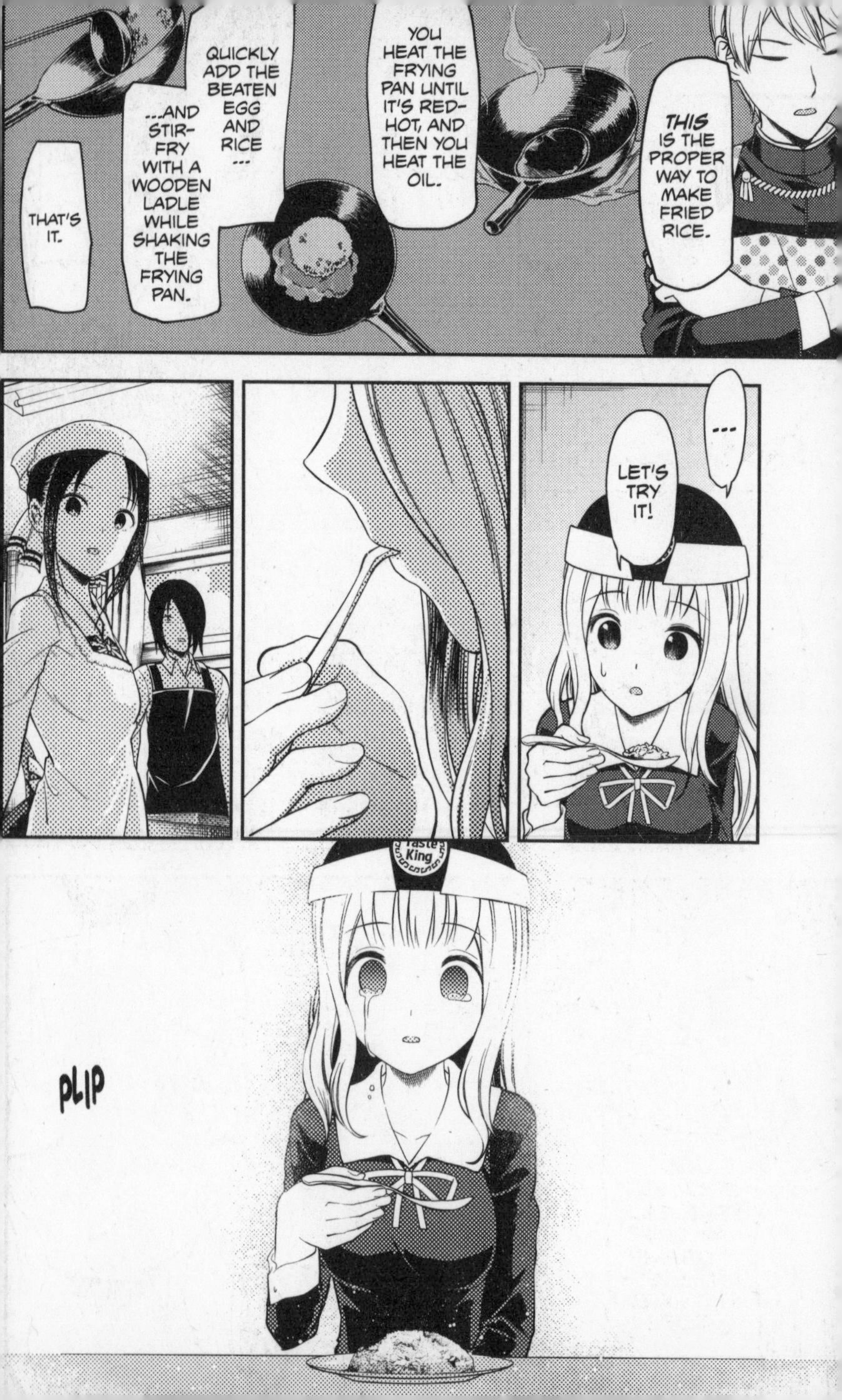
THIS IS THE PROPER WAY TO MAKE FRIED RICE.
YOU HEAT THE FRYING PAN UNTIL IT'S RED-HOT, AND THEN YOU HEAT THE OIL.
QUICKLY ADD THE BEATEN EGG AND RICE...
...AND STIR-FRY WITH A WOODEN LADLE WHILE SHAKING THE FRYING PAN.
THAT'S IT.
...
LET'S TRY IT!
Taste King
PLIP

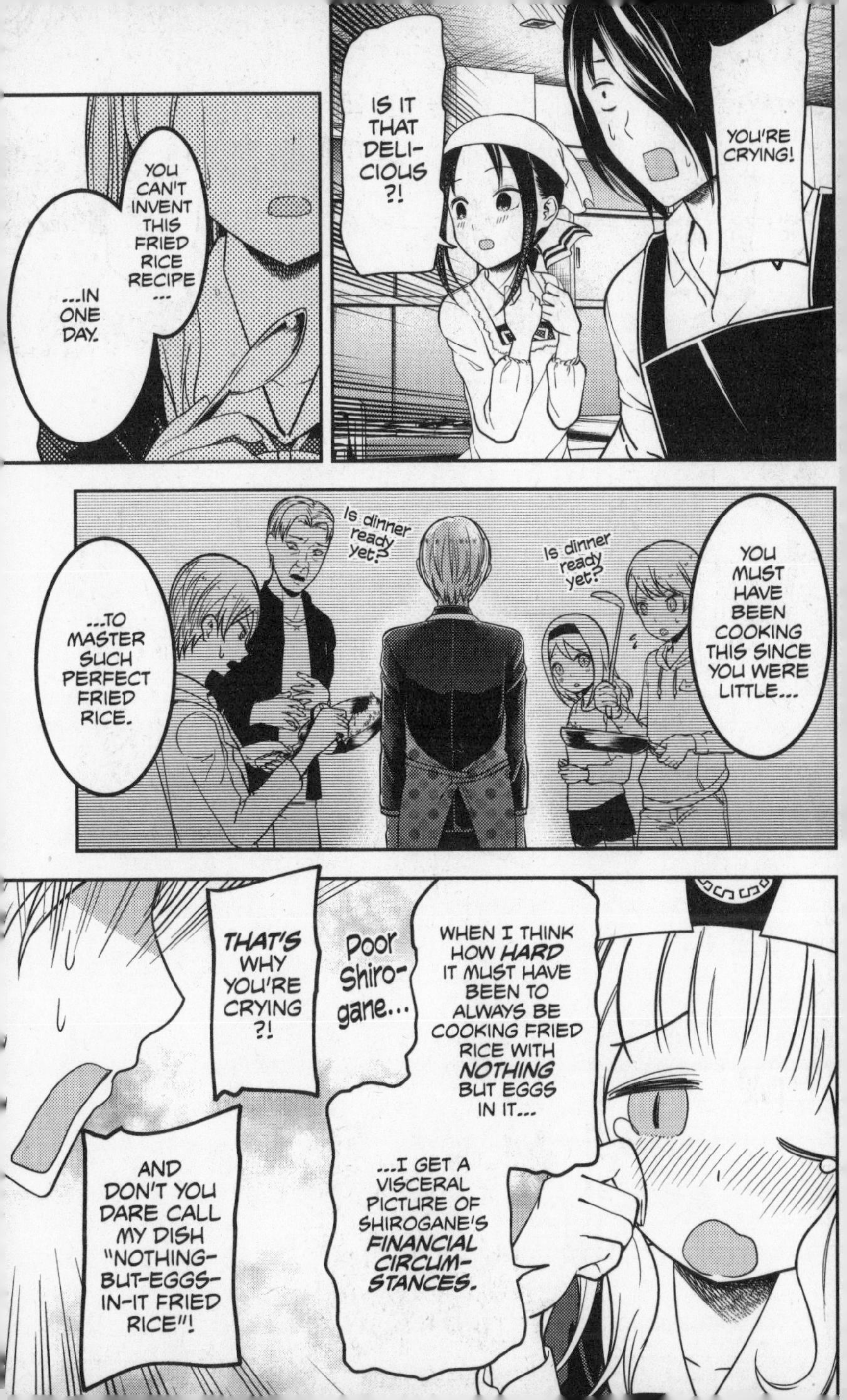

YOU'RE CRYING!
IS IT THAT DELICIOUS?!
YOU CAN'T INVENT THIS FRIED RICE RECIPE...
...IN ONE DAY.
YOU MUST HAVE BEEN COOKING THIS SINCE YOU WERE LITTLE...
Is dinner ready yet?
Is dinner ready yet?
...TO MASTER SUCH PERFECT FRIED RICE.
WHEN I THINK HOW *HARD* IT MUST HAVE BEEN TO ALWAYS BE COOKING FRIED RICE WITH *NOTHING* BUT EGGS IN IT...
Poor Shirogane...
THAT'S WHY YOU'RE CRYING?!
...I GET A VISCERAL PICTURE OF SHIROGANE'S *FINANCIAL CIRCUMSTANCES.*
AND DON'T YOU DARE CALL MY DISH "NOTHING-BUT-EGGS-IN-IT FRIED RICE"!

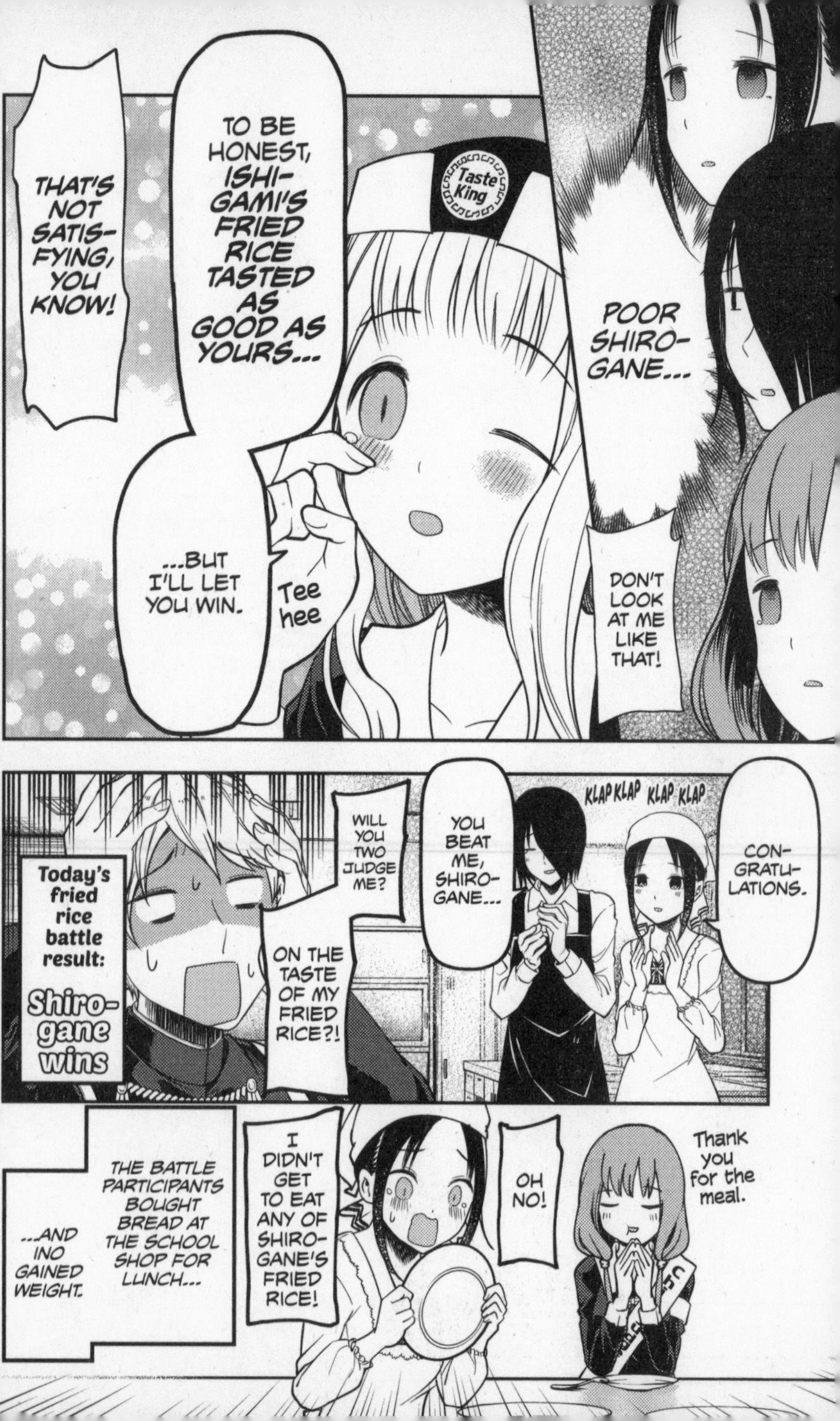
POOR SHIROGANE...
DON'T LOOK AT ME LIKE THAT!
TO BE HONEST, ISHIGAMI'S FRIED RICE TASTED AS GOOD AS YOURS...
THAT'S NOT SATISFYING, YOU KNOW!
...BUT I'LL LET YOU WIN.
Tee hee
Taste King
CONGRATULATIONS.
KLAP KLAP KLAP KLAP
YOU BEAT ME, SHIROGANE...
WILL YOU TWO JUDGE ME?
ON THE TASTE OF MY FRIED RICE?!
Today's fried rice battle result:
Shirogane wins
Thank you for the meal.
OH NO!
I DIDN'T GET TO EAT ANY OF SHIROGANE'S FRIED RICE!
THE BATTLE PARTICIPANTS BOUGHT BREAD AT THE SCHOOL SHOP FOR LUNCH...
...AND INO GAINED WEIGHT.

Time for...

...lunch.

?!

KAGUYA-SAMA

LOVE IS WAR

Battle 97 Nagisa Kashiwagi Wants to Kill

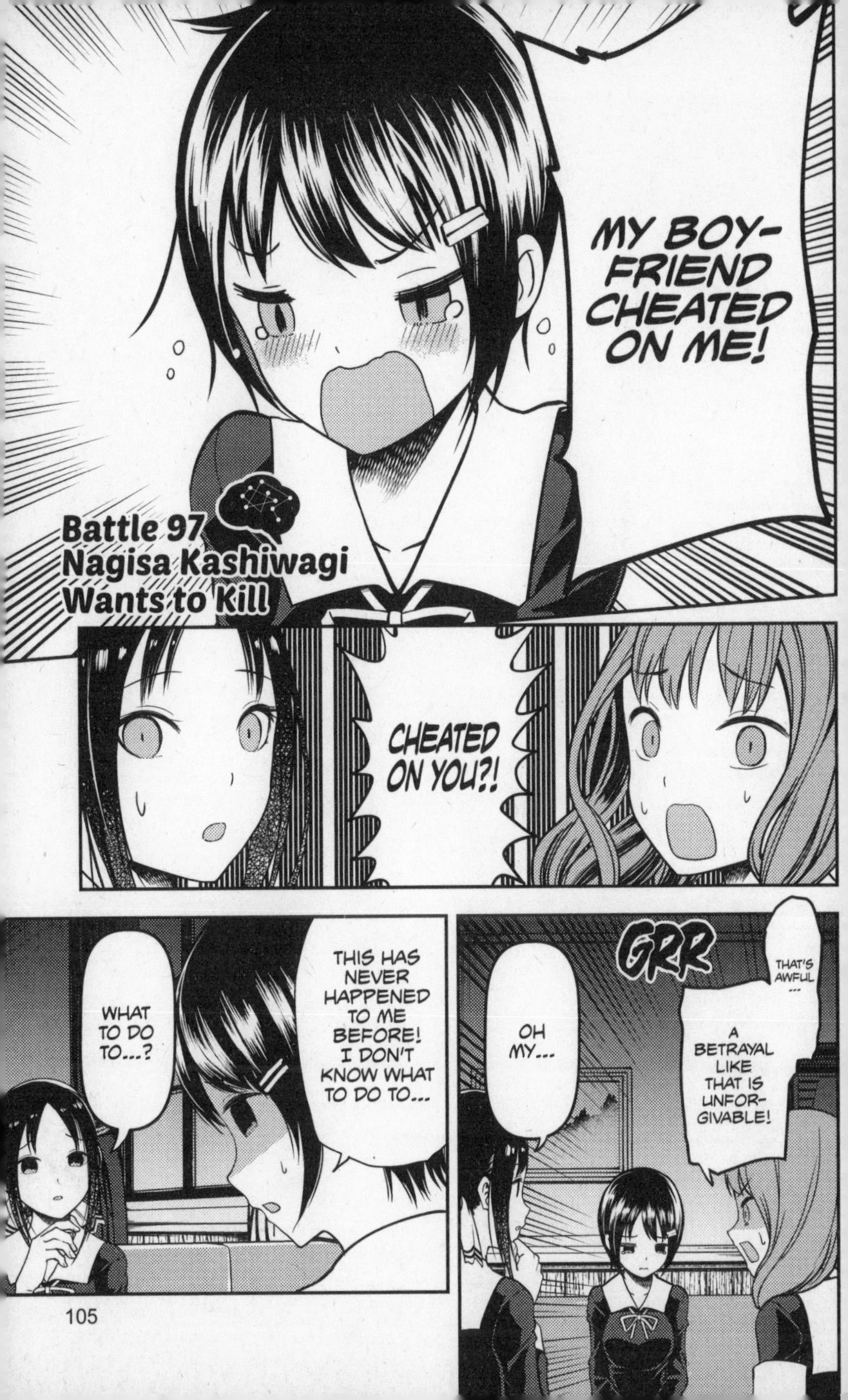
MY BOY-FRIEND CHEATED ON ME!
CHEATED ON YOU?!
GRR
THAT'S AWFUL...
A BETRAYAL LIKE THAT IS UNFORGIVABLE!
OH MY...
THIS HAS NEVER HAPPENED TO ME BEFORE! I DON'T KNOW WHAT TO DO TO...
WHAT TO DO TO...?

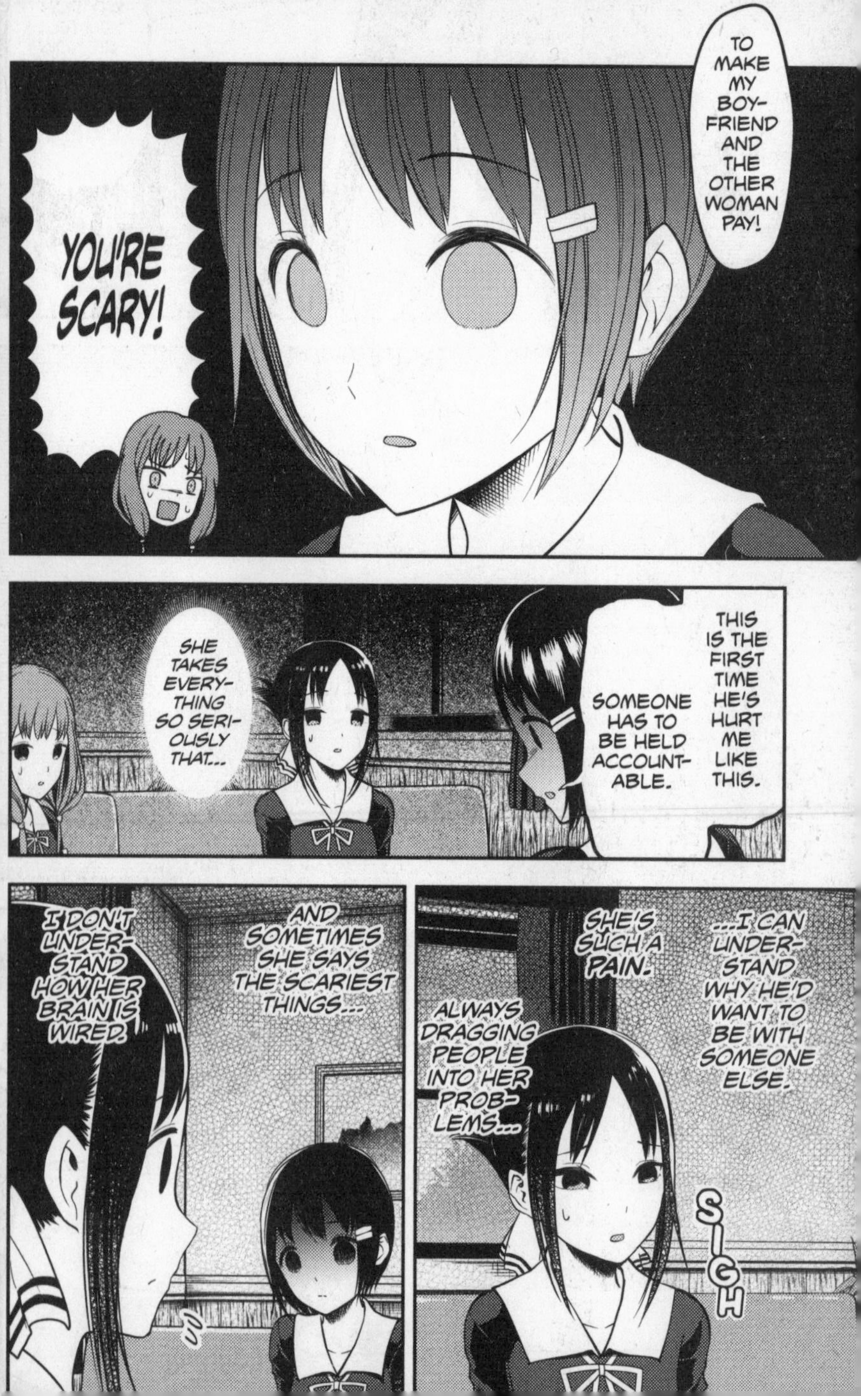
TO MAKE MY BOYFRIEND AND THE OTHER WOMAN PAY!
YOU'RE SCARY!
THIS IS THE FIRST TIME HE'S HURT ME LIKE THIS.
SOMEONE HAS TO BE HELD ACCOUNTABLE.
SHE TAKES EVERYTHING SO SERIOUSLY THAT...
...I CAN UNDERSTAND WHY HE'D WANT TO BE WITH SOMEONE ELSE.
SIGH
SHE'S SUCH A PAIN.
ALWAYS DRAGGING PEOPLE INTO HER PROBLEMS...
AND SOMETIMES SHE SAYS THE SCARIEST THINGS...
I DON'T UNDERSTAND HOW HER BRAIN IS WIRED.

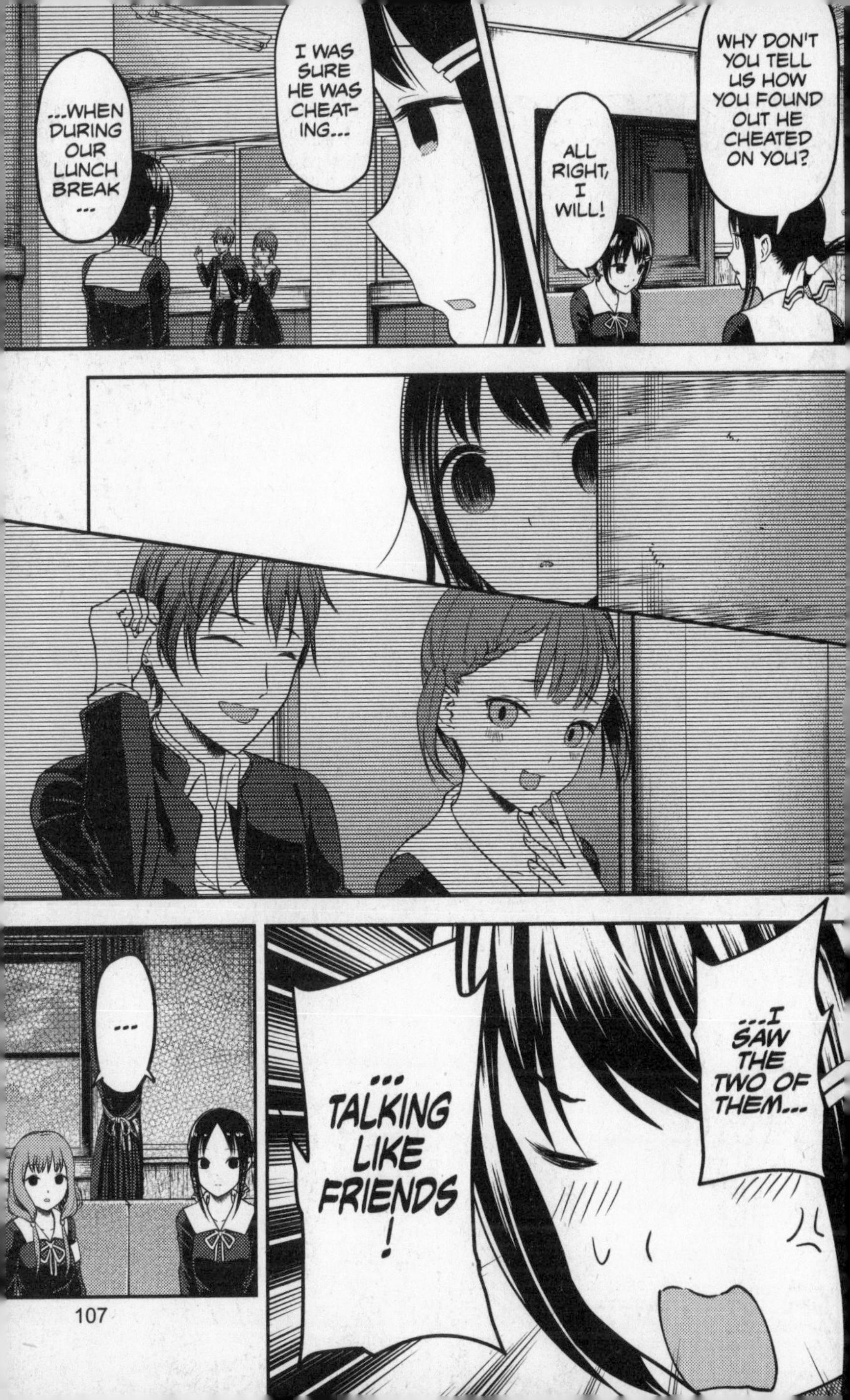
WHY DON'T YOU TELL US HOW YOU FOUND OUT HE CHEATED ON YOU?
ALL RIGHT, I WILL!
I WAS SURE HE WAS CHEAT-ING...
...WHEN DURING OUR LUNCH BREAK...
...I SAW THE TWO OF THEM...
...TALKING LIKE FRIENDS!
...

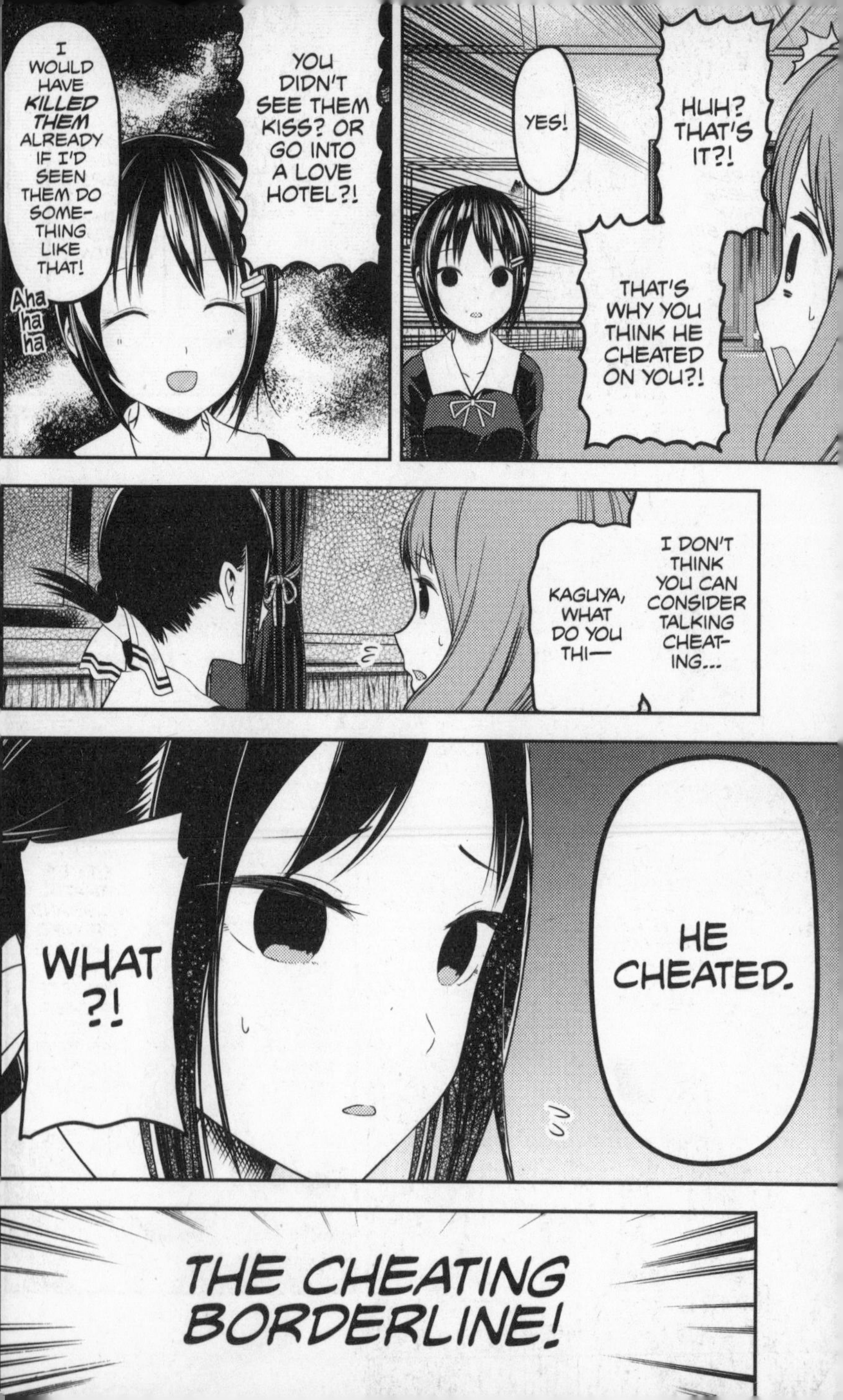
HUH? THAT'S IT?!
YES!
THAT'S WHY YOU THINK HE CHEATED ON YOU?!
YOU DIDN'T SEE THEM KISS? OR GO INTO A LOVE HOTEL?!
I WOULD HAVE KILLED THEM ALREADY IF I'D SEEN THEM DO SOMETHING LIKE THAT!
Aha ha ha
I DON'T THINK YOU CAN CONSIDER TALKING CHEATING...
KAGUYA, WHAT DO YOU THI—
HE CHEATED.
WHAT?!
THE CHEATING BORDERLINE!

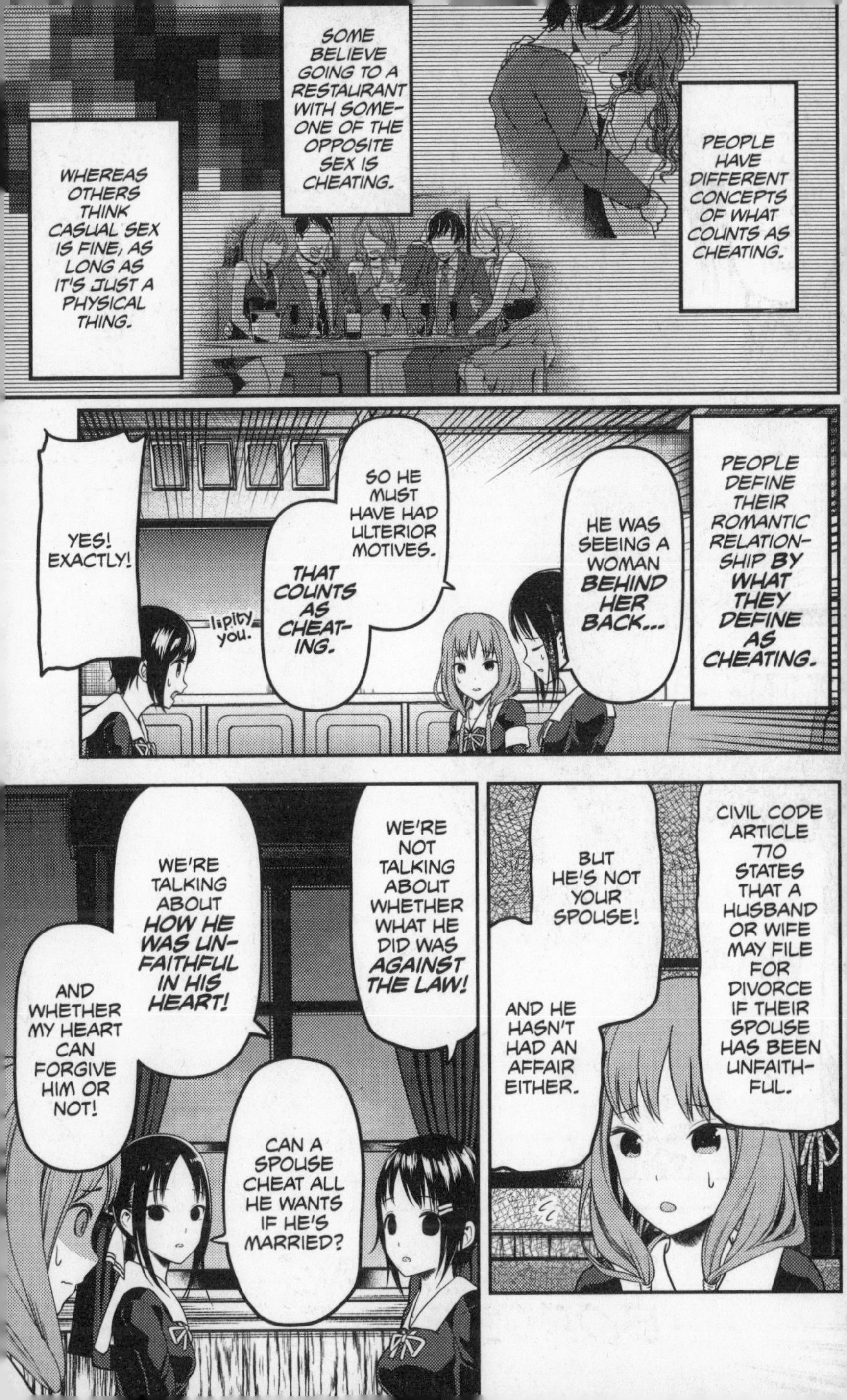
PEOPLE HAVE DIFFERENT CONCEPTS OF WHAT COUNTS AS CHEATING.
SOME BELIEVE GOING TO A RESTAURANT WITH SOMEONE OF THE OPPOSITE SEX IS CHEATING.
WHEREAS OTHERS THINK CASUAL SEX IS FINE, AS LONG AS IT'S JUST A PHYSICAL THING.
PEOPLE DEFINE THEIR ROMANTIC RELATIONSHIP BY WHAT THEY DEFINE AS CHEATING.
HE WAS SEEING A WOMAN BEHIND HER BACK...
SO HE MUST HAVE HAD ULTERIOR MOTIVES.
THAT COUNTS AS CHEATING.
I...pity you.
YES! EXACTLY!
CIVIL CODE ARTICLE 770 STATES THAT A HUSBAND OR WIFE MAY FILE FOR DIVORCE IF THEIR SPOUSE HAS BEEN UNFAITHFUL.
BUT HE'S NOT YOUR SPOUSE!
AND HE HASN'T HAD AN AFFAIR EITHER.
WE'RE NOT TALKING ABOUT WHETHER WHAT HE DID WAS AGAINST THE LAW!
WE'RE TALKING ABOUT HOW HE WAS UNFAITHFUL IN HIS HEART!
AND WHETHER MY HEART CAN FORGIVE HIM OR NOT!
CAN A SPOUSE CHEAT ALL HE WANTS IF HE'S MARRIED?

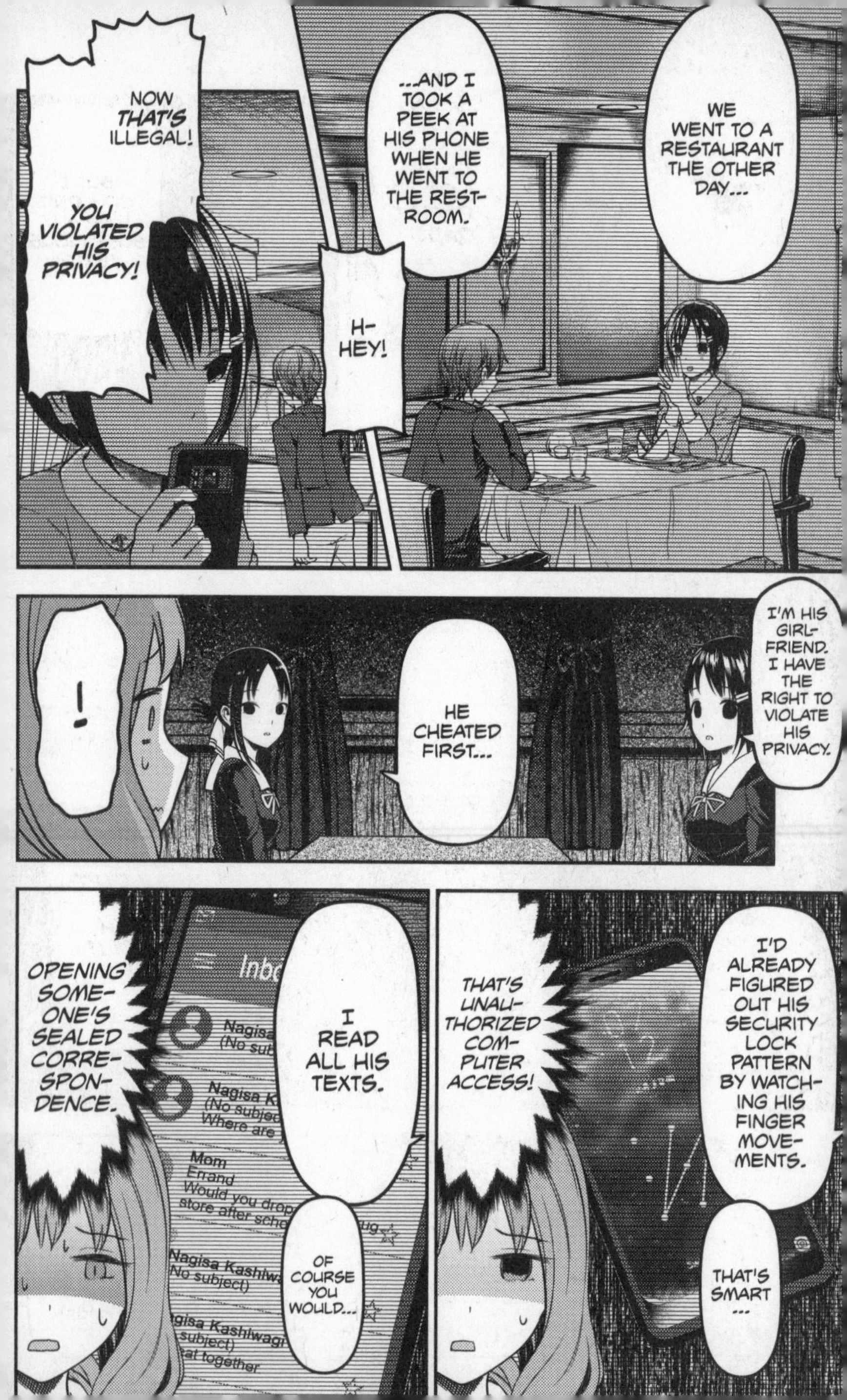
WE WENT TO A RESTAURANT THE OTHER DAY...
...AND I TOOK A PEEK AT HIS PHONE WHEN HE WENT TO THE REST-ROOM.
H-HEY!
NOW THAT'S ILLEGAL!
YOU VIOLATED HIS PRIVACY!
I'M HIS GIRL-FRIEND. I HAVE THE RIGHT TO VIOLATE HIS PRIVACY.
HE CHEATED FIRST...
!
I'D ALREADY FIGURED OUT HIS SECURITY LOCK PATTERN BY WATCHING HIS FINGER MOVE-MENTS.
THAT'S UNAUTHORIZED COM-PUTER ACCESS!
THAT'S SMART...
I READ ALL HIS TEXTS.
OPENING SOME-ONE'S SEALED CORRE-SPON-DENCE.
OF COURSE YOU WOULD...
Mom
Errand

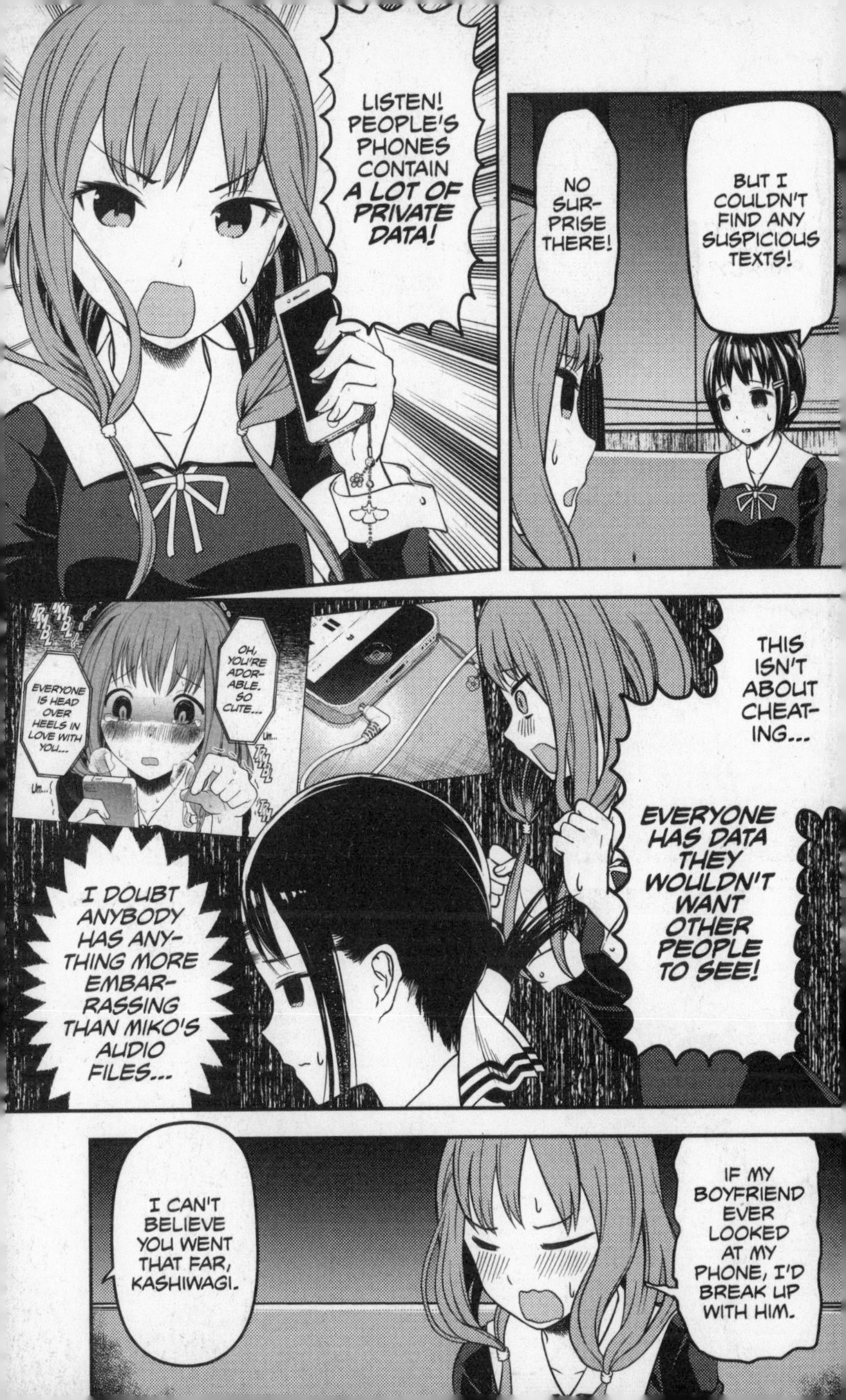
BUT I COULDN'T FIND ANY SUSPICIOUS TEXTS!
NO SURPRISE THERE!
LISTEN! PEOPLE'S PHONES CONTAIN A LOT OF PRIVATE DATA!
THIS ISN'T ABOUT CHEATING...
EVERYONE HAS DATA THEY WOULDN'T WANT OTHER PEOPLE TO SEE!
OH, YOU'RE ADORABLE. SO CUTE...
EVERYONE IS HEAD OVER HEELS IN LOVE WITH YOU...
Um...
Um...
I DOUBT ANYBODY HAS ANYTHING MORE EMBARRASSING THAN MIKO'S AUDIO FILES...
IF MY BOYFRIEND EVER LOOKED AT MY PHONE, I'D BREAK UP WITH HIM.
I CAN'T BELIEVE YOU WENT THAT FAR, KASHIWAGI.

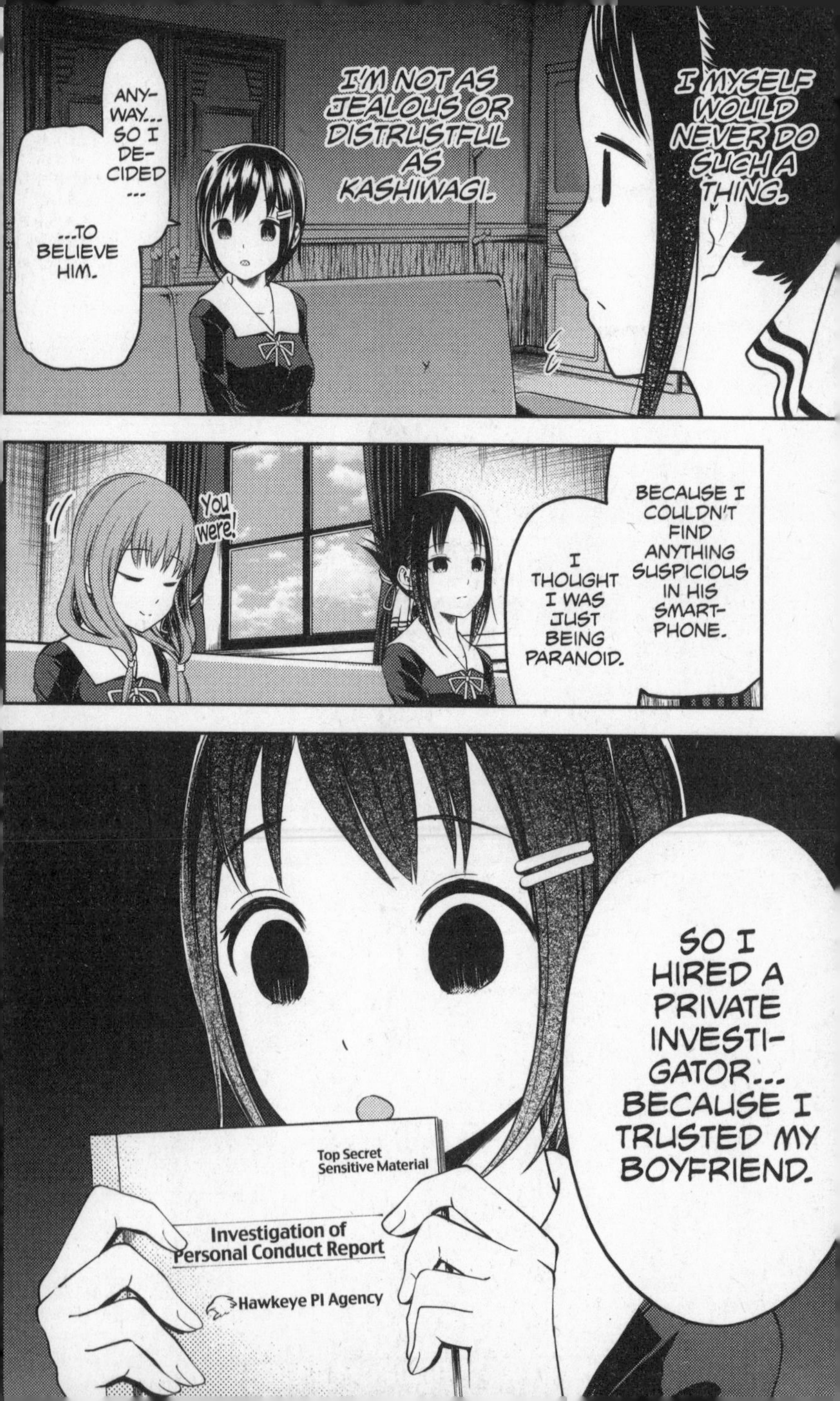
I MYSELF WOULD NEVER DO SUCH A THING.
I'M NOT AS JEALOUS OR DISTRUSTFUL AS KASHIWAGI.
ANYWAY... SO I DECIDED...
...TO BELIEVE HIM.
BECAUSE I COULDN'T FIND ANYTHING SUSPICIOUS IN HIS SMARTPHONE.
I THOUGHT I WAS JUST BEING PARANOID.
You were!
SO I HIRED A PRIVATE INVESTIGATOR... BECAUSE I TRUSTED MY BOYFRIEND.
Top Secret Sensitive Material
Investigation of Personal Conduct Report
Hawkeye PI Agency

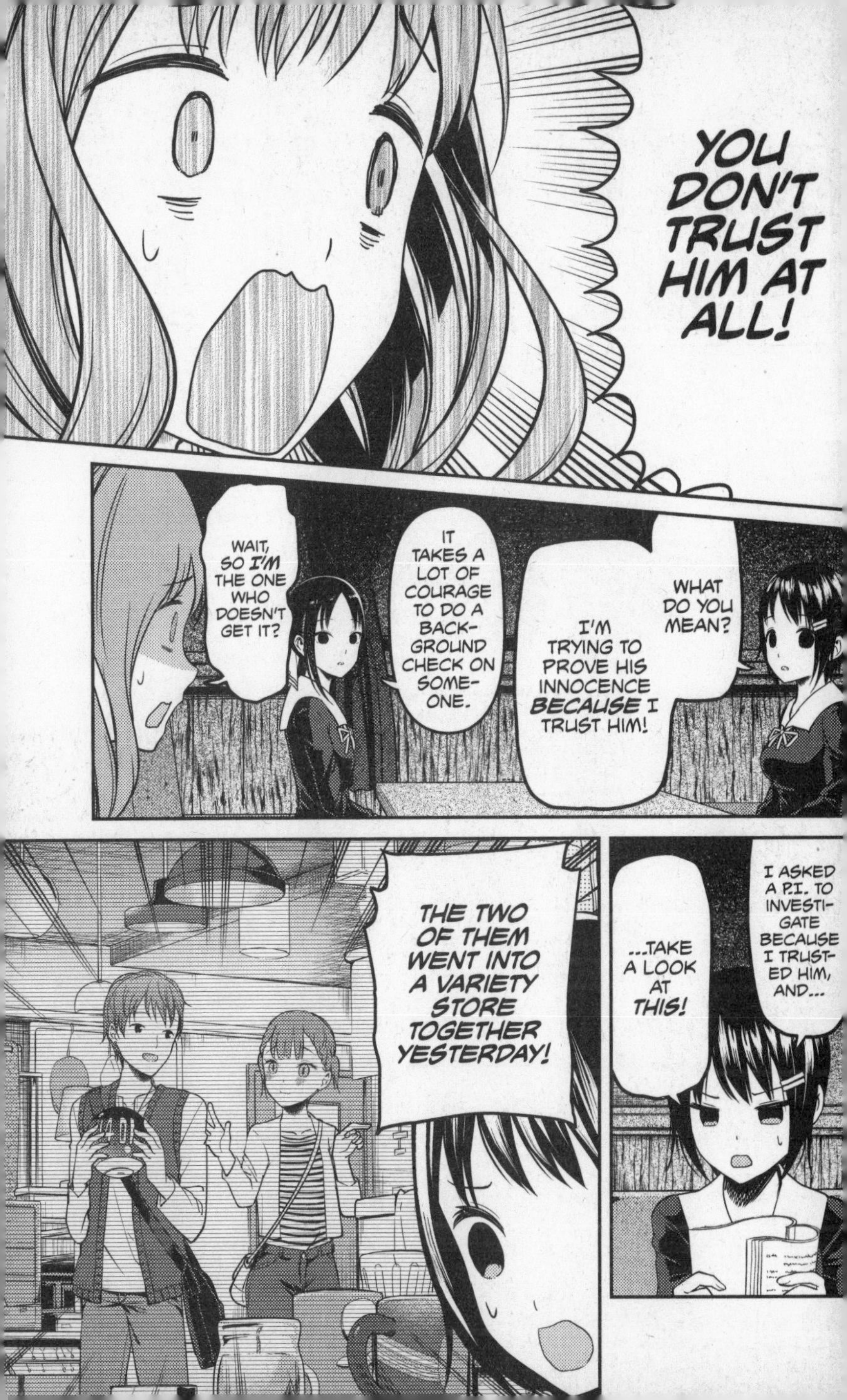
YOU DON'T TRUST HIM AT ALL!
WHAT DO YOU MEAN?
I'M TRYING TO PROVE HIS INNOCENCE *BECAUSE* I TRUST HIM!
IT TAKES A LOT OF COURAGE TO DO A BACK-GROUND CHECK ON SOME-ONE.
WAIT, SO *I'M* THE ONE WHO DOESN'T GET IT?
I ASKED A P.I. TO INVESTI-GATE BECAUSE I TRUST-ED HIM, AND...
...TAKE A LOOK AT *THIS!*
THE TWO OF THEM WENT INTO A VARIETY STORE TOGETHER YESTERDAY!

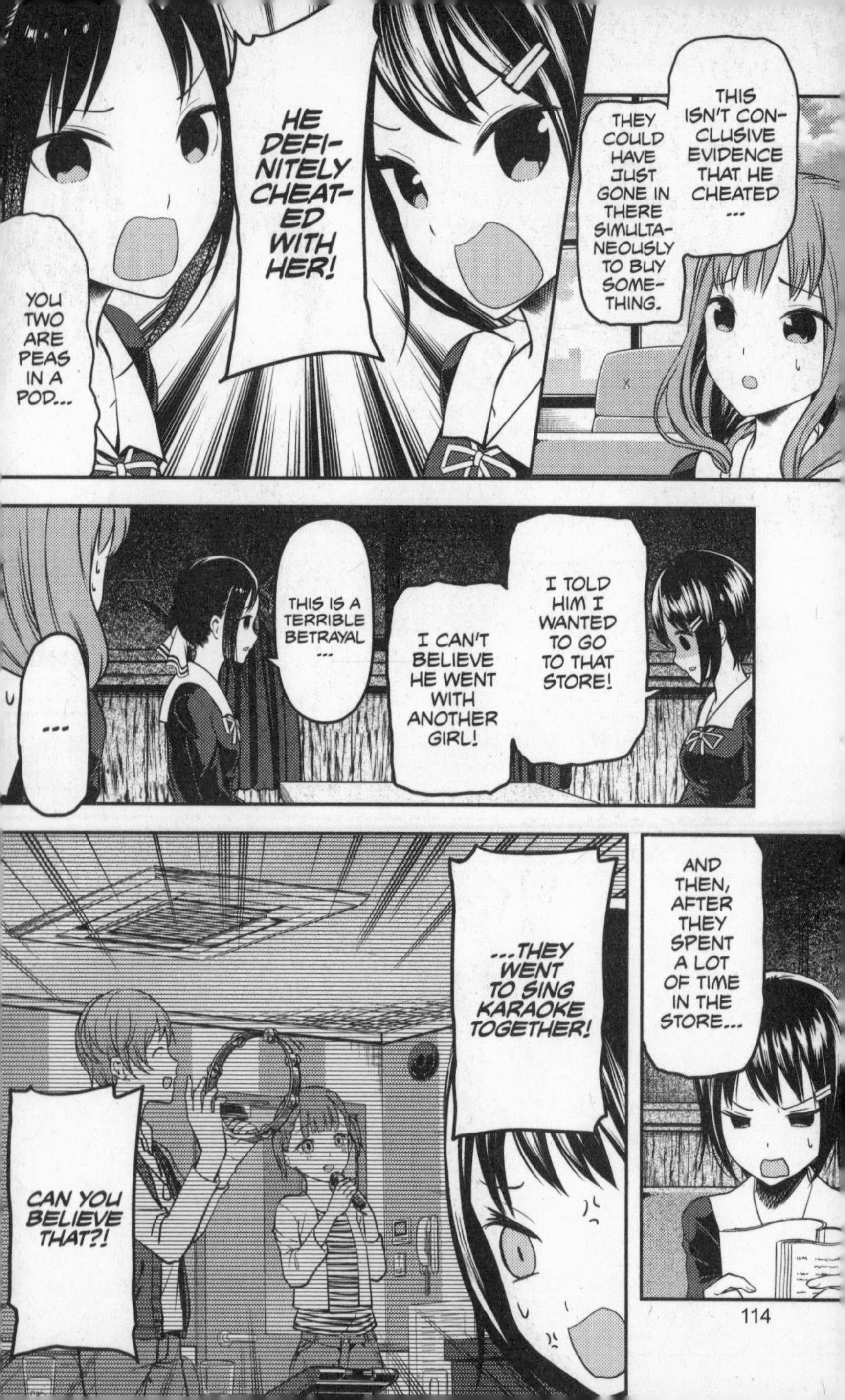
THIS ISN'T CON-CLUSIVE EVIDENCE THAT HE CHEATED...
THEY COULD HAVE JUST GONE IN THERE SIMULTA-NEOUSLY TO BUY SOME-THING.
HE DEFI-NITELY CHEAT-ED WITH HER!
YOU TWO ARE PEAS IN A POD...
I TOLD HIM I WANTED TO GO TO THAT STORE!
I CAN'T BELIEVE HE WENT WITH ANOTHER GIRL!
THIS IS A TERRIBLE BETRAYAL...
...
AND THEN, AFTER THEY SPENT A LOT OF TIME IN THE STORE...
...THEY WENT TO SING KARAOKE TOGETHER!
CAN YOU BELIEVE THAT?!

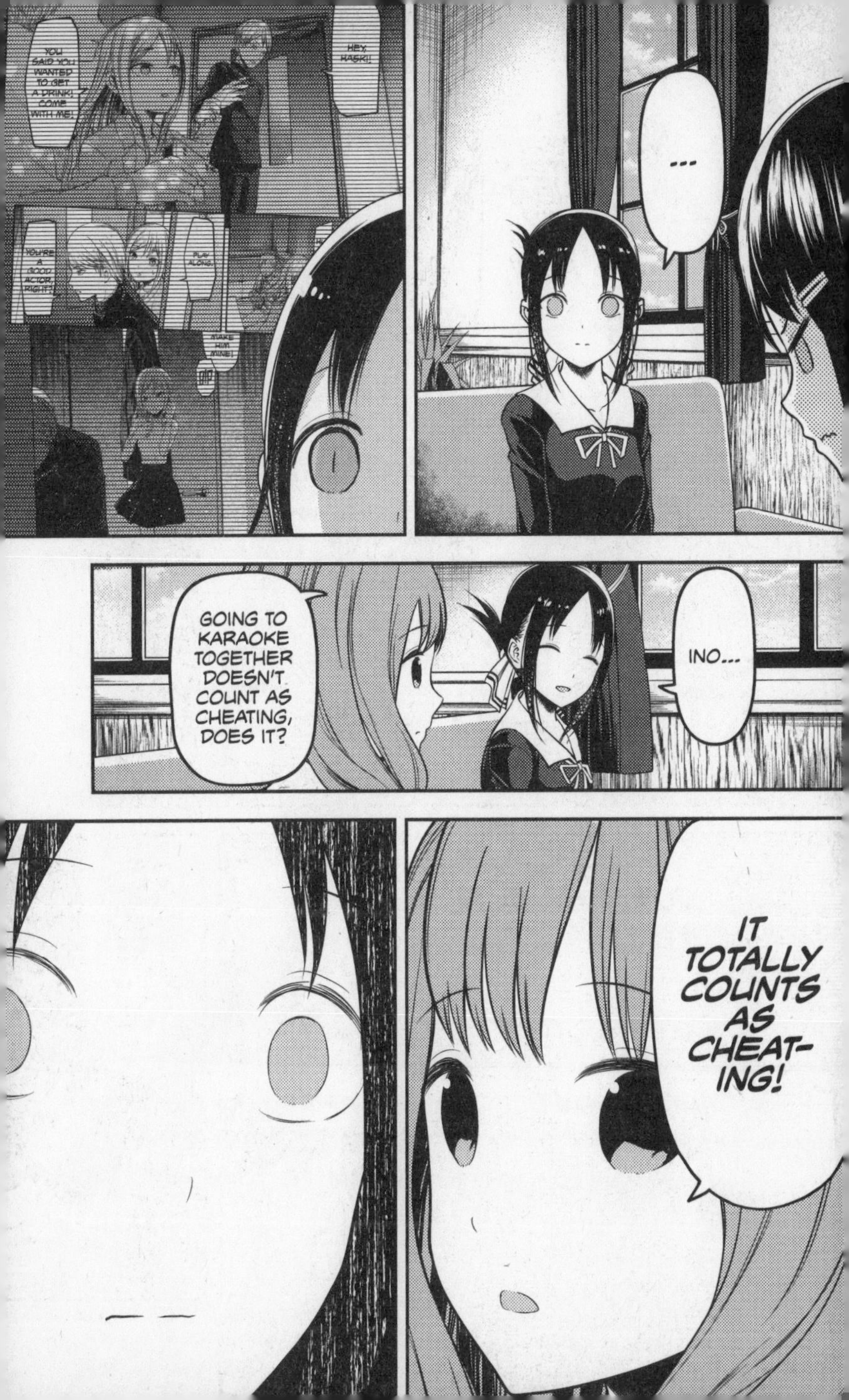
...
HEY, HASK!!
YOU SAID YOU WANTED TO GET A DRINK! COME WITH ME!
PLAY ALONG.
YOU'RE A GOOD ACTOR, RIGHT?!
MAKE HIM MINE!
INO...
GOING TO KARAOKE TOGETHER DOESN'T COUNT AS CHEATING, DOES IT?
IT TOTALLY COUNTS AS CHEAT-ING!
——

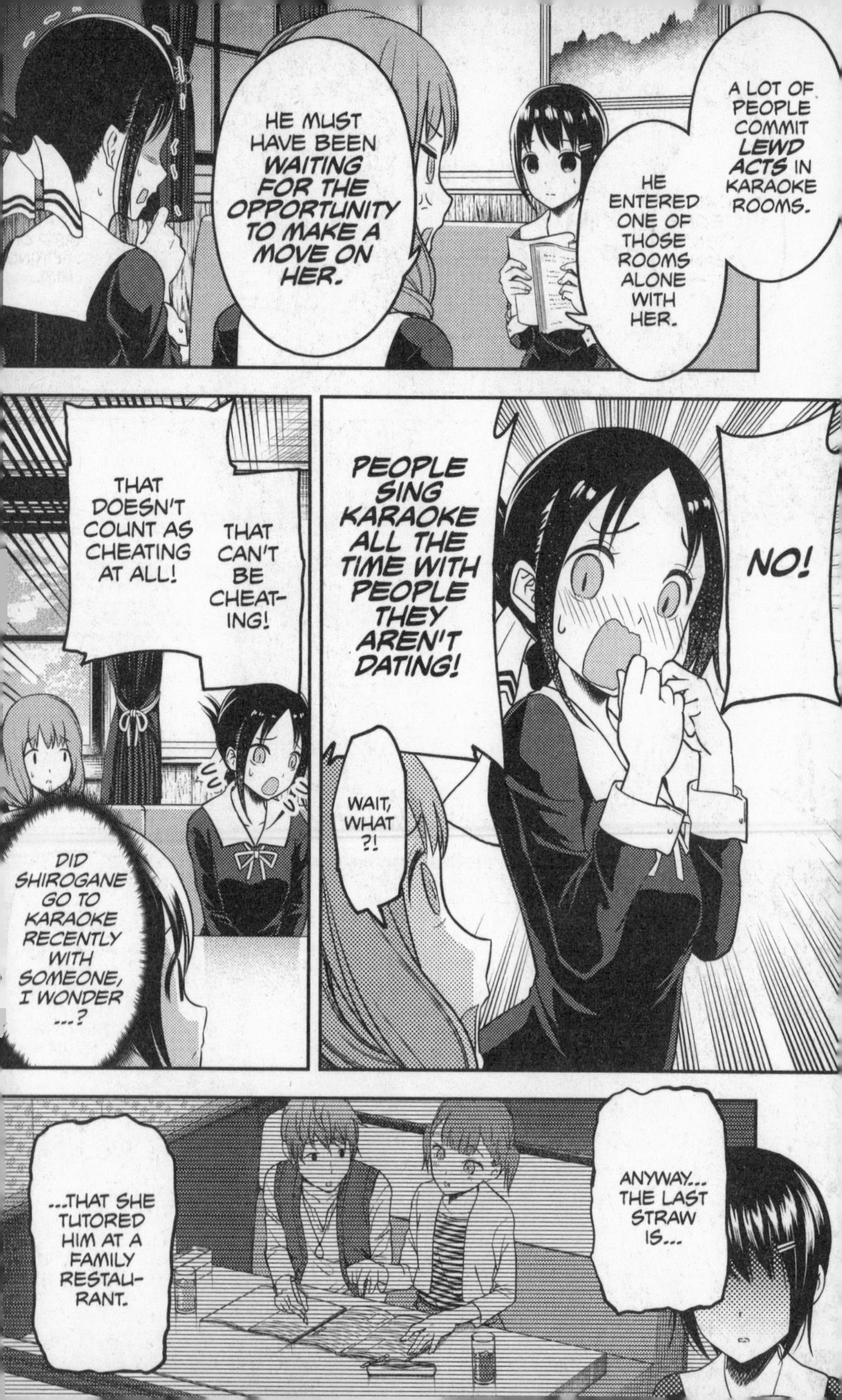
A LOT OF PEOPLE COMMIT LEWD ACTS IN KARAOKE ROOMS.
HE ENTERED ONE OF THOSE ROOMS ALONE WITH HER.
HE MUST HAVE BEEN WAITING FOR THE OPPORTUNITY TO MAKE A MOVE ON HER.
NO!
PEOPLE SING KARAOKE ALL THE TIME WITH PEOPLE THEY AREN'T DATING!
WAIT, WHAT?!
THAT CAN'T BE CHEAT-ING!
THAT DOESN'T COUNT AS CHEATING AT ALL!
DID SHIROGANE GO TO KARAOKE RECENTLY WITH SOMEONE, I WONDER...?
ANYWAY... THE LAST STRAW IS...
...THAT SHE TUTORED HIM AT A FAMILY RESTAU-RANT.

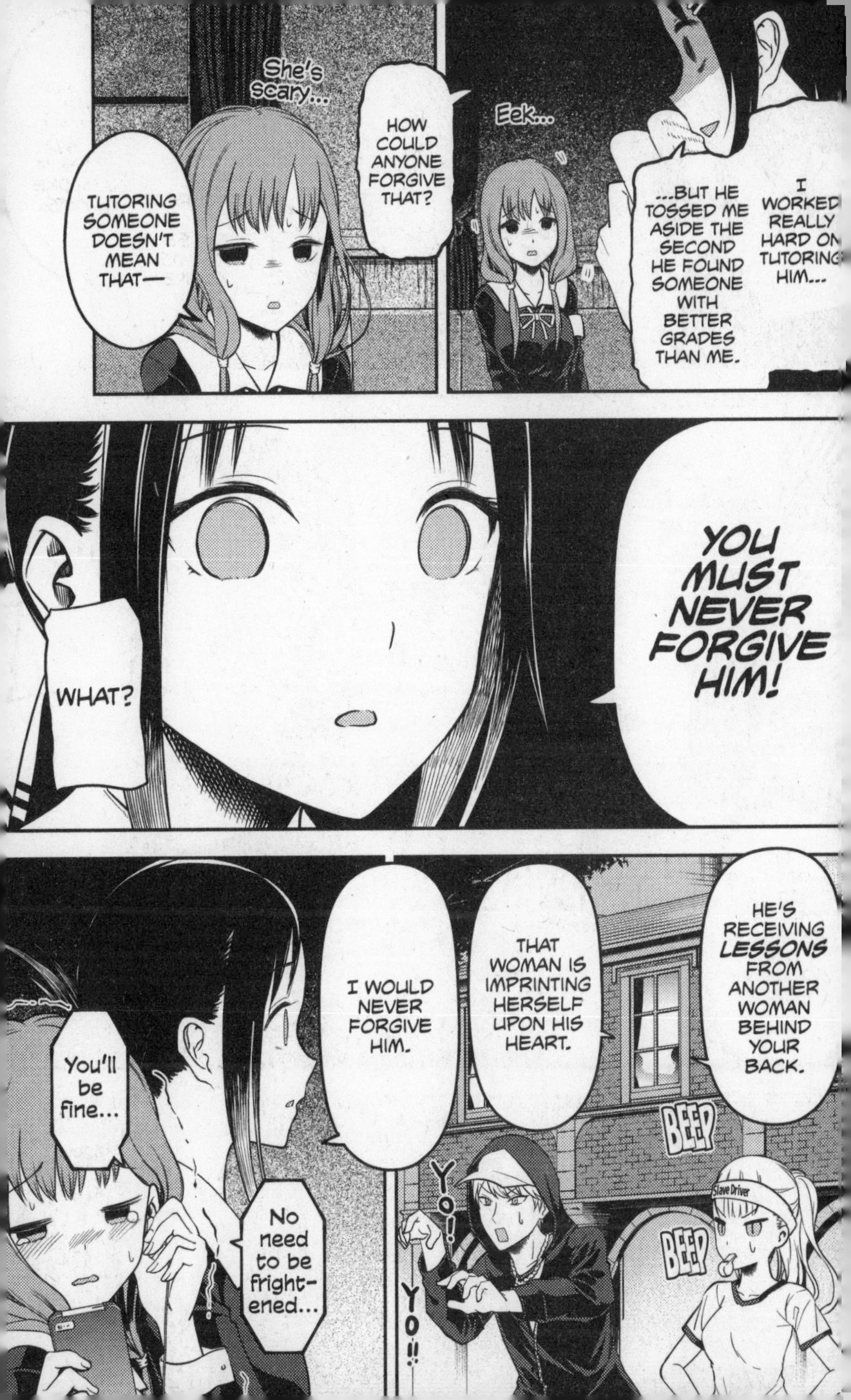
I WORKED REALLY HARD ON TUTORING HIM...
...BUT HE TOSSED ME ASIDE THE SECOND HE FOUND SOMEONE WITH BETTER GRADES THAN ME.
Eek...
HOW COULD ANYONE FORGIVE THAT?
She's scary...
TUTORING SOMEONE DOESN'T MEAN THAT—
YOU MUST NEVER FORGIVE HIM!
WHAT?
HE'S RECEIVING LESSONS FROM ANOTHER WOMAN BEHIND YOUR BACK.
THAT WOMAN IS IMPRINTING HERSELF UPON HIS HEART.
I WOULD NEVER FORGIVE HIM.
BEEP
BEEP
Slave Driver
YO!
YO!!
No need to be frightened...
You'll be fine...

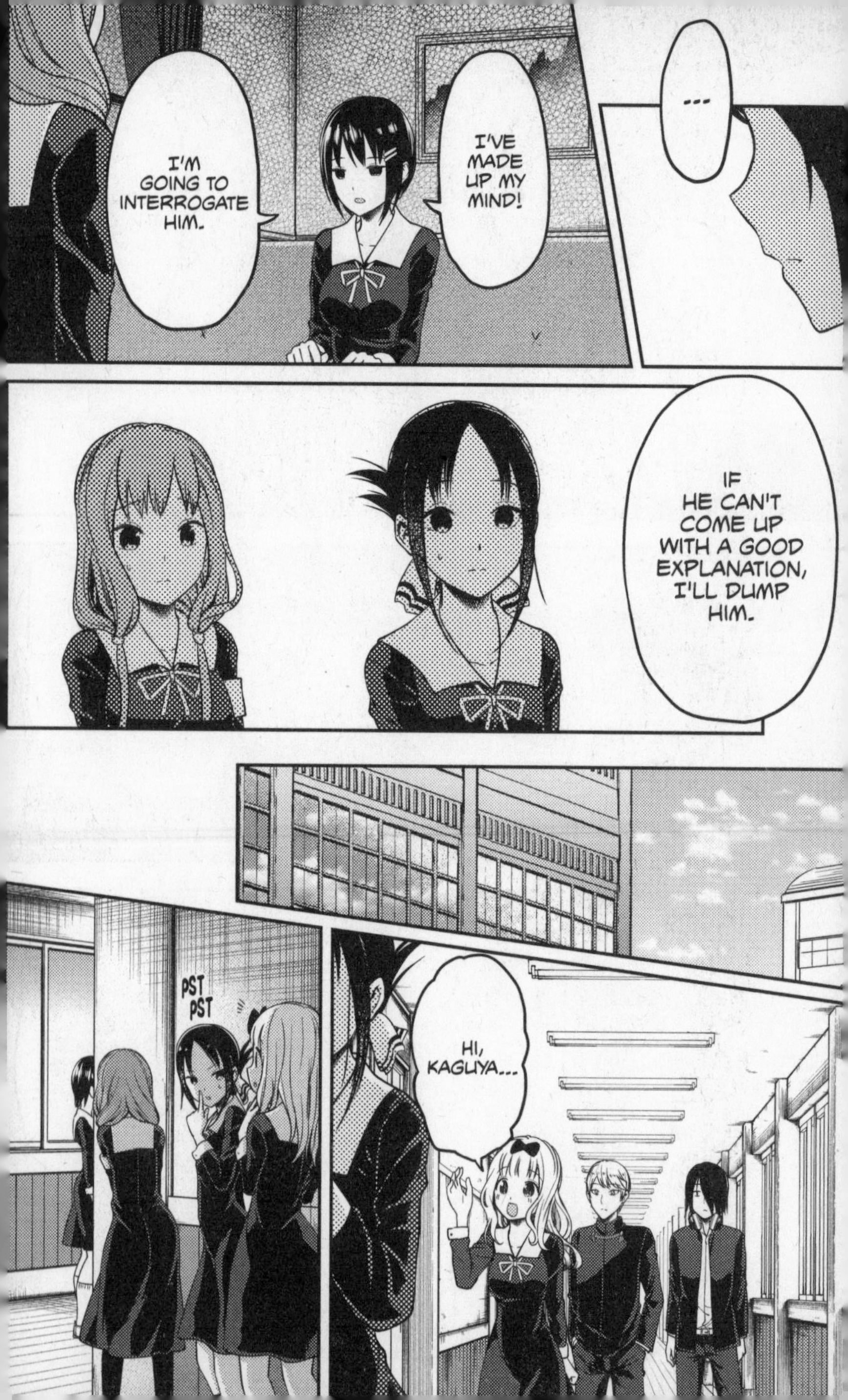
...
I'VE MADE UP MY MIND!
I'M GOING TO INTERROGATE HIM.
IF HE CAN'T COME UP WITH A GOOD EXPLANATION, I'LL DUMP HIM.
HI, KAGUYA...
PST PST

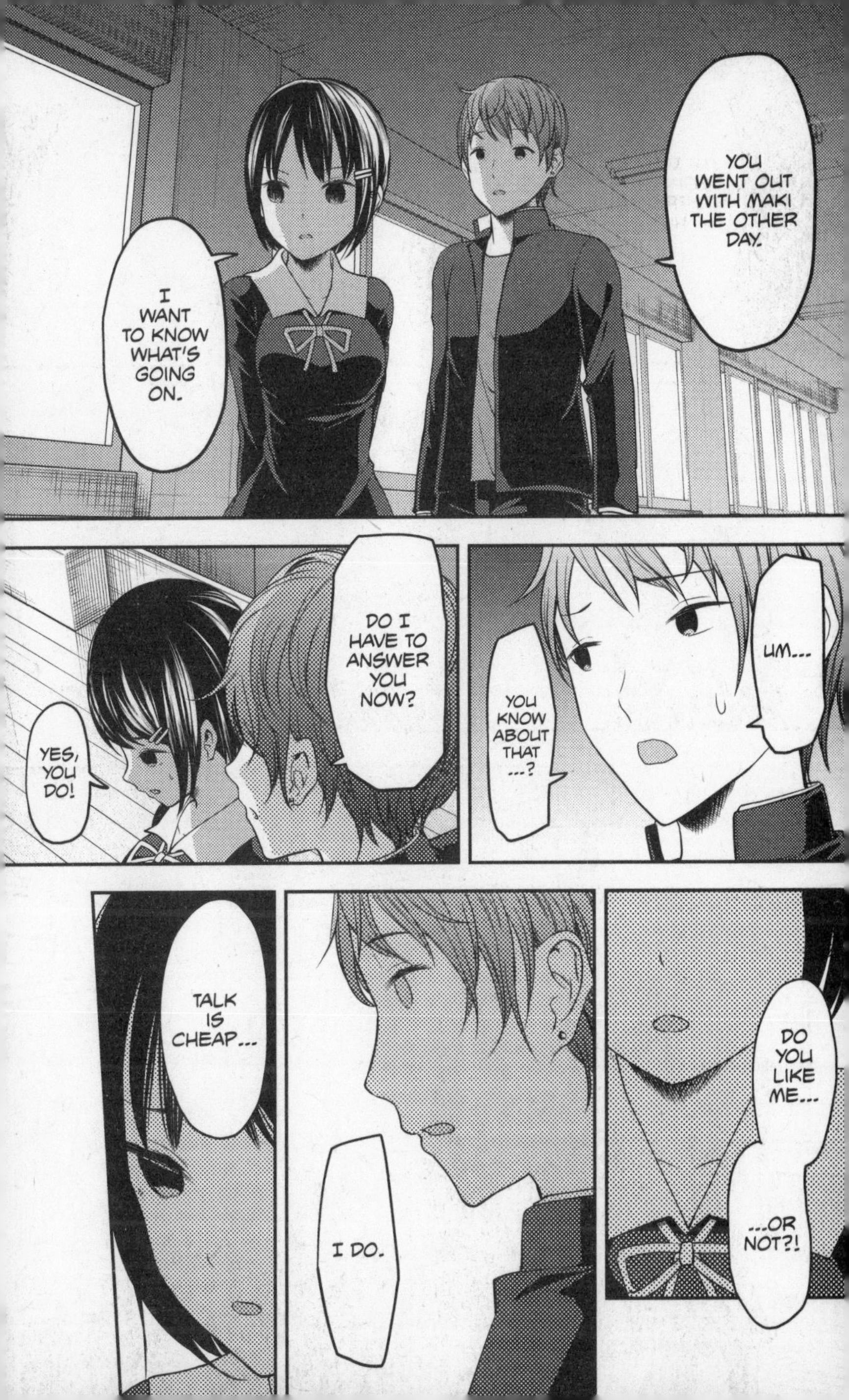
YOU WENT OUT WITH MAKI THE OTHER DAY.
I WANT TO KNOW WHAT'S GOING ON.
UM...
YOU KNOW ABOUT THAT...?
DO I HAVE TO ANSWER YOU NOW?
YES, YOU DO!
DO YOU LIKE ME...
...OR NOT?!
I DO.
TALK IS CHEAP...

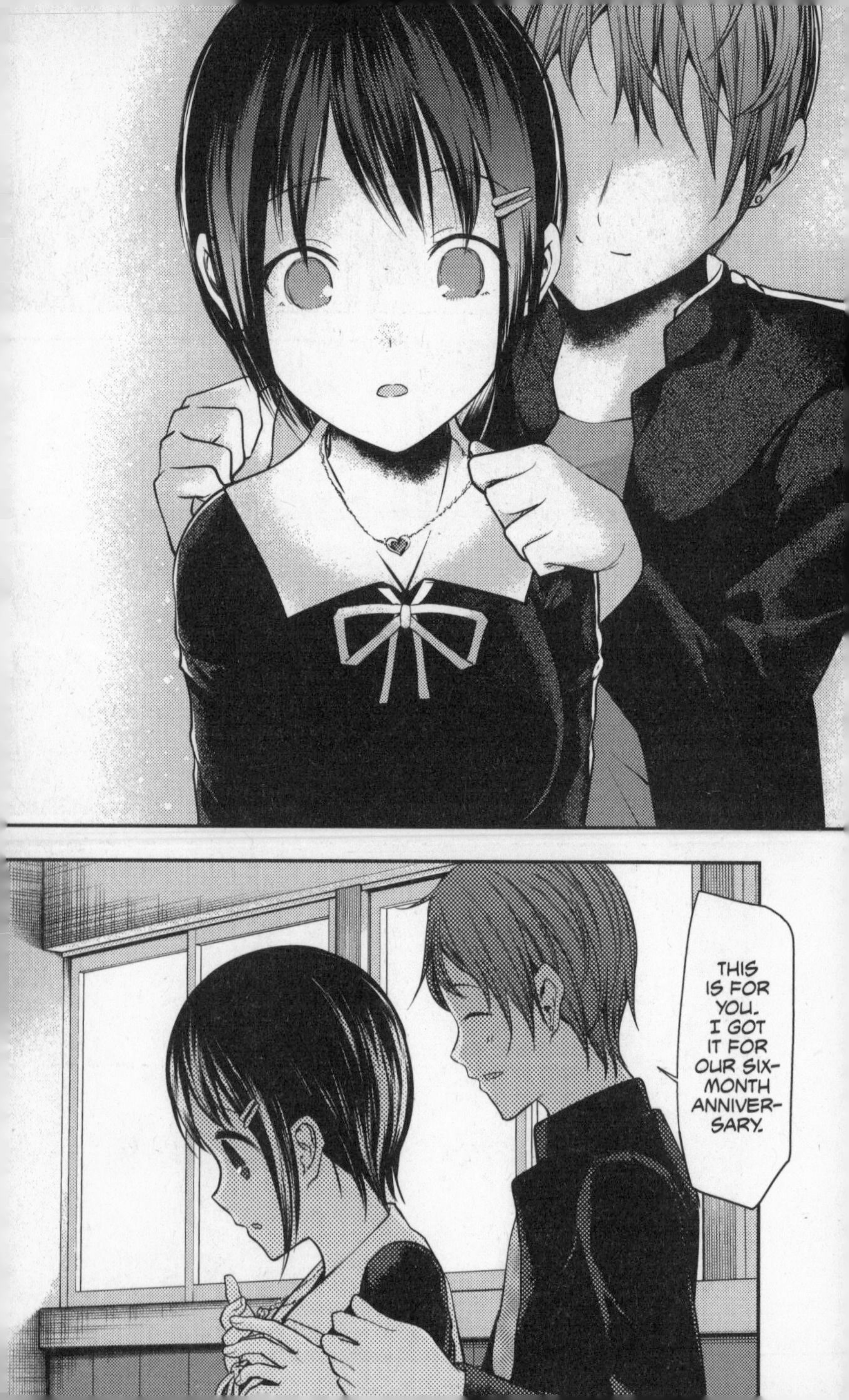
THIS IS FOR YOU. I GOT IT FOR OUR SIX-MONTH ANNIVERSARY.

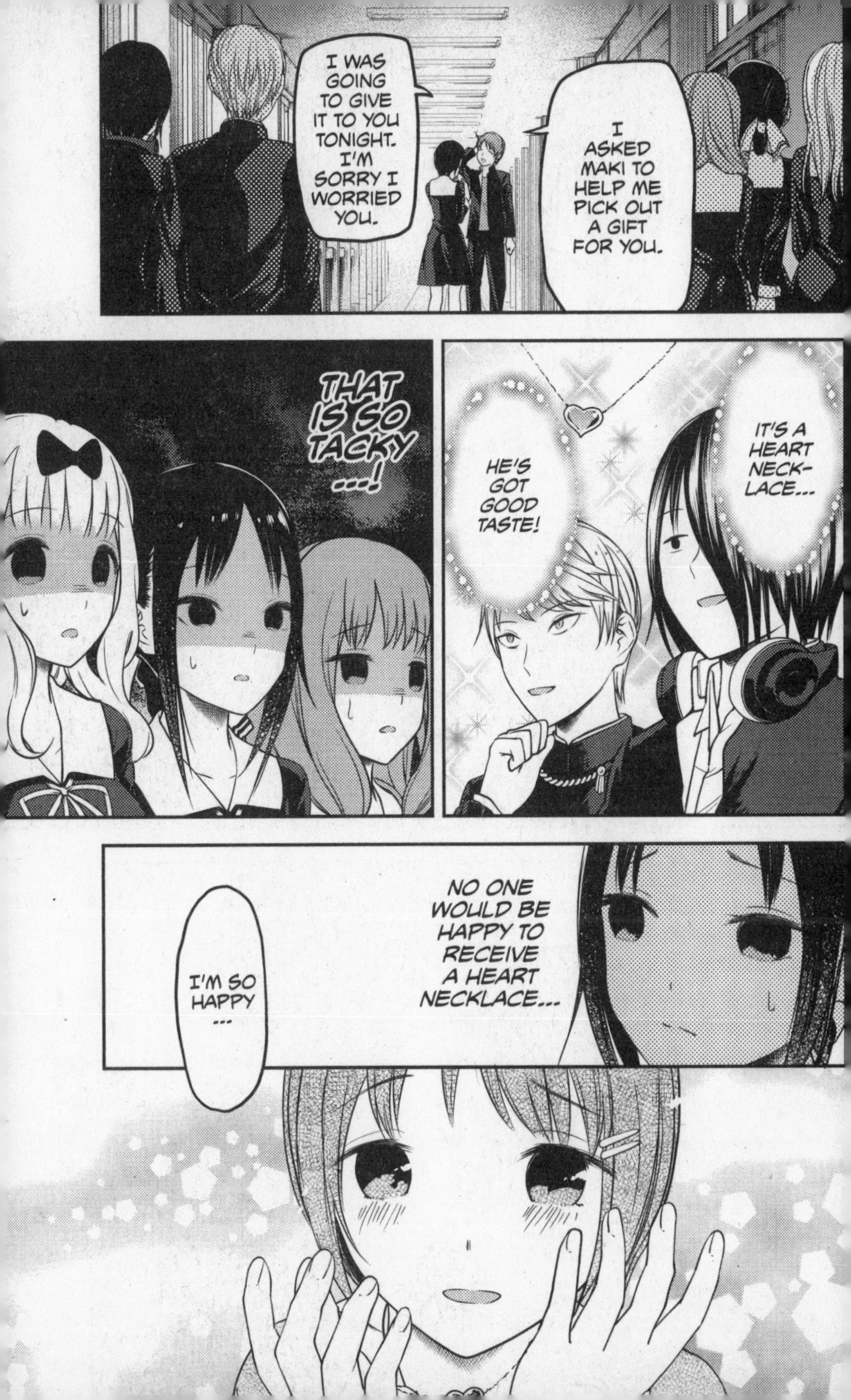
I ASKED MAKI TO HELP ME PICK OUT A GIFT FOR YOU.
I WAS GOING TO GIVE IT TO YOU TONIGHT. I'M SORRY I WORRIED YOU.
IT'S A HEART NECK-LACE...
HE'S GOT GOOD TASTE!
THAT IS SO TACKY...!
NO ONE WOULD BE HAPPY TO RECEIVE A HEART NECKLACE...
I'M SO HAPPY...

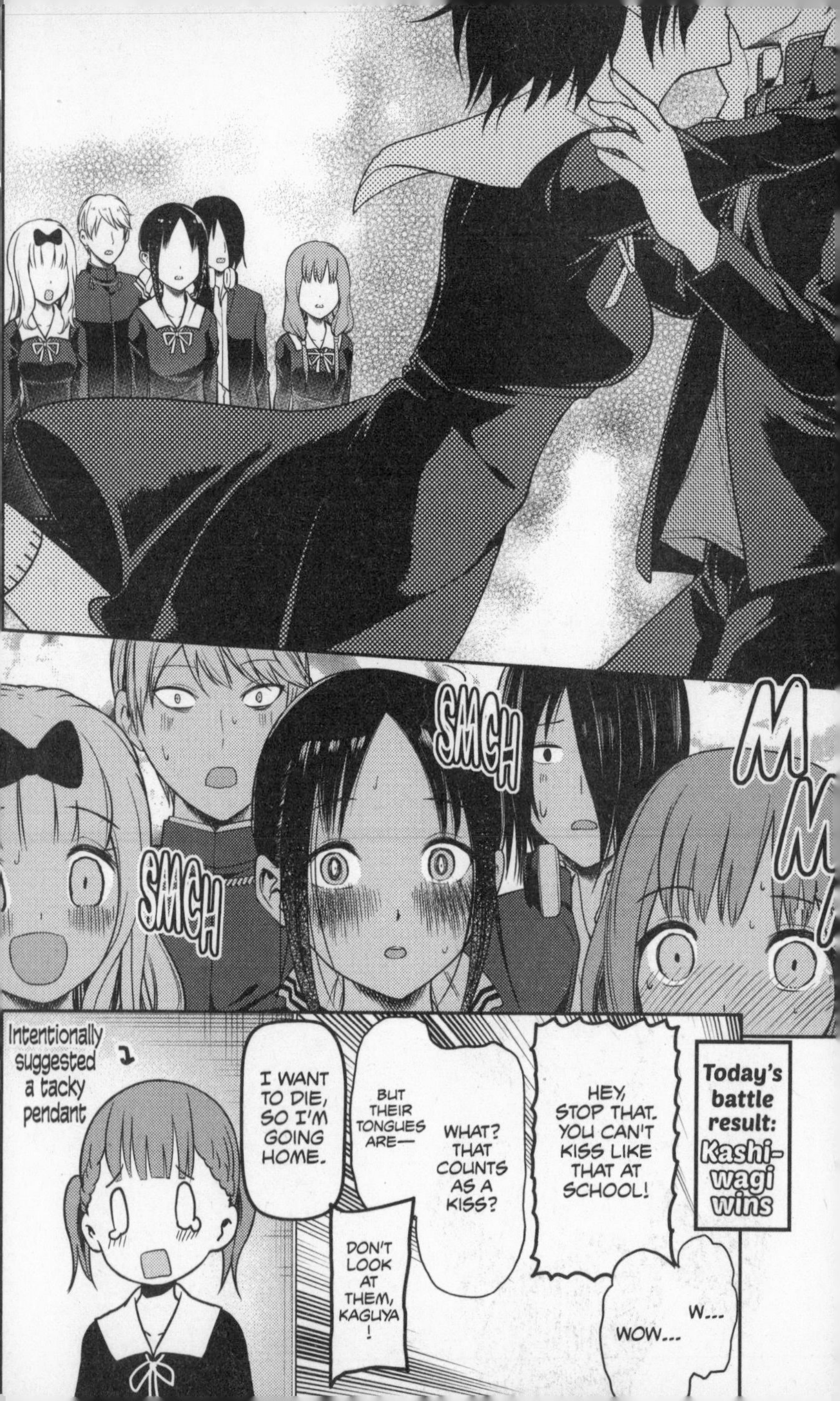

MM
SMCH
SMCH
Today's battle result: Kashiwagi wins
HEY, STOP THAT. YOU CAN'T KISS LIKE THAT AT SCHOOL!
W... WOW...
WHAT? THAT COUNTS AS A KISS?
BUT THEIR TONGUES ARE—
DON'T LOOK AT THEM, KAGUYA!
I WANT TO DIE, SO I'M GOING HOME.
Intentionally suggested a tacky pendant

This
doesn't
go with
most
of my
clothes.
♡

Oh.

KAGUYA-SAMA LOVE IS WAR

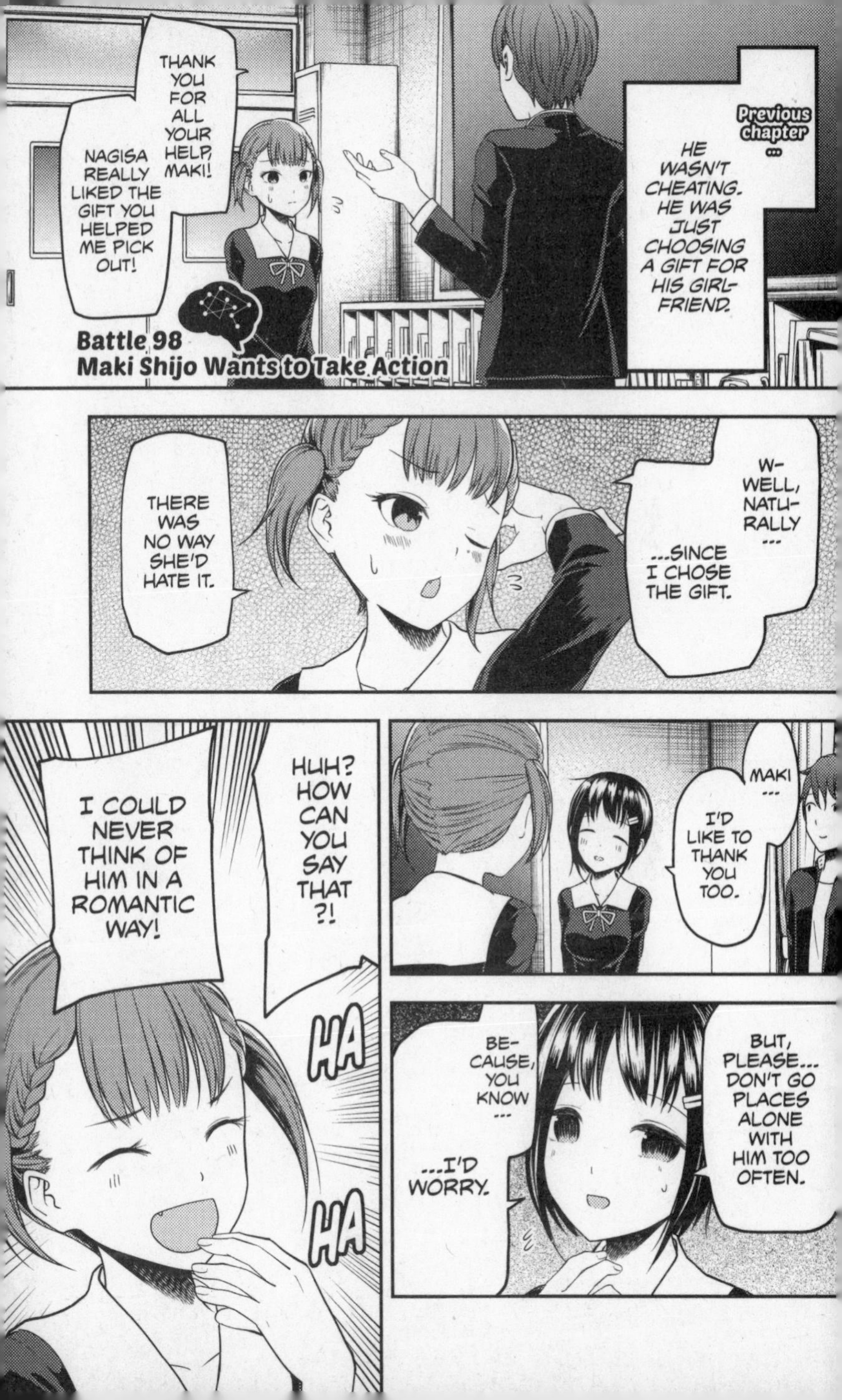

Previous chapter ...
HE WASN'T CHEATING. HE WAS JUST CHOOSING A GIFT FOR HIS GIRL-FRIEND.
THANK YOU FOR ALL YOUR HELP, MAKI!
NAGISA REALLY LIKED THE GIFT YOU HELPED ME PICK OUT!
Battle 98
Maki Shijo Wants to Take Action
W-WELL, NATURALLY ...
...SINCE I CHOSE THE GIFT.
THERE WAS NO WAY SHE'D HATE IT.
MAKI ...
I'D LIKE TO THANK YOU TOO.
BUT, PLEASE... DON'T GO PLACES ALONE WITH HIM TOO OFTEN.
BE-CAUSE, YOU KNOW ...
...I'D WORRY.
HUH? HOW CAN YOU SAY THAT ?!
I COULD NEVER THINK OF HIM IN A ROMANTIC WAY!
HA
HA

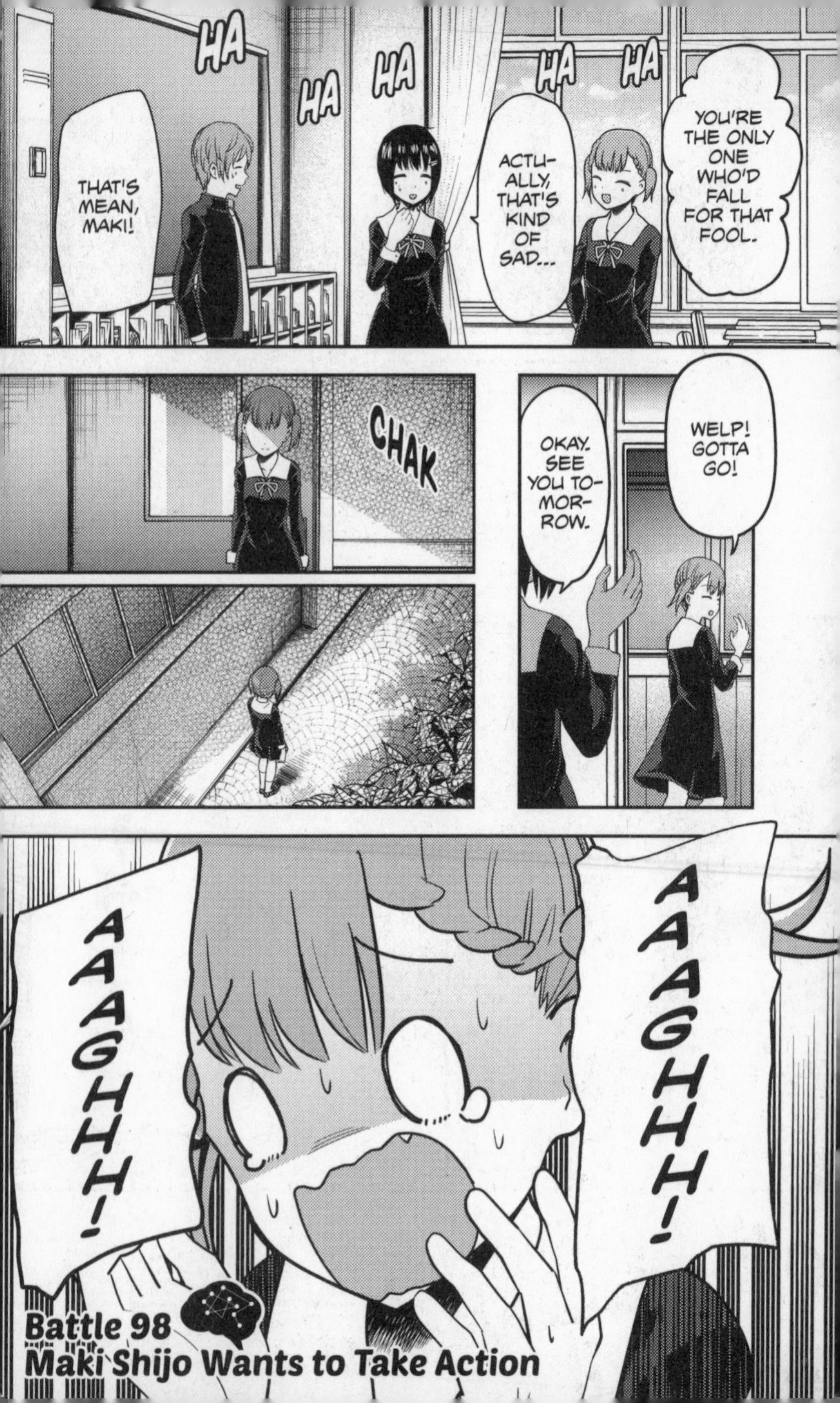
HA
HA
HA
HA
YOU'RE THE ONLY ONE WHO'D FALL FOR THAT FOOL.
ACTU-ALLY, THAT'S KIND OF SAD...
THAT'S MEAN, MAKI!
WELP! GOTTA GO!
OKAY. SEE YOU TO-MOR-ROW.
CHAK
AAAGHHH!
AAAGHHH!

Battle 98
Maki Shijo Wants to Take Action

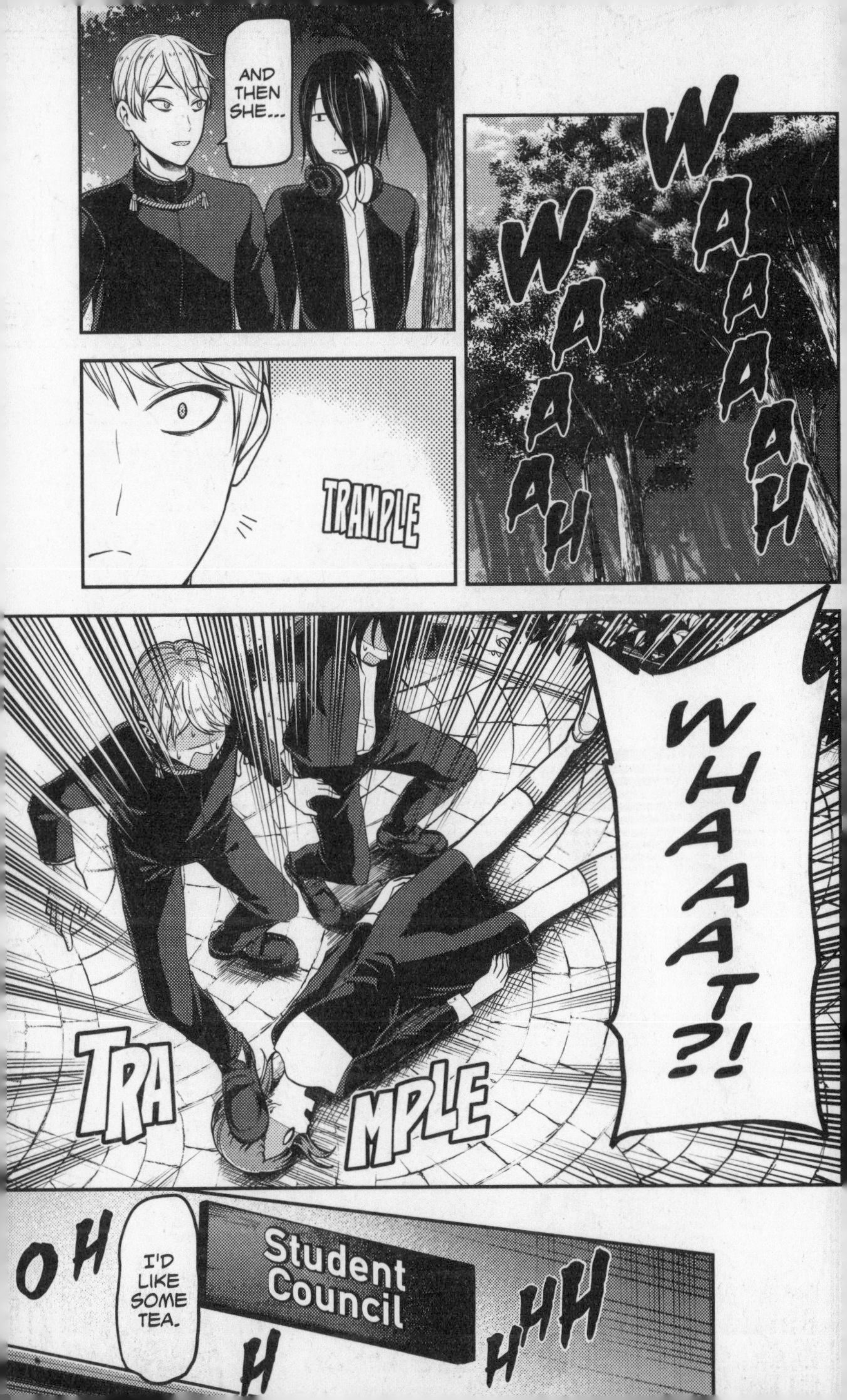
WAAAAH
WAAAH
AND THEN SHE...
TRAMPLE
WHAAAAT?!
TRAMPLE
OHHHHHH
I'D LIKE SOME TEA.
Student Council

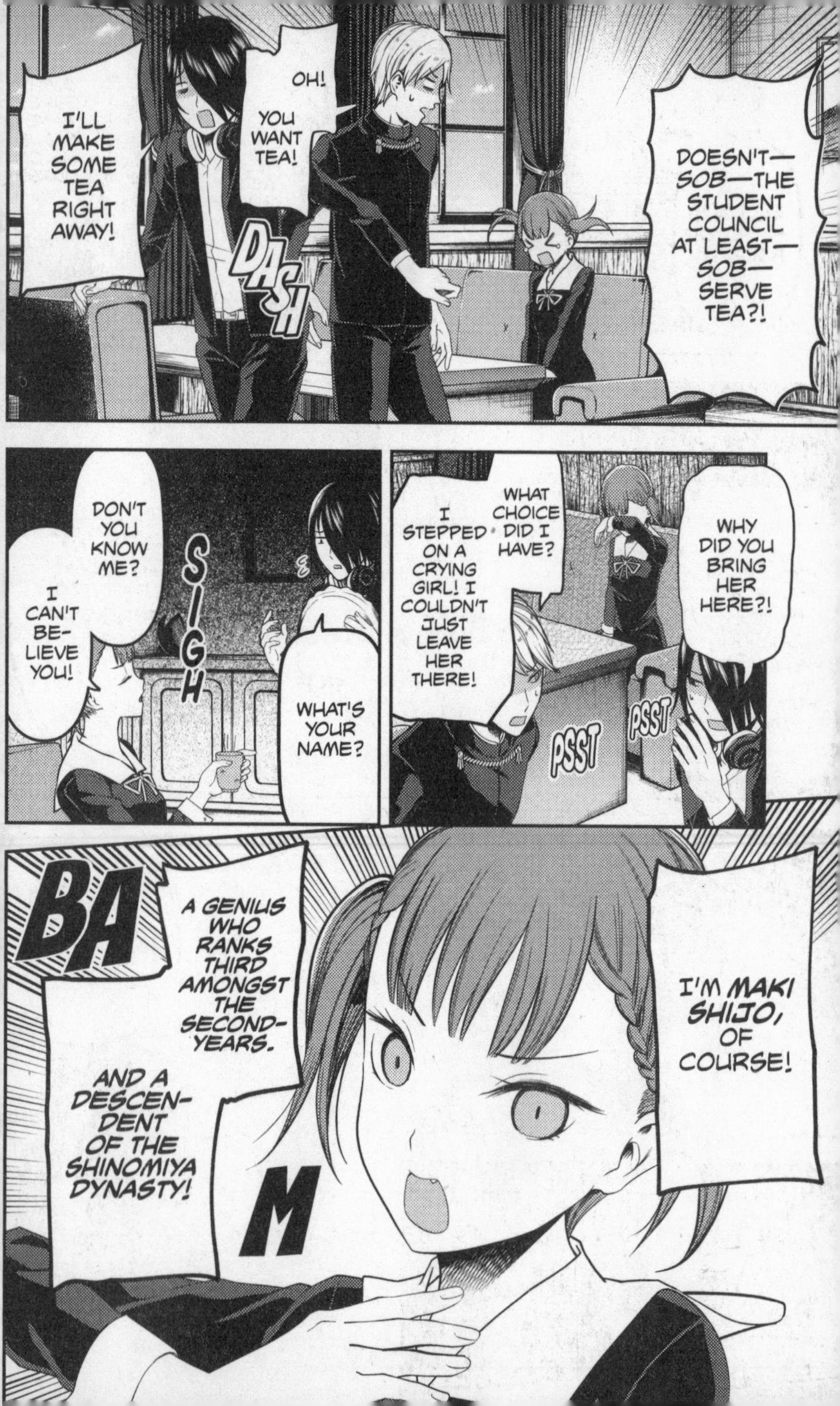
DOESN'T—SOB—THE STUDENT COUNCIL AT LEAST—SOB—SERVE TEA?!
OH!
YOU WANT TEA!
I'LL MAKE SOME TEA RIGHT AWAY!
DASH
WHY DID YOU BRING HER HERE?!
PSST
WHAT CHOICE DID I HAVE?
I STEPPED ON A CRYING GIRL! I COULDN'T JUST LEAVE HER THERE!
PSST
WHAT'S YOUR NAME?
SIGH
DON'T YOU KNOW ME?
I CAN'T BE-LIEVE YOU!
I'M MAKI SHIJO, OF COURSE!
A GENIUS WHO RANKS THIRD AMONGST THE SECOND-YEARS.
AND A DESCENDENT OF THE SHINOMIYA DYNASTY!
BA
M

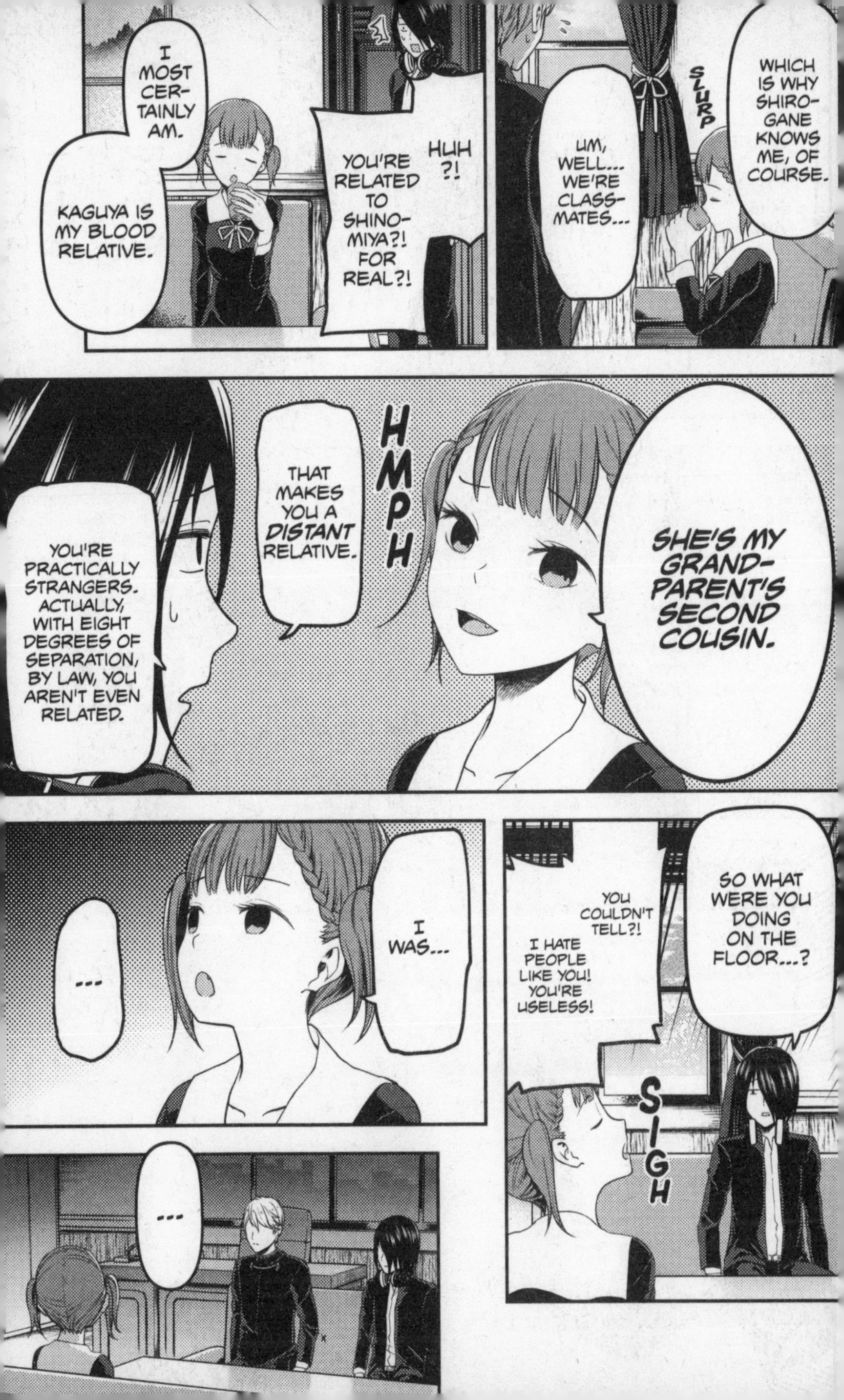
WHICH IS WHY SHIROGANE KNOWS ME, OF COURSE.
SLURP
UM, WELL... WE'RE CLASSMATES...
HUH?!
YOU'RE RELATED TO SHINOMIYA?! FOR REAL?!
I MOST CERTAINLY AM.
KAGUYA IS MY BLOOD RELATIVE.
SHE'S MY GRANDPARENT'S SECOND COUSIN.
HMPH
THAT MAKES YOU A DISTANT RELATIVE.
YOU'RE PRACTICALLY STRANGERS. ACTUALLY, WITH EIGHT DEGREES OF SEPARATION, BY LAW, YOU AREN'T EVEN RELATED.
SO WHAT WERE YOU DOING ON THE FLOOR...?
YOU COULDN'T TELL?!
I HATE PEOPLE LIKE YOU! YOU'RE USELESS!
SIGH
I WAS...
...
...

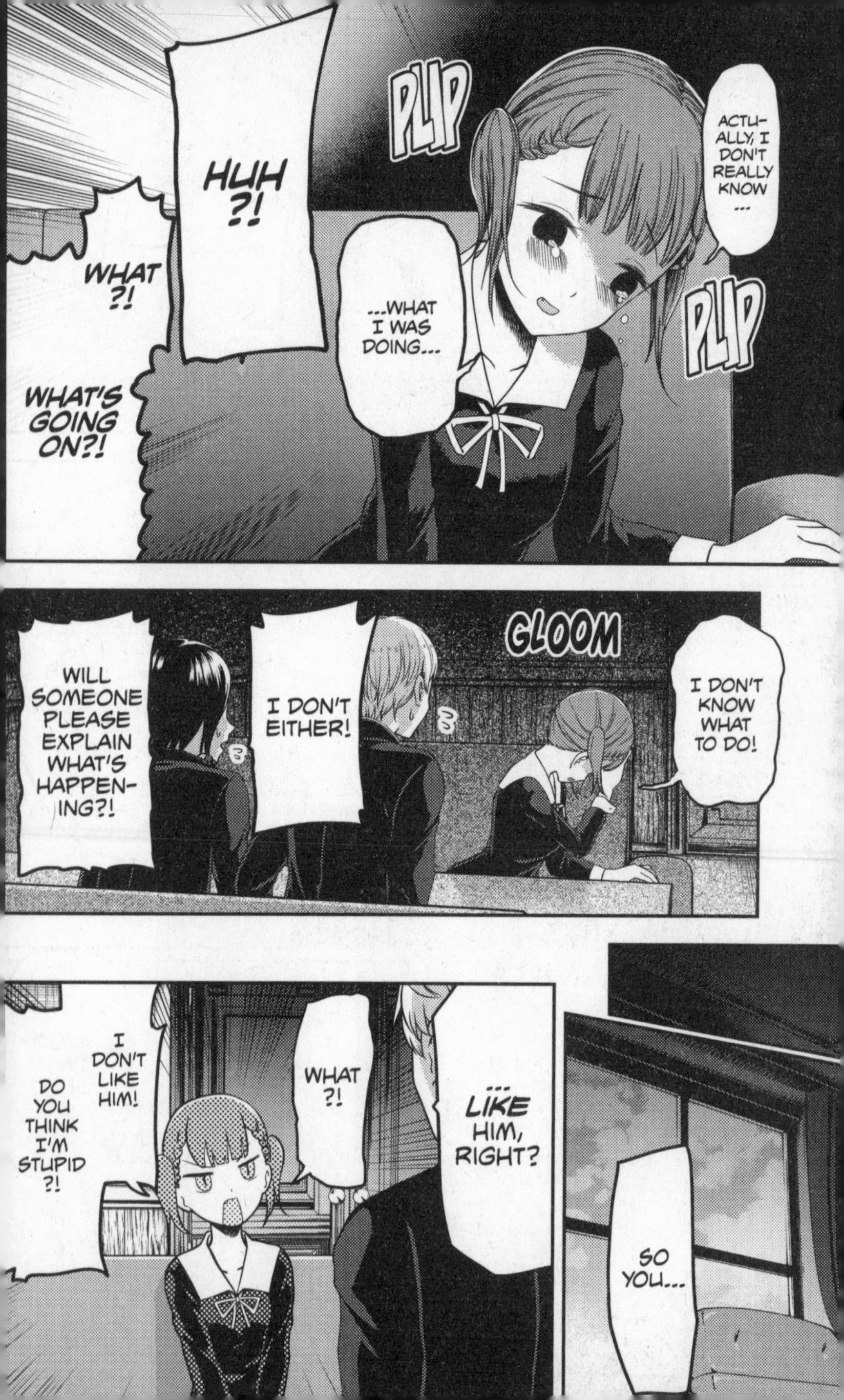
PLIP
ACTU-ALLY, I DON'T REALLY KNOW...
PLIP
...WHAT I WAS DOING...
HUH?!
WHAT?!
WHAT'S GOING ON?!
GLOOM
I DON'T KNOW WHAT TO DO!
I DON'T EITHER!
WILL SOMEONE PLEASE EXPLAIN WHAT'S HAPPEN-ING?!
SO YOU...
...LIKE HIM, RIGHT?
WHAT?!
I DON'T LIKE HIM!
DO YOU THINK I'M STUPID?!

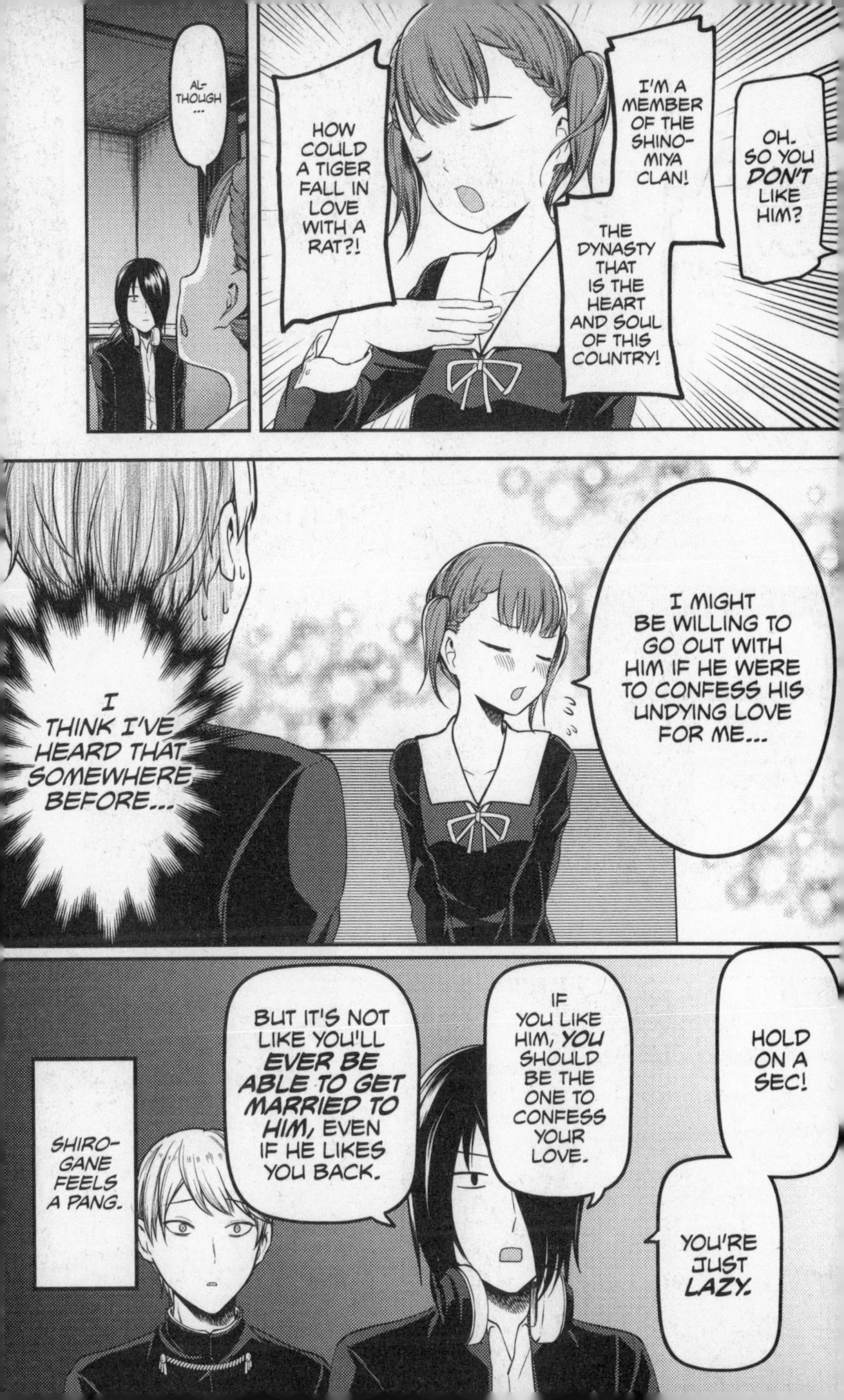
OH. SO YOU *DON'T* LIKE HIM?
I'M A MEMBER OF THE SHINOMIYA CLAN!
THE DYNASTY THAT IS THE HEART AND SOUL OF THIS COUNTRY!
HOW COULD A TIGER FALL IN LOVE WITH A RAT?!
ALTHOUGH...
I MIGHT BE WILLING TO GO OUT WITH HIM IF HE WERE TO CONFESS HIS UNDYING LOVE FOR ME...
I THINK I'VE HEARD THAT SOMEWHERE BEFORE...
HOLD ON A SEC!
YOU'RE JUST *LAZY.*
IF YOU LIKE HIM, *YOU* SHOULD BE THE ONE TO CONFESS YOUR LOVE.
BUT IT'S NOT LIKE YOU'LL *EVER BE ABLE TO GET MARRIED TO HIM,* EVEN IF HE LIKES YOU BACK.
SHIROGANE FEELS A PANG.

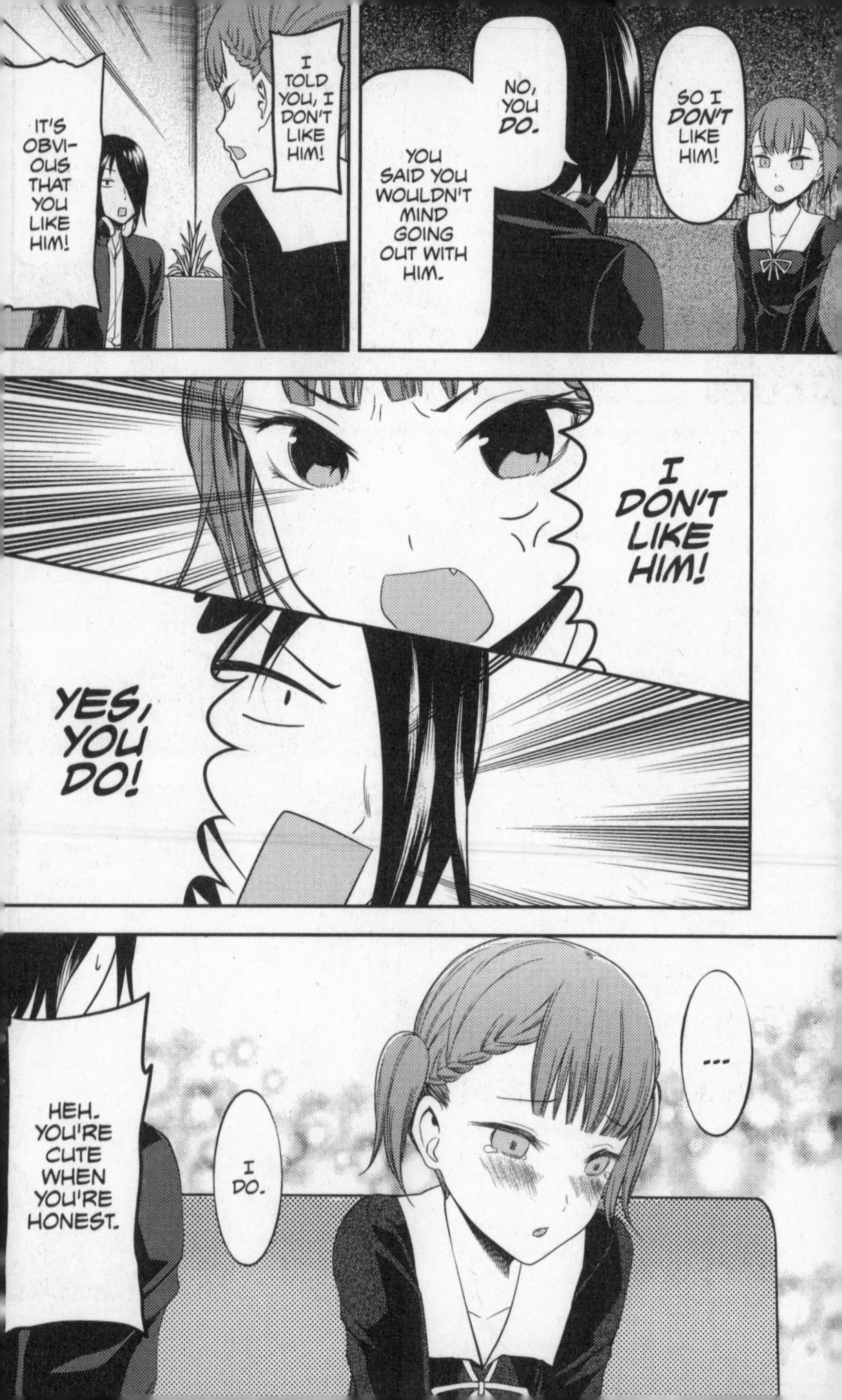
SO I DON'T LIKE HIM!
NO, YOU DO.
YOU SAID YOU WOULDN'T MIND GOING OUT WITH HIM.
I TOLD YOU, I DON'T LIKE HIM!
IT'S OBVIOUS THAT YOU LIKE HIM!
I DON'T LIKE HIM!
YES, YOU DO!
...
I DO.
HEH. YOU'RE CUTE WHEN YOU'RE HONEST.

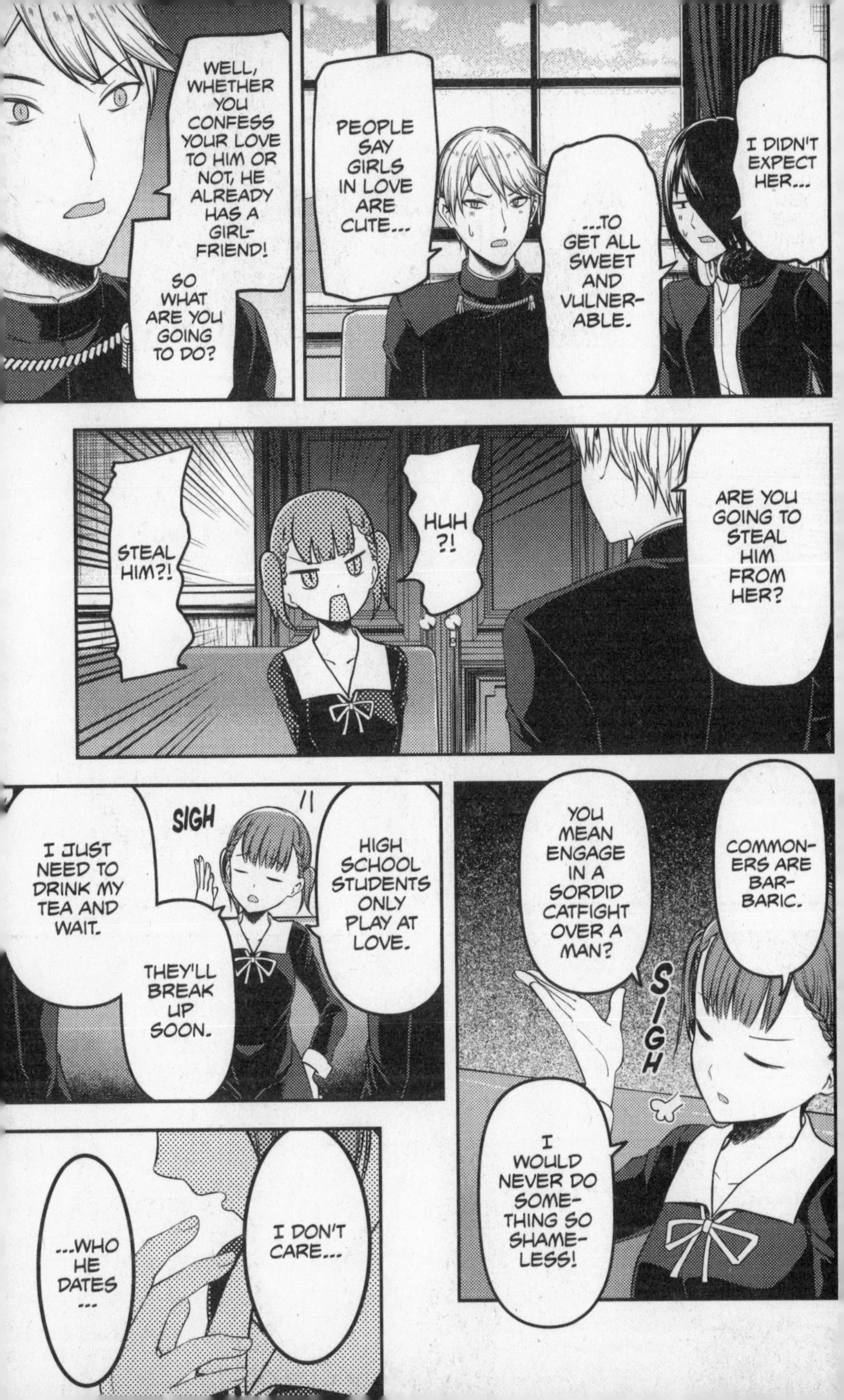
I DIDN'T EXPECT HER...
...TO GET ALL SWEET AND VULNERABLE.
PEOPLE SAY GIRLS IN LOVE ARE CUTE...
WELL, WHETHER YOU CONFESS YOUR LOVE TO HIM OR NOT, HE ALREADY HAS A GIRLFRIEND!
SO WHAT ARE YOU GOING TO DO?
ARE YOU GOING TO STEAL HIM FROM HER?
HUH?!
STEAL HIM?!
COMMONERS ARE BARBARIC.
YOU MEAN ENGAGE IN A SORDID CATFIGHT OVER A MAN?
SIGH
I WOULD NEVER DO SOMETHING SO SHAMELESS!
SIGH
HIGH SCHOOL STUDENTS ONLY PLAY AT LOVE.
I JUST NEED TO DRINK MY TEA AND WAIT.
THEY'LL BREAK UP SOON.
I DON'T CARE...
...WHO HE DATES...

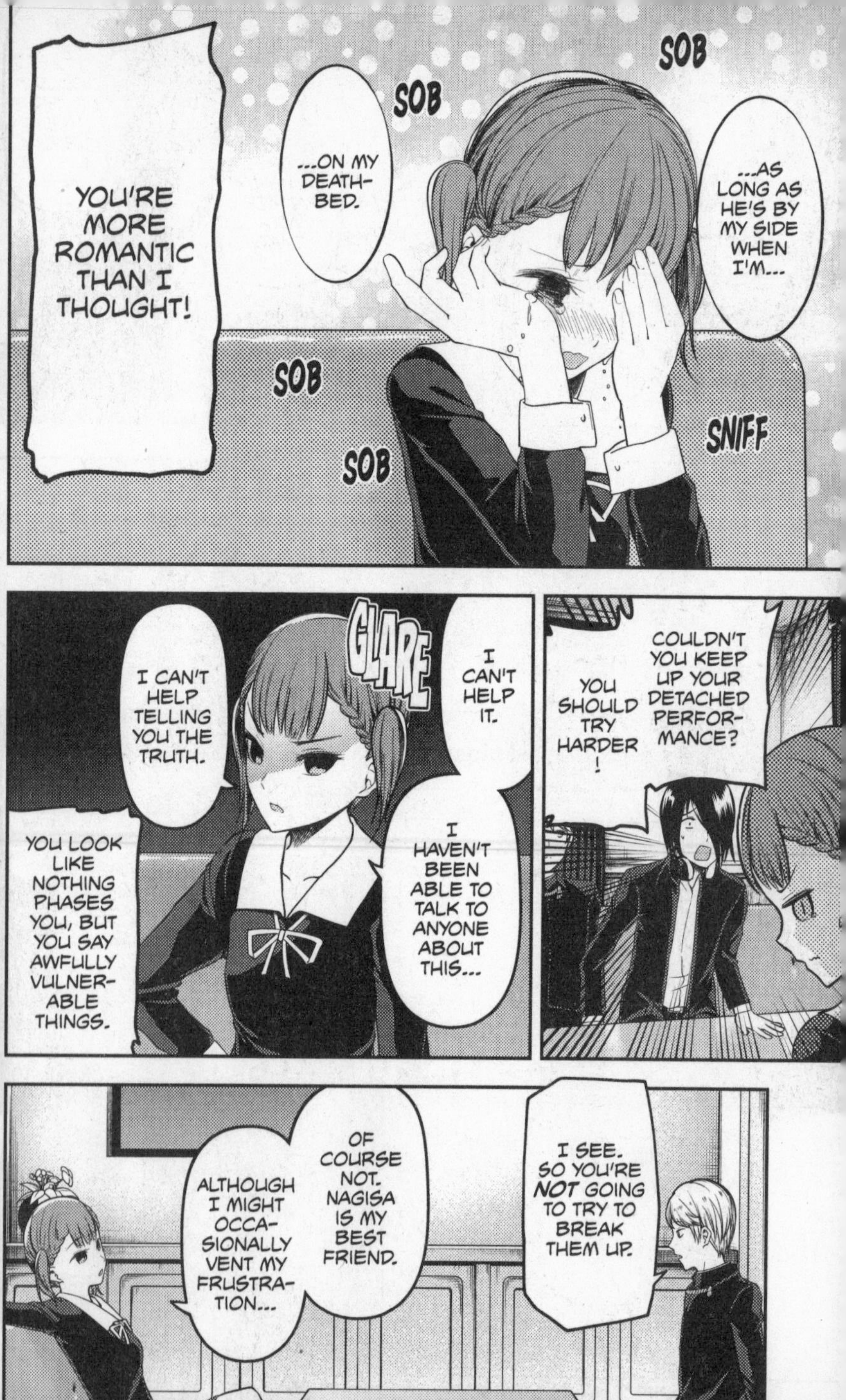
...AS LONG AS HE'S BY MY SIDE WHEN I'M...
SOB
SOB
...ON MY DEATHBED.
SNIFF
SOB
SOB
YOU'RE MORE ROMANTIC THAN I THOUGHT!
COULDN'T YOU KEEP UP YOUR DETACHED PERFORMANCE?
YOU SHOULD TRY HARDER!
GLARE
I CAN'T HELP IT.
I CAN'T HELP TELLING YOU THE TRUTH.
I HAVEN'T BEEN ABLE TO TALK TO ANYONE ABOUT THIS...
YOU LOOK LIKE NOTHING PHASES YOU, BUT YOU SAY AWFULLY VULNERABLE THINGS.
I SEE. SO YOU'RE *NOT* GOING TO TRY TO BREAK THEM UP.
OF COURSE NOT. NAGISA IS MY BEST FRIEND.
ALTHOUGH I MIGHT OCCASIONALLY VENT MY FRUSTRATION...

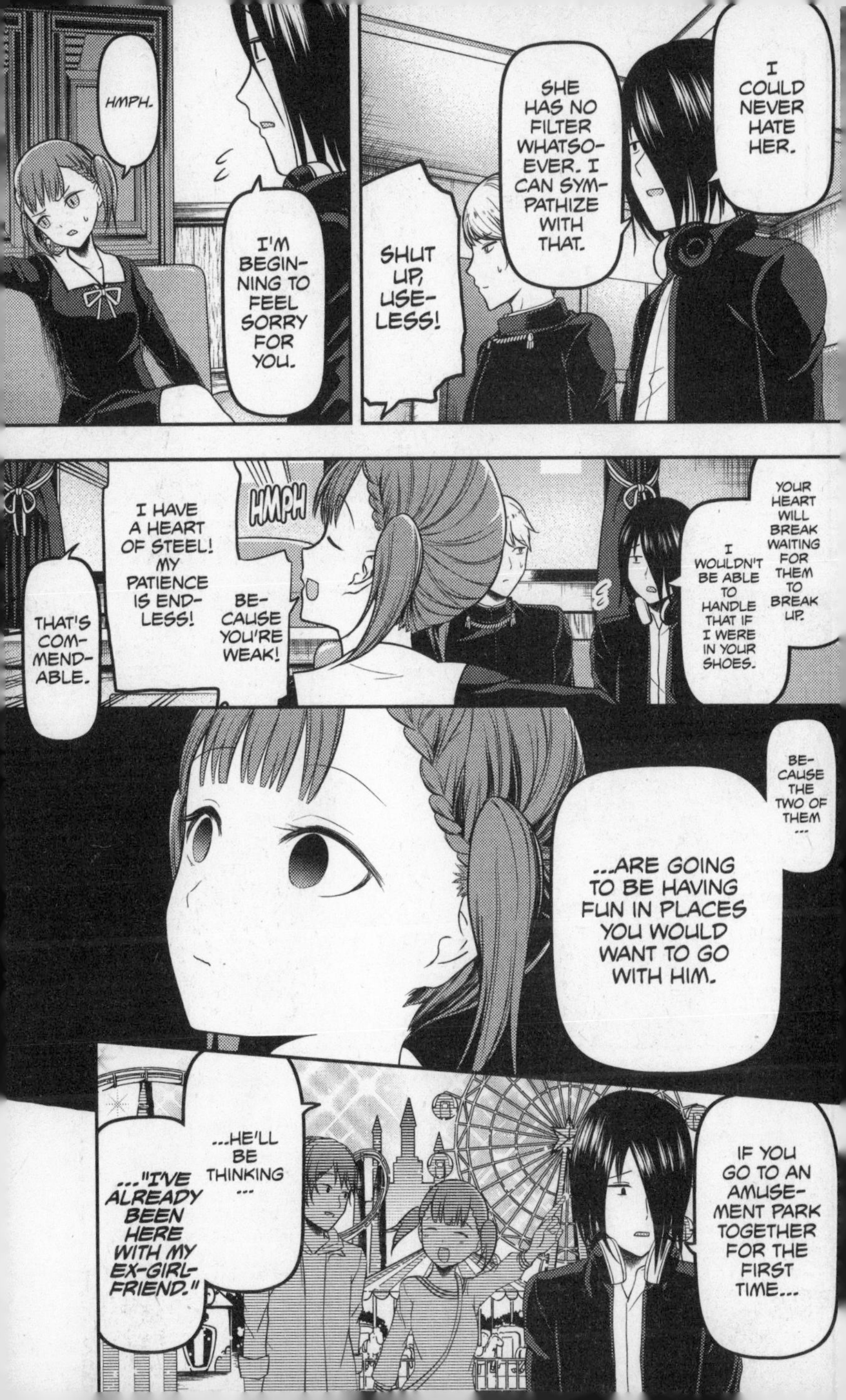
I COULD NEVER HATE HER.
SHE HAS NO FILTER WHATSOEVER. I CAN SYMPATHIZE WITH THAT.
SHUT UP, USELESS!
I'M BEGINNING TO FEEL SORRY FOR YOU.
HMPH.
YOUR HEART WILL BREAK WAITING FOR THEM TO BREAK UP.
I WOULDN'T BE ABLE TO HANDLE THAT IF I WERE IN YOUR SHOES.
BECAUSE YOU'RE WEAK!
HMPH
I HAVE A HEART OF STEEL! MY PATIENCE IS ENDLESS!
THAT'S COMMENDABLE.
BECAUSE THE TWO OF THEM...
...ARE GOING TO BE HAVING FUN IN PLACES YOU WOULD WANT TO GO WITH HIM.
IF YOU GO TO AN AMUSEMENT PARK TOGETHER FOR THE FIRST TIME...
...HE'LL BE THINKING...
..."I'VE ALREADY BEEN HERE WITH MY EX-GIRLFRIEND."

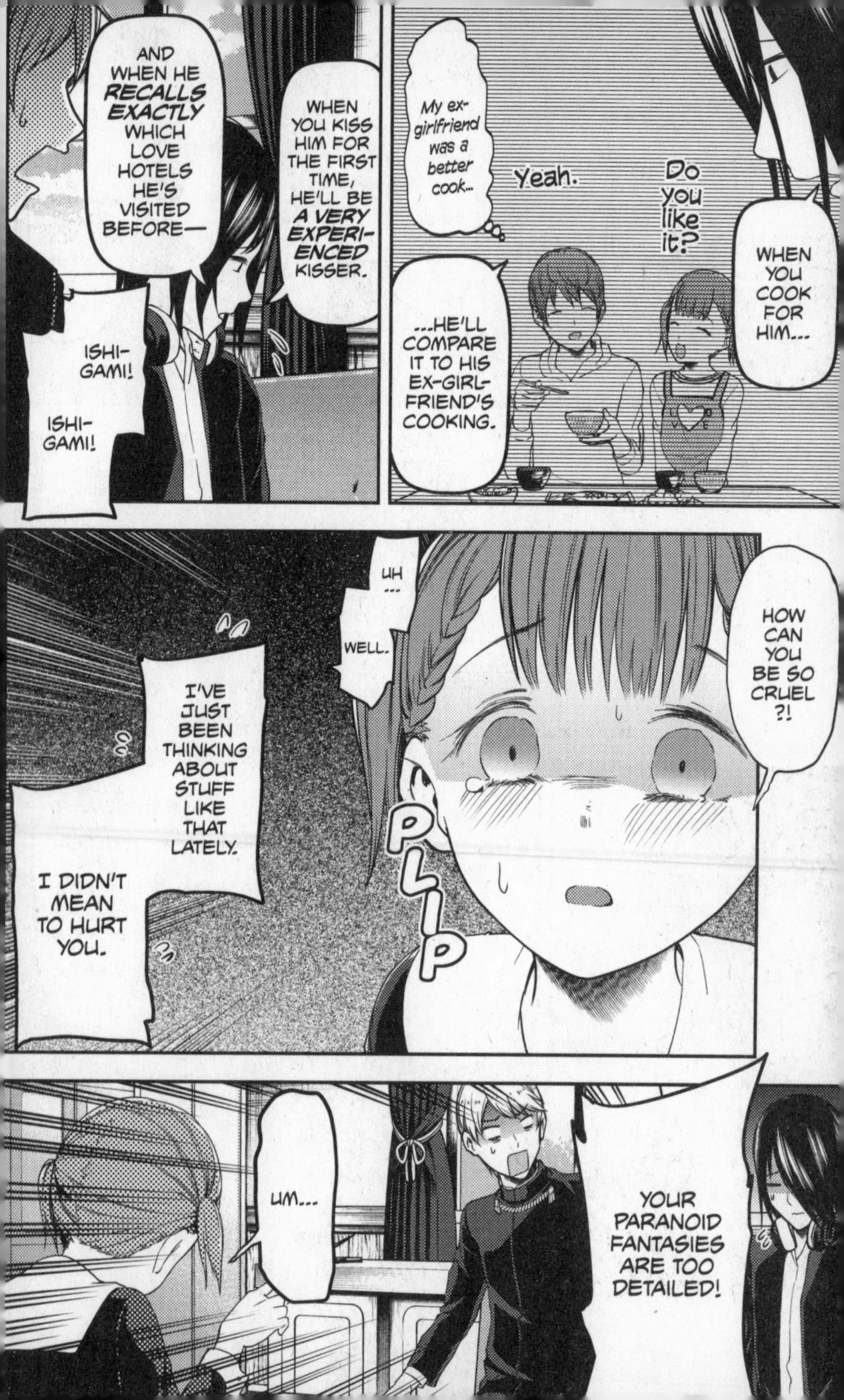
WHEN YOU COOK FOR HIM...
Do you like it?
Yeah.
My ex-girlfriend was a better cook...
...HE'LL COMPARE IT TO HIS EX-GIRLFRIEND'S COOKING.
WHEN YOU KISS HIM FOR THE FIRST TIME, HE'LL BE A VERY EXPERIENCED KISSER.
AND WHEN HE RECALLS EXACTLY WHICH LOVE HOTELS HE'S VISITED BEFORE—
ISHI-GAMI!
ISHI-GAMI!
HOW CAN YOU BE SO CRUEL?!
PLIP
UH... WELL.
I'VE JUST BEEN THINKING ABOUT STUFF LIKE THAT LATELY.
I DIDN'T MEAN TO HURT YOU.
YOUR PARANOID FANTASIES ARE TOO DETAILED!
UM...

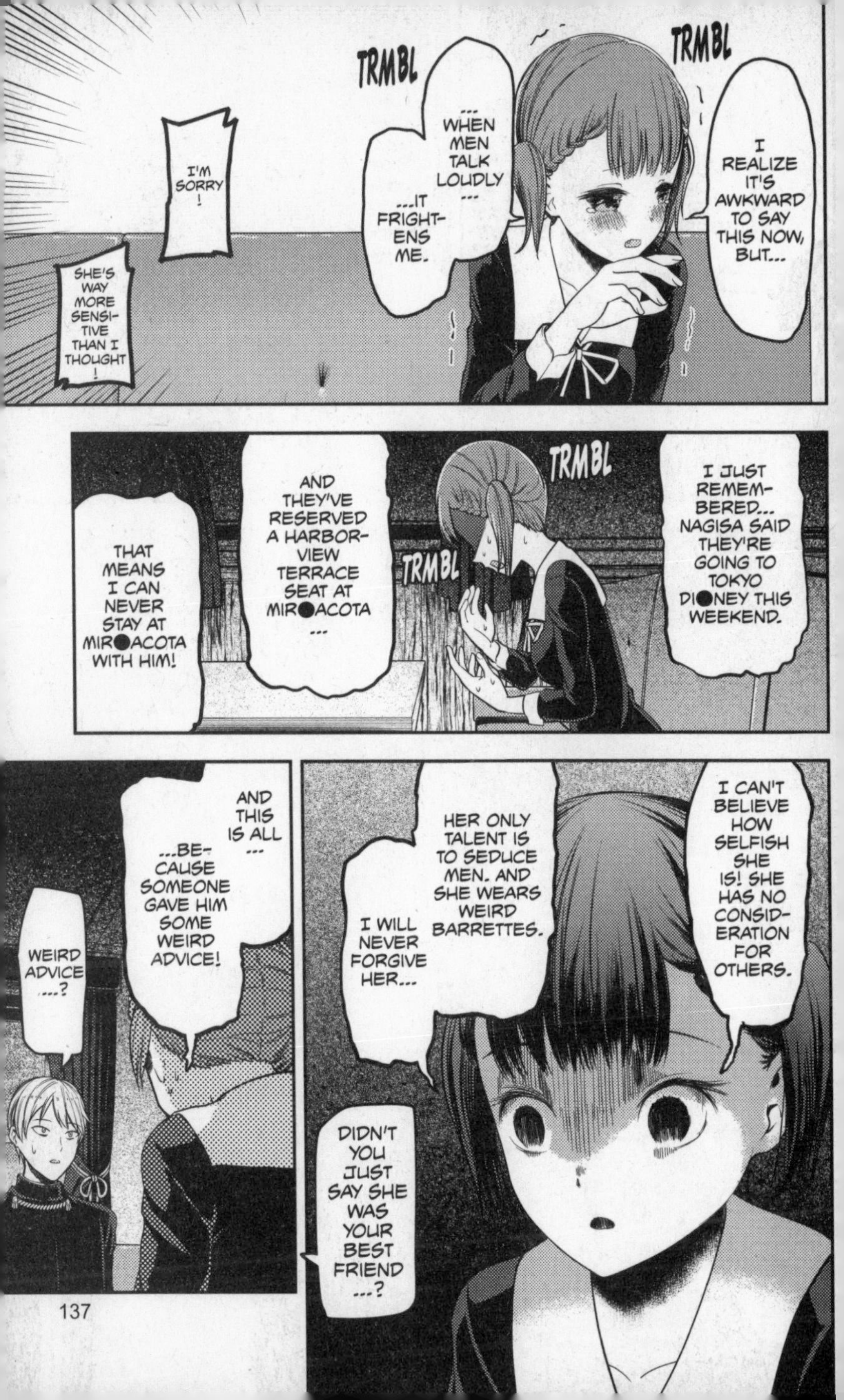
TRMBL
I REALIZE IT'S AWKWARD TO SAY THIS NOW, BUT...
TRMBL
...WHEN MEN TALK LOUDLY...
...IT FRIGHTENS ME.
I'M SORRY!
SHE'S WAY MORE SENSITIVE THAN I THOUGHT!
I JUST REMEMBERED... NAGISA SAID THEY'RE GOING TO TOKYO DI●NEY THIS WEEKEND.
TRMBL
TRMBL
AND THEY'VE RESERVED A HARBOR-VIEW TERRACE SEAT AT MIR●ACOTA...
THAT MEANS I CAN NEVER STAY AT MIR●ACOTA WITH HIM!
I CAN'T BELIEVE HOW SELFISH SHE IS! SHE HAS NO CONSIDERATION FOR OTHERS.
HER ONLY TALENT IS TO SEDUCE MEN. AND SHE WEARS WEIRD BARRETTES.
I WILL NEVER FORGIVE HER...
DIDN'T YOU JUST SAY SHE WAS YOUR BEST FRIEND...?
AND THIS IS ALL...
...BECAUSE SOMEONE GAVE HIM SOME WEIRD ADVICE!
WEIRD ADVICE...?

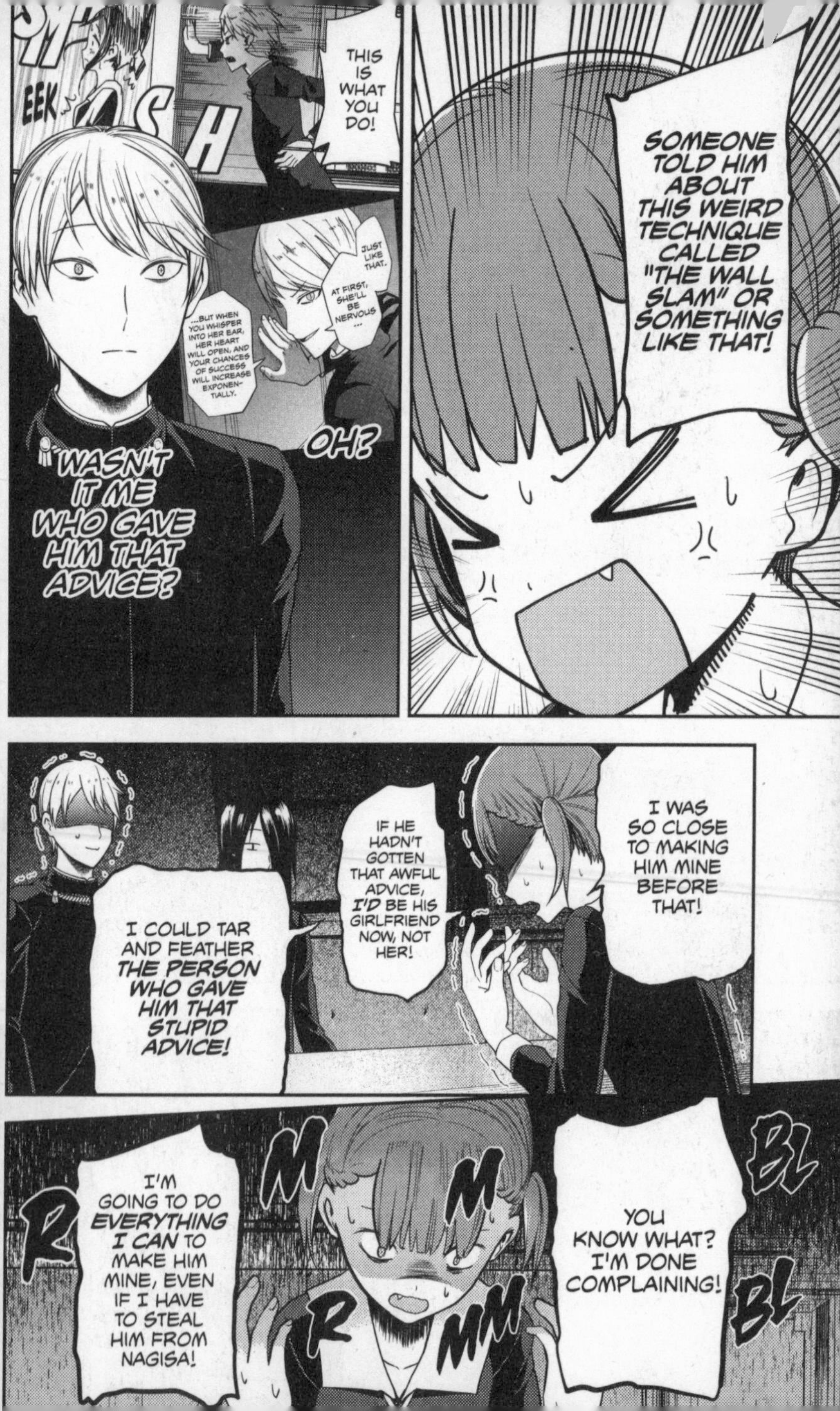

SOMEONE TOLD HIM ABOUT THIS WEIRD TECHNIQUE CALLED "THE WALL SLAM" OR SOMETHING LIKE THAT!
SH
EEK
SH
THIS IS WHAT YOU DO!
JUST LIKE THAT.
AT FIRST, SHE'LL BE NERVOUS...
...BUT WHEN YOU WHISPER INTO HER EAR, HER HEART WILL OPEN, AND YOUR CHANCES OF SUCCESS WILL INCREASE EXPONENTIALLY.
OH?
WASN'T IT ME WHO GAVE HIM THAT ADVICE?
I WAS SO CLOSE TO MAKING HIM MINE BEFORE THAT!
IF HE HADN'T GOTTEN THAT AWFUL ADVICE, *I'D* BE HIS GIRLFRIEND NOW, NOT HER!
I COULD TAR AND FEATHER ***THE PERSON WHO GAVE HIM THAT STUPID ADVICE!***
BL
BL
YOU KNOW WHAT? I'M DONE COMPLAINING!
M
M
MM
R
R
I'M GOING TO DO ***EVERYTHING I CAN*** TO MAKE HIM MINE, EVEN IF I HAVE TO STEAL HIM FROM NAGISA!

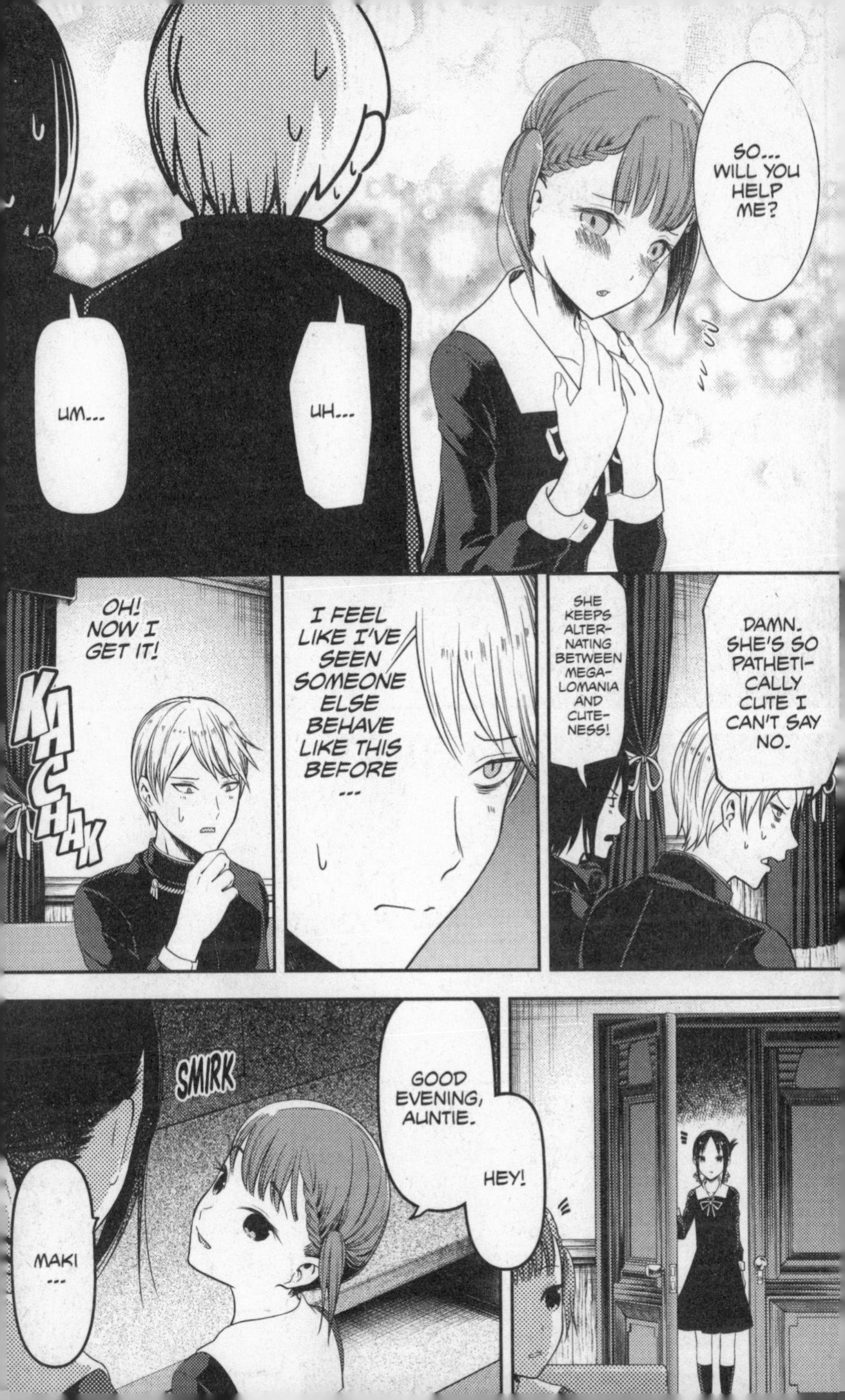
SO... WILL YOU HELP ME?
UH...
UM...
DAMN. SHE'S SO PATHETI-CALLY CUTE I CAN'T SAY NO.
SHE KEEPS ALTER-NATING BETWEEN MEGA-LOMANIA AND CUTE-NESS!
I FEEL LIKE I'VE SEEN SOMEONE ELSE BEHAVE LIKE THIS BEFORE ...
OH! NOW I GET IT!
KACHAK
GOOD EVENING, AUNTIE.
SMIRK
HEY!
MAKI ...

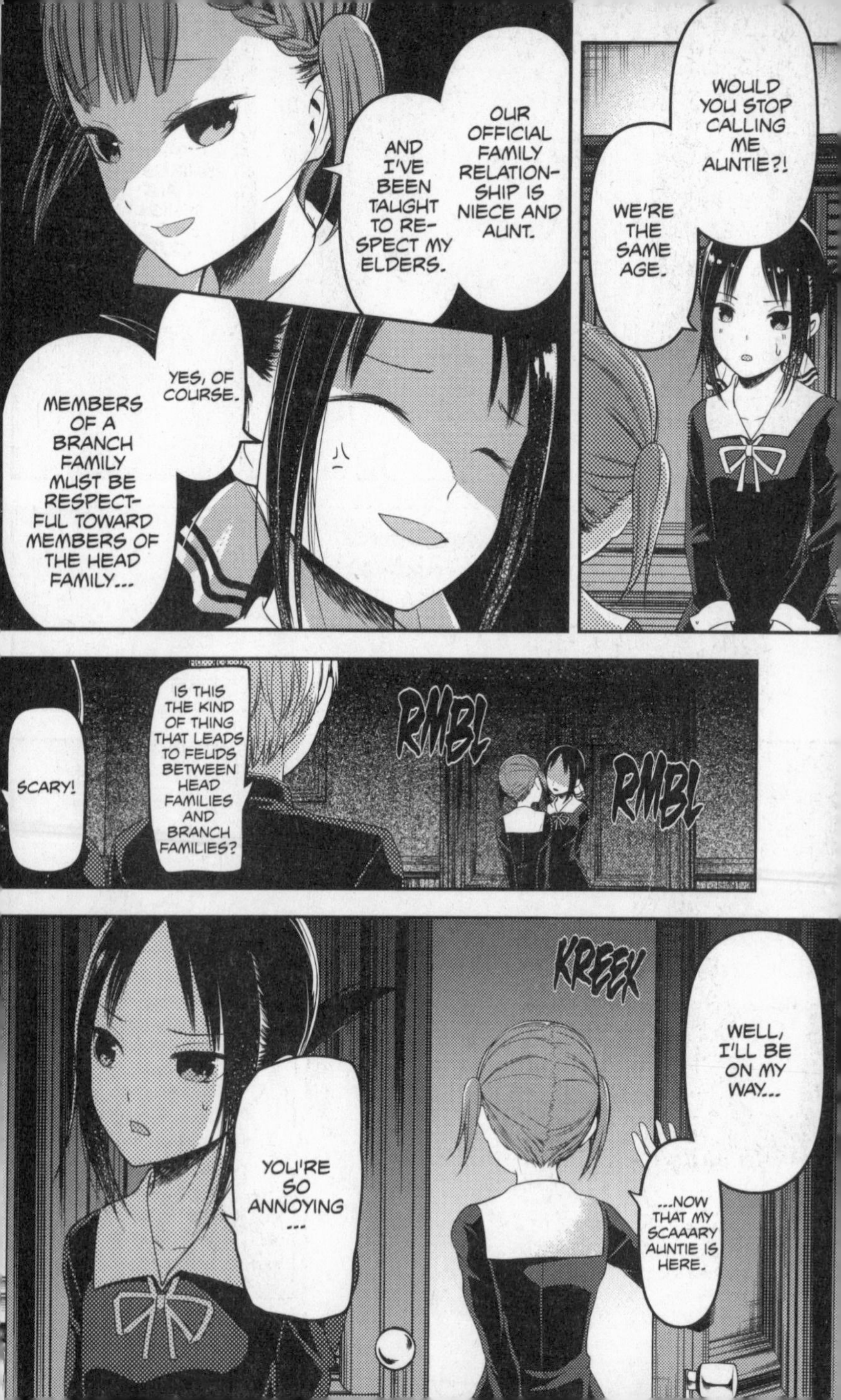
WOULD YOU STOP CALLING ME AUNTIE?!
WE'RE THE SAME AGE.
OUR OFFICIAL FAMILY RELATIONSHIP IS NIECE AND AUNT.
AND I'VE BEEN TAUGHT TO RESPECT MY ELDERS.
YES, OF COURSE.
MEMBERS OF A BRANCH FAMILY MUST BE RESPECTFUL TOWARD MEMBERS OF THE HEAD FAMILY...
RMBL
RMBL
IS THIS THE KIND OF THING THAT LEADS TO FEUDS BETWEEN HEAD FAMILIES AND BRANCH FAMILIES?
SCARY!
KREEK
WELL, I'LL BE ON MY WAY...
...NOW THAT MY SCAAARY AUNTIE IS HERE.
YOU'RE SO ANNOYING...

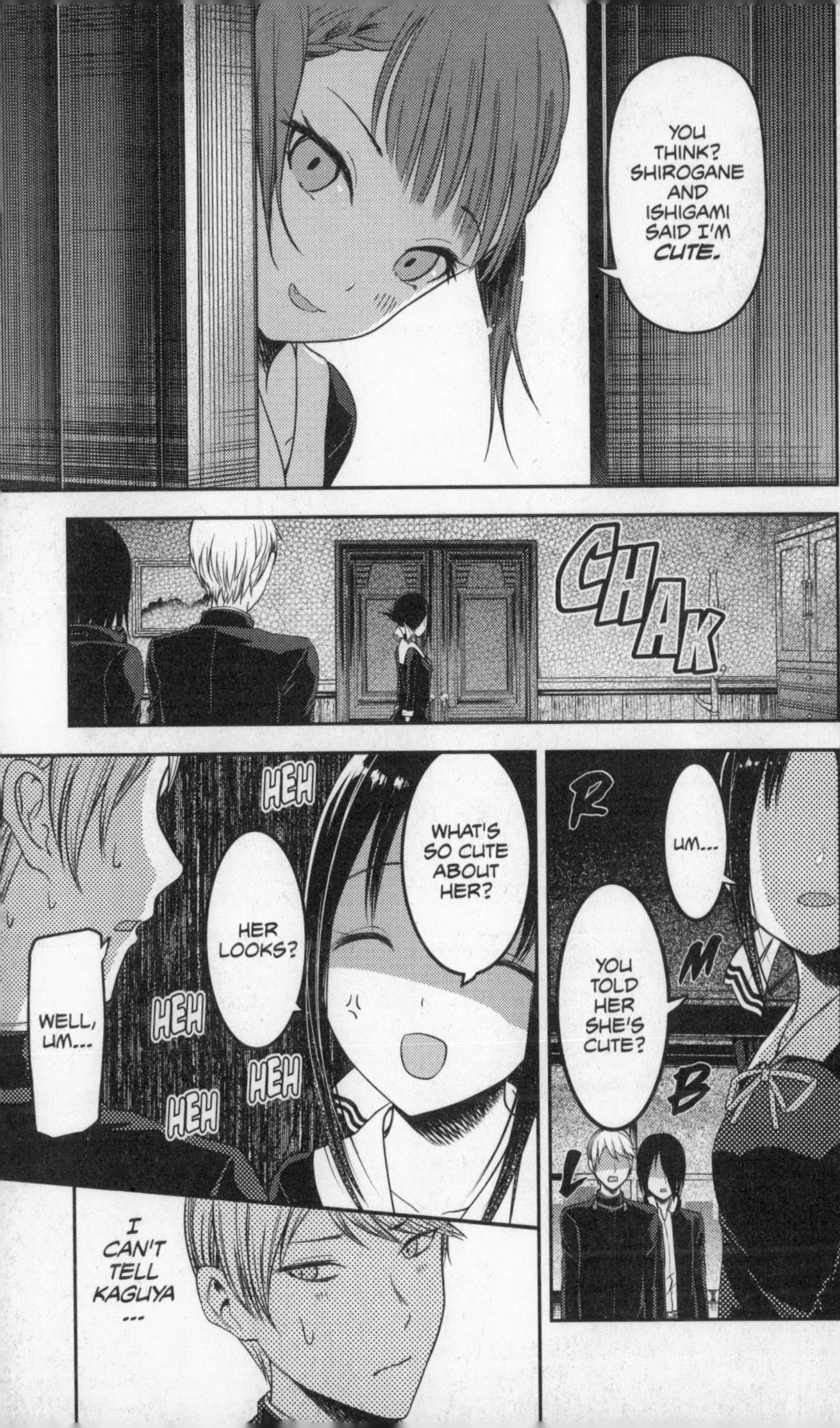
YOU THINK? SHIROGANE AND ISHIGAMI SAID I'M CUTE.
CHAK
RMBL
UM...
YOU TOLD HER SHE'S CUTE?
WHAT'S SO CUTE ABOUT HER?
HEH
HER LOOKS?
HEH
HEH
HEH
WELL, UM...
I CAN'T TELL KAGUYA...

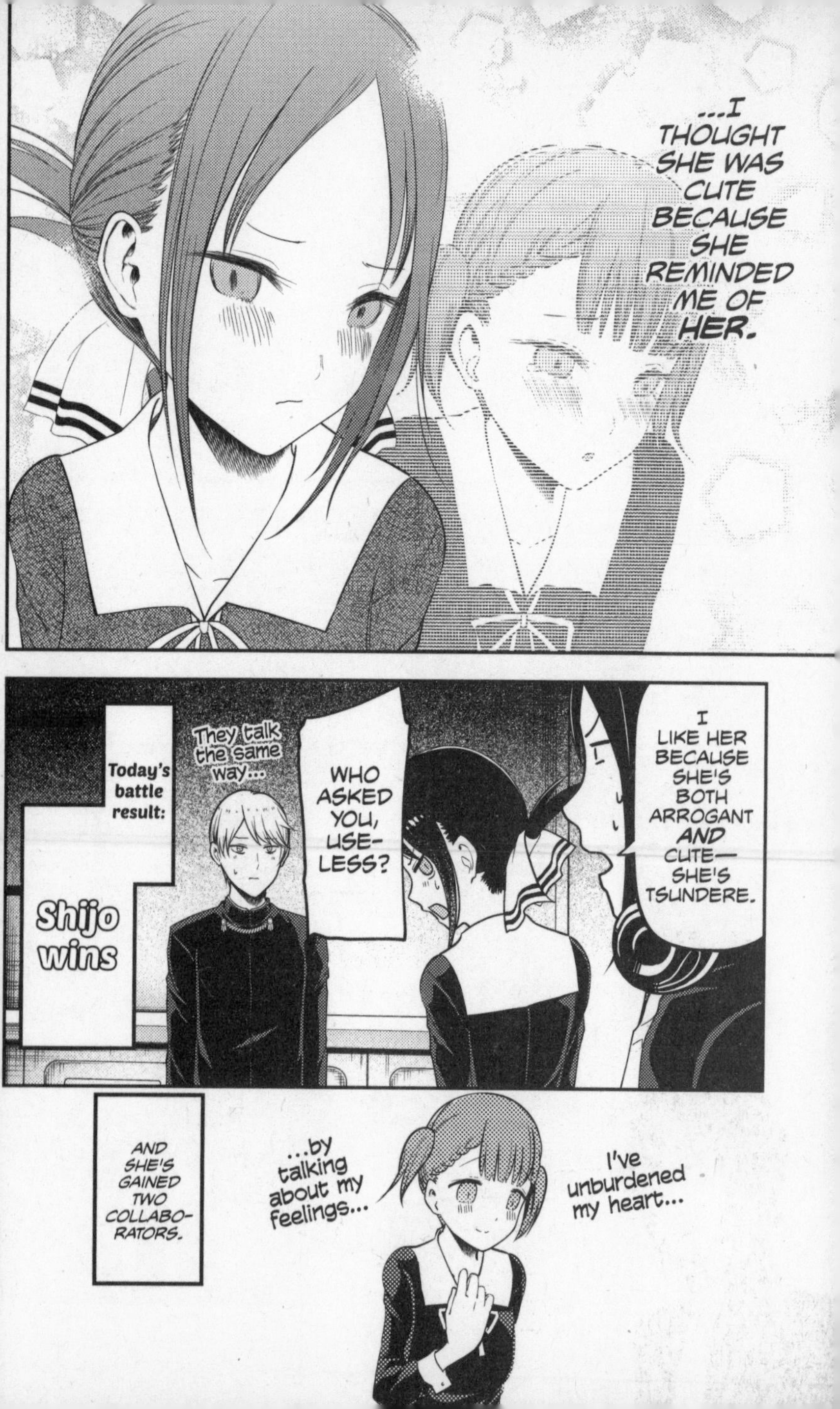
...I THOUGHT SHE WAS CUTE BECAUSE SHE REMINDED ME OF HER.
I LIKE HER BECAUSE SHE'S BOTH ARROGANT AND CUTE—SHE'S TSUNDERE.
WHO ASKED YOU, USELESS?
They talk the same way...
Today's battle result:
Shijo wins
I've unburdened my heart...
...by talking about my feelings...
AND SHE'S GAINED TWO COLLABORATORS.

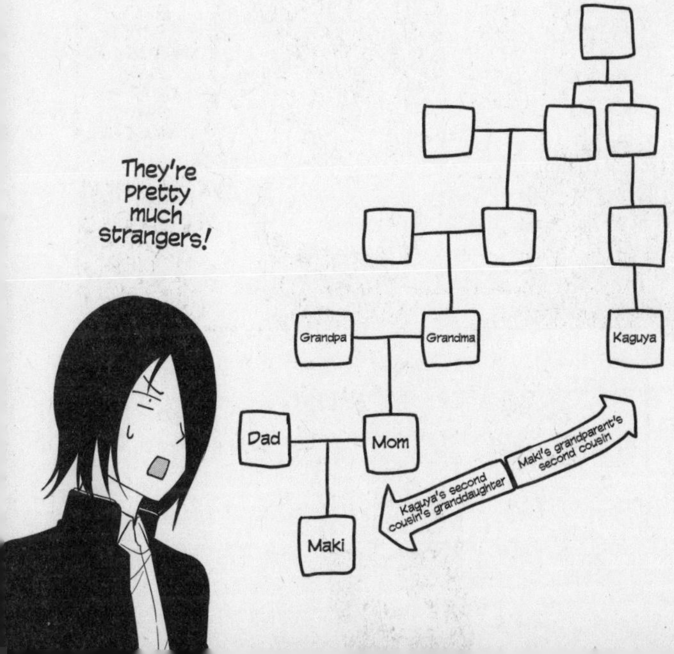
They're pretty much strangers!
Grandpa
Grandma
Kaguya
Dad
Mom
Maki
Maki's grandparent's second cousin
Kaguya's second cousin's granddaughter

KAGUYA-SAMA
LOVE IS WAR

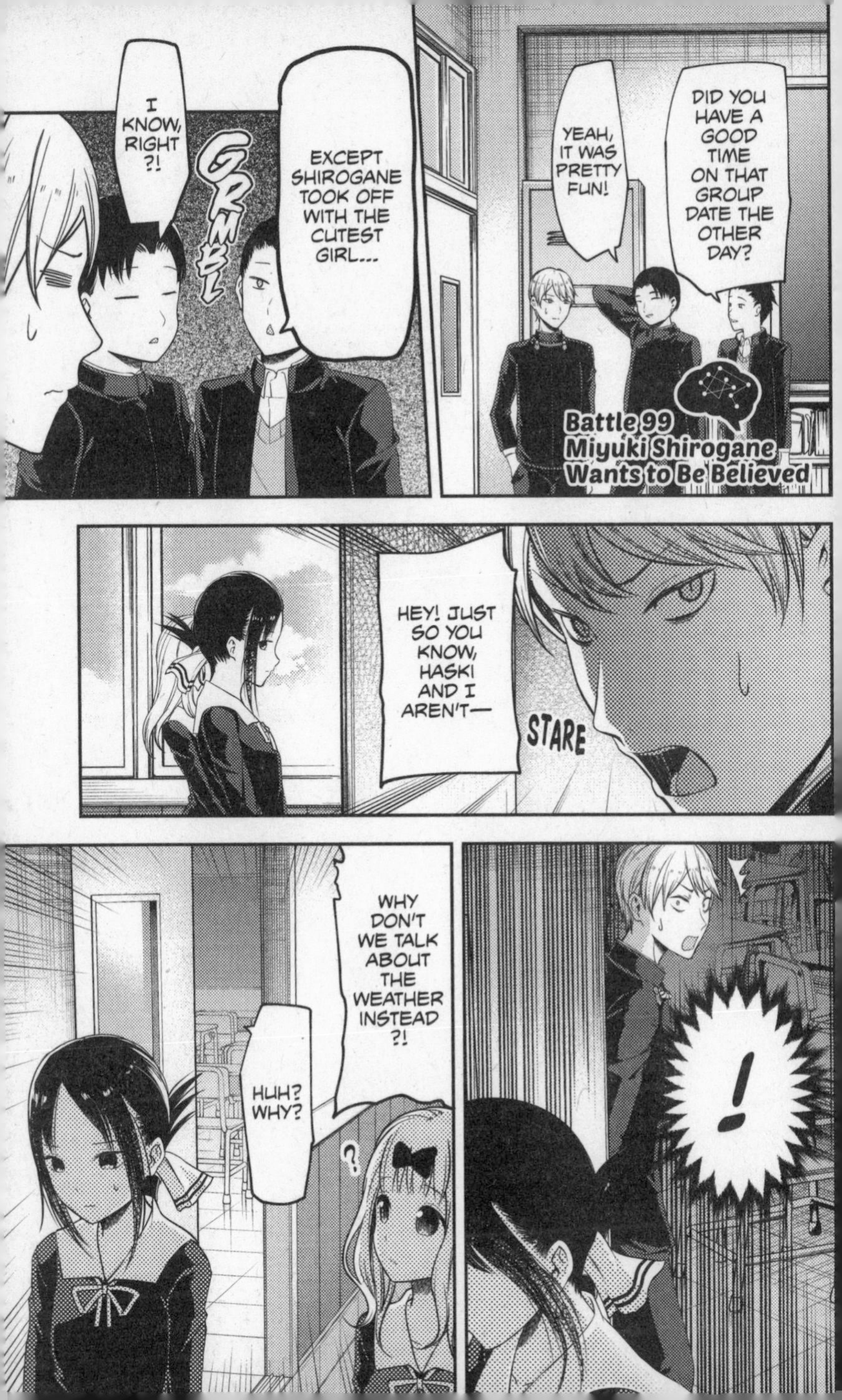
DID YOU HAVE A GOOD TIME ON THAT GROUP DATE THE OTHER DAY?
YEAH, IT WAS PRETTY FUN!
Battle 99
Miyuki Shirogane Wants to Be Believed
EXCEPT SHIROGANE TOOK OFF WITH THE CUTEST GIRL...
GRMBL
I KNOW, RIGHT?!
HEY! JUST SO YOU KNOW, HASKI AND I AREN'T—
STARE
!
WHY DON'T WE TALK ABOUT THE WEATHER INSTEAD?!
HUH? WHY?
?

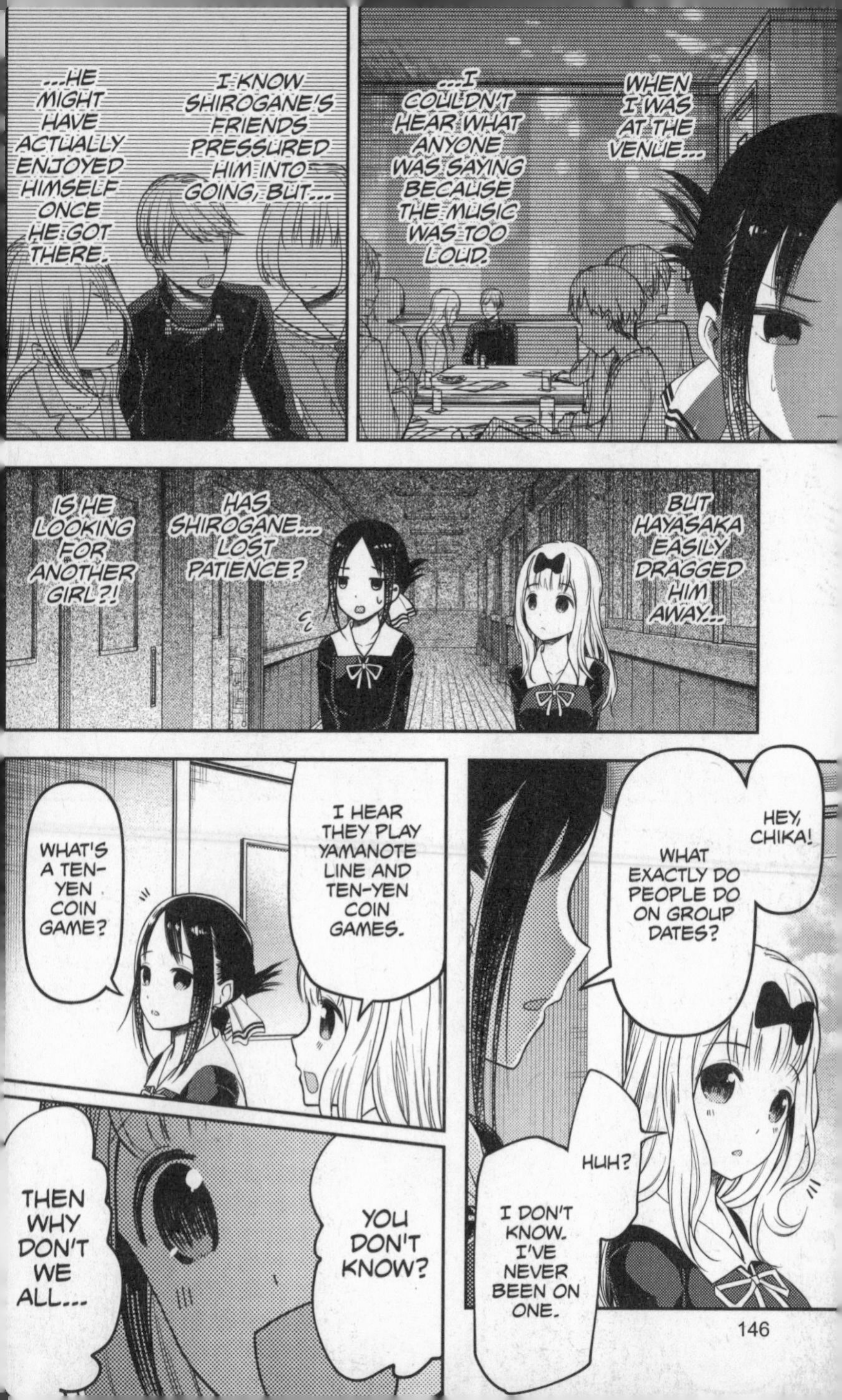
WHEN I WAS AT THE VENUE...
...I COULDN'T HEAR WHAT ANYONE WAS SAYING BECAUSE THE MUSIC WAS TOO LOUD.
I KNOW SHIROGANE'S FRIENDS PRESSURED HIM INTO GOING, BUT...
...HE MIGHT HAVE ACTUALLY ENJOYED HIMSELF ONCE HE GOT THERE.
BUT HAYASAKA EASILY DRAGGED HIM AWAY...
HAS SHIROGANE... LOST PATIENCE?
IS HE LOOKING FOR ANOTHER GIRL?!
HEY, CHIKA!
WHAT EXACTLY DO PEOPLE DO ON GROUP DATES?
HUH?
I DON'T KNOW. I'VE NEVER BEEN ON ONE.
I HEAR THEY PLAY YAMANOTE LINE AND TEN-YEN COIN GAMES.
WHAT'S A TEN-YEN COIN GAME?
YOU DON'T KNOW?
THEN WHY DON'T WE ALL...

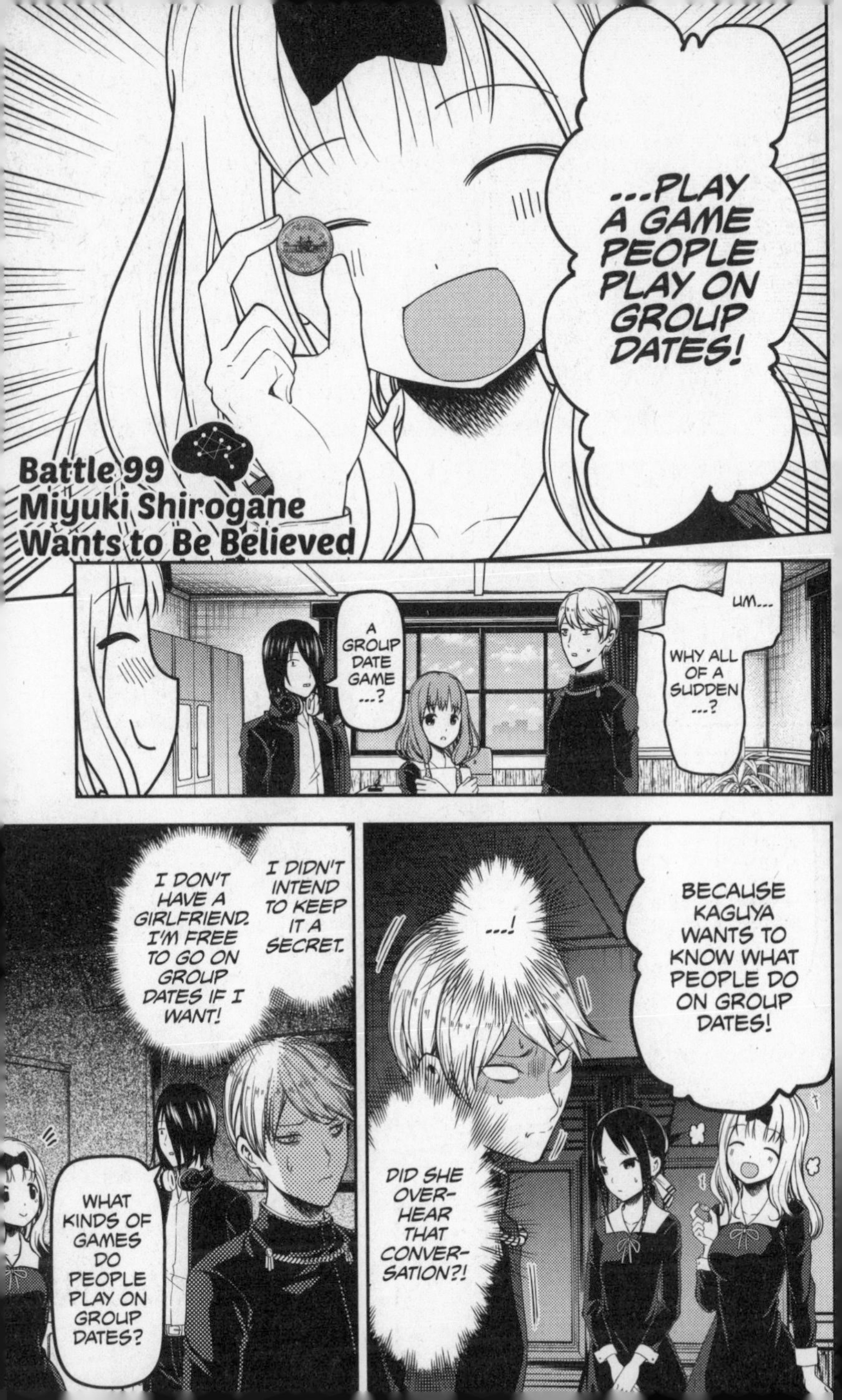
...PLAY A GAME PEOPLE PLAY ON GROUP DATES!
Battle 99 Miyuki Shirogane Wants to Be Believed
UM...
WHY ALL OF A SUDDEN...?
A GROUP DATE GAME...?
BECAUSE KAGUYA WANTS TO KNOW WHAT PEOPLE DO ON GROUP DATES!
...!
DID SHE OVERHEAR THAT CONVERSATION?!
I DIDN'T INTEND TO KEEP IT A SECRET.
I DON'T HAVE A GIRLFRIEND. I'M FREE TO GO ON GROUP DATES IF I WANT!
WHAT KINDS OF GAMES DO PEOPLE PLAY ON GROUP DATES?

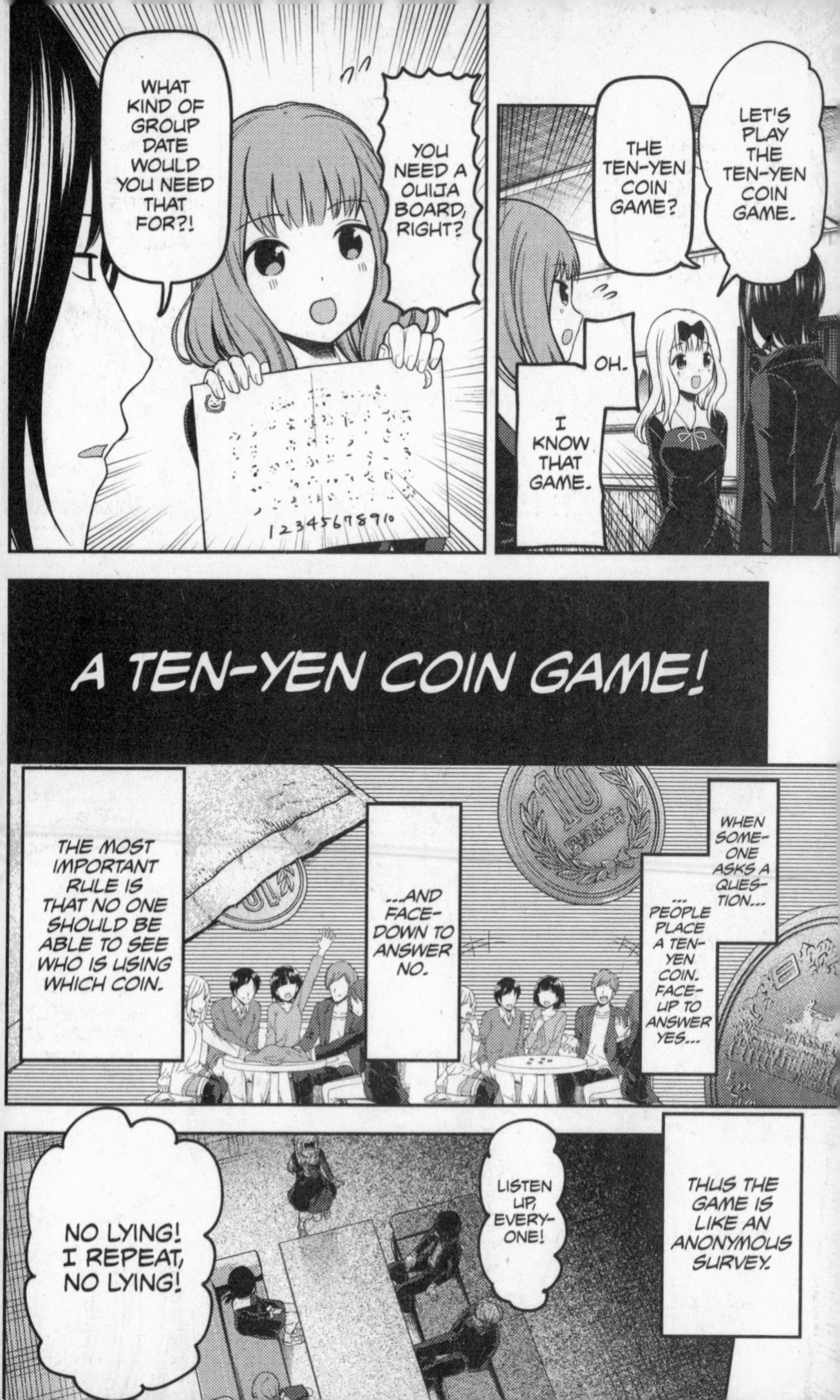
LET'S PLAY THE TEN-YEN COIN GAME.
THE TEN-YEN COIN GAME?
OH.
I KNOW THAT GAME.
YOU NEED A OUIJA BOARD, RIGHT?
12345678910
WHAT KIND OF GROUP DATE WOULD YOU NEED THAT FOR?!
A TEN-YEN COIN GAME!
WHEN SOMEONE ASKS A QUESTION...
...PEOPLE PLACE A TEN-YEN COIN. FACE-UP TO ANSWER YES...
...AND FACE-DOWN TO ANSWER NO.
THE MOST IMPORTANT RULE IS THAT NO ONE SHOULD BE ABLE TO SEE WHO IS USING WHICH COIN.
THUS THE GAME IS LIKE AN ANONYMOUS SURVEY.
LISTEN UP, EVERYONE!
NO LYING! I REPEAT, NO LYING!

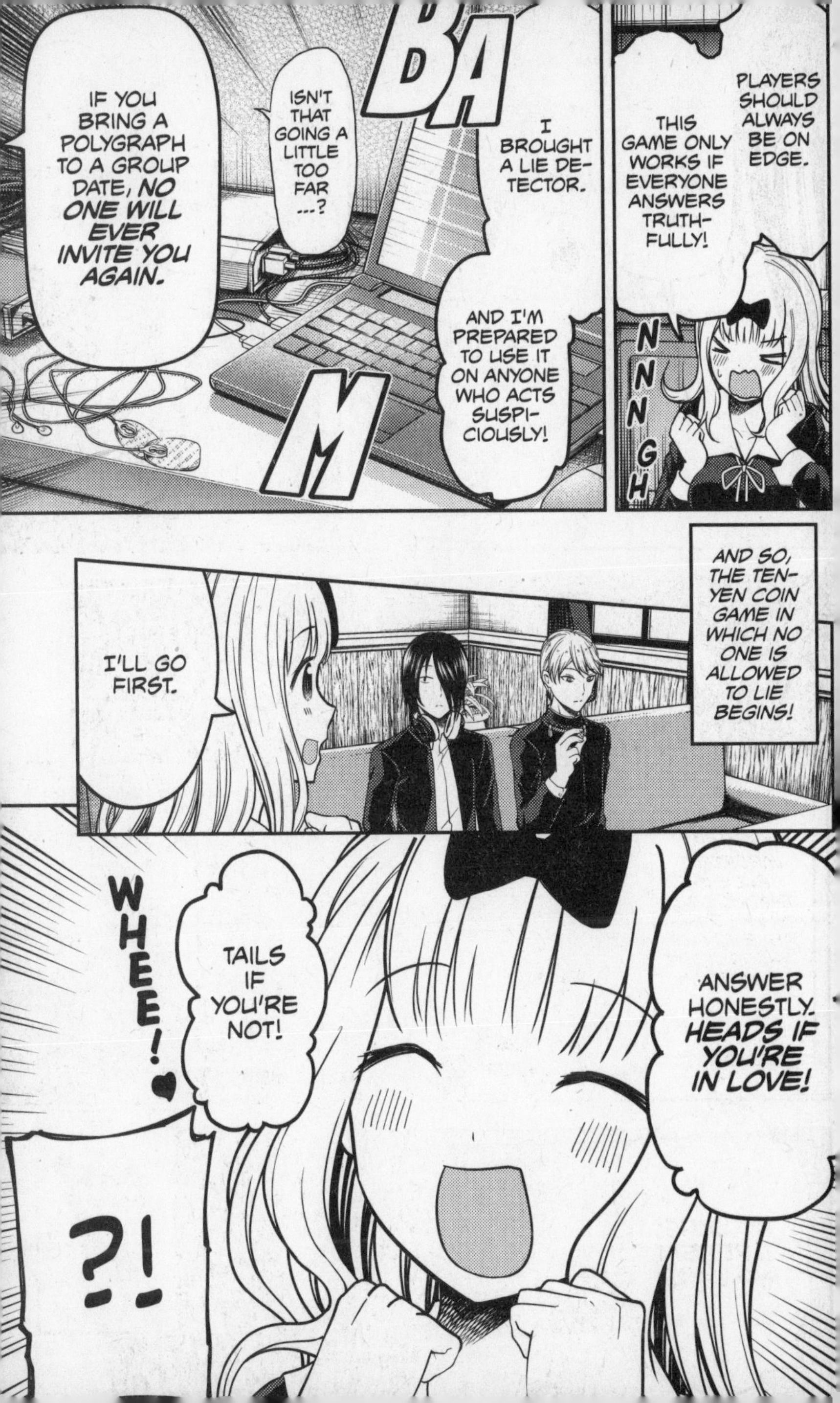
PLAYERS SHOULD ALWAYS BE ON EDGE.
THIS GAME ONLY WORKS IF EVERYONE ANSWERS TRUTHFULLY!
NNNNGH
BAM
I BROUGHT A LIE DETECTOR.
AND I'M PREPARED TO USE IT ON ANYONE WHO ACTS SUSPICIOUSLY!
ISN'T THAT GOING A LITTLE TOO FAR...?
IF YOU BRING A POLYGRAPH TO A GROUP DATE, NO ONE WILL EVER INVITE YOU AGAIN.
AND SO, THE TEN-YEN COIN GAME IN WHICH NO ONE IS ALLOWED TO LIE BEGINS!
I'LL GO FIRST.
ANSWER HONESTLY. HEADS IF YOU'RE IN LOVE!
TAILS IF YOU'RE NOT!
WHEE! ♥
?!

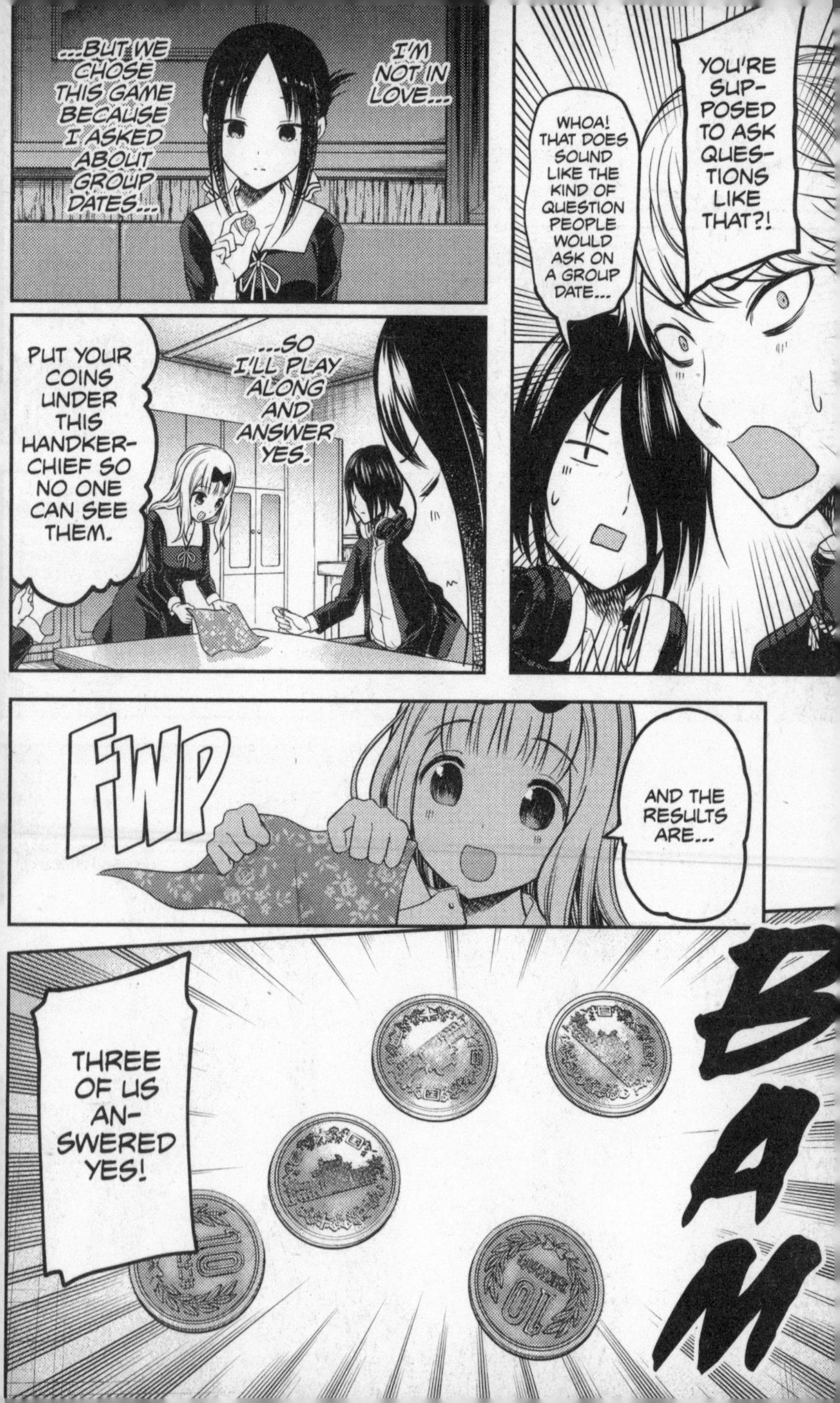

YOU'RE SUP-POSED TO ASK QUES-TIONS LIKE THAT?!
WHOA! THAT DOES SOUND LIKE THE KIND OF QUESTION PEOPLE WOULD ASK ON A GROUP DATE...
I'M NOT IN LOVE...
...BUT WE CHOSE THIS GAME BECAUSE I ASKED ABOUT GROUP DATES...
...SO I'LL PLAY ALONG AND ANSWER YES.
PUT YOUR COINS UNDER THIS HANDKER-CHIEF SO NO ONE CAN SEE THEM.
AND THE RESULTS ARE...
FWP
BAM
THREE OF US AN-SWERED YES!

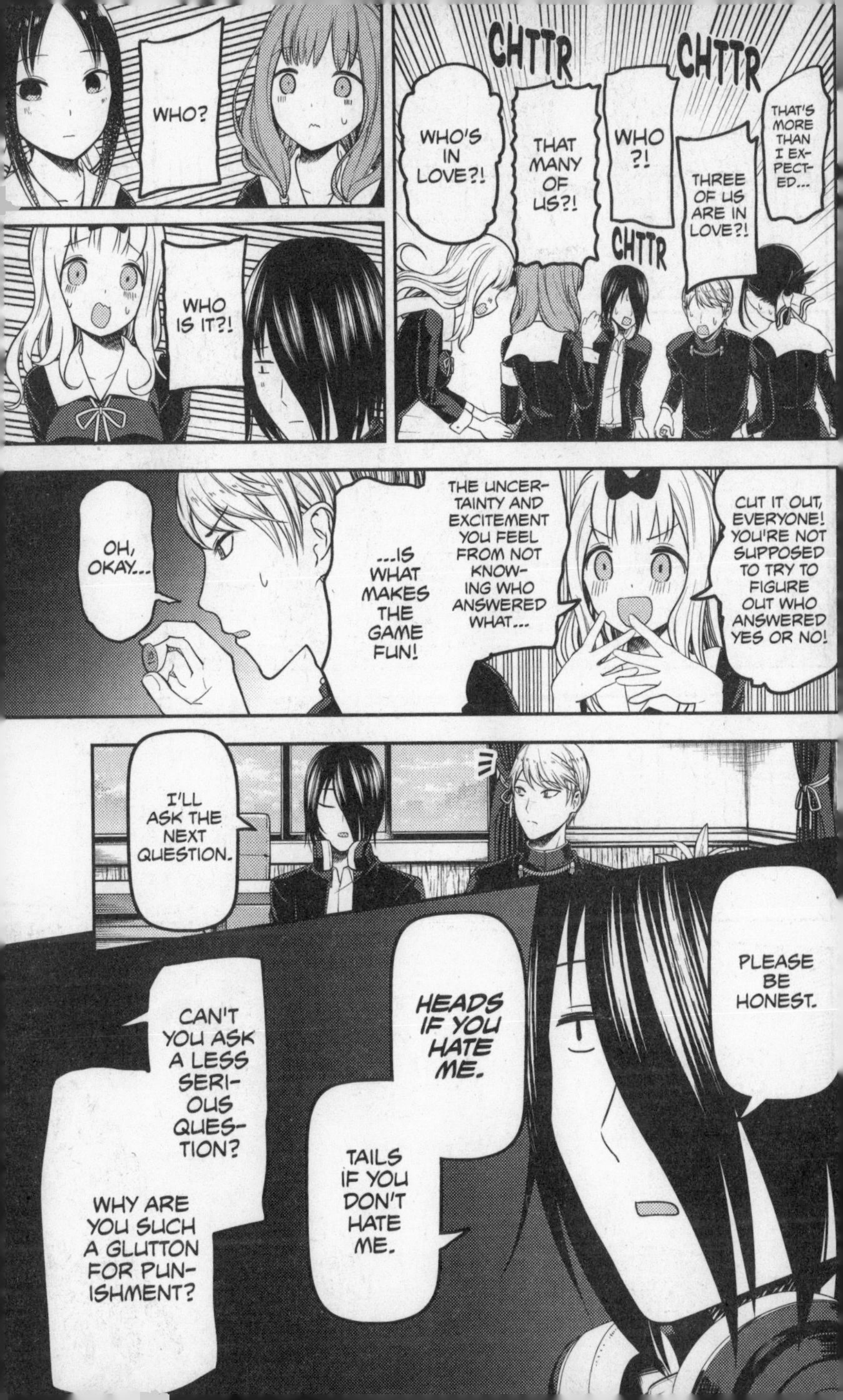
CHTTR
CHTTR
THAT'S MORE THAN I EXPECTED...
THREE OF US ARE IN LOVE?!
WHO?!
CHTTR
THAT MANY OF US?!
WHO'S IN LOVE?!
WHO?
WHO IS IT?!
CUT IT OUT, EVERYONE! YOU'RE NOT SUPPOSED TO TRY TO FIGURE OUT WHO ANSWERED YES OR NO!
THE UNCERTAINTY AND EXCITEMENT YOU FEEL FROM NOT KNOWING WHO ANSWERED WHAT...
...IS WHAT MAKES THE GAME FUN!
OH, OKAY...
I'LL ASK THE NEXT QUESTION.
PLEASE BE HONEST.
HEADS IF YOU HATE ME.
TAILS IF YOU DON'T HATE ME.
CAN'T YOU ASK A LESS SERIOUS QUESTION?
WHY ARE YOU SUCH A GLUTTON FOR PUNISHMENT?

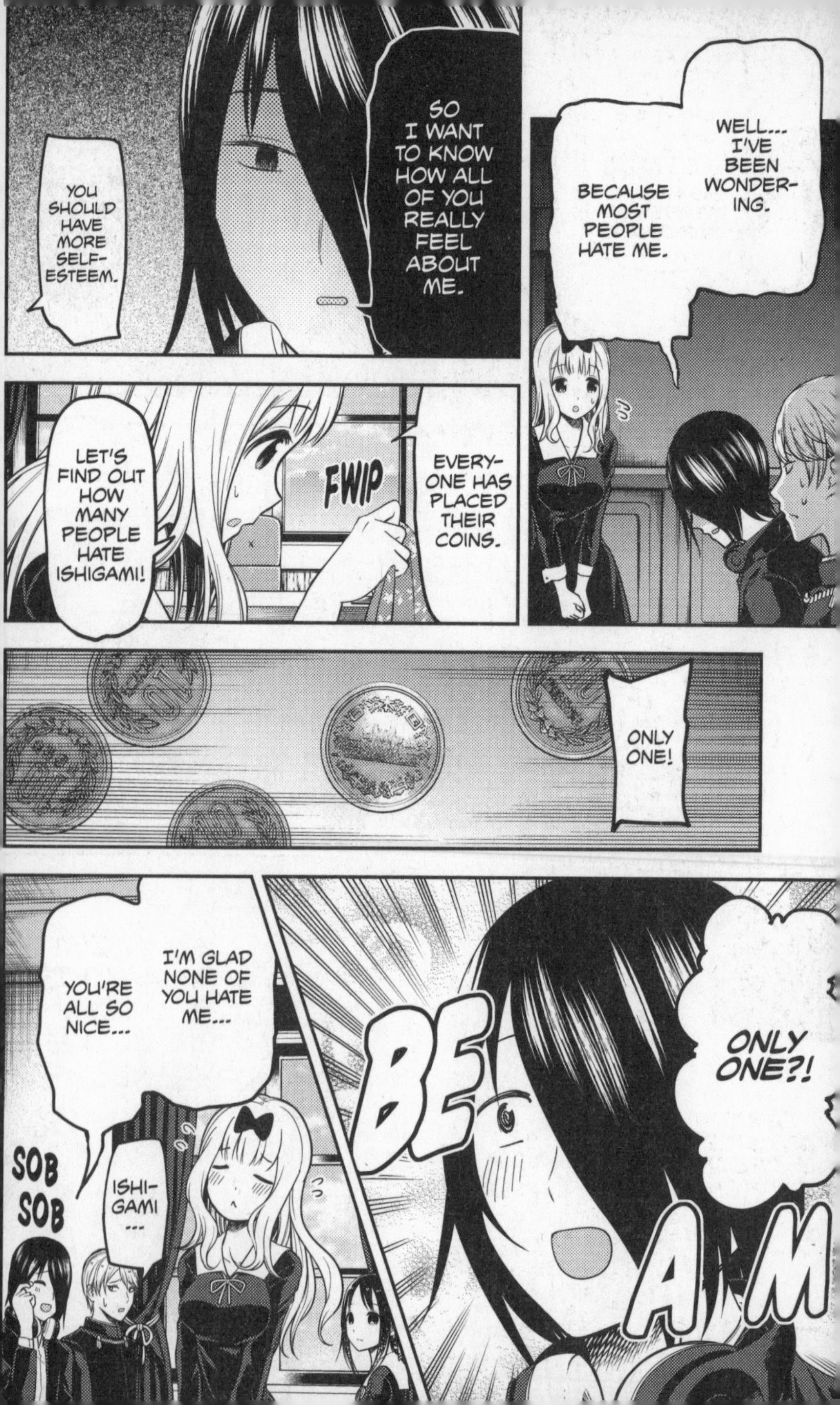
WELL... I'VE BEEN WONDERING.
BECAUSE MOST PEOPLE HATE ME.
SO I WANT TO KNOW HOW ALL OF YOU REALLY FEEL ABOUT ME.
YOU SHOULD HAVE MORE SELF-ESTEEM.
EVERYONE HAS PLACED THEIR COINS.
FWIP
LET'S FIND OUT HOW MANY PEOPLE HATE ISHIGAMI!
ONLY ONE!
ONLY ONE?!
BEAM
I'M GLAD NONE OF YOU HATE ME...
YOU'RE ALL SO NICE...
ISHIGAMI...
SOB SOB

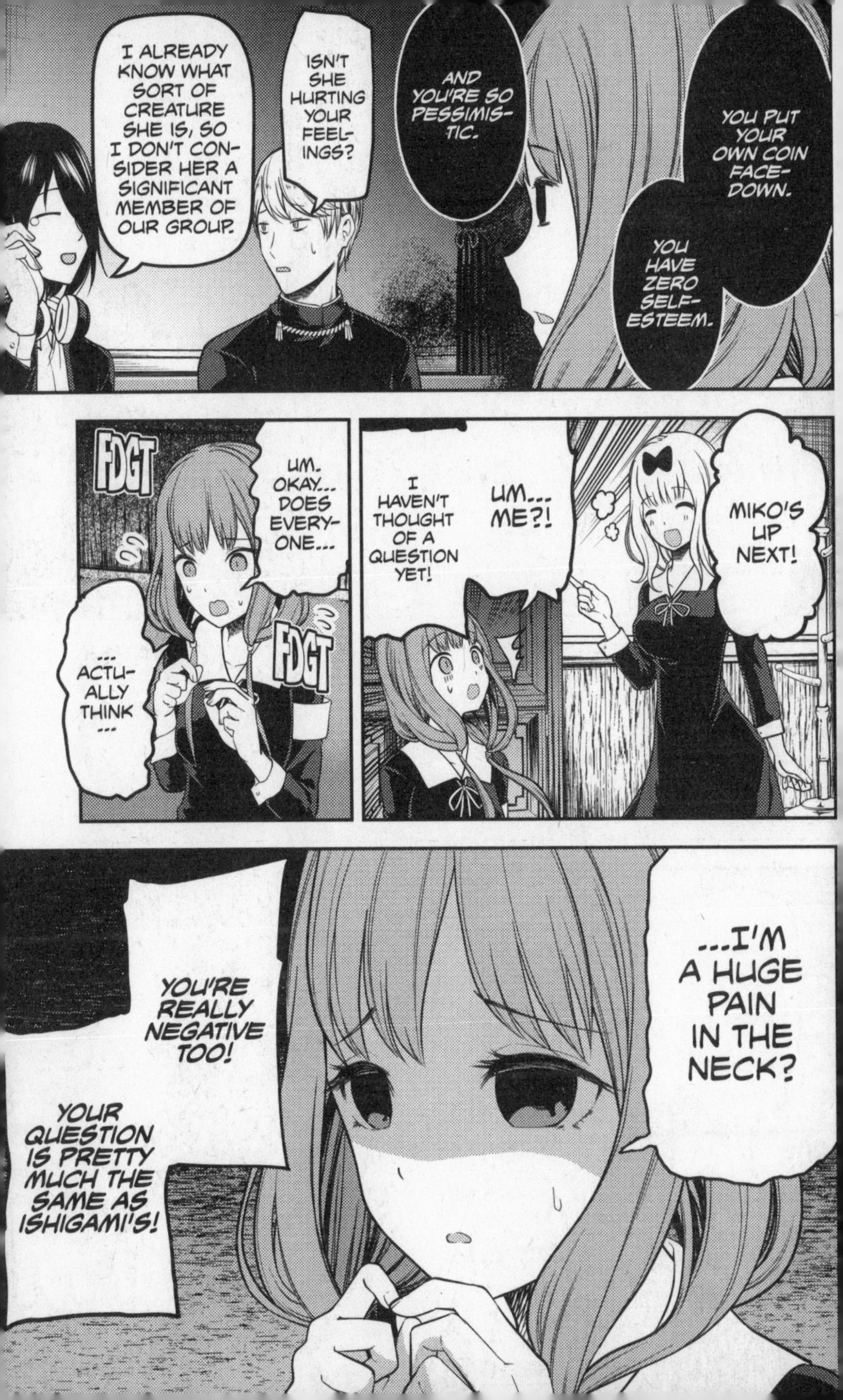
YOU PUT YOUR OWN COIN FACE-DOWN.
YOU HAVE ZERO SELF-ESTEEM.
AND YOU'RE SO PESSIMISTIC.
ISN'T SHE HURTING YOUR FEELINGS?
I ALREADY KNOW WHAT SORT OF CREATURE SHE IS, SO I DON'T CONSIDER HER A SIGNIFICANT MEMBER OF OUR GROUP.
MIKO'S UP NEXT!
UM... ME?!
I HAVEN'T THOUGHT OF A QUESTION YET!
UM. OKAY... DOES EVERYONE...
FDGT
FDGT
...ACTUALLY THINK...
...I'M A HUGE PAIN IN THE NECK?
YOU'RE REALLY NEGATIVE TOO!
YOUR QUESTION IS PRETTY MUCH THE SAME AS ISHIGAMI'S!

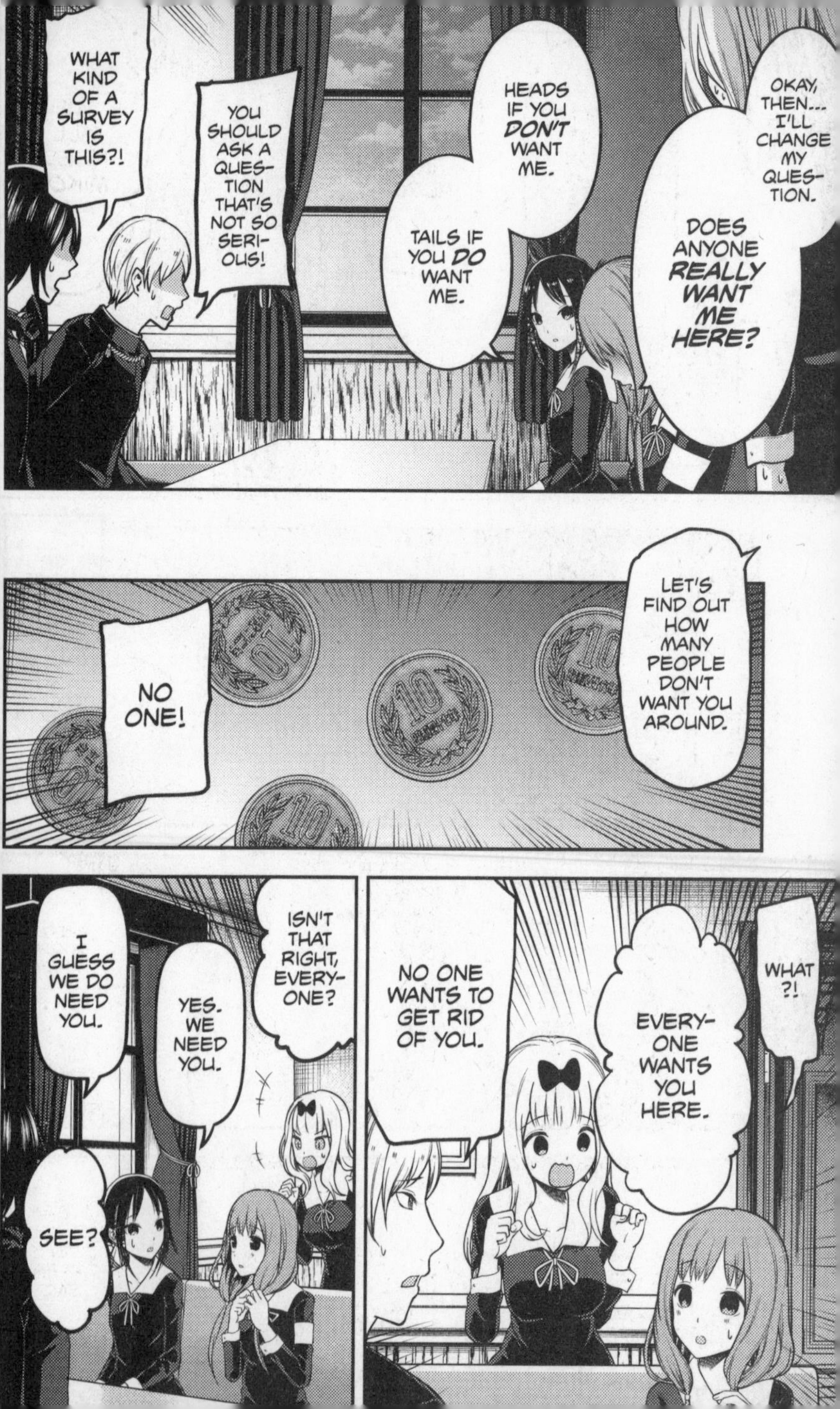
OKAY, THEN... I'LL CHANGE MY QUESTION.
DOES ANYONE *REALLY WANT ME HERE?*
HEADS IF YOU *DON'T* WANT ME.
TAILS IF YOU *DO* WANT ME.
YOU SHOULD ASK A QUESTION THAT'S NOT SO SERIOUS!
WHAT KIND OF A SURVEY IS THIS?!
LET'S FIND OUT HOW MANY PEOPLE DON'T WANT YOU AROUND.
NO ONE!
WHAT?!
EVERYONE WANTS YOU HERE.
NO ONE WANTS TO GET RID OF YOU.
ISN'T THAT RIGHT, EVERYONE?
YES. WE NEED YOU.
I GUESS WE DO NEED YOU.
SEE?

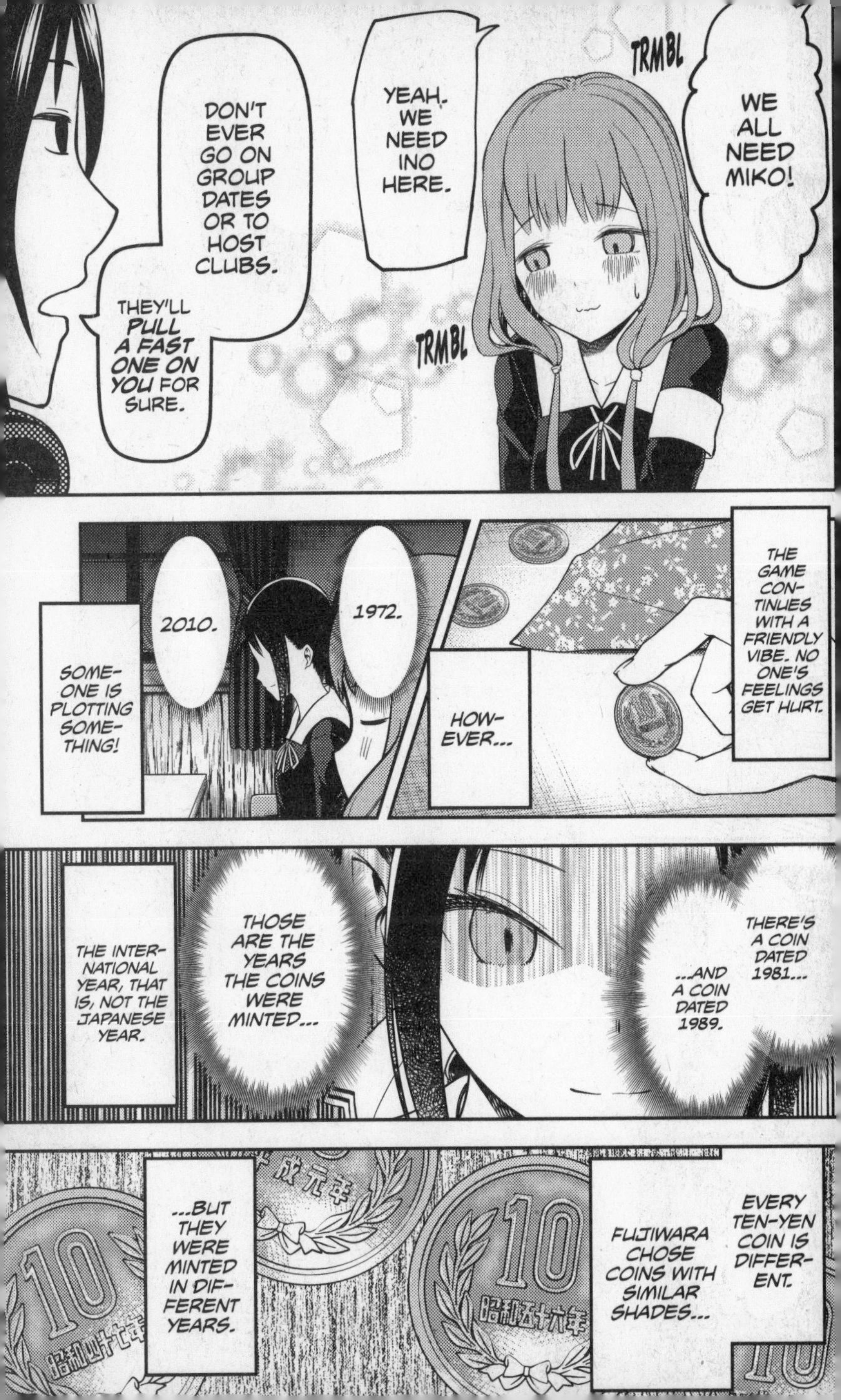
TRMBL
WE ALL NEED MIKO!
TRMBL
YEAH. WE NEED INO HERE.
DON'T EVER GO ON GROUP DATES OR TO HOST CLUBS.
THEY'LL PULL A FAST ONE ON YOU FOR SURE.
THE GAME CONTINUES WITH A FRIENDLY VIBE. NO ONE'S FEELINGS GET HURT.
HOWEVER...
1972.
2010.
SOMEONE IS PLOTTING SOMETHING!
THERE'S A COIN DATED 1981...
...AND A COIN DATED 1989.
THOSE ARE THE YEARS THE COINS WERE MINTED...
THE INTERNATIONAL YEAR, THAT IS, NOT THE JAPANESE YEAR.
EVERY TEN-YEN COIN IS DIFFERENT.
FUJIWARA CHOSE COINS WITH SIMILAR SHADES...
...BUT THEY WERE MINTED IN DIFFERENT YEARS.

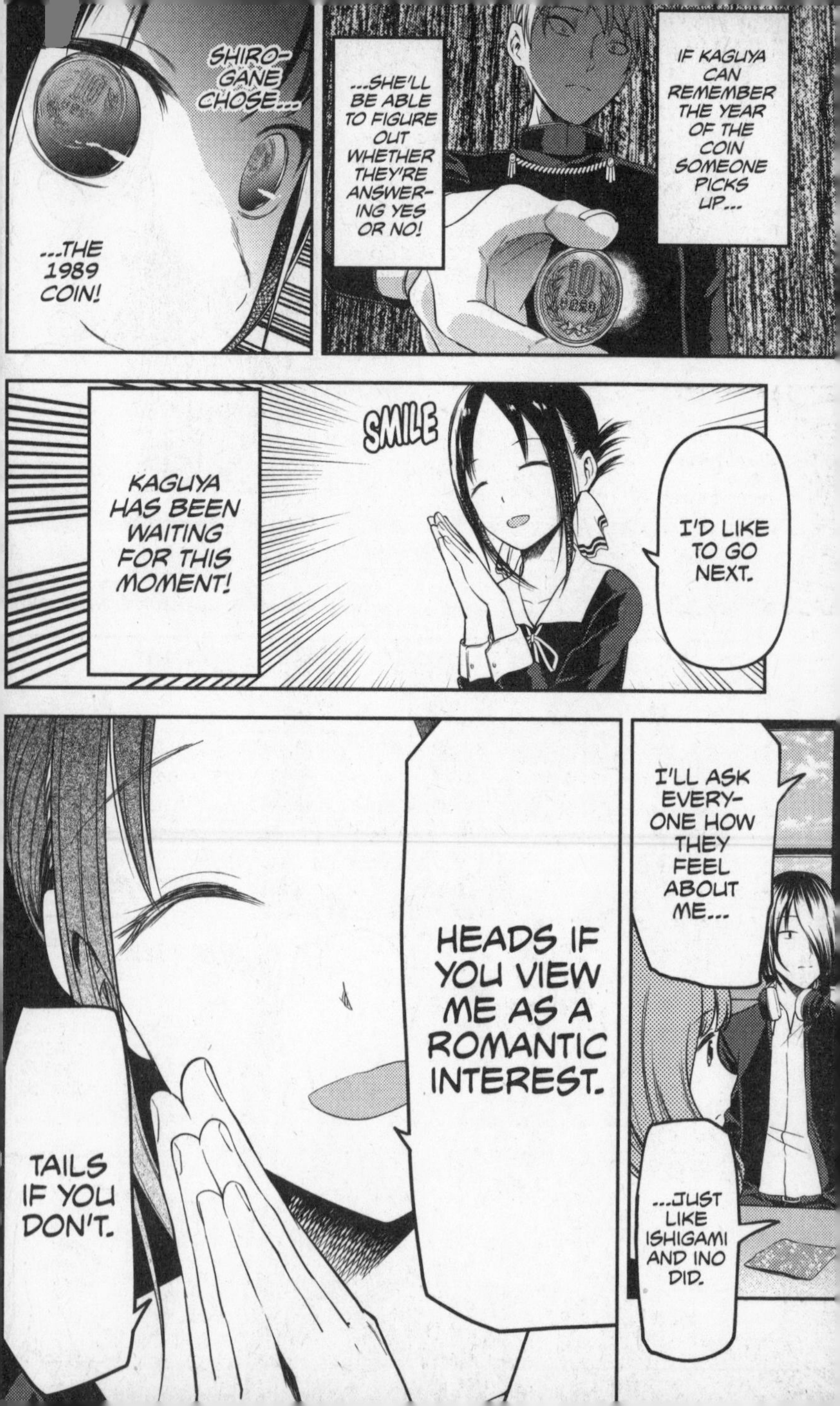
IF KAGUYA CAN REMEMBER THE YEAR OF THE COIN SOMEONE PICKS UP...
...SHE'LL BE ABLE TO FIGURE OUT WHETHER THEY'RE ANSWERING YES OR NO!
SHIROGANE CHOSE...
...THE 1989 COIN!
I'D LIKE TO GO NEXT.
SMILE
KAGUYA HAS BEEN WAITING FOR THIS MOMENT!
I'LL ASK EVERYONE HOW THEY FEEL ABOUT ME...
...JUST LIKE ISHIGAMI AND INO DID.
HEADS IF YOU VIEW ME AS A ROMANTIC INTEREST.
TAILS IF YOU DON'T.

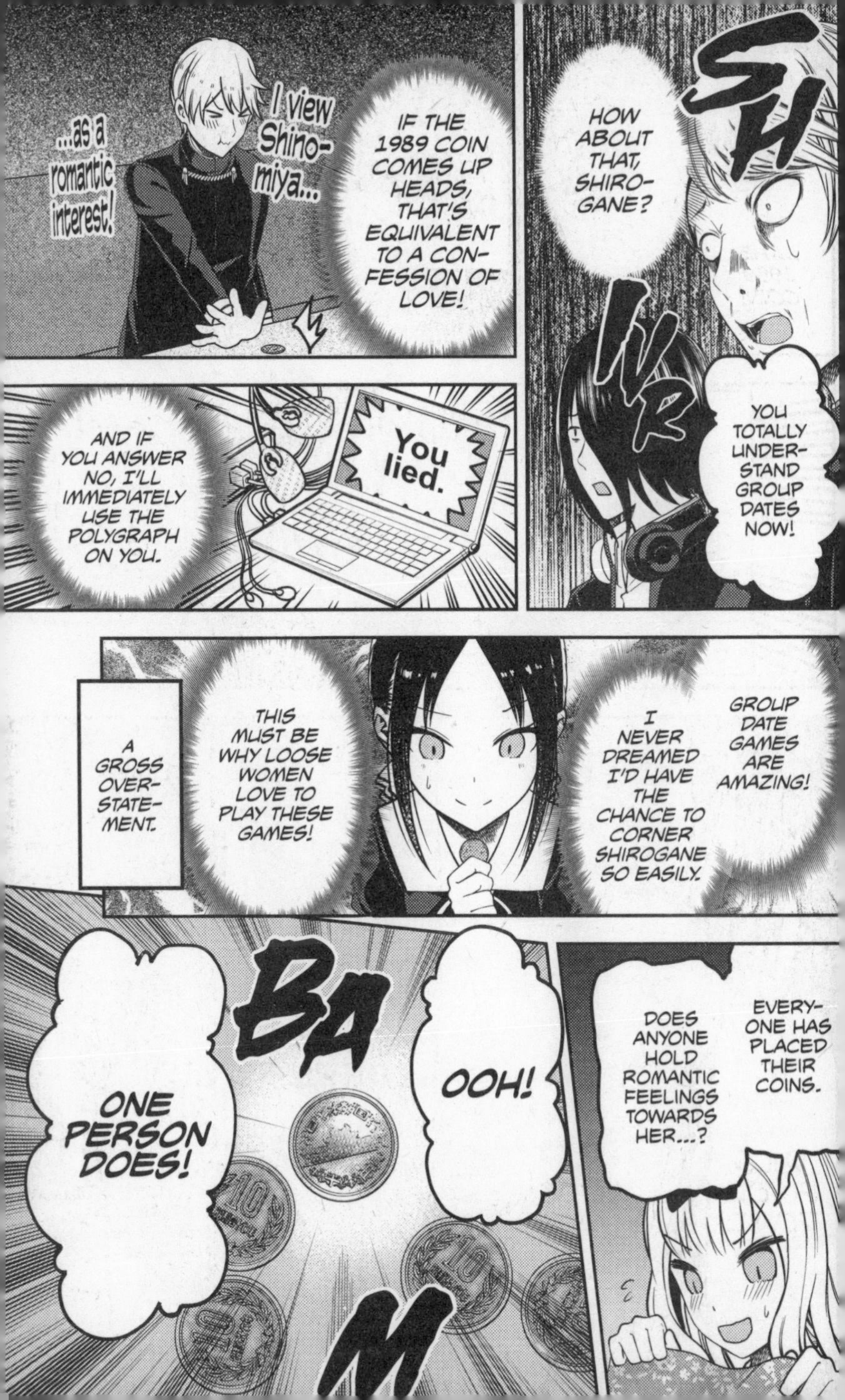
HOW ABOUT THAT, SHIROGANE?
YOU TOTALLY UNDERSTAND GROUP DATES NOW!
IF THE 1989 COIN COMES UP HEADS, THAT'S EQUIVALENT TO A CONFESSION OF LOVE!
I view Shinomiya...
...as a romantic interest!
AND IF YOU ANSWER NO, I'LL IMMEDIATELY USE THE POLYGRAPH ON YOU.
You lied.
GROUP DATE GAMES ARE AMAZING!
I NEVER DREAMED I'D HAVE THE CHANCE TO CORNER SHIROGANE SO EASILY.
THIS MUST BE WHY LOOSE WOMEN LOVE TO PLAY THESE GAMES!
A GROSS OVERSTATEMENT.
EVERYONE HAS PLACED THEIR COINS.
DOES ANYONE HOLD ROMANTIC FEELINGS TOWARDS HER...?
OOH!
BAM
ONE PERSON DOES!

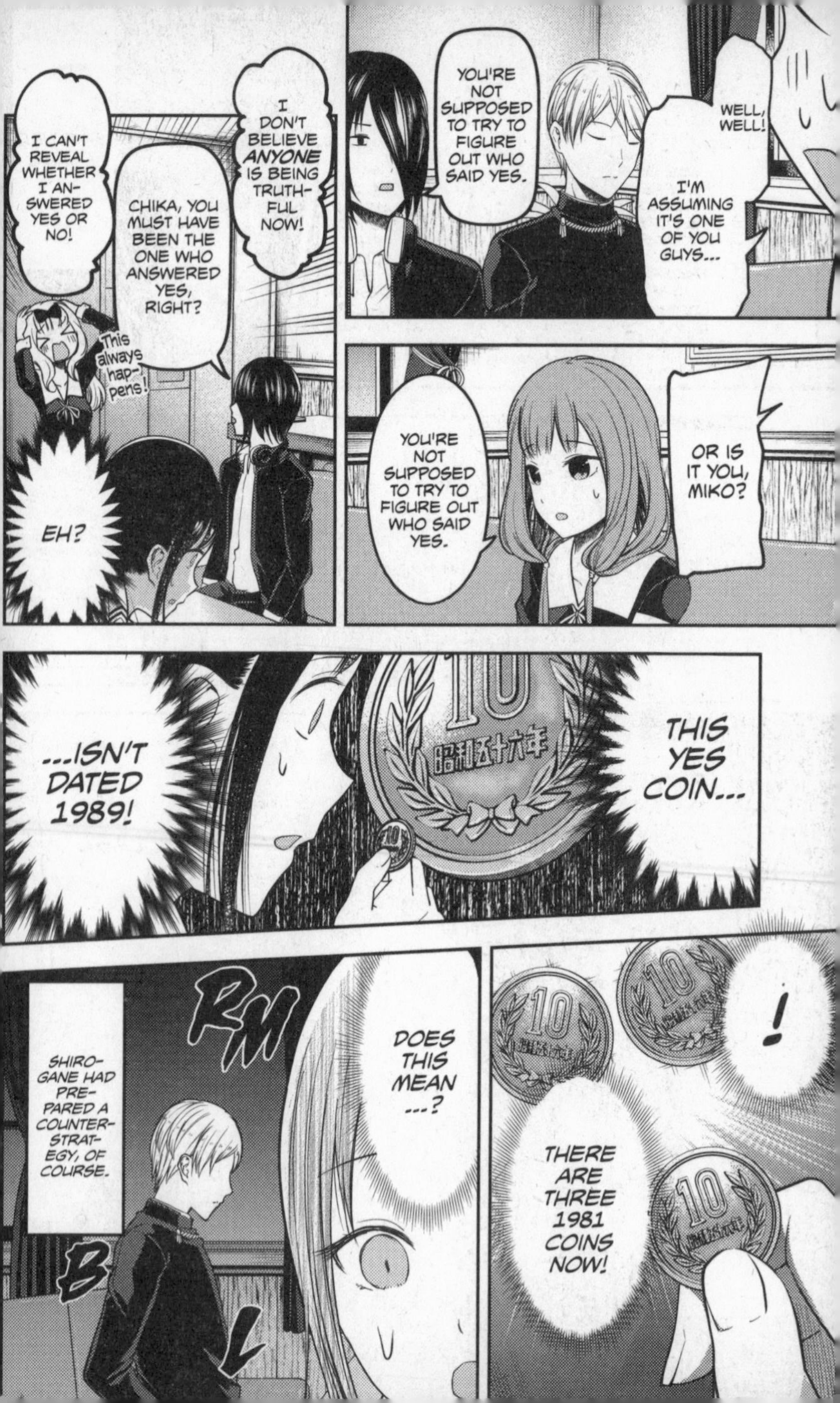

WELL, WELL!
I'M ASSUMING IT'S ONE OF YOU GUYS...
YOU'RE NOT SUPPOSED TO TRY TO FIGURE OUT WHO SAID YES.
OR IS IT YOU, MIKO?
YOU'RE NOT SUPPOSED TO TRY TO FIGURE OUT WHO SAID YES.
I DON'T BELIEVE *ANYONE* IS BEING TRUTHFUL NOW!
CHIKA, YOU MUST HAVE BEEN THE ONE WHO ANSWERED YES, RIGHT?
I CAN'T REVEAL WHETHER I ANSWERED YES OR NO!
This always happens!
EH?
THIS YES COIN...
10
昭和五十六年
...ISN'T DATED 1989!
!
THERE ARE THREE 1981 COINS NOW!
DOES THIS MEAN...?
RM
SHIROGANE HAD PREPARED A COUNTERSTRATEGY, OF COURSE.
B

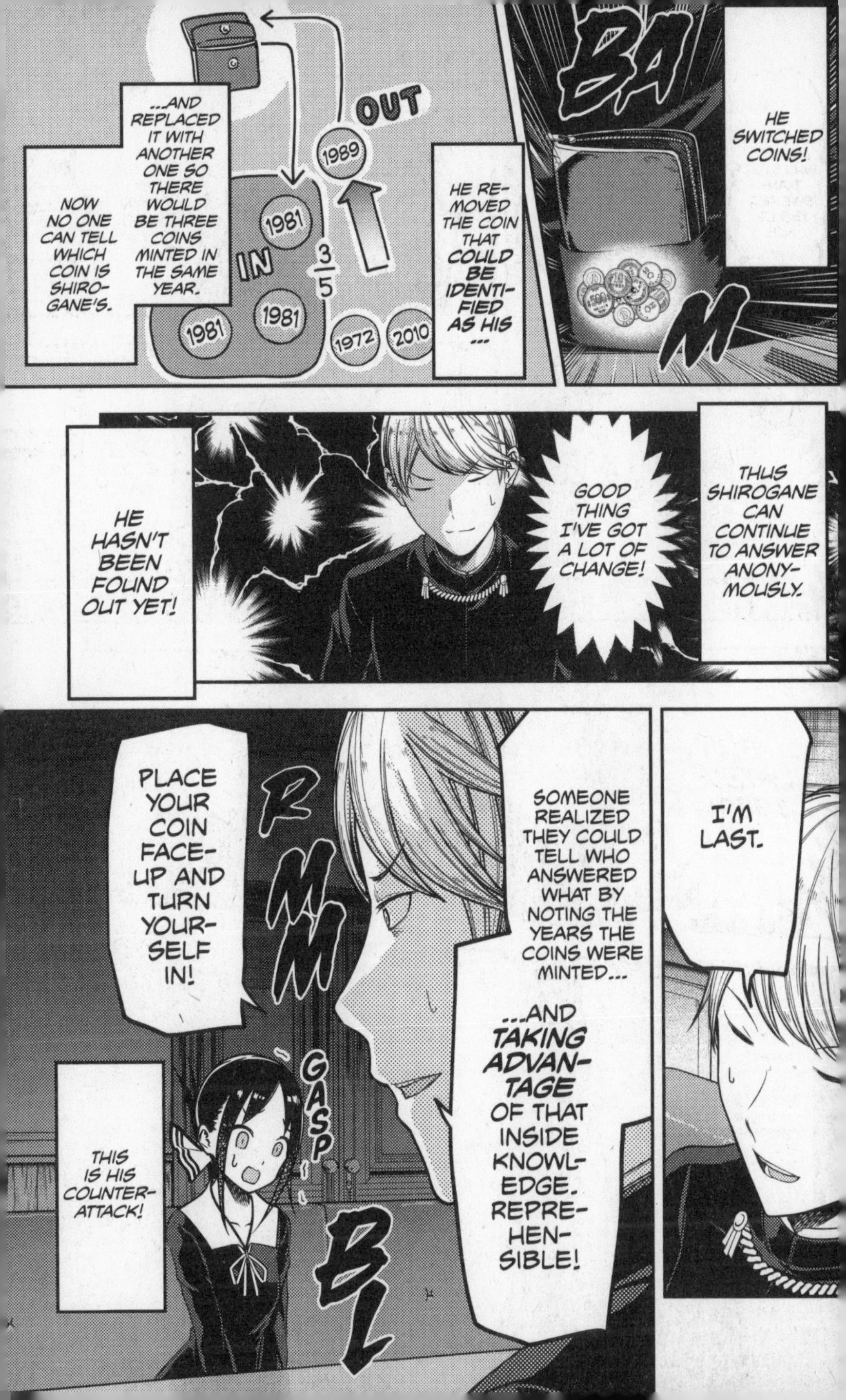
BAM
HE SWITCHED COINS!
HE REMOVED THE COIN THAT COULD BE IDENTIFIED AS HIS...
OUT
1989
3/5
IN
1981
1981
1981
1972
2010
...AND REPLACED IT WITH ANOTHER ONE SO THERE WOULD BE THREE COINS MINTED IN THE SAME YEAR.
NOW NO ONE CAN TELL WHICH COIN IS SHIROGANE'S.
THUS SHIROGANE CAN CONTINUE TO ANSWER ANONYMOUSLY.
GOOD THING I'VE GOT A LOT OF CHANGE!
HE HASN'T BEEN FOUND OUT YET!
I'M LAST.
SOMEONE REALIZED THEY COULD TELL WHO ANSWERED WHAT BY NOTING THE YEARS THE COINS WERE MINTED...
...AND TAKING ADVANTAGE OF THAT INSIDE KNOWLEDGE. REPREHENSIBLE!
RMMM
PLACE YOUR COIN FACE-UP AND TURN YOURSELF IN!
GASP
BL
THIS IS HIS COUNTER-ATTACK!

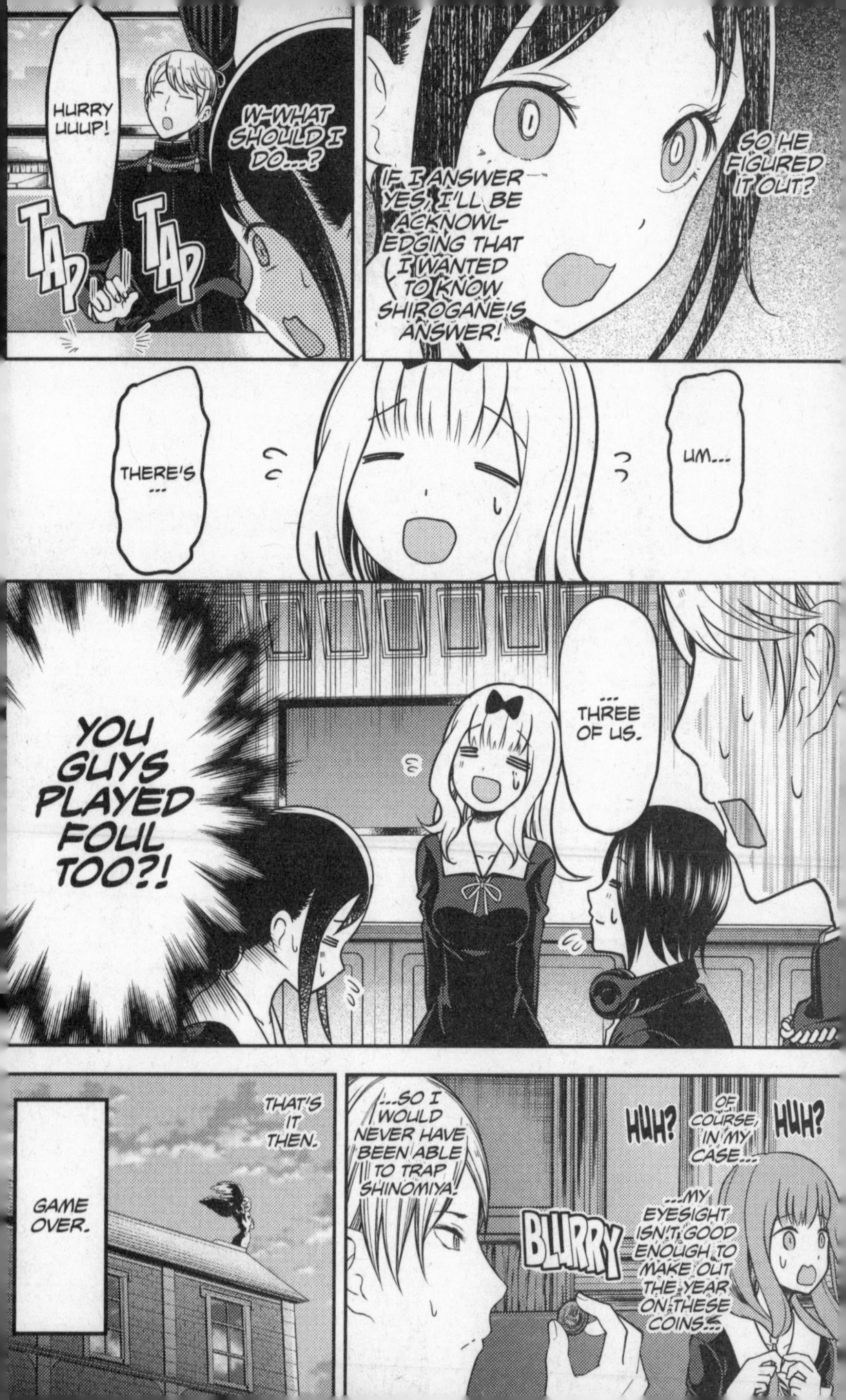
SO HE FIGURED IT OUT?
IF I ANSWER YES, I'LL BE ACKNOWLEDGING THAT I WANTED TO KNOW SHIROGANE'S ANSWER!
W-WHAT SHOULD I DO...?
HURRY UUUP!
TAP
TAP
UM...
THERE'S ...
...THREE OF US.
YOU GUYS PLAYED FOUL TOO?!
HUH?
OF COURSE, IN MY CASE...
HUH?
...MY EYESIGHT ISN'T GOOD ENOUGH TO MAKE OUT THE YEAR ON THESE COINS...
BLURRY
...SO I WOULD NEVER HAVE BEEN ABLE TO TRAP SHINOMIYA!
THAT'S IT THEN.
GAME OVER.

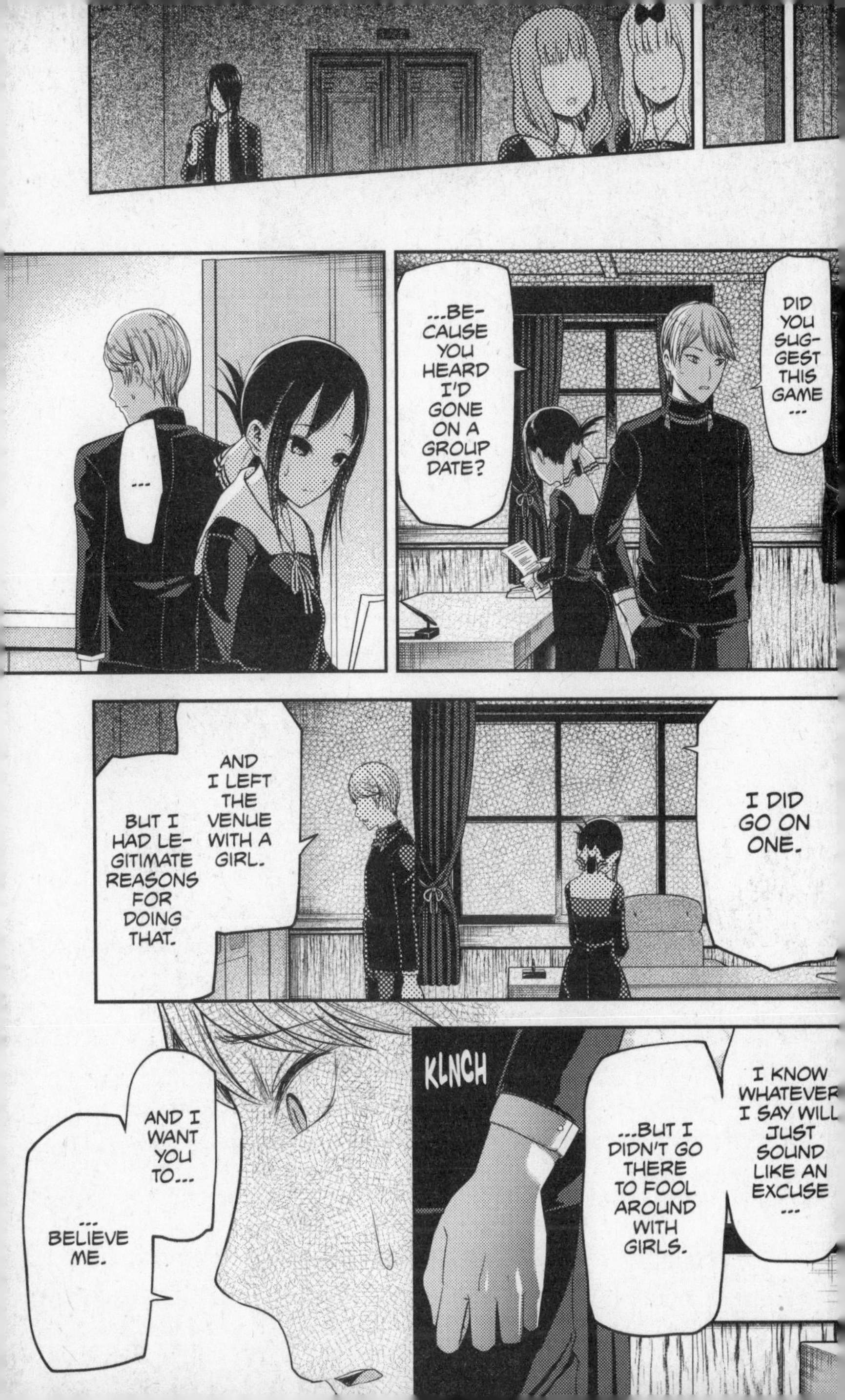
DID YOU SUGGEST THIS GAME...
...BECAUSE YOU HEARD I'D GONE ON A GROUP DATE?
...
I DID GO ON ONE.
AND I LEFT THE VENUE WITH A GIRL.
BUT I HAD LEGITIMATE REASONS FOR DOING THAT.
KLNCH
I KNOW WHATEVER I SAY WILL JUST SOUND LIKE AN EXCUSE...
...BUT I DIDN'T GO THERE TO FOOL AROUND WITH GIRLS.
AND I WANT YOU TO...
...BELIEVE ME.

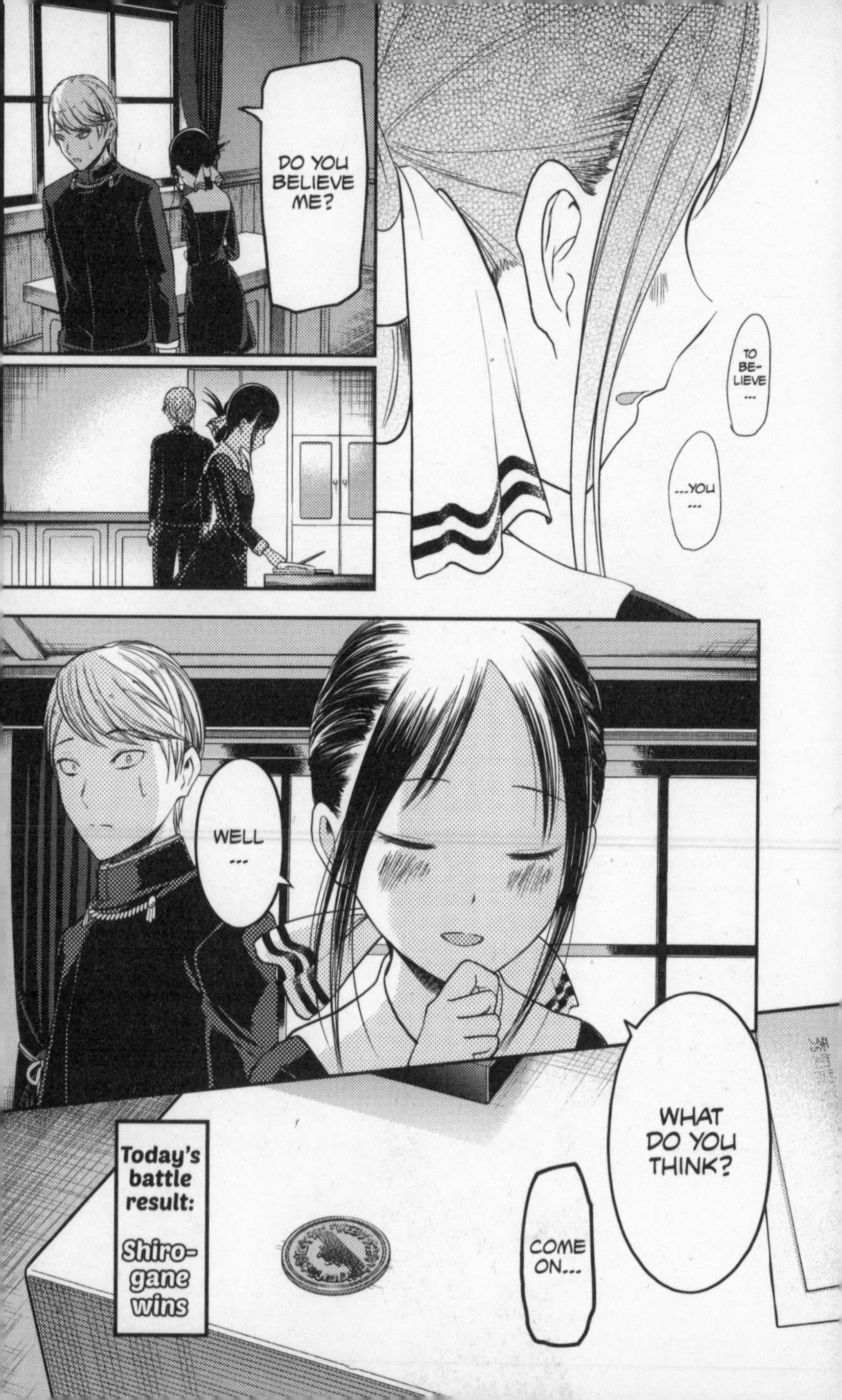
TO BE-LIEVE ...
...YOU ...
DO YOU BELIEVE ME?
WELL ...
WHAT DO YOU THINK?
COME ON...
Today's battle result:
Shiro-gane wins

Shirogane took the 1989 coin.
Did he choose that one to figure out who would answer yes or no?
Hm...
SHE CAN'T FIGURE OUT WHAT EXACTLY JUST HAP-PENED.

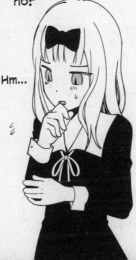

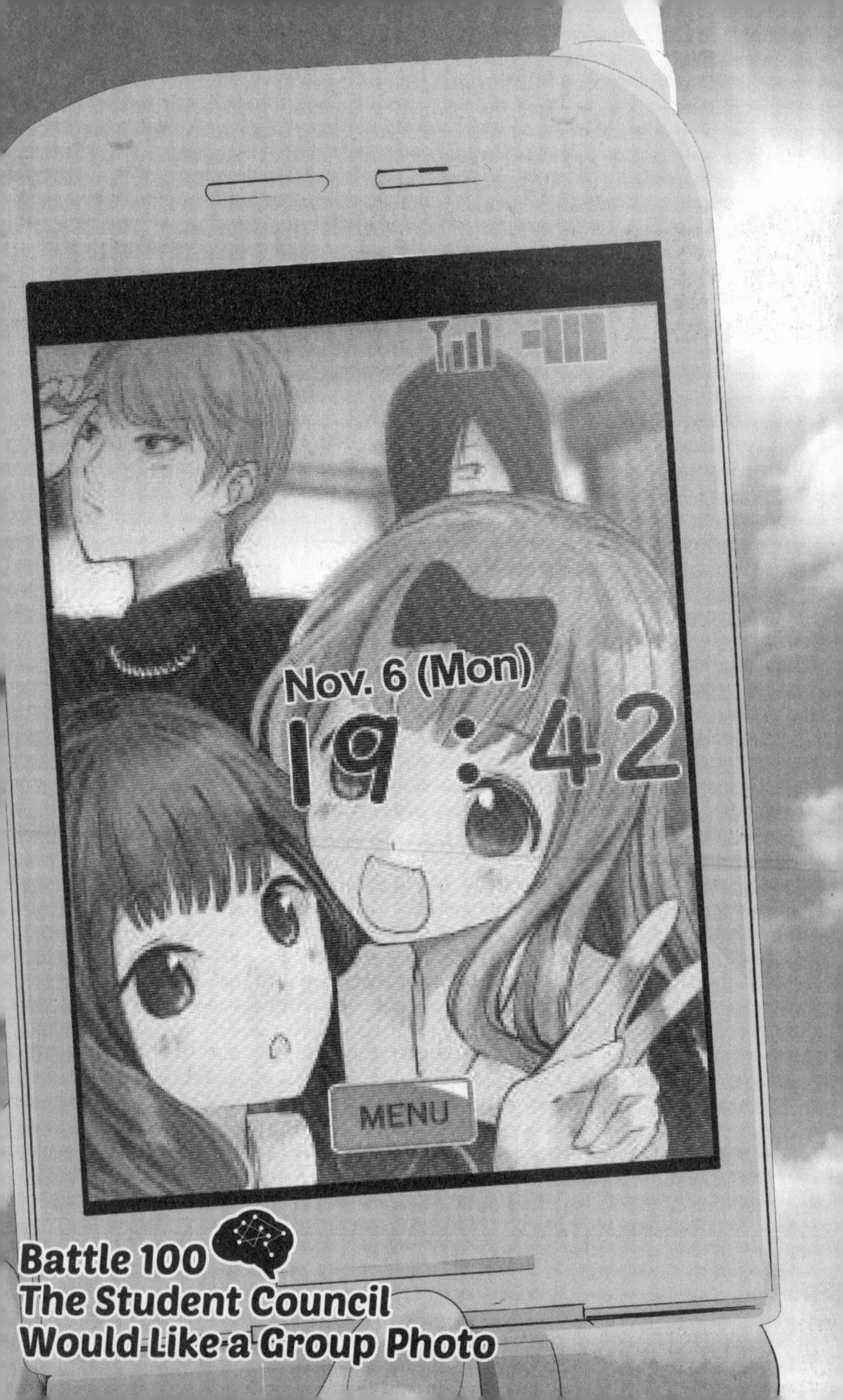
Nov. 6 (Mon)
19:42
MENU
Battle 100
The Student Council Would Like a Group Photo

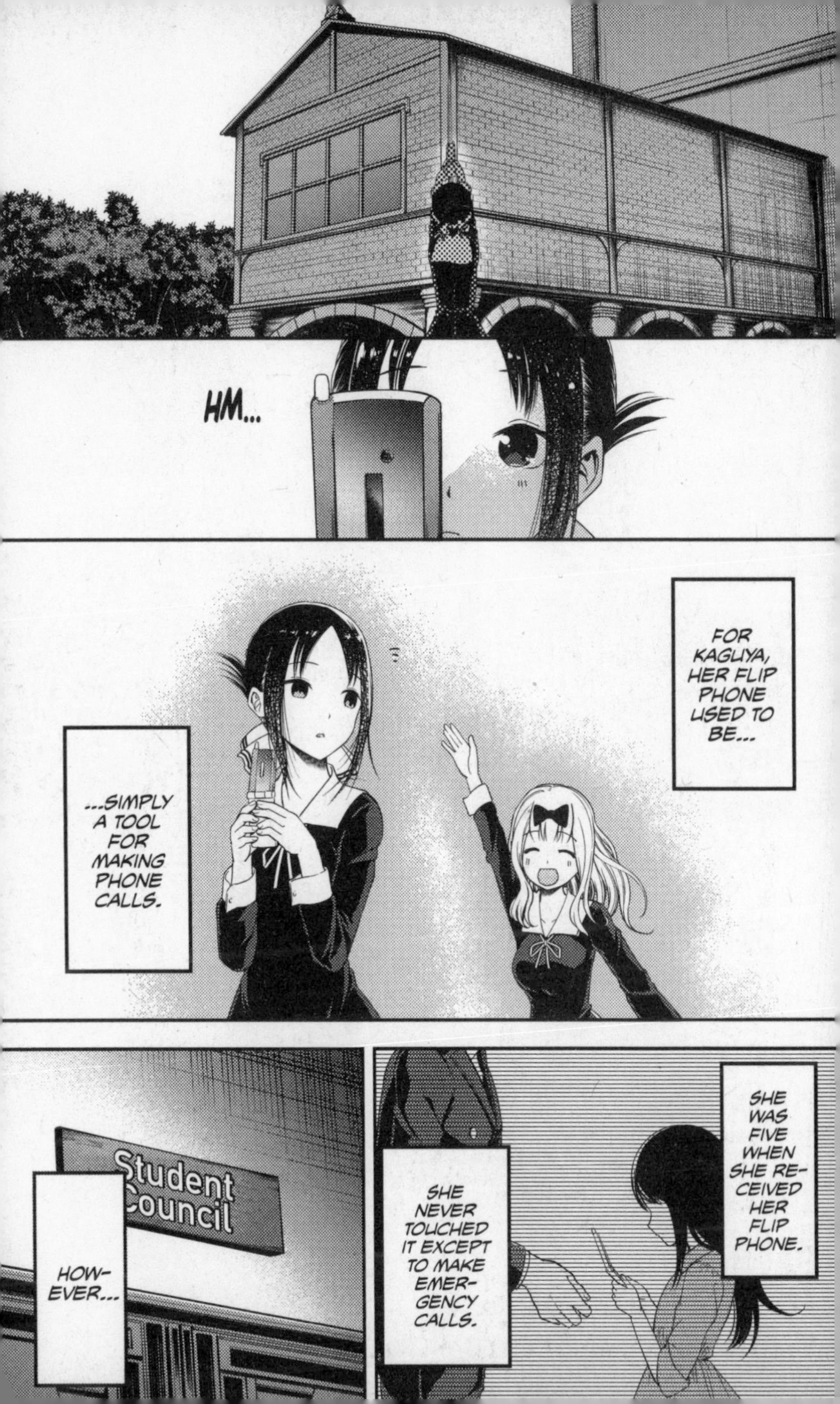
HM...
FOR KAGUYA, HER FLIP PHONE USED TO BE...
...SIMPLY A TOOL FOR MAKING PHONE CALLS.
SHE WAS FIVE WHEN SHE RE-CEIVED HER FLIP PHONE.
SHE NEVER TOUCHED IT EXCEPT TO MAKE EMER-GENCY CALLS.
Student Council
HOW-EVER...

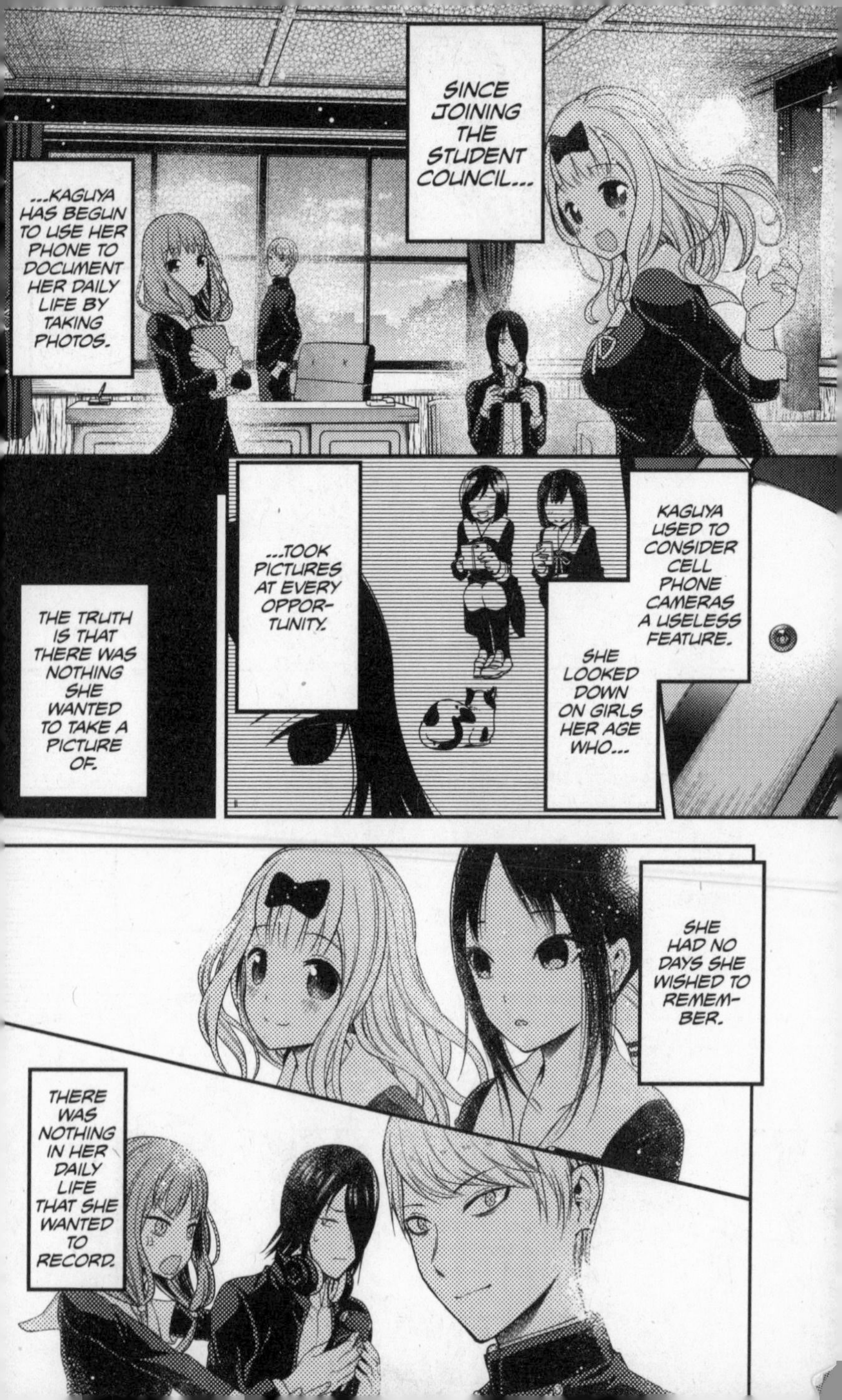
SINCE JOINING THE STUDENT COUNCIL...
...KAGUYA HAS BEGUN TO USE HER PHONE TO DOCUMENT HER DAILY LIFE BY TAKING PHOTOS.
KAGUYA USED TO CONSIDER CELL PHONE CAMERAS A USELESS FEATURE.
SHE LOOKED DOWN ON GIRLS HER AGE WHO...
...TOOK PICTURES AT EVERY OPPORTUNITY.
THE TRUTH IS THAT THERE WAS NOTHING SHE WANTED TO TAKE A PICTURE OF.
SHE HAD NO DAYS SHE WISHED TO REMEMBER.
THERE WAS NOTHING IN HER DAILY LIFE THAT SHE WANTED TO RECORD.

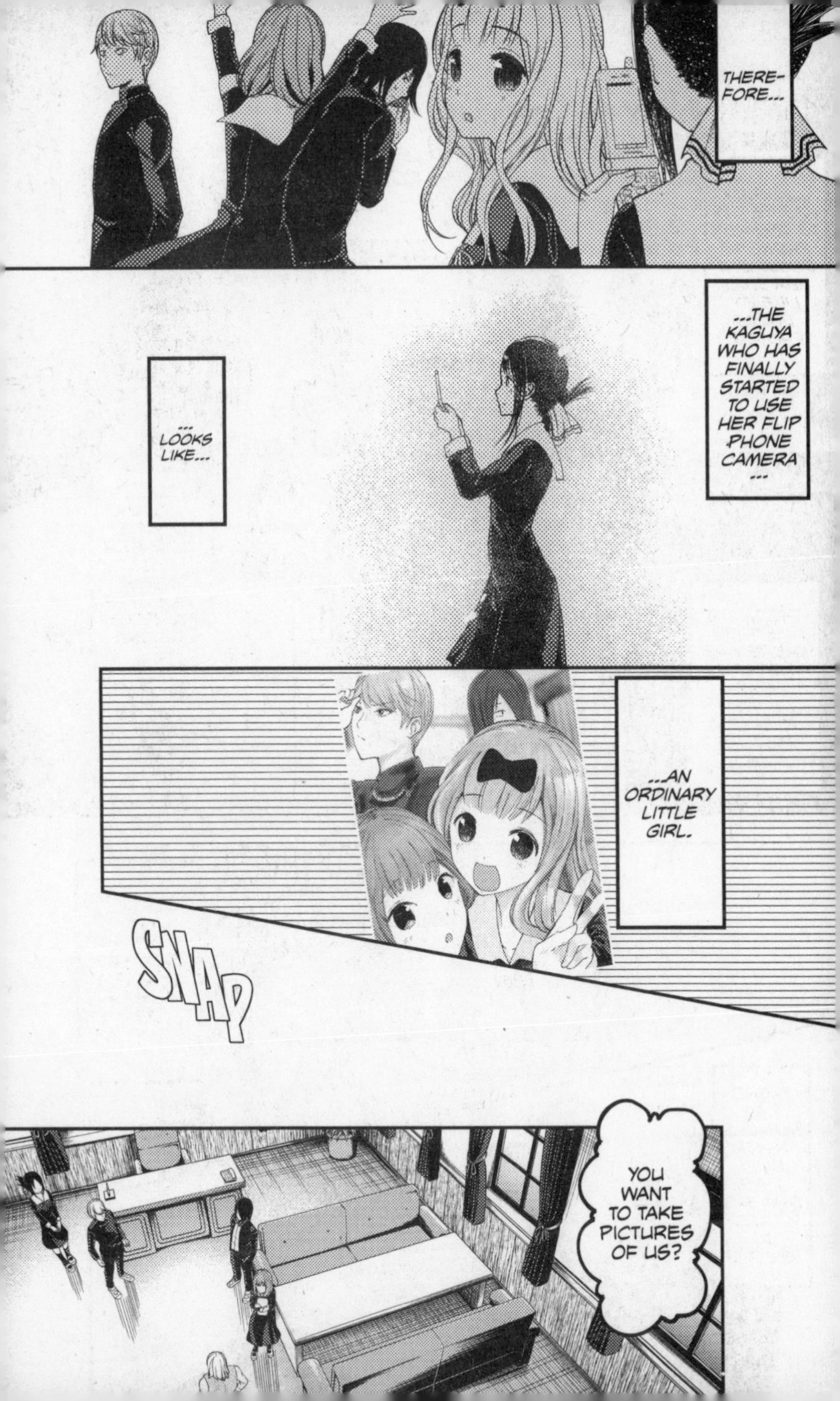
THEREFORE...
...THE KAGUYA WHO HAS FINALLY STARTED TO USE HER FLIP PHONE CAMERA...
...LOOKS LIKE...
...AN ORDINARY LITTLE GIRL.
SNAP
YOU WANT TO TAKE PICTURES OF US?

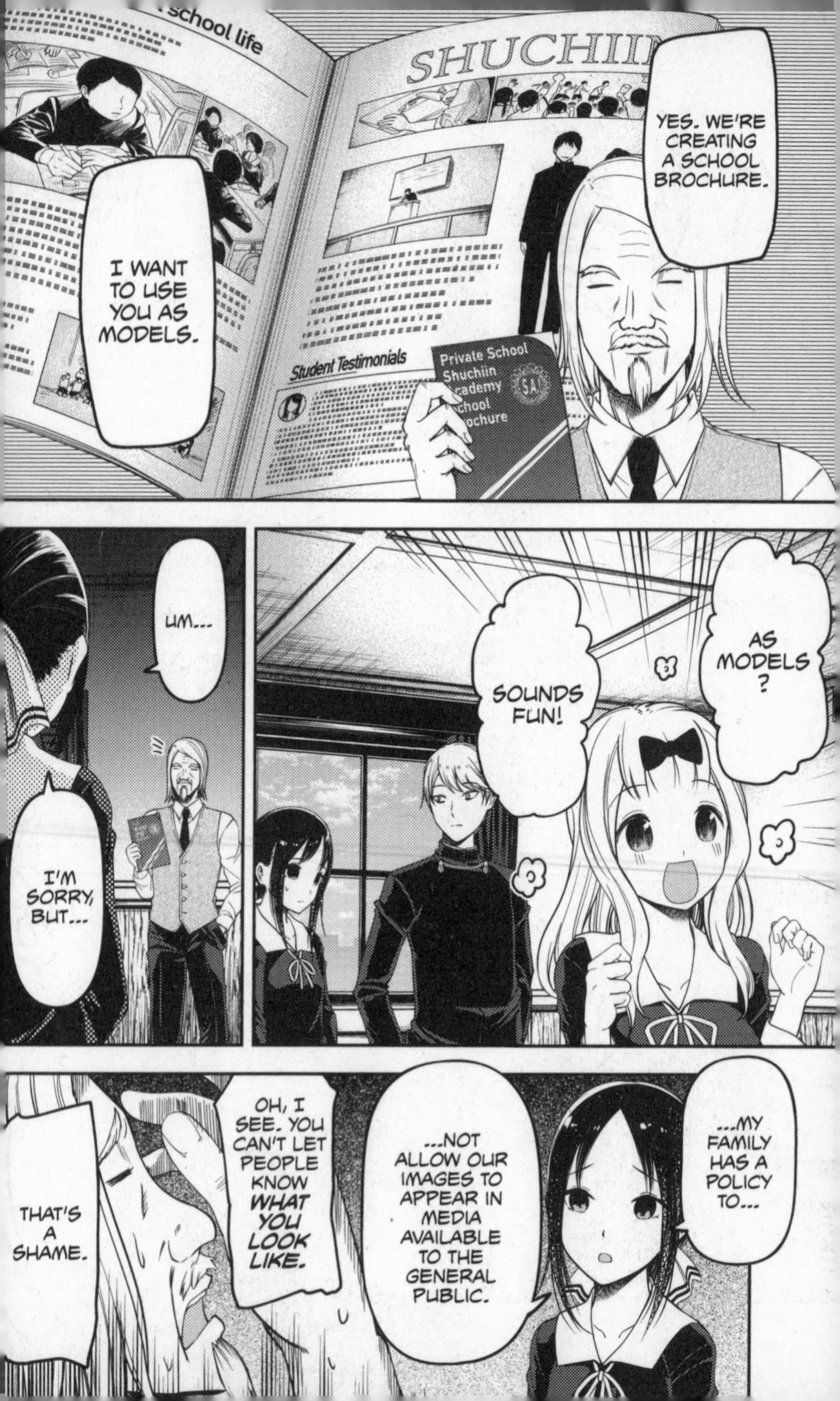
school life
Private School
Shuchiin
Student Testimonials
YES. WE'RE CREATING A SCHOOL BROCHURE.
I WANT TO USE YOU AS MODELS.
AS MODELS?
SOUNDS FUN!
UM...
I'M SORRY, BUT...
...MY FAMILY HAS A POLICY TO...
...NOT ALLOW OUR IMAGES TO APPEAR IN MEDIA AVAILABLE TO THE GENERAL PUBLIC.
OH, I SEE. YOU CAN'T LET PEOPLE KNOW *WHAT YOU LOOK LIKE*.
THAT'S A SHAME.

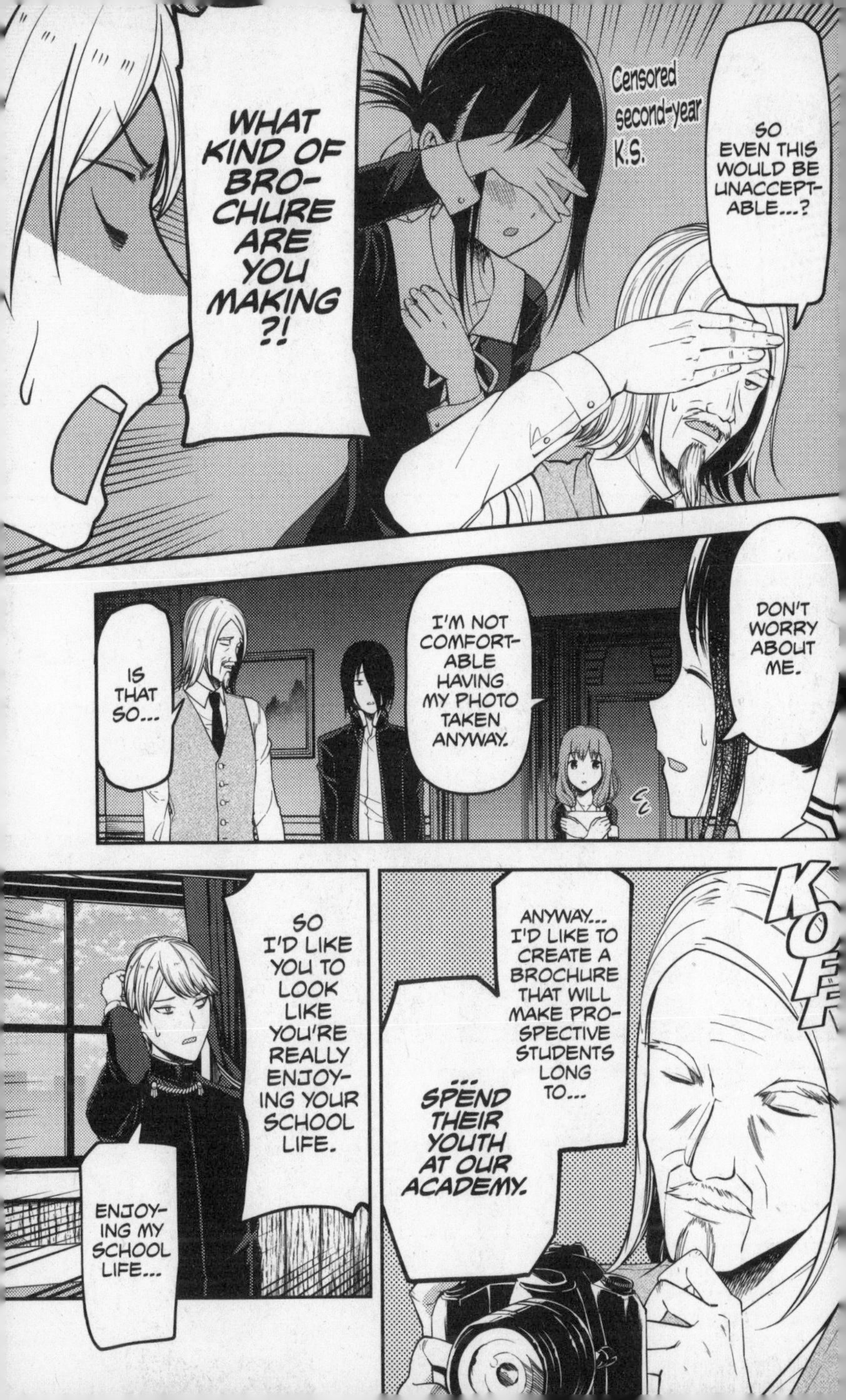
SO EVEN THIS WOULD BE UNACCEPTABLE...?
Censored second-year K.S.
WHAT KIND OF BROCHURE ARE YOU MAKING?!
DON'T WORRY ABOUT ME.
I'M NOT COMFORTABLE HAVING MY PHOTO TAKEN ANYWAY.
IS THAT SO...
KOFF
ANYWAY... I'D LIKE TO CREATE A BROCHURE THAT WILL MAKE PROSPECTIVE STUDENTS LONG TO...
...SPEND THEIR YOUTH AT OUR ACADEMY.
SO I'D LIKE YOU TO LOOK LIKE YOU'RE REALLY ENJOYING YOUR SCHOOL LIFE.
ENJOYING MY SCHOOL LIFE...

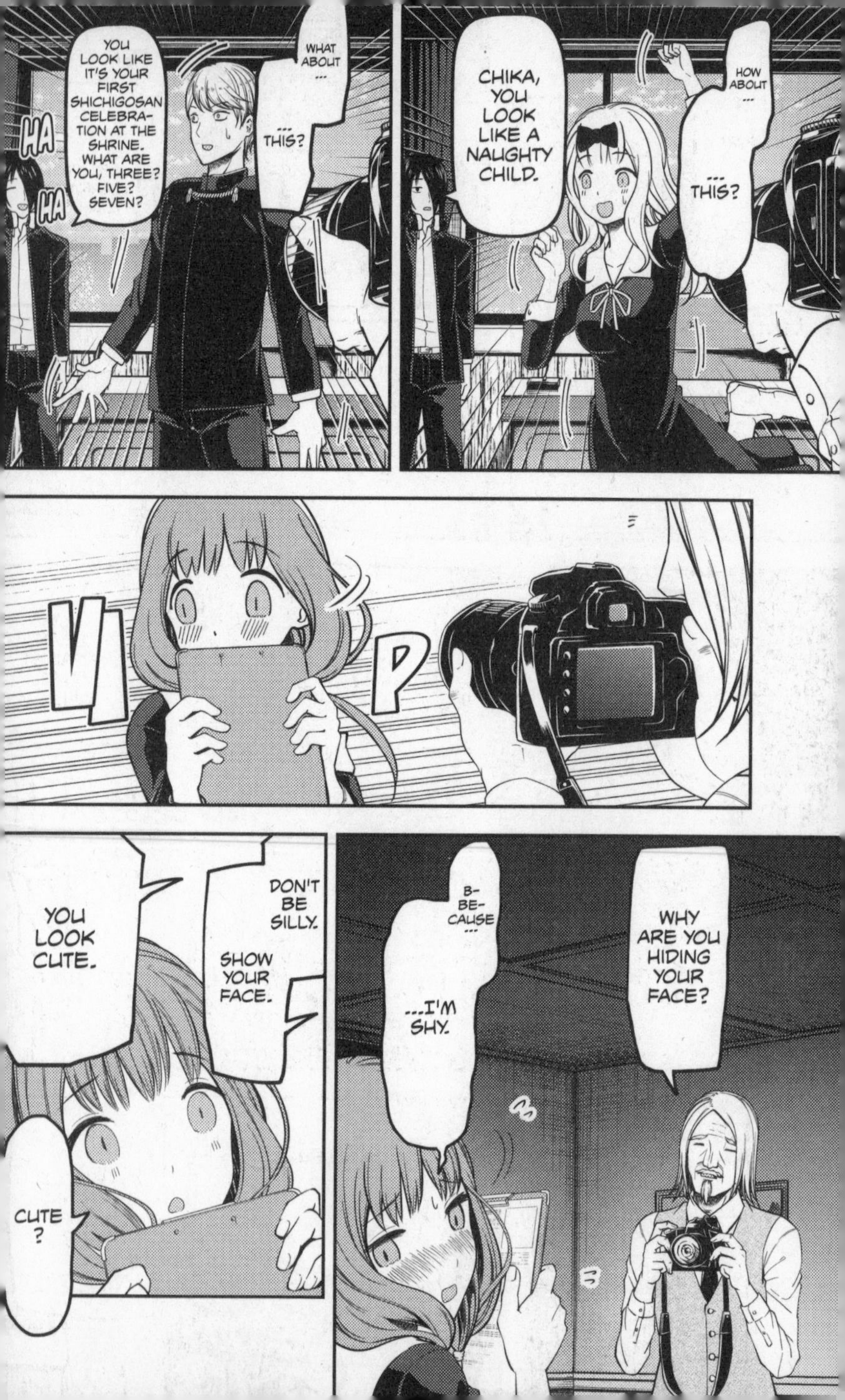
HOW ABOUT ...
... THIS?
CHIKA, YOU LOOK LIKE A NAUGHTY CHILD.
WHAT ABOUT ...
... THIS?
YOU LOOK LIKE IT'S YOUR FIRST SHICHIGOSAN CELEBRATION AT THE SHRINE. WHAT ARE YOU, THREE? FIVE? SEVEN?
HA HA
V P
WHY ARE YOU HIDING YOUR FACE?
B-BE-CAUSE ...
...I'M SHY.
DON'T BE SILLY.
SHOW YOUR FACE.
YOU LOOK CUTE.
CUTE?

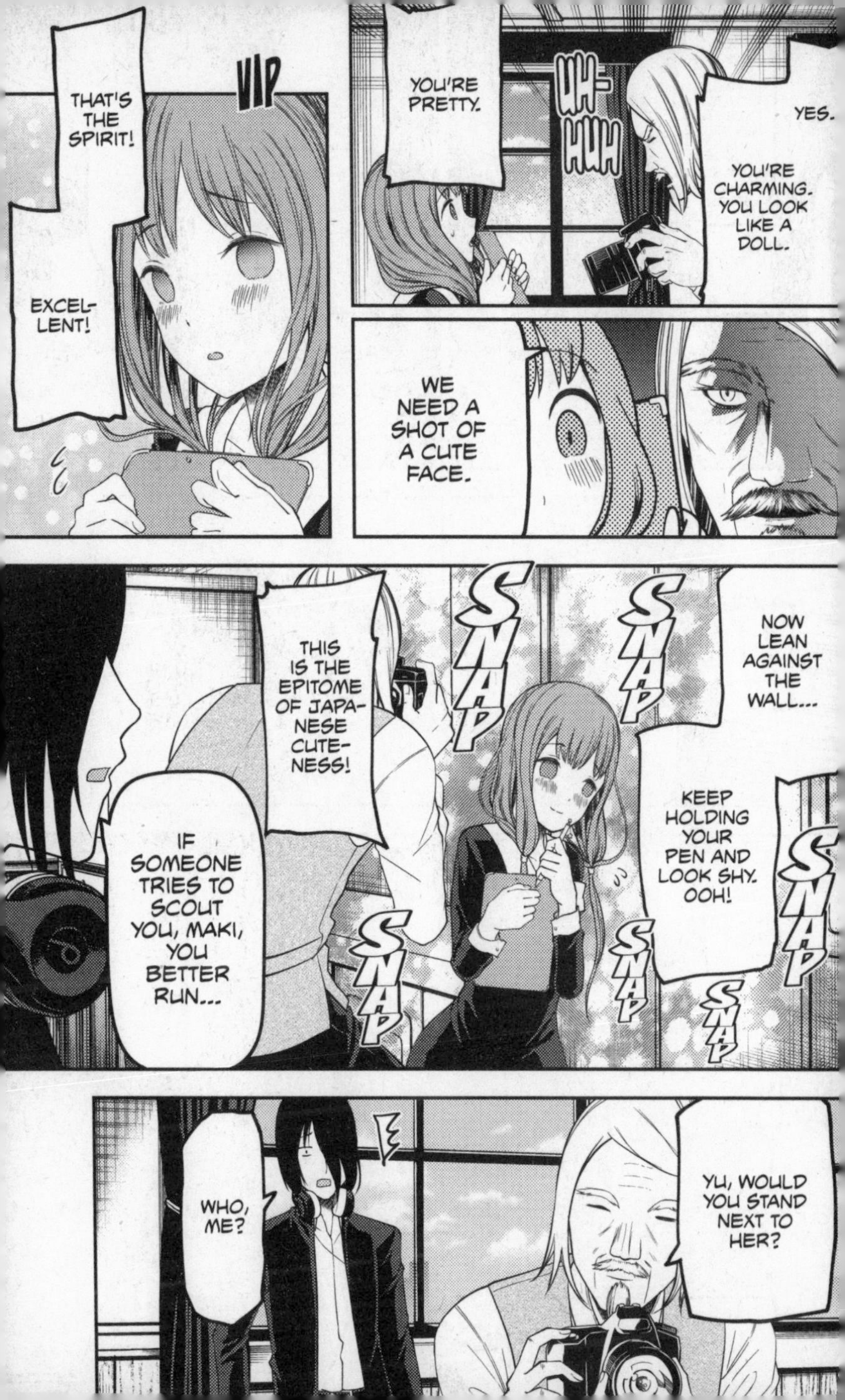
YES.
YOU'RE CHARMING. YOU LOOK LIKE A DOLL.
UH-HUH
YOU'RE PRETTY.
WE NEED A SHOT OF A CUTE FACE.
VIP
THAT'S THE SPIRIT!
EXCEL-LENT!
NOW LEAN AGAINST THE WALL...
SNAP
SNAP
KEEP HOLDING YOUR PEN AND LOOK SHY. OOH!
SNAP
SNAP
SNAP
THIS IS THE EPITOME OF JAPANESE CUTENESS!
SNAP
IF SOMEONE TRIES TO SCOUT YOU, MAKI, YOU BETTER RUN...
YU, WOULD YOU STAND NEXT TO HER?
WHO, ME?

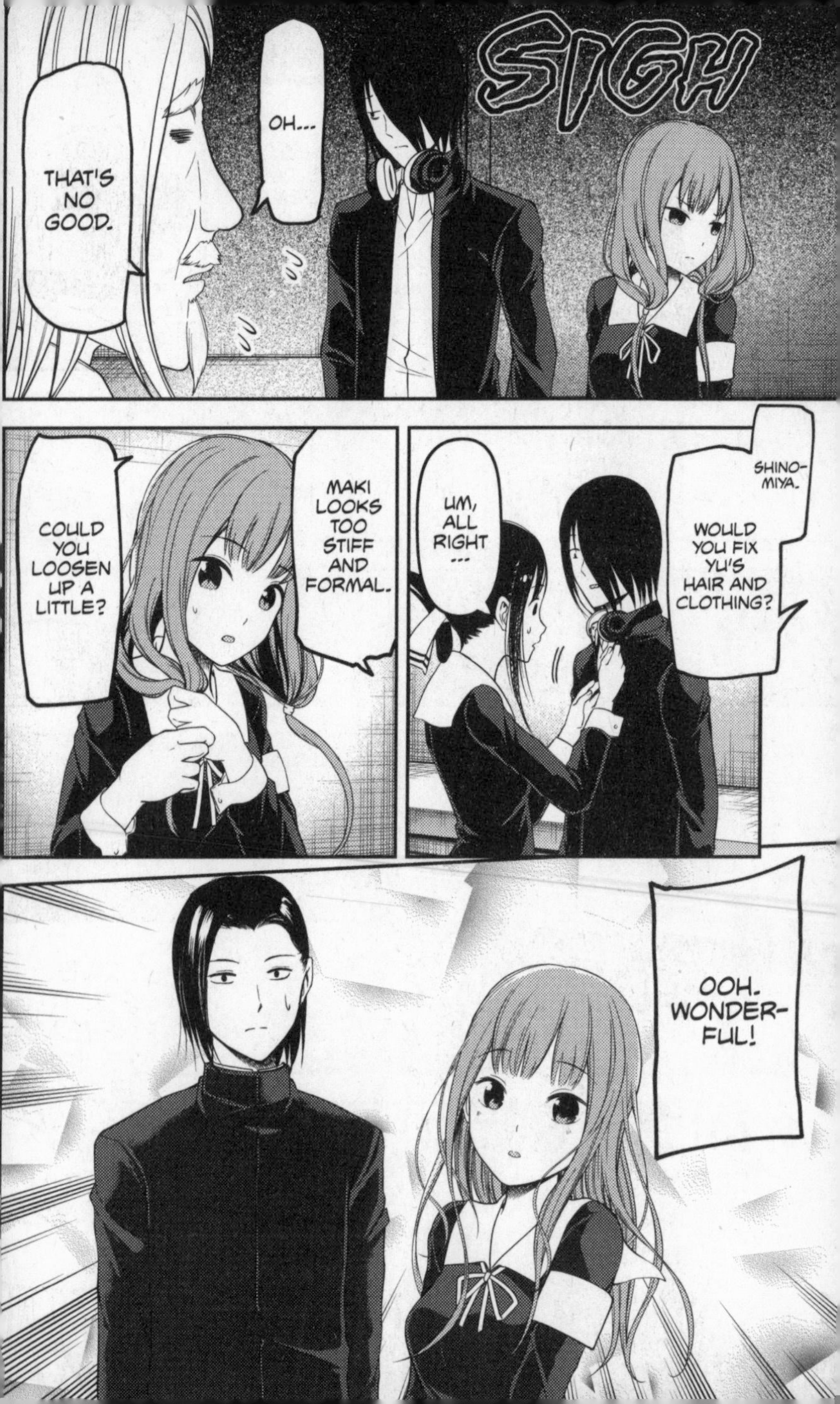
SIGH
OH...
THAT'S NO GOOD.
SHINO-MIYA.
WOULD YOU FIX YU'S HAIR AND CLOTHING?
UM, ALL RIGHT ...
MAKI LOOKS TOO STIFF AND FORMAL.
COULD YOU LOOSEN UP A LITTLE?
OOH. WONDER-FUL!

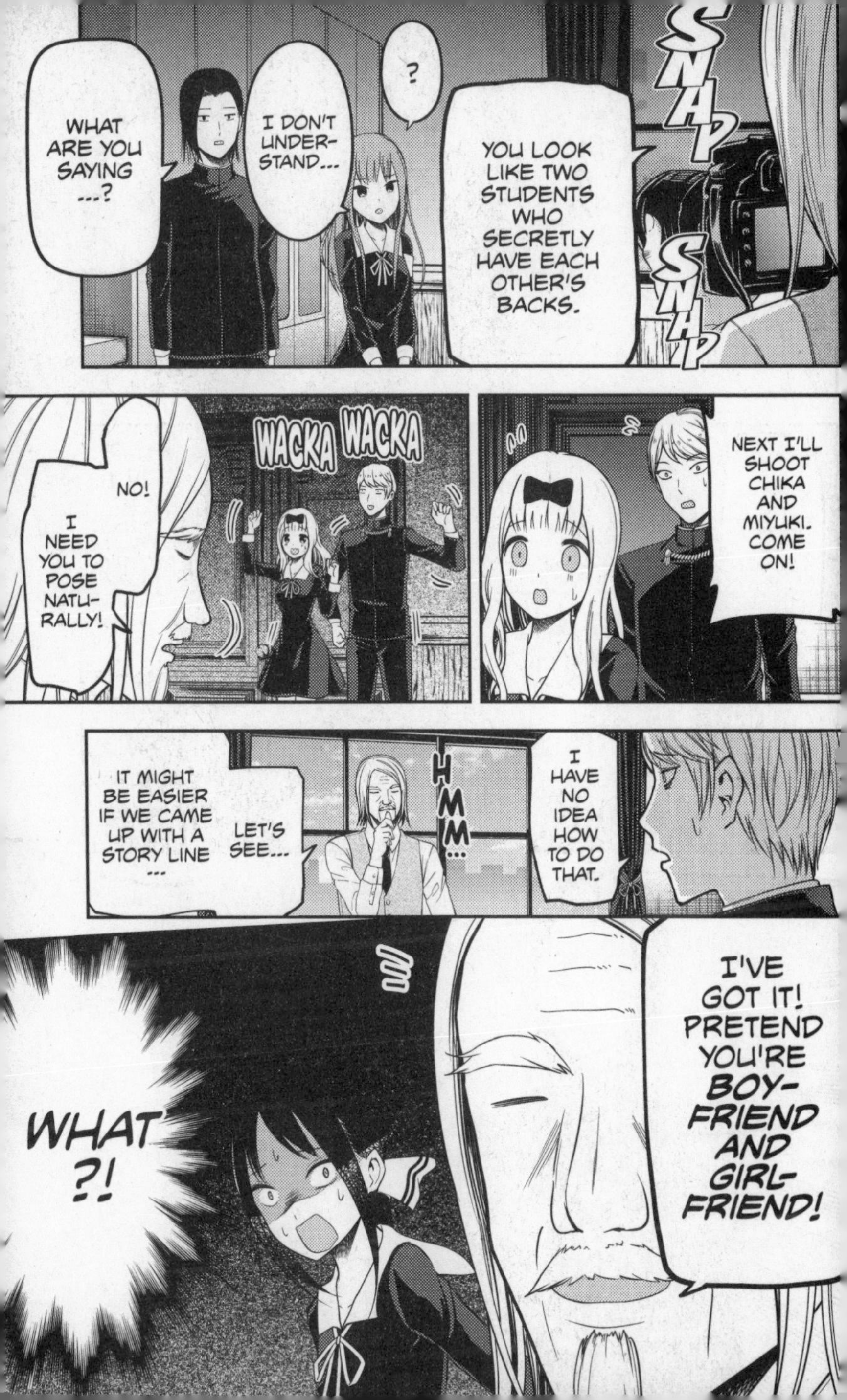
SNAP
SNAP
YOU LOOK LIKE TWO STUDENTS WHO SECRETLY HAVE EACH OTHER'S BACKS.
?
I DON'T UNDER-STAND...
WHAT ARE YOU SAYING ...?
NEXT I'LL SHOOT CHIKA AND MIYUKI. COME ON!
WACKA WACKA
NO!
I NEED YOU TO POSE NATU-RALLY!
I HAVE NO IDEA HOW TO DO THAT.
HMM...
LET'S SEE...
IT MIGHT BE EASIER IF WE CAME UP WITH A STORY LINE ...
I'VE GOT IT! PRETEND YOU'RE BOY-FRIEND AND GIRL-FRIEND!
WHAT ?!

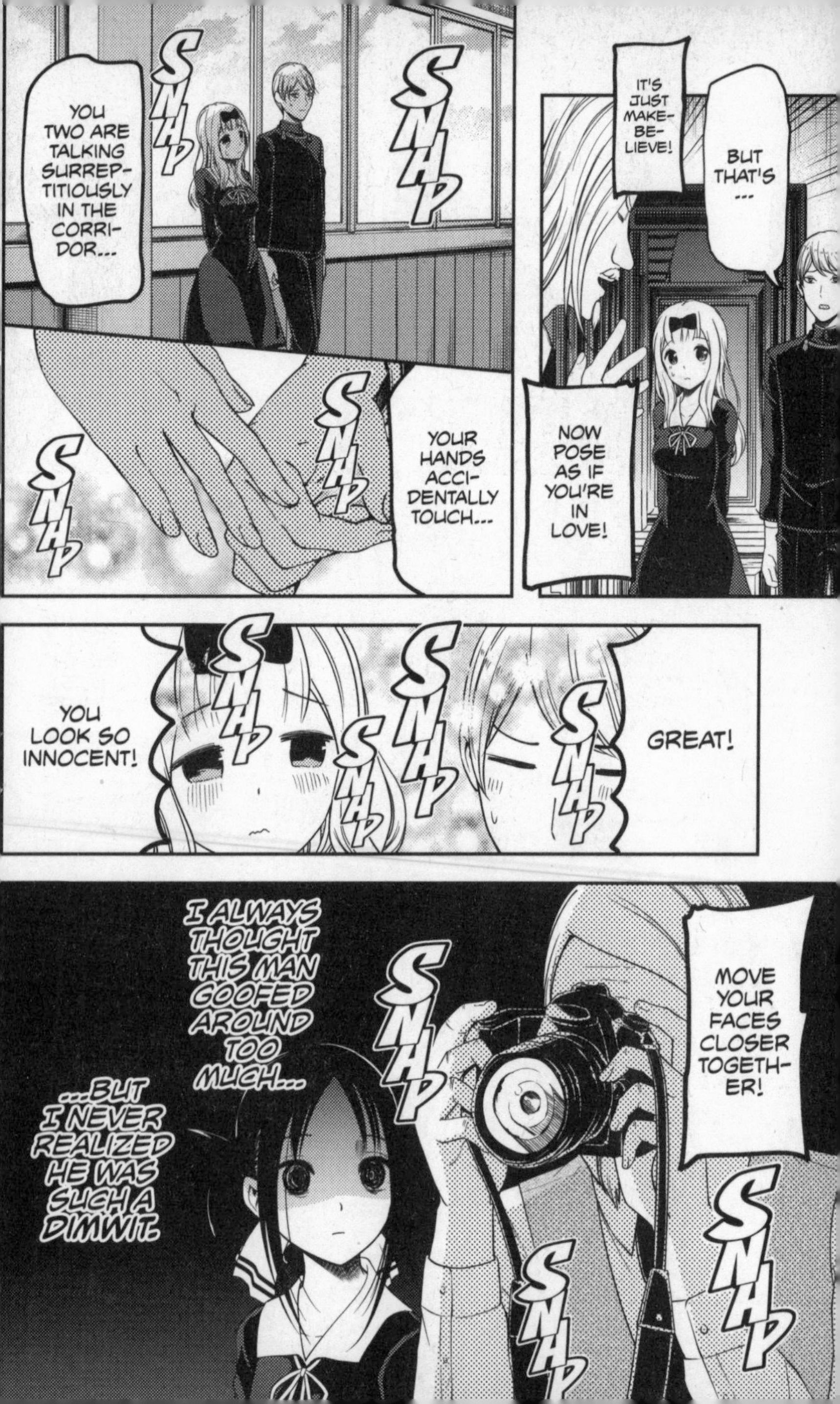
BUT THAT'S...
IT'S JUST MAKE-BELIEVE!
NOW POSE AS IF YOU'RE IN LOVE!
SNAP
YOU TWO ARE TALKING SURREPTITIOUSLY IN THE CORRIDOR...
SNAP
YOUR HANDS ACCIDENTALLY TOUCH...
SNAP
SNAP
GREAT!
SNAP
SNAP
SNAP
SNAP
YOU LOOK SO INNOCENT!
MOVE YOUR FACES CLOSER TOGETHER!
SNAP
SNAP
SNAP
I ALWAYS THOUGHT THIS MAN GOOFED AROUND TOO MUCH...
...BUT I NEVER REALIZED HE WAS SUCH A DIMWIT.

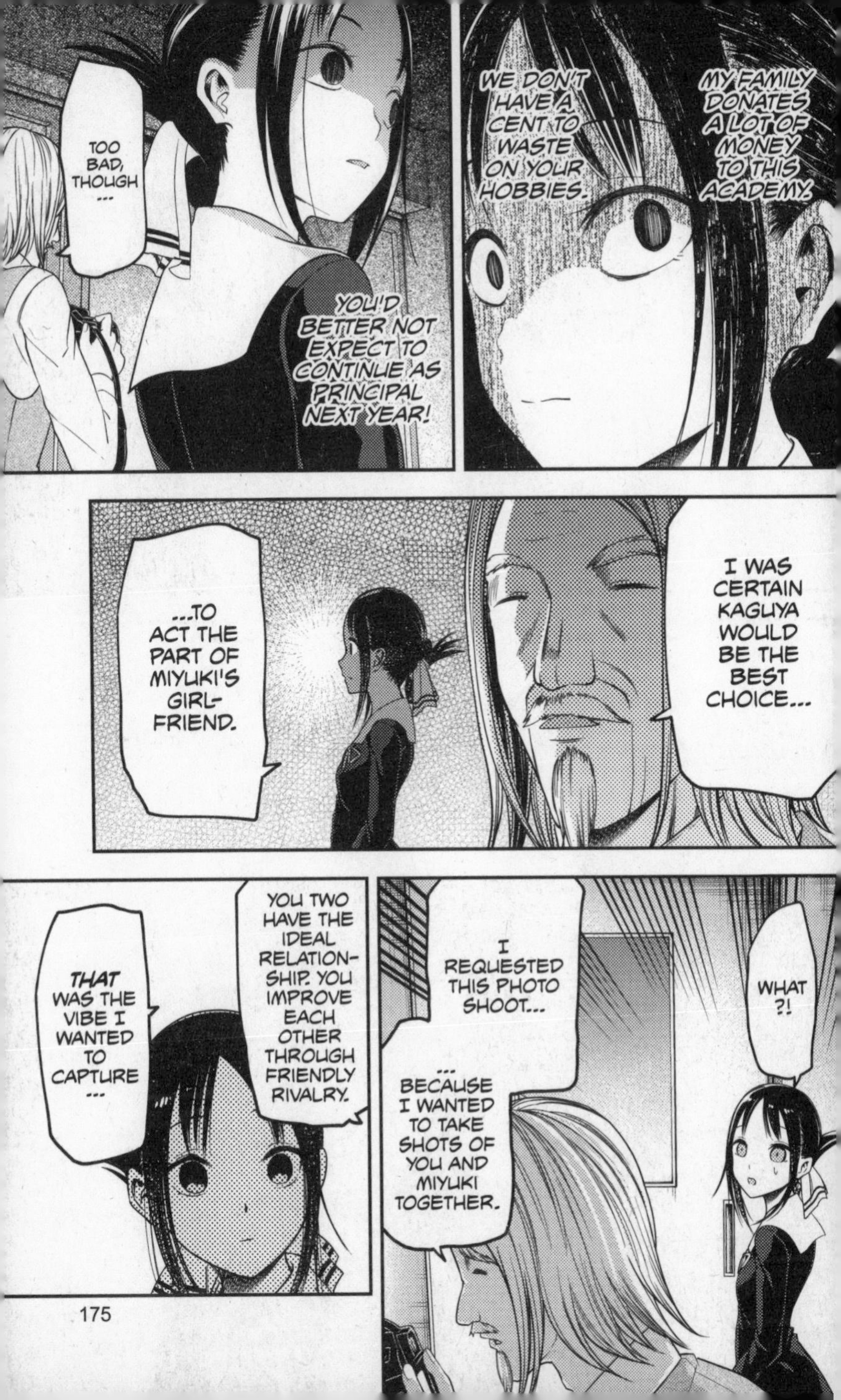
MY FAMILY DONATES A LOT OF MONEY TO THIS ACADEMY.
WE DON'T HAVE A CENT TO WASTE ON YOUR HOBBIES.
TOO BAD, THOUGH...
YOU'D BETTER NOT EXPECT TO CONTINUE AS PRINCIPAL NEXT YEAR!
I WAS CERTAIN KAGUYA WOULD BE THE BEST CHOICE...
...TO ACT THE PART OF MIYUKI'S GIRL-FRIEND.
WHAT?!
I REQUESTED THIS PHOTO SHOOT...
...BECAUSE I WANTED TO TAKE SHOTS OF YOU AND MIYUKI TOGETHER.
YOU TWO HAVE THE IDEAL RELATION-SHIP. YOU IMPROVE EACH OTHER THROUGH FRIENDLY RIVALRY.
THAT WAS THE VIBE I WANTED TO CAPTURE...

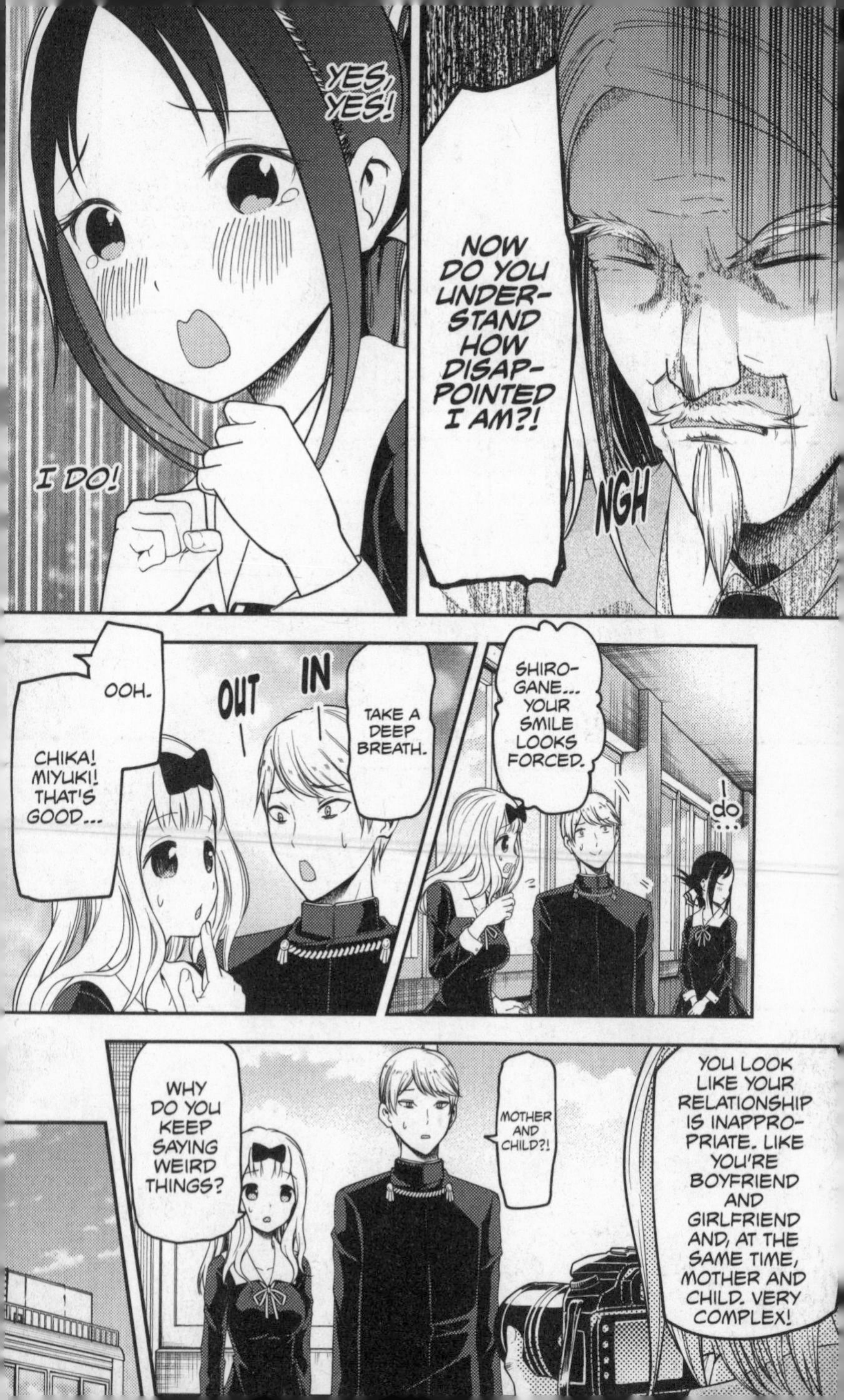
NOW DO YOU UNDER-STAND HOW DISAP-POINTED I AM?!
NGH
YES, YES!
I DO!
SHIRO-GANE... YOUR SMILE LOOKS FORCED.
I do...
TAKE A DEEP BREATH.
IN
OUT
OOH.
CHIKA! MIYUKI! THAT'S GOOD...
YOU LOOK LIKE YOUR RELATIONSHIP IS INAPPRO-PRIATE. LIKE YOU'RE BOYFRIEND AND GIRLFRIEND AND, AT THE SAME TIME, MOTHER AND CHILD. VERY COMPLEX!
MOTHER AND CHILD?!
WHY DO YOU KEEP SAYING WEIRD THINGS?

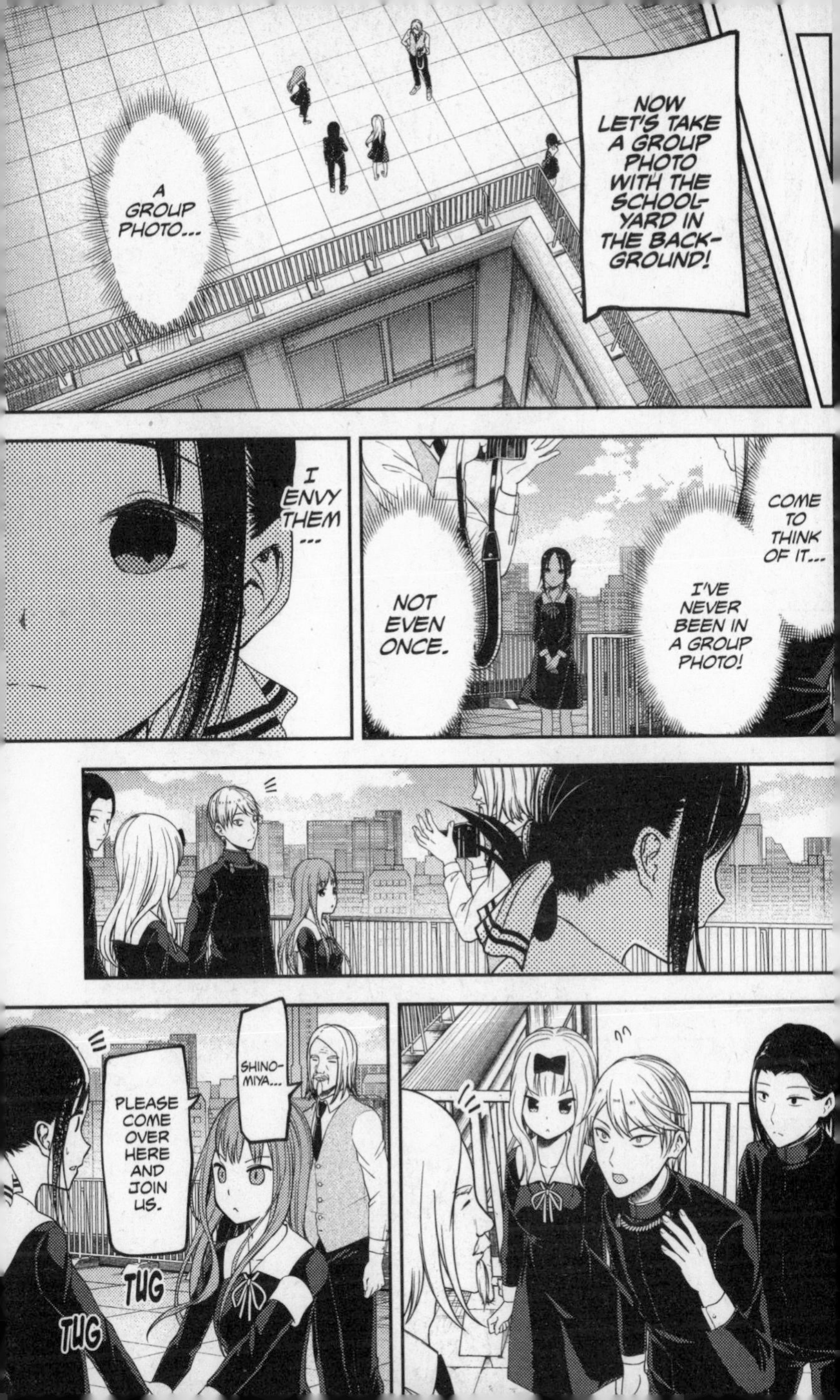
NOW LET'S TAKE A GROUP PHOTO WITH THE SCHOOLYARD IN THE BACKGROUND!
A GROUP PHOTO...
COME TO THINK OF IT...
I'VE NEVER BEEN IN A GROUP PHOTO!
NOT EVEN ONCE.
I ENVY THEM...
SHINOMIYA...
PLEASE COME OVER HERE AND JOIN US.
TUG
TUG

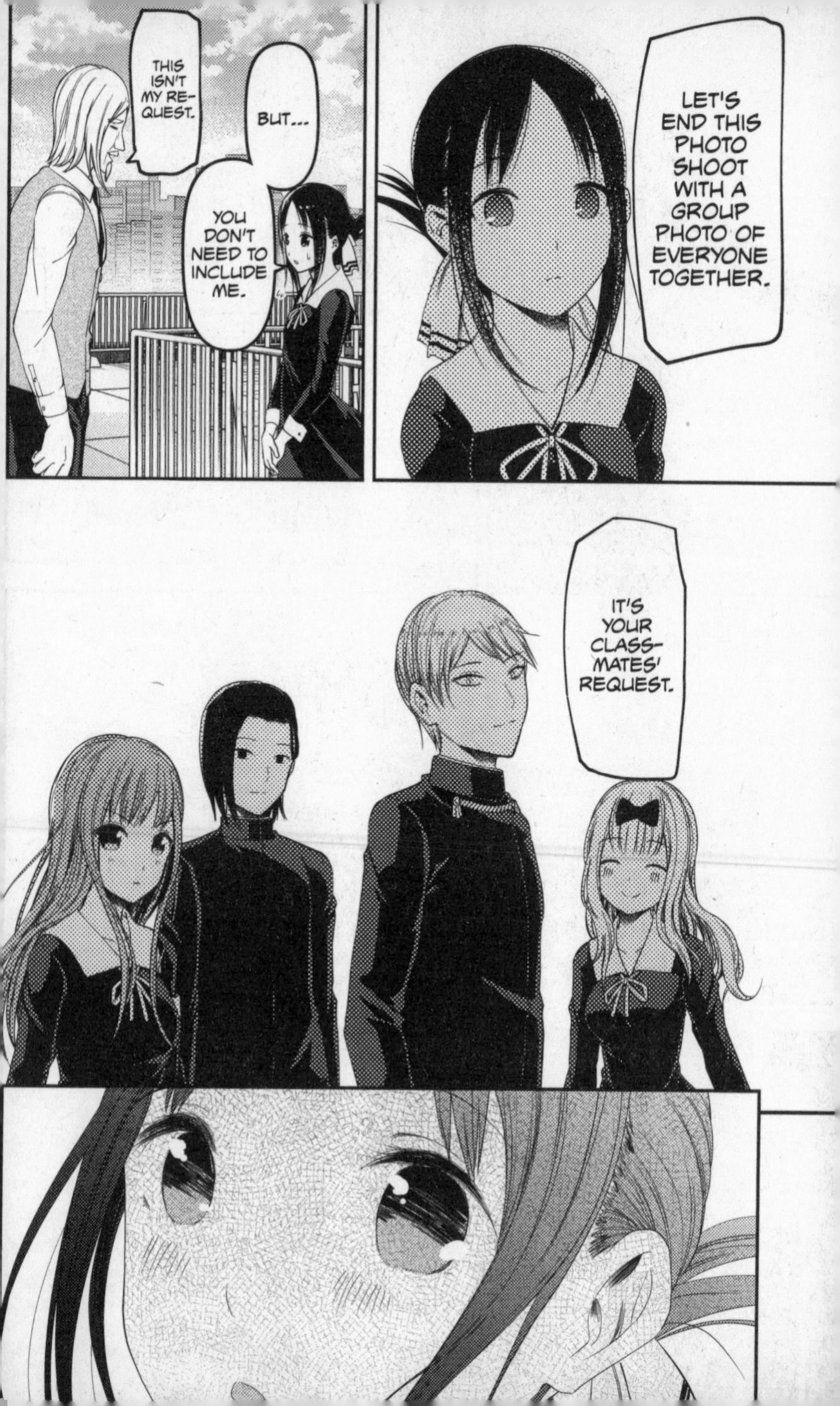
LET'S END THIS PHOTO SHOOT WITH A GROUP PHOTO OF EVERYONE TOGETHER.
BUT...
YOU DON'T NEED TO INCLUDE ME.
THIS ISN'T MY RE-QUEST.
IT'S YOUR CLASS-MATES' REQUEST.

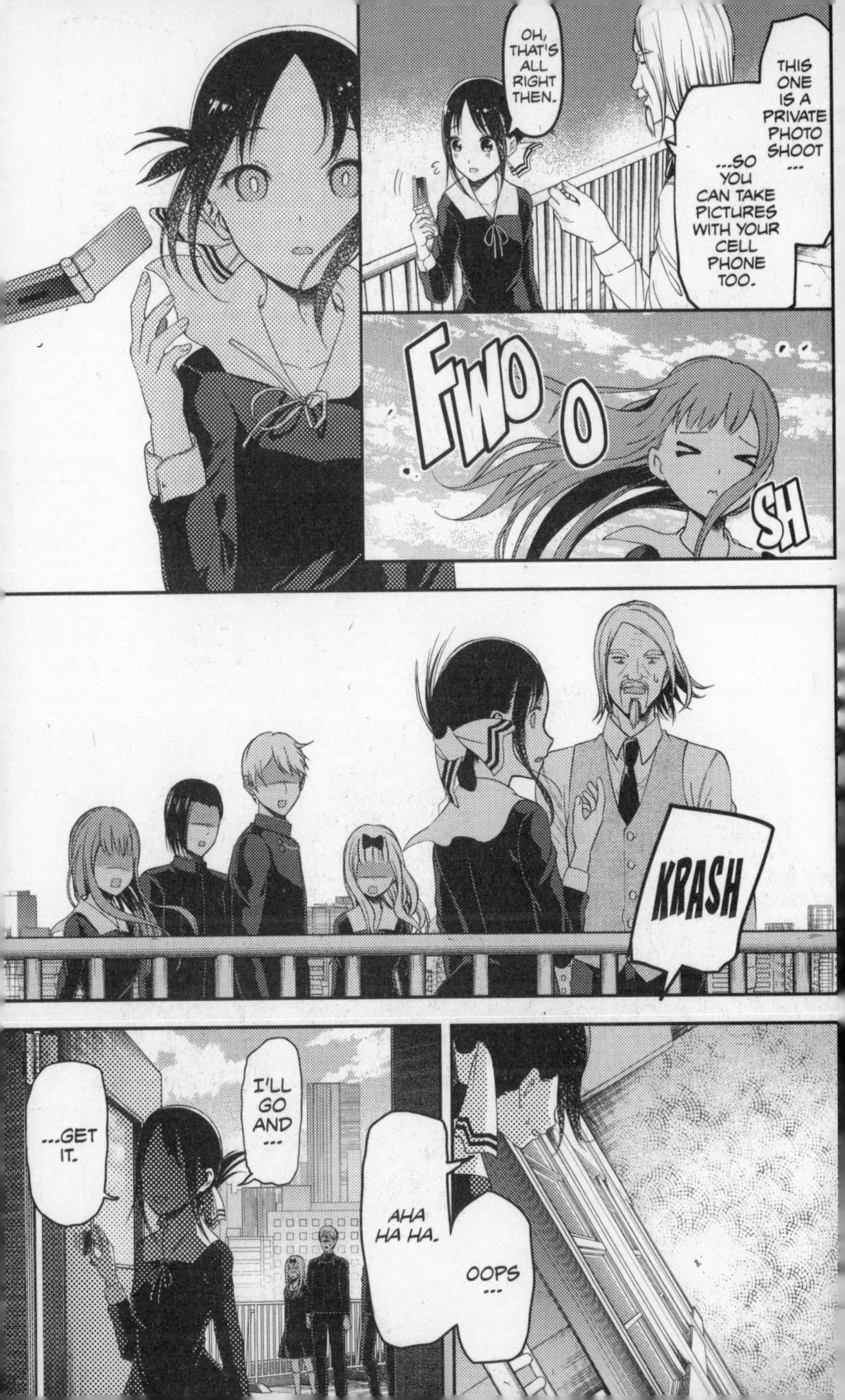
THIS ONE IS A PRIVATE PHOTO SHOOT...
...SO YOU CAN TAKE PICTURES WITH YOUR CELL PHONE TOO.
OH, THAT'S ALL RIGHT THEN.
FWOO
SH
KRASH
AHA HA HA.
OOPS...
I'LL GO AND...
...GET IT.

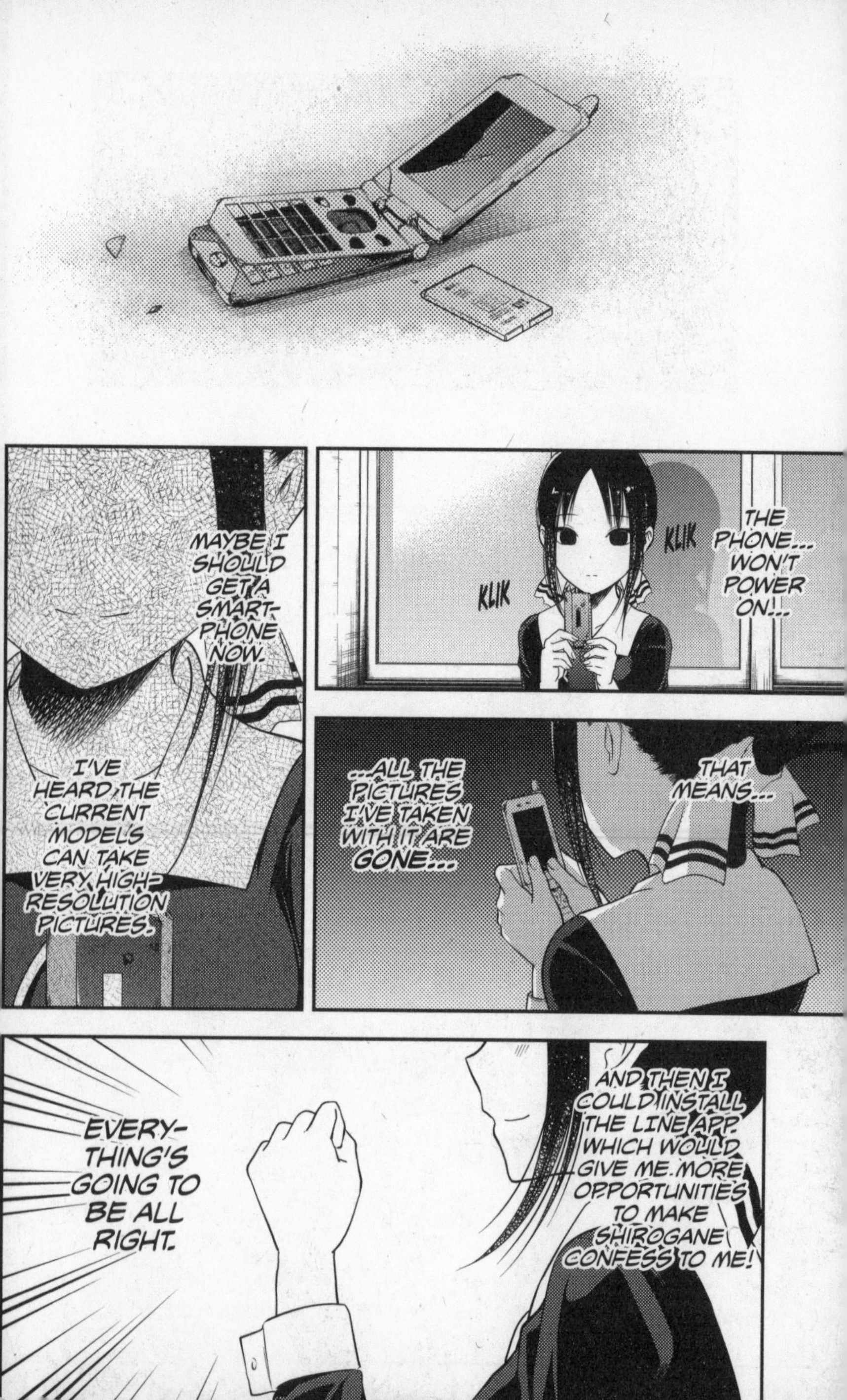
THE PHONE... WON'T POWER ON...
KLIK
KLIK
THAT MEANS...
...ALL THE PICTURES I'VE TAKEN WITH IT ARE GONE...
MAYBE I SHOULD GET A SMART-PHONE NOW.
I'VE HEARD THE CURRENT MODELS CAN TAKE VERY HIGH-RESOLUTION PICTURES.
AND THEN I COULD INSTALL THE LINE APP WHICH WOULD GIVE ME MORE OPPORTUNITIES TO MAKE SHIROGANE CONFESS TO ME!
EVERY-THING'S GOING TO BE ALL RIGHT.

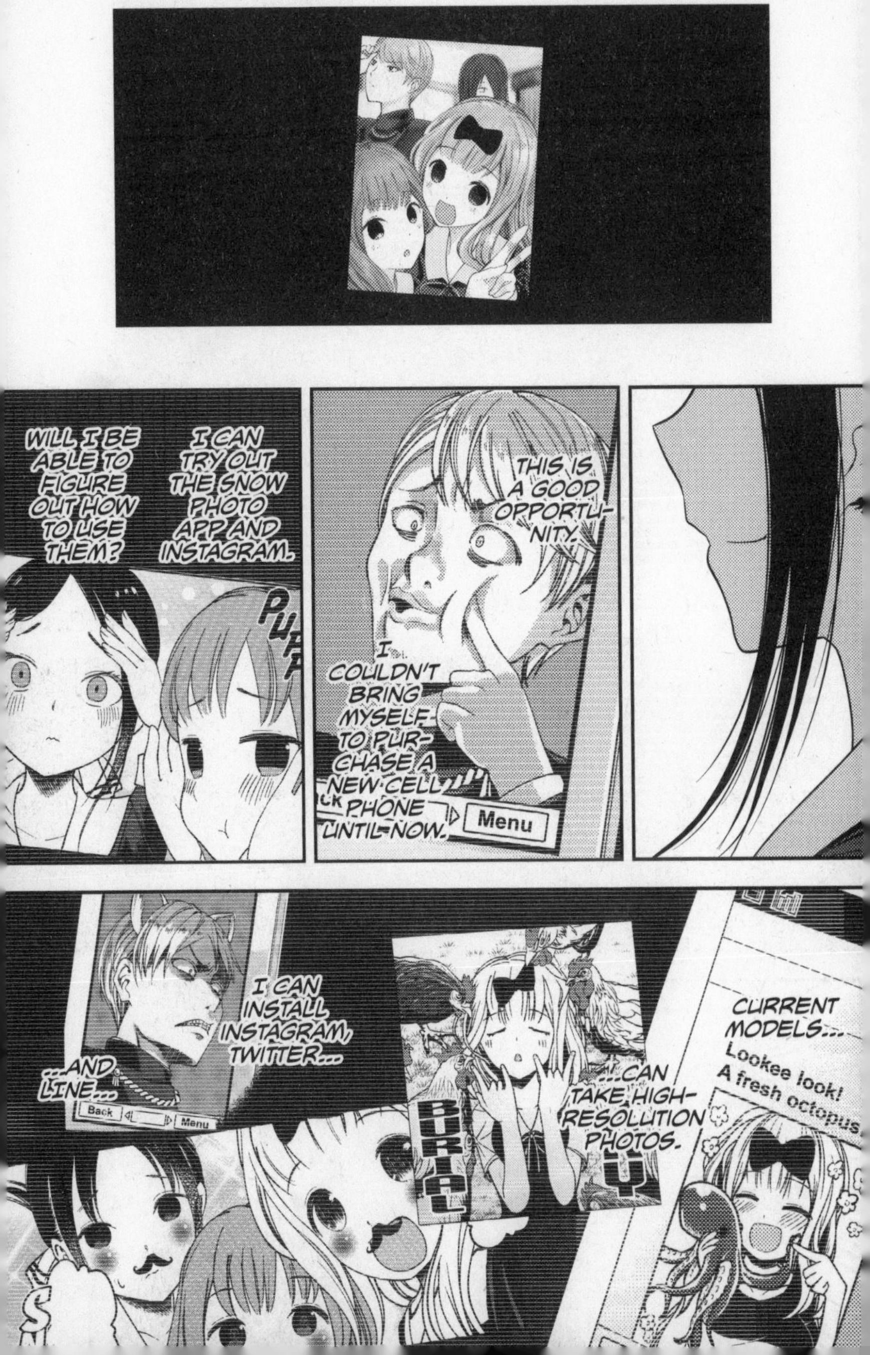
THIS IS A GOOD OPPORTUNITY.
I COULDN'T BRING MYSELF TO PURCHASE A NEW CELL PHONE UNTIL NOW.
Menu
I CAN TRY OUT THE SNOW PHOTO APP AND INSTAGRAM.
WILL I BE ABLE TO FIGURE OUT HOW TO USE THEM?
CURRENT MODELS...
Lookee look!
A fresh octopus.
...CAN TAKE HIGH-RESOLUTION PHOTOS.
I CAN INSTALL INSTAGRAM, TWITTER...
...AND LINE...
Back
Menu

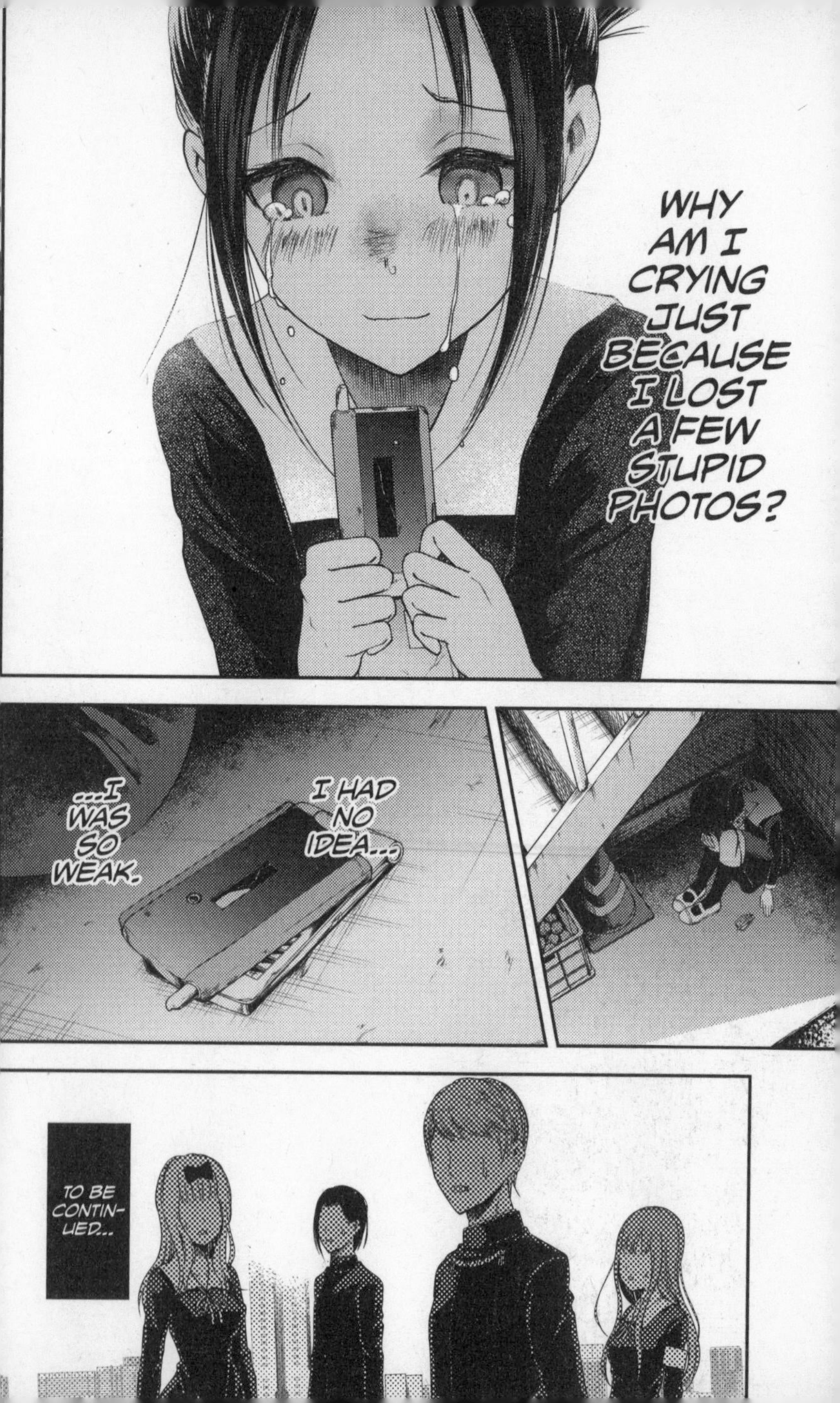
WHY AM I CRYING JUST BECAUSE I LOST A FEW STUPID PHOTOS?
I HAD NO IDEA...
...I WAS SO WEAK.
TO BE CONTIN-UED...

KAGUYA-SAMA

LOVE IS WAR

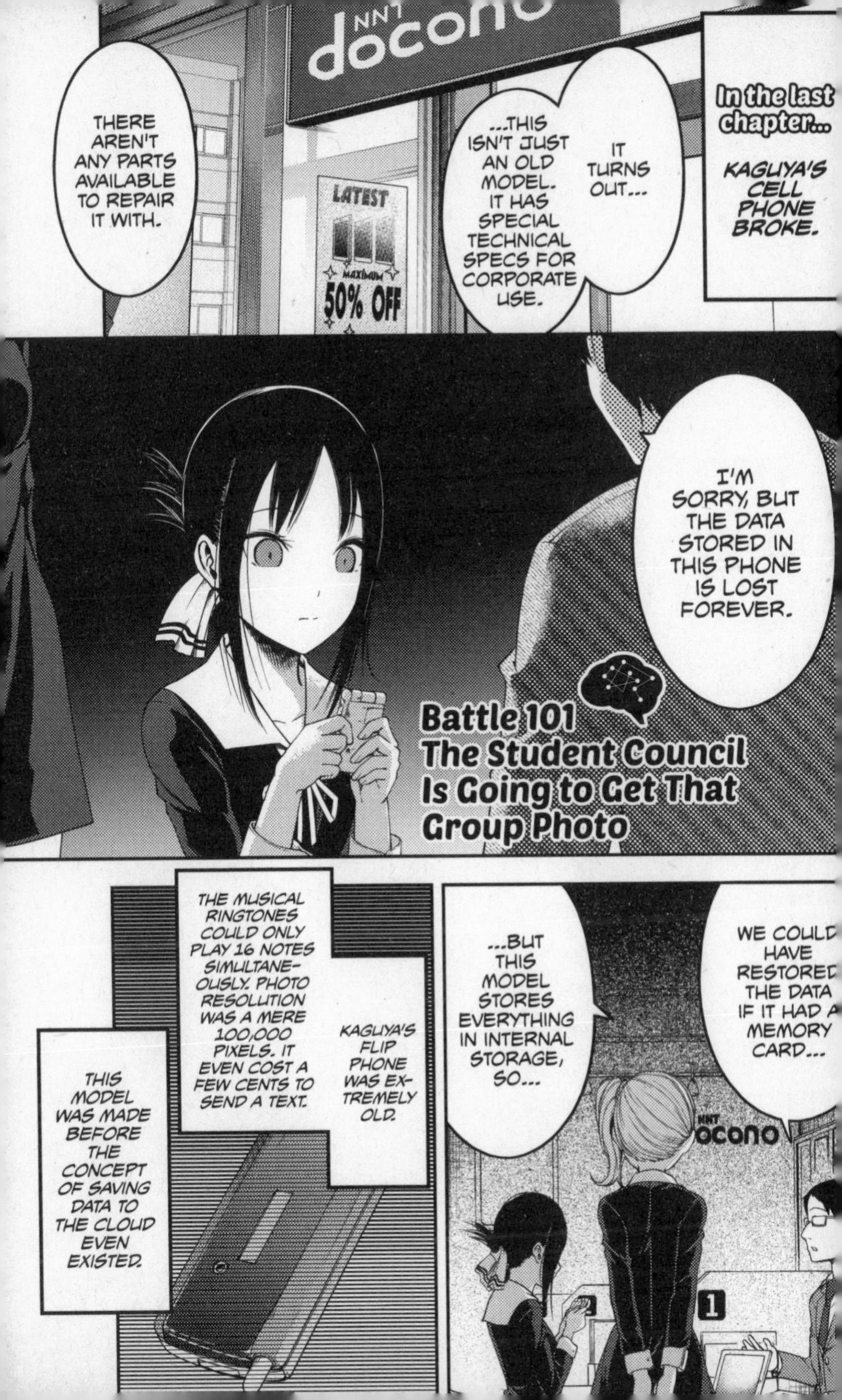
In the last chapter...
KAGUYA'S CELL PHONE BROKE.
IT TURNS OUT...
...THIS ISN'T JUST AN OLD MODEL. IT HAS SPECIAL TECHNICAL SPECS FOR CORPORATE USE.
LATEST
MAXIMUM
50% OFF
THERE AREN'T ANY PARTS AVAILABLE TO REPAIR IT WITH.
I'M SORRY, BUT THE DATA STORED IN THIS PHONE IS LOST FOREVER.
Battle 101
The Student Council Is Going to Get That Group Photo
WE COULD HAVE RESTORED THE DATA IF IT HAD A MEMORY CARD...
...BUT THIS MODEL STORES EVERYTHING IN INTERNAL STORAGE, SO...
KAGUYA'S FLIP PHONE WAS EXTREMELY OLD.
THE MUSICAL RINGTONES COULD ONLY PLAY 16 NOTES SIMULTANEOUSLY. PHOTO RESOLUTION WAS A MERE 100,000 PIXELS. IT EVEN COST A FEW CENTS TO SEND A TEXT.
THIS MODEL WAS MADE BEFORE THE CONCEPT OF SAVING DATA TO THE CLOUD EVEN EXISTED.

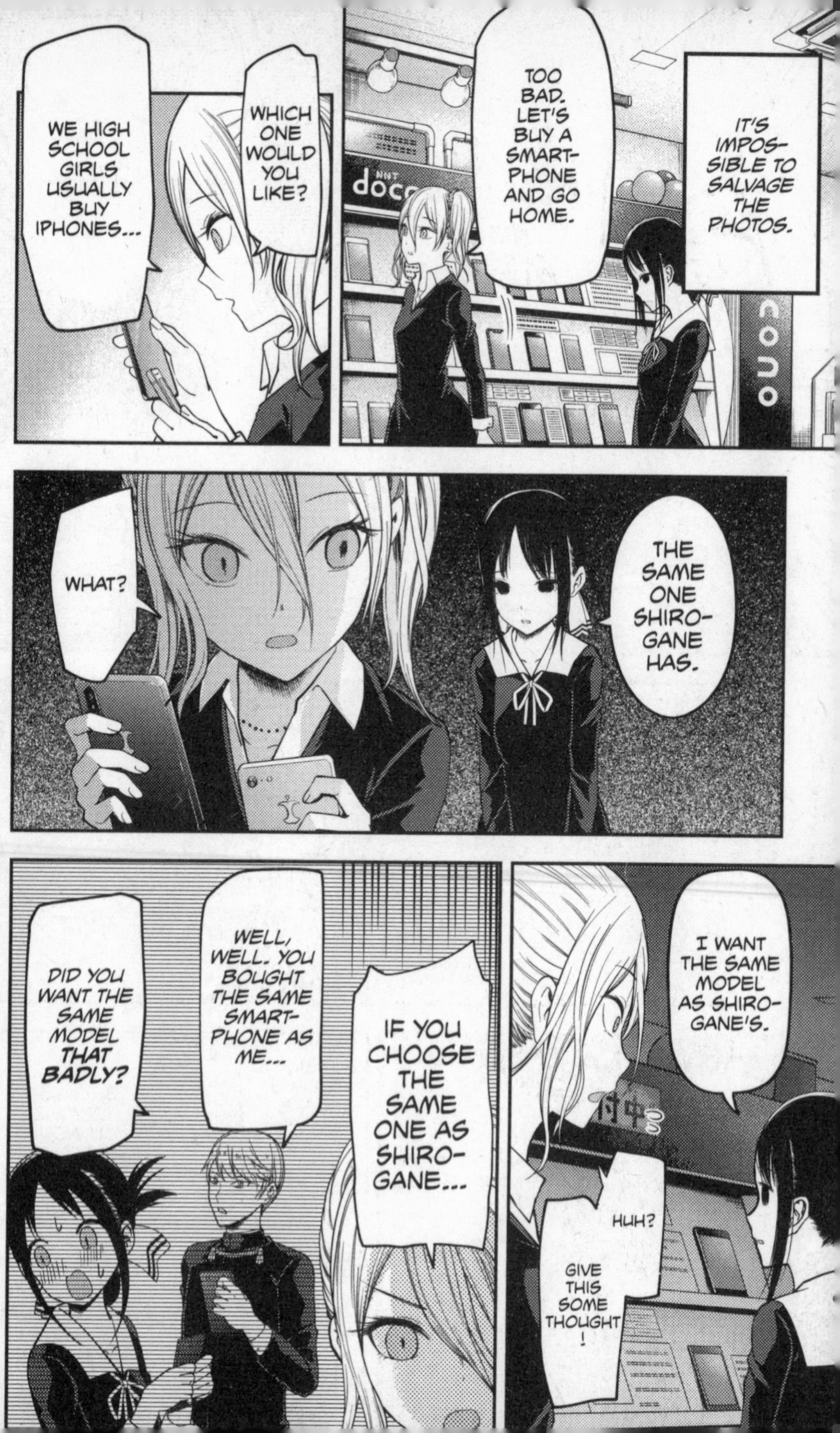
IT'S IMPOSSIBLE TO SALVAGE THE PHOTOS.
TOO BAD. LET'S BUY A SMARTPHONE AND GO HOME.
WHICH ONE WOULD YOU LIKE?
WE HIGH SCHOOL GIRLS USUALLY BUY IPHONES...
THE SAME ONE SHIROGANE HAS.
WHAT?
I WANT THE SAME MODEL AS SHIROGANE'S.
HUH?
GIVE THIS SOME THOUGHT!
IF YOU CHOOSE THE SAME ONE AS SHIROGANE...
WELL, WELL. YOU BOUGHT THE SAME SMARTPHONE AS ME...
DID YOU WANT THE SAME MODEL THAT BADLY?

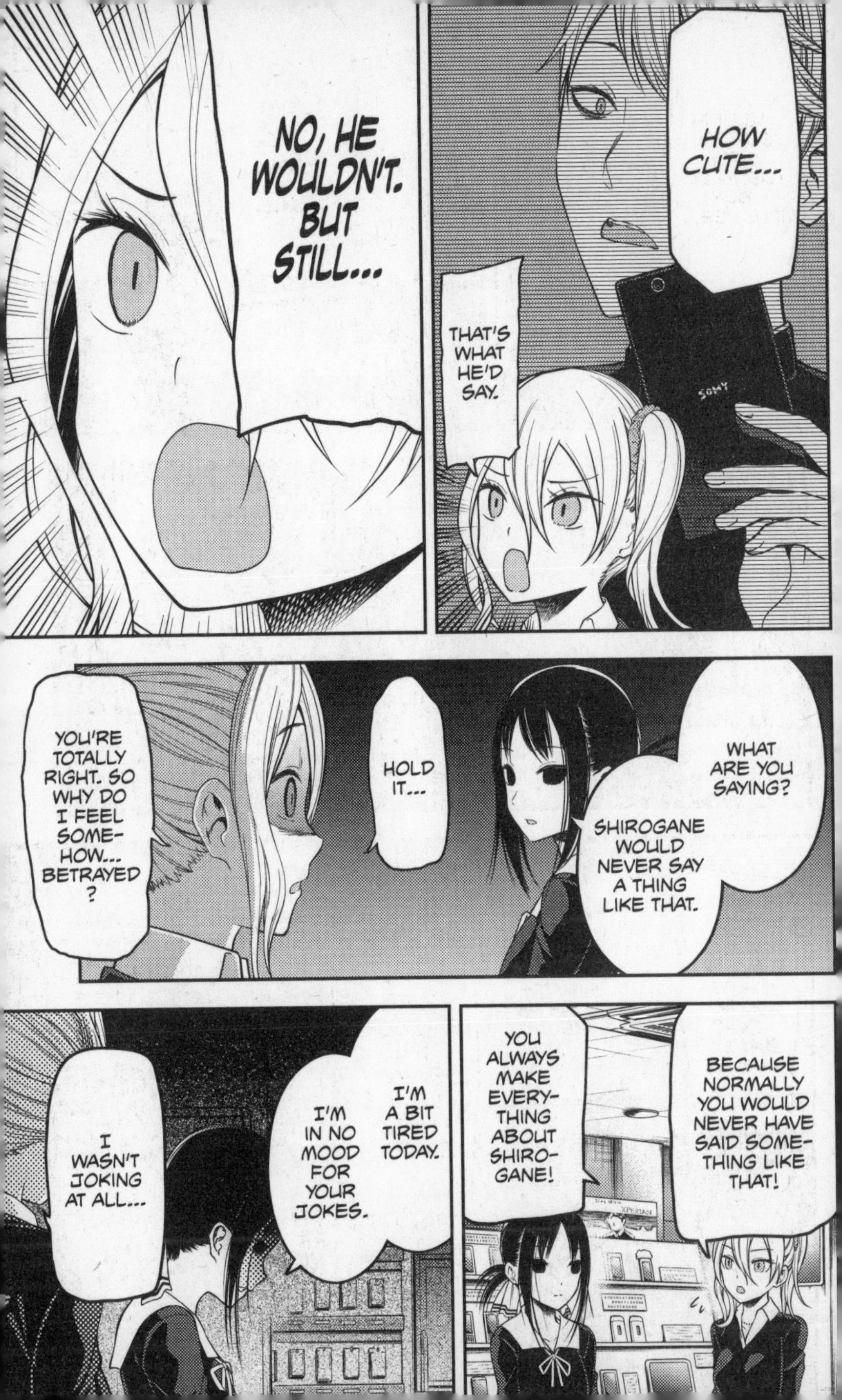
HOW CUTE...
THAT'S WHAT HE'D SAY.
NO, HE WOULDN'T. BUT STILL...
WHAT ARE YOU SAYING?
SHIROGANE WOULD NEVER SAY A THING LIKE THAT.
HOLD IT...
YOU'RE TOTALLY RIGHT. SO WHY DO I FEEL SOME-HOW... BETRAYED?
BECAUSE NORMALLY YOU WOULD NEVER HAVE SAID SOME-THING LIKE THAT!
YOU ALWAYS MAKE EVERY-THING ABOUT SHIRO-GANE!
I'M A BIT TIRED TODAY.
I'M IN NO MOOD FOR YOUR JOKES.
I WASN'T JOKING AT ALL...

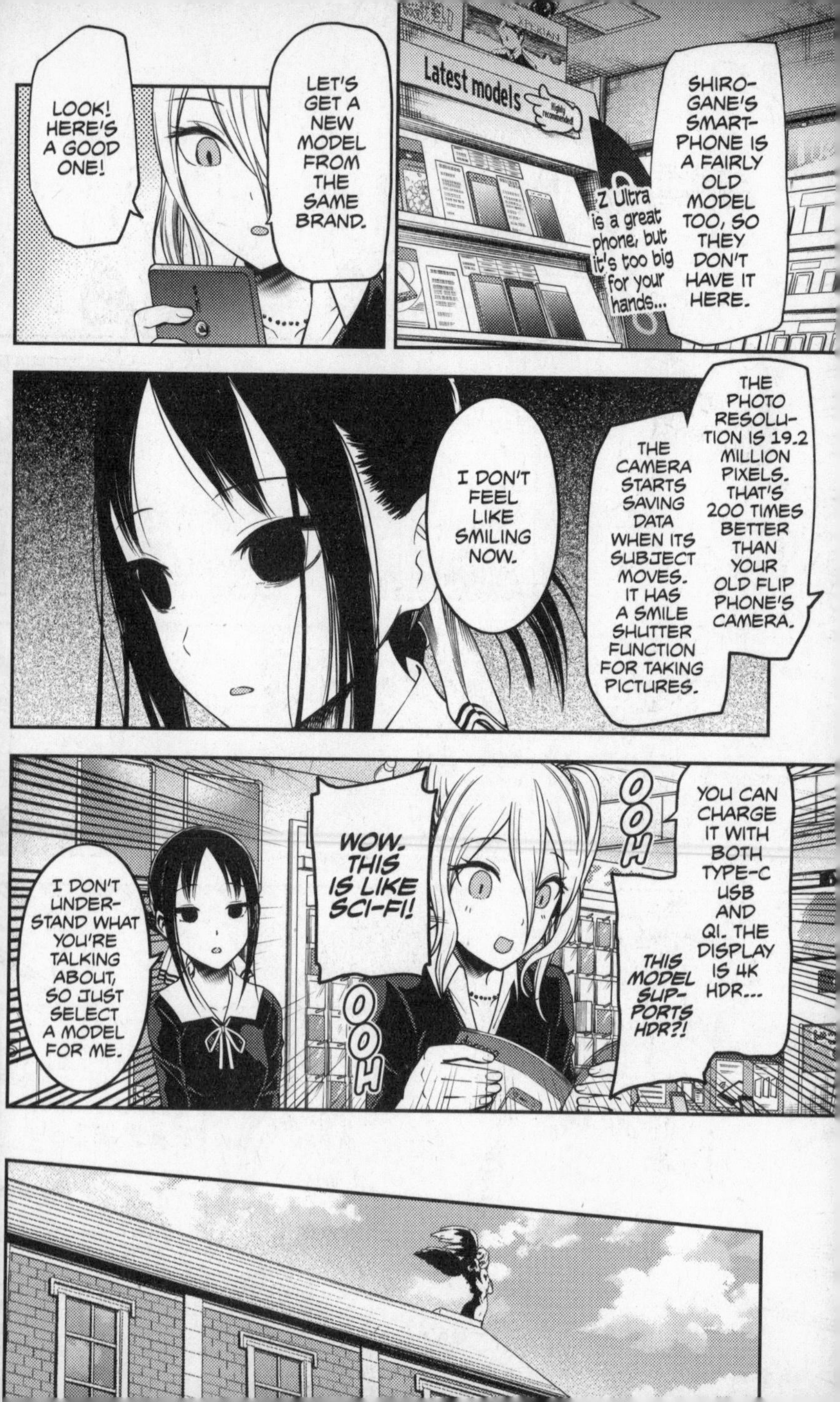
Latest models
Highly recommended!
SHIRO-GANE'S SMART-PHONE IS A FAIRLY OLD MODEL TOO, SO THEY DON'T HAVE IT HERE.
Z Ultra is a great phone, but it's too big for your hands...
LET'S GET A NEW MODEL FROM THE SAME BRAND.
LOOK! HERE'S A GOOD ONE!
THE PHOTO RESOLU-TION IS 19.2 MILLION PIXELS. THAT'S 200 TIMES BETTER THAN YOUR OLD FLIP PHONE'S CAMERA.
THE CAMERA STARTS SAVING DATA WHEN ITS SUBJECT MOVES. IT HAS A SMILE SHUTTER FUNCTION FOR TAKING PICTURES.
I DON'T FEEL LIKE SMILING NOW.
YOU CAN CHARGE IT WITH BOTH TYPE-C USB AND QI. THE DISPLAY IS 4K HDR...
THIS MODEL SUP-PORTS HDR?!
OOOH
WOW. THIS IS LIKE SCI-FI!
OOOH
I DON'T UNDER-STAND WHAT YOU'RE TALKING ABOUT, SO JUST SELECT A MODEL FOR ME.

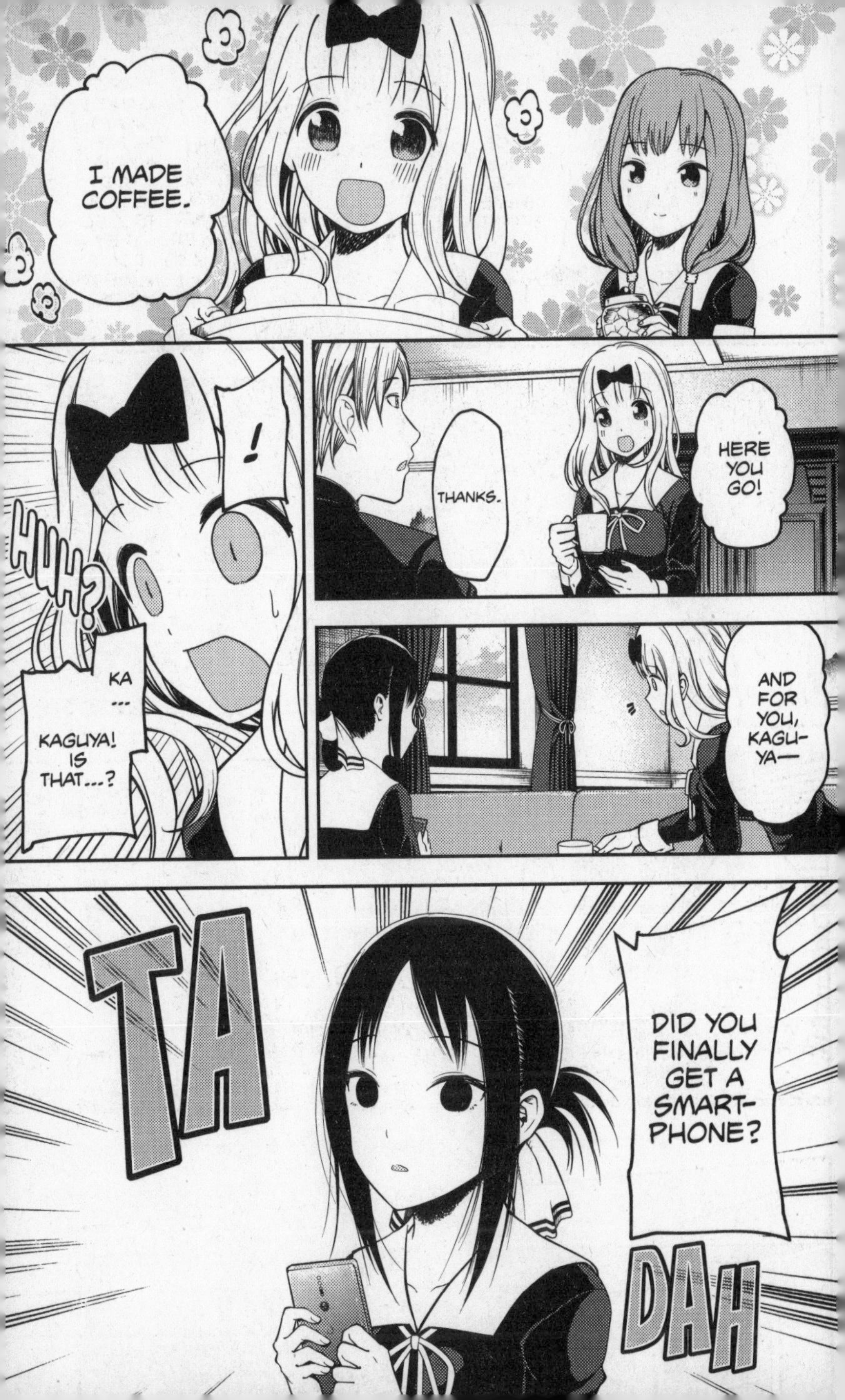
I MADE COFFEE.
HERE YOU GO!
THANKS.
AND FOR YOU, KAGU-YA—
!
HUH?
KA... KAGUYA! IS THAT...?
DID YOU FINALLY GET A SMART-PHONE?
TA
DAH

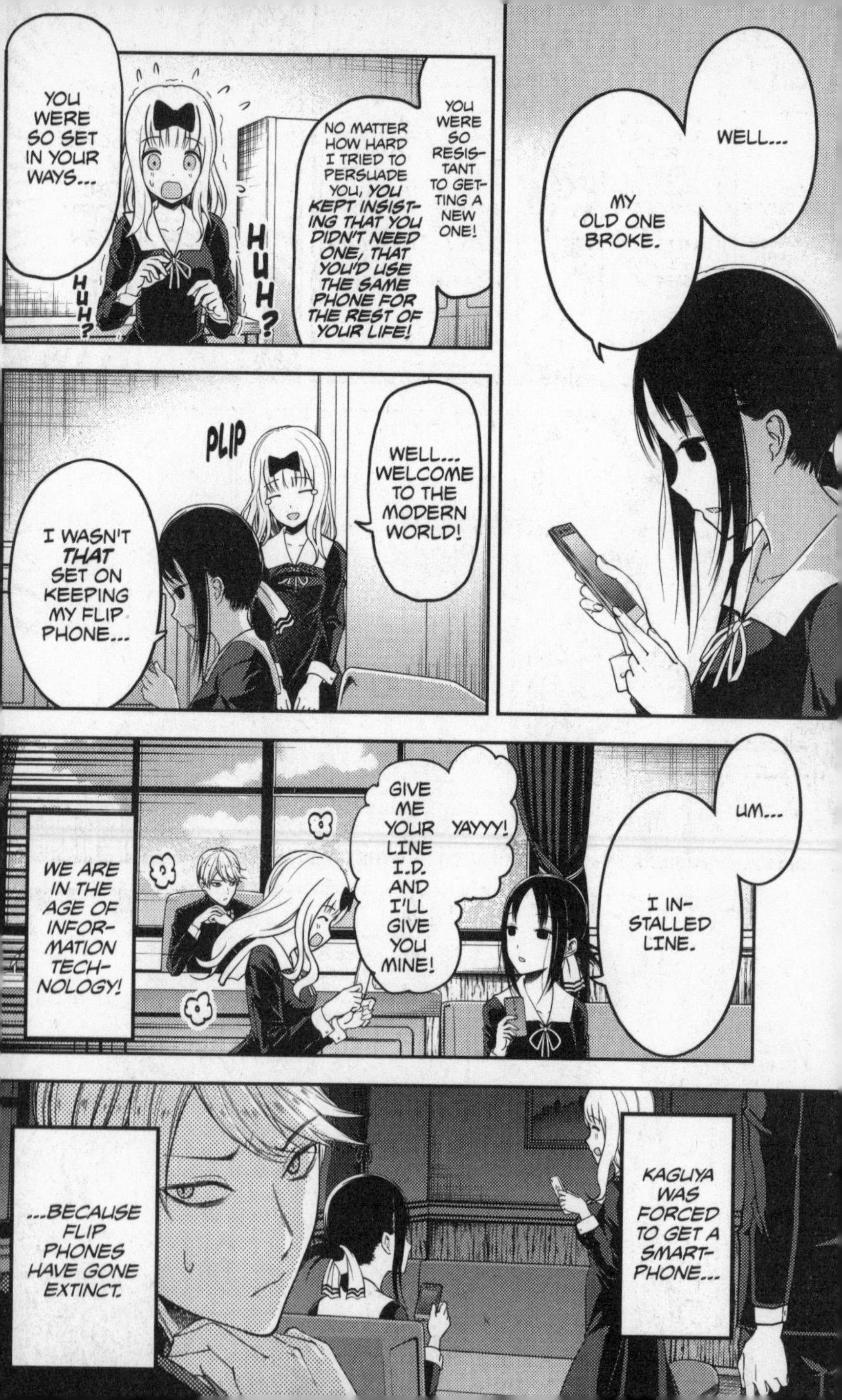
WELL...
MY OLD ONE BROKE.
YOU WERE SO RESISTANT TO GETTING A NEW ONE!
NO MATTER HOW HARD I TRIED TO PERSUADE YOU, YOU KEPT INSISTING THAT YOU DIDN'T NEED ONE, THAT YOU'D USE THE SAME PHONE FOR THE REST OF YOUR LIFE!
HUH?
HUH?
YOU WERE SO SET IN YOUR WAYS...
WELL... WELCOME TO THE MODERN WORLD!
PLIP
I WASN'T THAT SET ON KEEPING MY FLIP PHONE...
UM...
I INSTALLED LINE.
YAYYY!
GIVE ME YOUR LINE I.D. AND I'LL GIVE YOU MINE!
WE ARE IN THE AGE OF INFORMATION TECHNOLOGY!
KAGUYA WAS FORCED TO GET A SMARTPHONE...
...BECAUSE FLIP PHONES HAVE GONE EXTINCT.

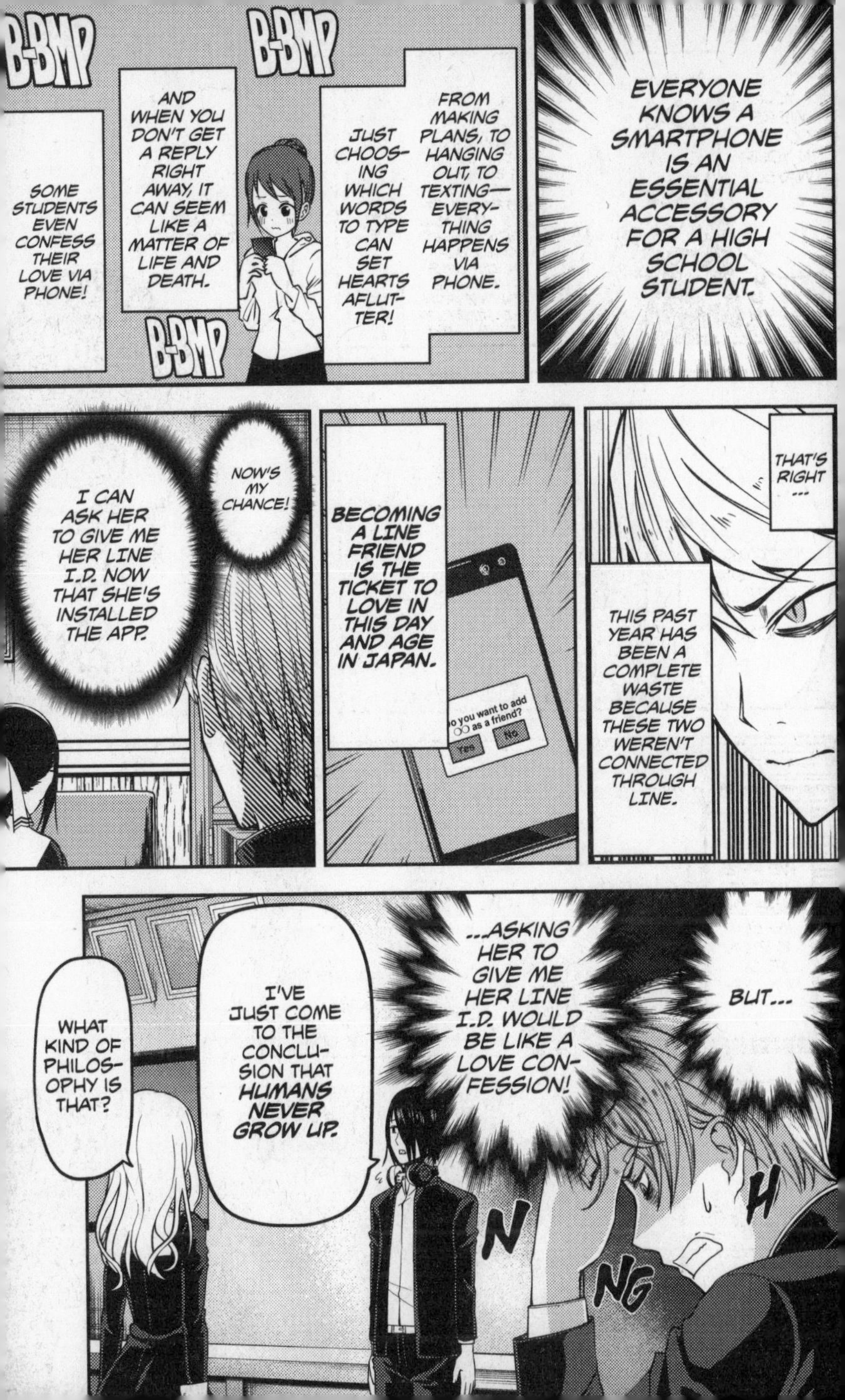

EVERYONE KNOWS A SMARTPHONE IS AN ESSENTIAL ACCESSORY FOR A HIGH SCHOOL STUDENT.
B-BMP
FROM MAKING PLANS, TO HANGING OUT, TO TEXTING—EVERYTHING HAPPENS VIA PHONE.
JUST CHOOSING WHICH WORDS TO TYPE CAN SET HEARTS AFLUTTER!
AND WHEN YOU DON'T GET A REPLY RIGHT AWAY, IT CAN SEEM LIKE A MATTER OF LIFE AND DEATH.
B-BMP
SOME STUDENTS EVEN CONFESS THEIR LOVE VIA PHONE!
B-BMP
THAT'S RIGHT...
THIS PAST YEAR HAS BEEN A COMPLETE WASTE BECAUSE THESE TWO WEREN'T CONNECTED THROUGH LINE.
BECOMING A LINE FRIEND IS THE TICKET TO LOVE IN THIS DAY AND AGE IN JAPAN.
o you want to add ○○ as a friend?
Yes
No
NOW'S MY CHANCE!
I CAN ASK HER TO GIVE ME HER LINE I.D. NOW THAT SHE'S INSTALLED THE APP.
BUT...
...ASKING HER TO GIVE ME HER LINE I.D. WOULD BE LIKE A LOVE CONFESSION!
H
NNG
I'VE JUST COME TO THE CONCLUSION THAT HUMANS NEVER GROW UP.
WHAT KIND OF PHILOSOPHY IS THAT?

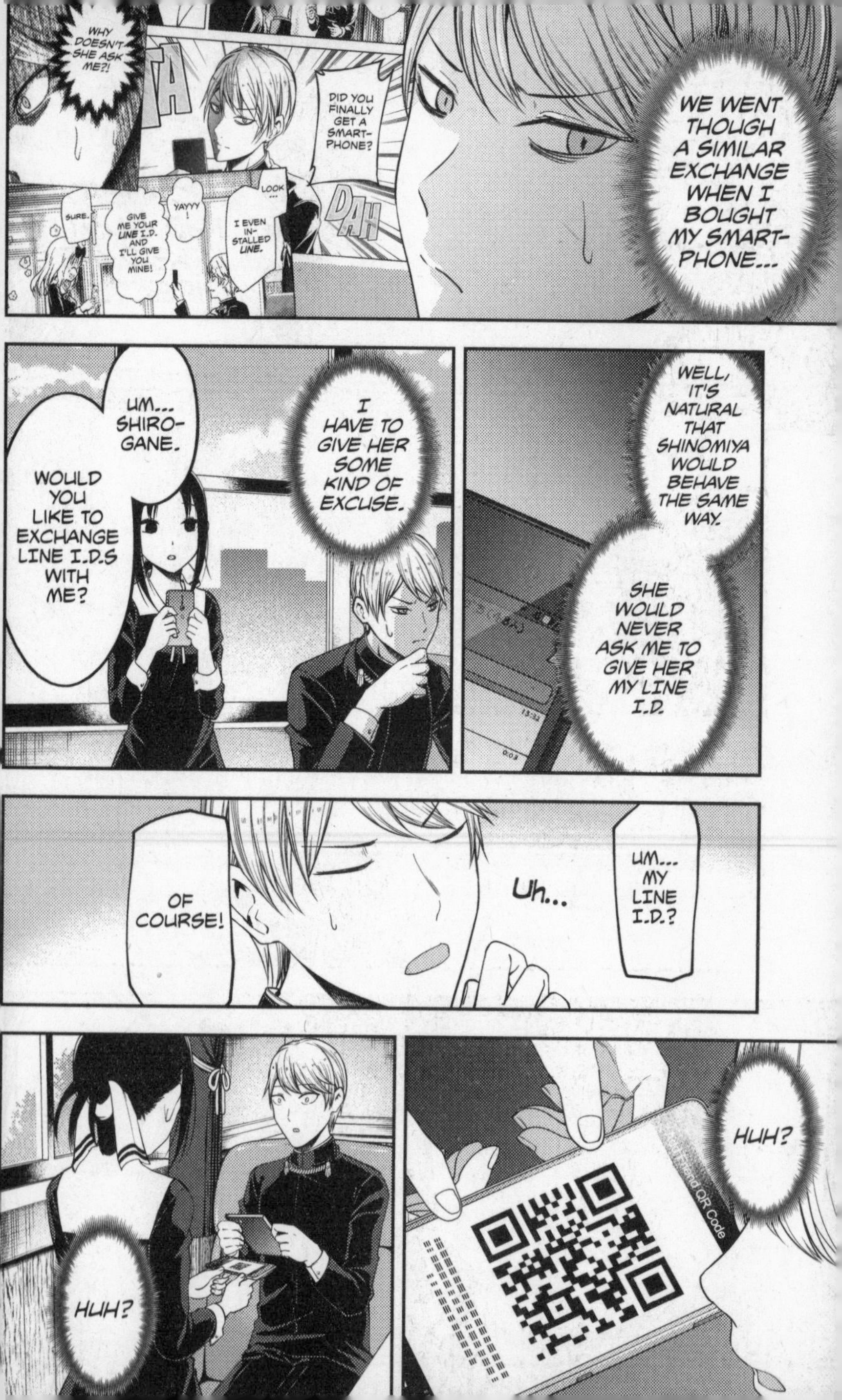
WE WENT THOUGH A SIMILAR EXCHANGE WHEN I BOUGHT MY SMART-PHONE...
DID YOU FINALLY GET A SMART-PHONE?
TA
DAH
LOOK...
I EVEN IN-STALLED LINE.
WHY DOESN'T SHE ASK ME?!
YAYYY!
GIVE ME YOUR LINE I.D. AND I'LL GIVE YOU MINE!
SURE.
WELL, IT'S NATURAL THAT SHINOMIYA WOULD BEHAVE THE SAME WAY.
SHE WOULD NEVER ASK ME TO GIVE HER MY LINE I.D.
I HAVE TO GIVE HER SOME KIND OF EXCUSE.
UM... SHIRO-GANE.
WOULD YOU LIKE TO EXCHANGE LINE I.D.S WITH ME?
UM... MY LINE I.D.?
Uh...
OF COURSE!
HUH?
QR Code
HUH?

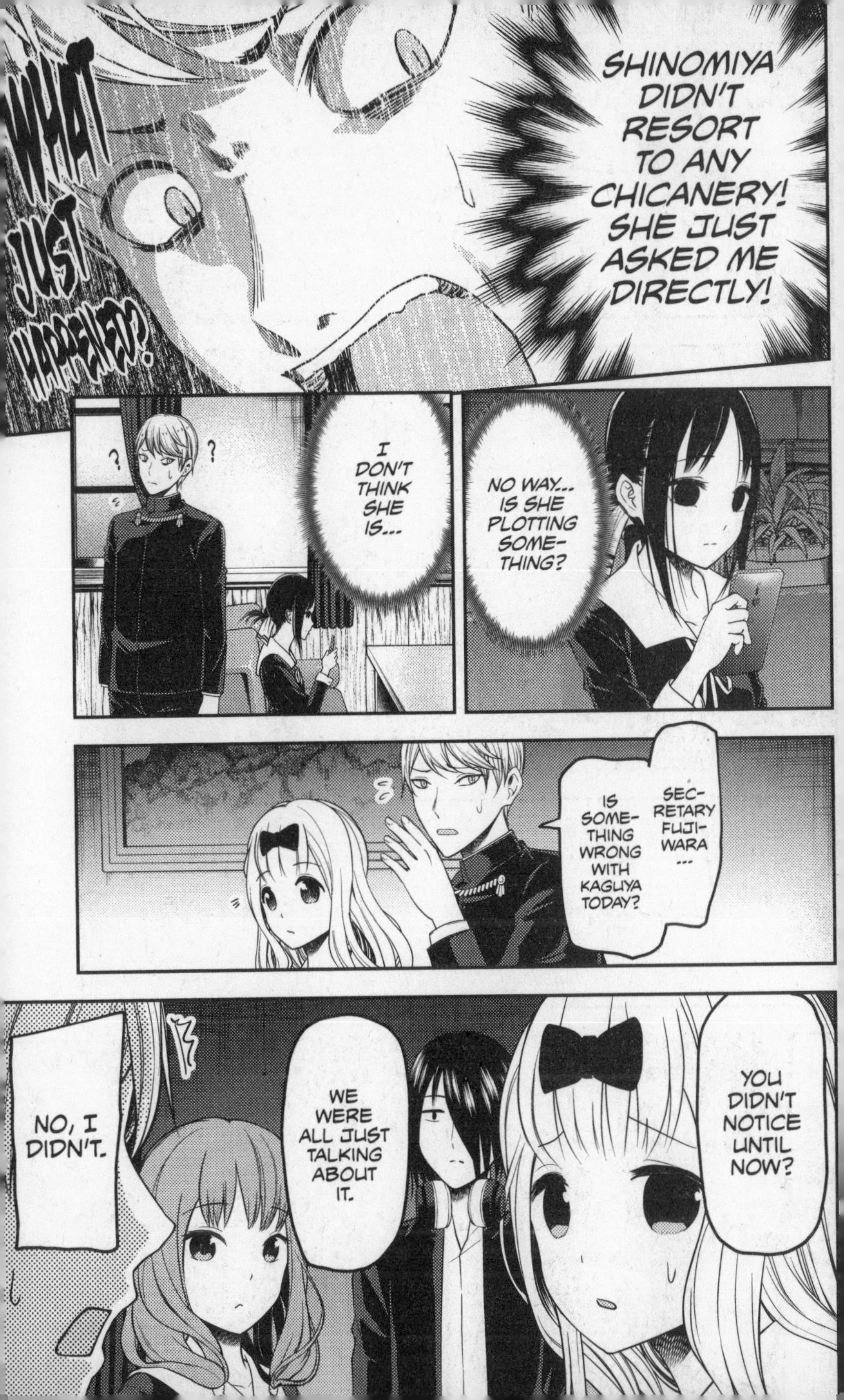
SHINOMIYA DIDN'T RESORT TO ANY CHICANERY! SHE JUST ASKED ME DIRECTLY!
WHAT JUST HAPPENED?!
NO WAY... IS SHE PLOTTING SOME-THING?
I DON'T THINK SHE IS...
SEC-RETARY FUJI-WARA...
IS SOME-THING WRONG WITH KAGUYA TODAY?
YOU DIDN'T NOTICE UNTIL NOW?
WE WERE ALL JUST TALKING ABOUT IT.
NO, I DIDN'T.

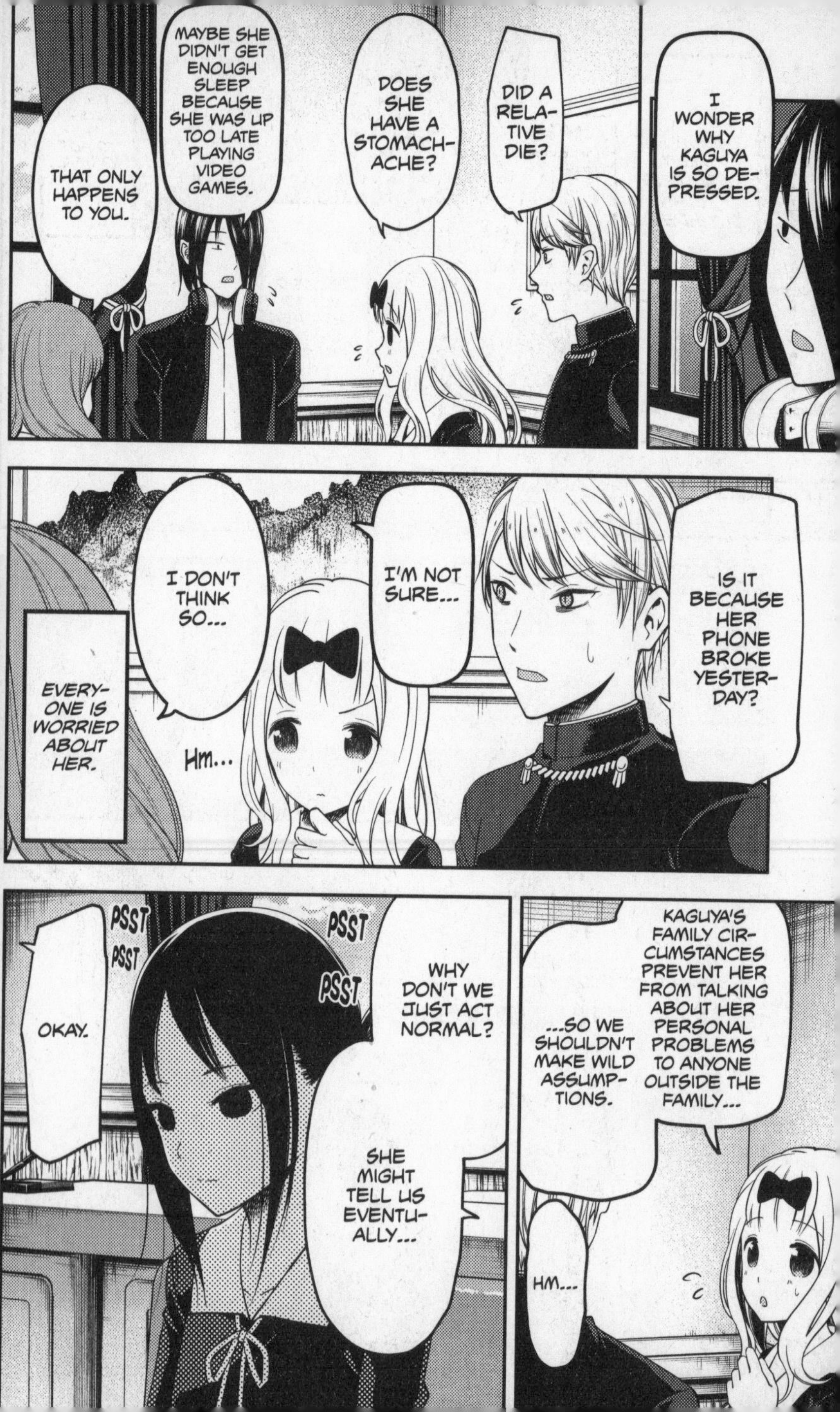

I WONDER WHY KAGUYA IS SO DEPRESSED.
DID A RELATIVE DIE?
DOES SHE HAVE A STOMACHACHE?
MAYBE SHE DIDN'T GET ENOUGH SLEEP BECAUSE SHE WAS UP TOO LATE PLAYING VIDEO GAMES.
THAT ONLY HAPPENS TO YOU.
IS IT BECAUSE HER PHONE BROKE YESTERDAY?
I'M NOT SURE...
I DON'T THINK SO...
Hm...
EVERYONE IS WORRIED ABOUT HER.
KAGUYA'S FAMILY CIRCUMSTANCES PREVENT HER FROM TALKING ABOUT HER PERSONAL PROBLEMS TO ANYONE OUTSIDE THE FAMILY...
...SO WE SHOULDN'T MAKE WILD ASSUMPTIONS.
HM...
WHY DON'T WE JUST ACT NORMAL?
SHE MIGHT TELL US EVENTUALLY...
PSST
PSST
PSST
PSST
OKAY.

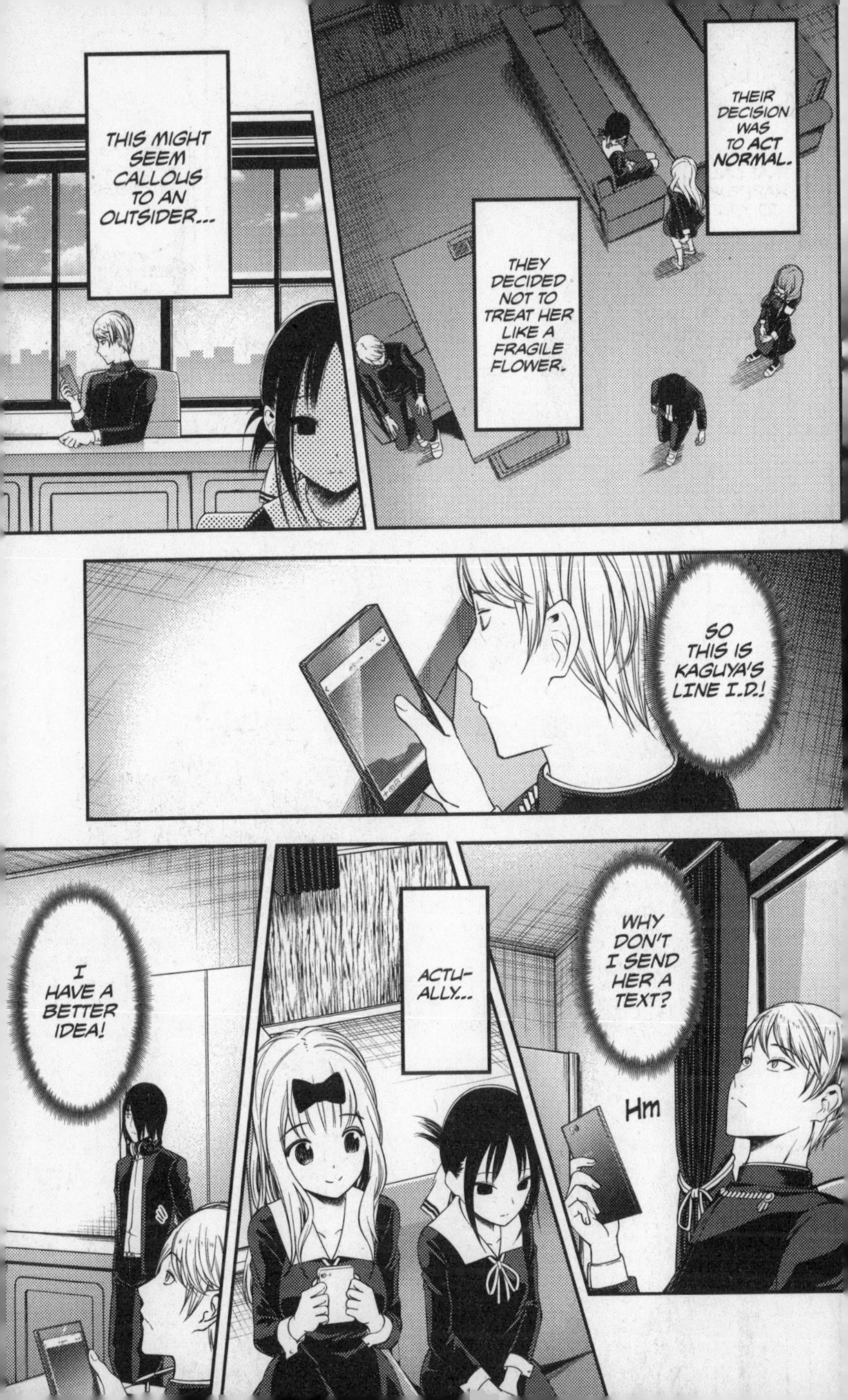
THEIR DECISION WAS TO ACT NORMAL.
THEY DECIDED NOT TO TREAT HER LIKE A FRAGILE FLOWER.
THIS MIGHT SEEM CALLOUS TO AN OUTSIDER...
SO THIS IS KAGUYA'S LINE I.D.!
WHY DON'T I SEND HER A TEXT?
Hm
ACTU-ALLY...
I HAVE A BETTER IDEA!

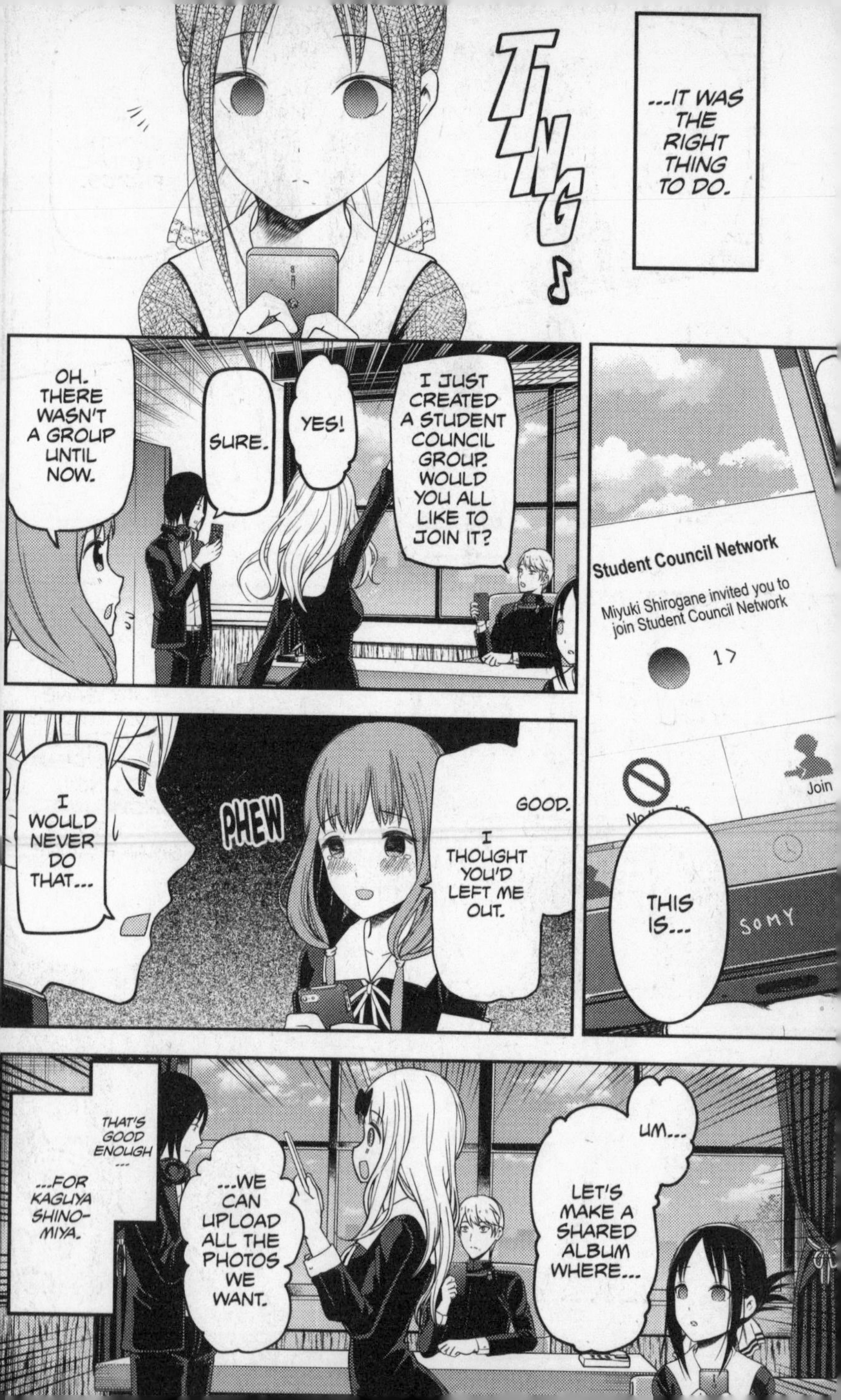
...IT WAS THE RIGHT THING TO DO.
TING
Student Council Network
Miyuki Shirogane invited you to join Student Council Network
1>
Join
THIS IS...
SOMY
I JUST CREATED A STUDENT COUNCIL GROUP. WOULD YOU ALL LIKE TO JOIN IT?
YES!
SURE.
OH. THERE WASN'T A GROUP UNTIL NOW.
GOOD. I THOUGHT YOU'D LEFT ME OUT.
PHEW
I WOULD NEVER DO THAT...
UM...
LET'S MAKE A SHARED ALBUM WHERE...
...WE CAN UPLOAD ALL THE PHOTOS WE WANT.
THAT'S GOOD ENOUGH...
...FOR KAGUYA SHINOMIYA.

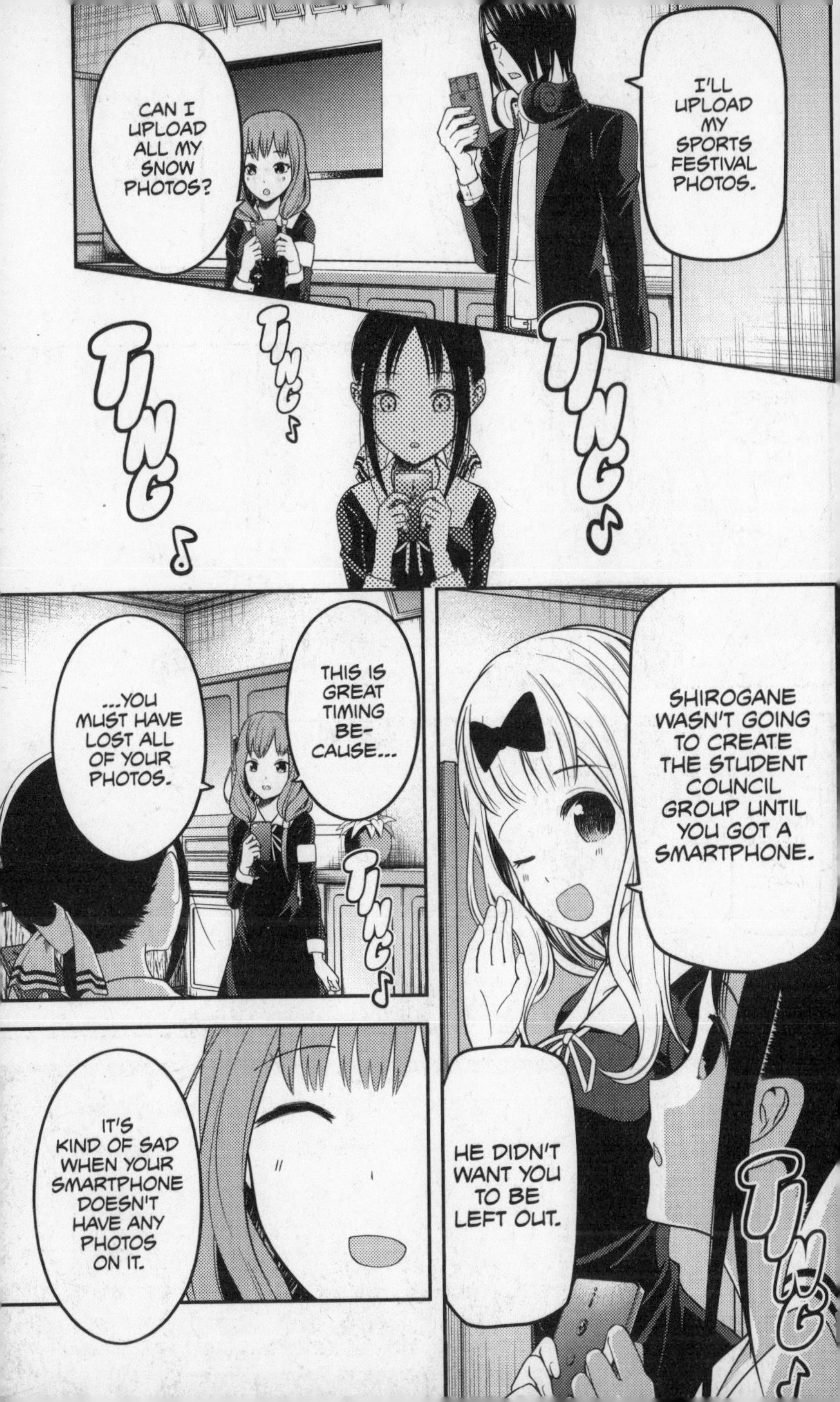
I'LL UPLOAD MY SPORTS FESTIVAL PHOTOS.
CAN I UPLOAD ALL MY SNOW PHOTOS?
TING♪
TING♪
TING♪
SHIROGANE WASN'T GOING TO CREATE THE STUDENT COUNCIL GROUP UNTIL YOU GOT A SMARTPHONE.
HE DIDN'T WANT YOU TO BE LEFT OUT.
TING♪
THIS IS GREAT TIMING BE-CAUSE...
...YOU MUST HAVE LOST ALL OF YOUR PHOTOS.
TING♪
IT'S KIND OF SAD WHEN YOUR SMARTPHONE DOESN'T HAVE ANY PHOTOS ON IT.

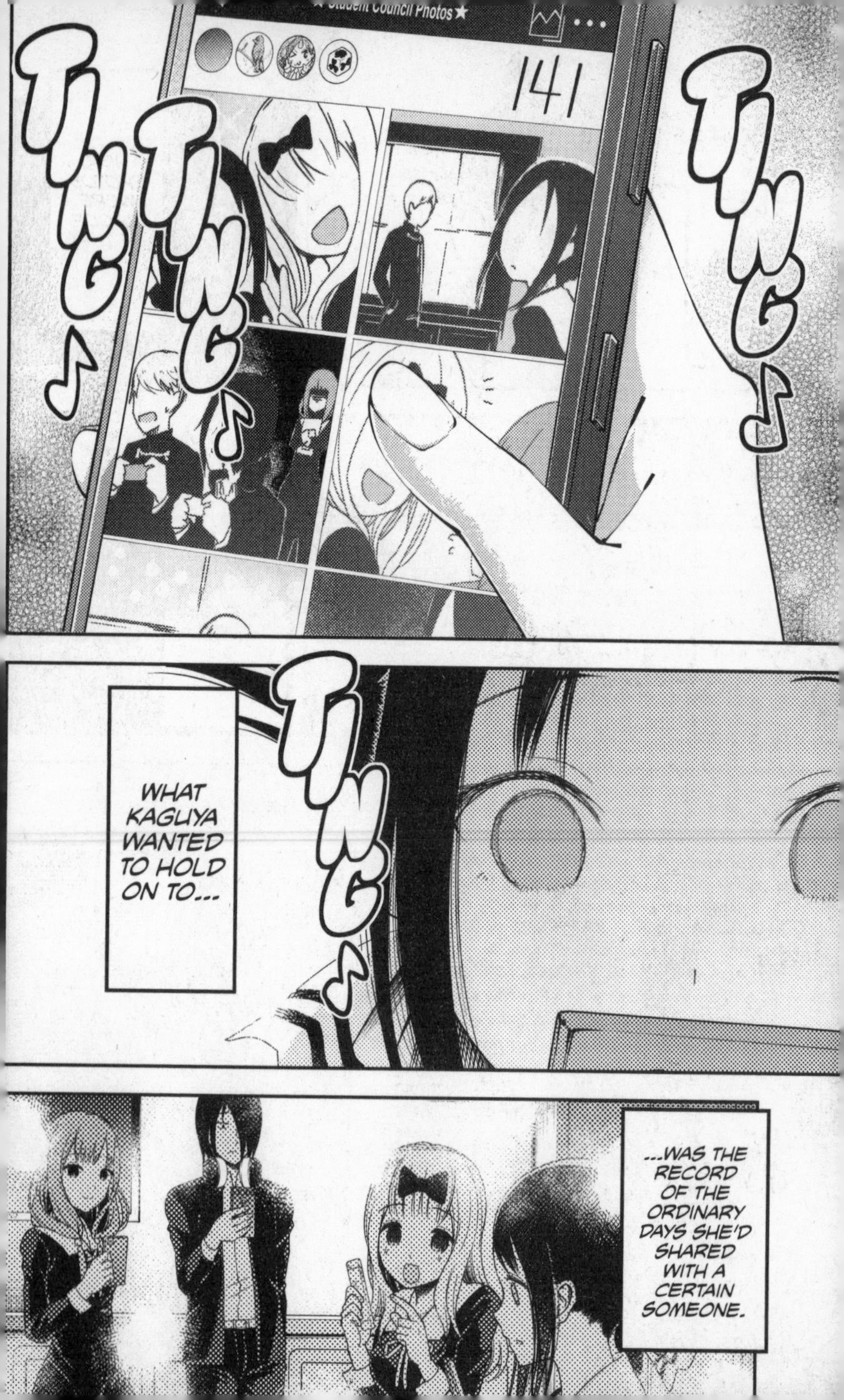
Student Council Photos★
141
TING♪
TING♪
TING♪
TING♪
WHAT KAGUYA WANTED TO HOLD ON TO...
...WAS THE RECORD OF THE ORDINARY DAYS SHE'D SHARED WITH A CERTAIN SOMEONE.

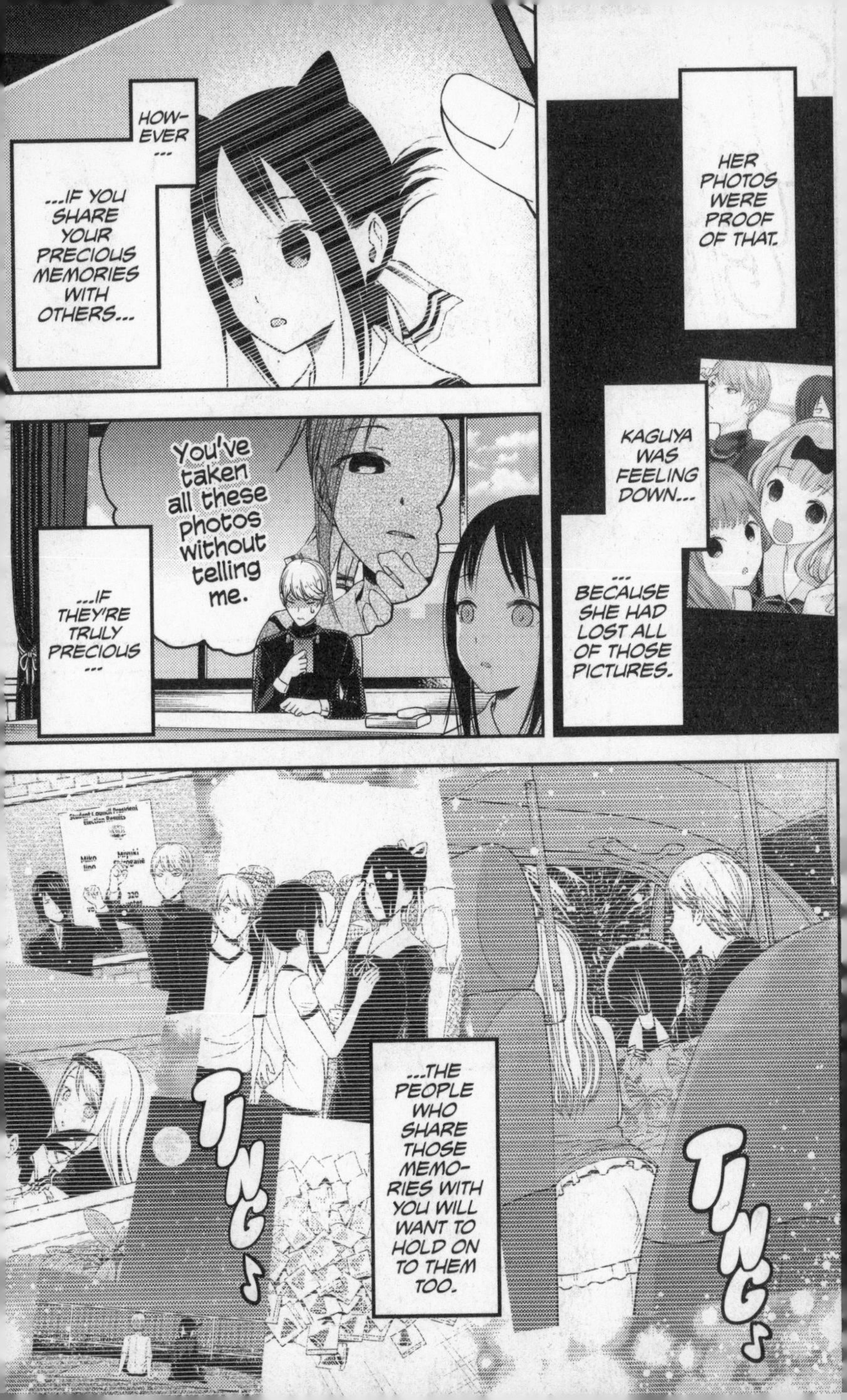
HER PHOTOS WERE PROOF OF THAT.
KAGUYA WAS FEELING DOWN...
...BECAUSE SHE HAD LOST ALL OF THOSE PICTURES.
HOW-EVER...
...IF YOU SHARE YOUR PRECIOUS MEMORIES WITH OTHERS...
You've taken all these photos without telling me.
...IF THEY'RE TRULY PRECIOUS...
TING
...THE PEOPLE WHO SHARE THOSE MEMO-RIES WITH YOU WILL WANT TO HOLD ON TO THEM TOO.
TING

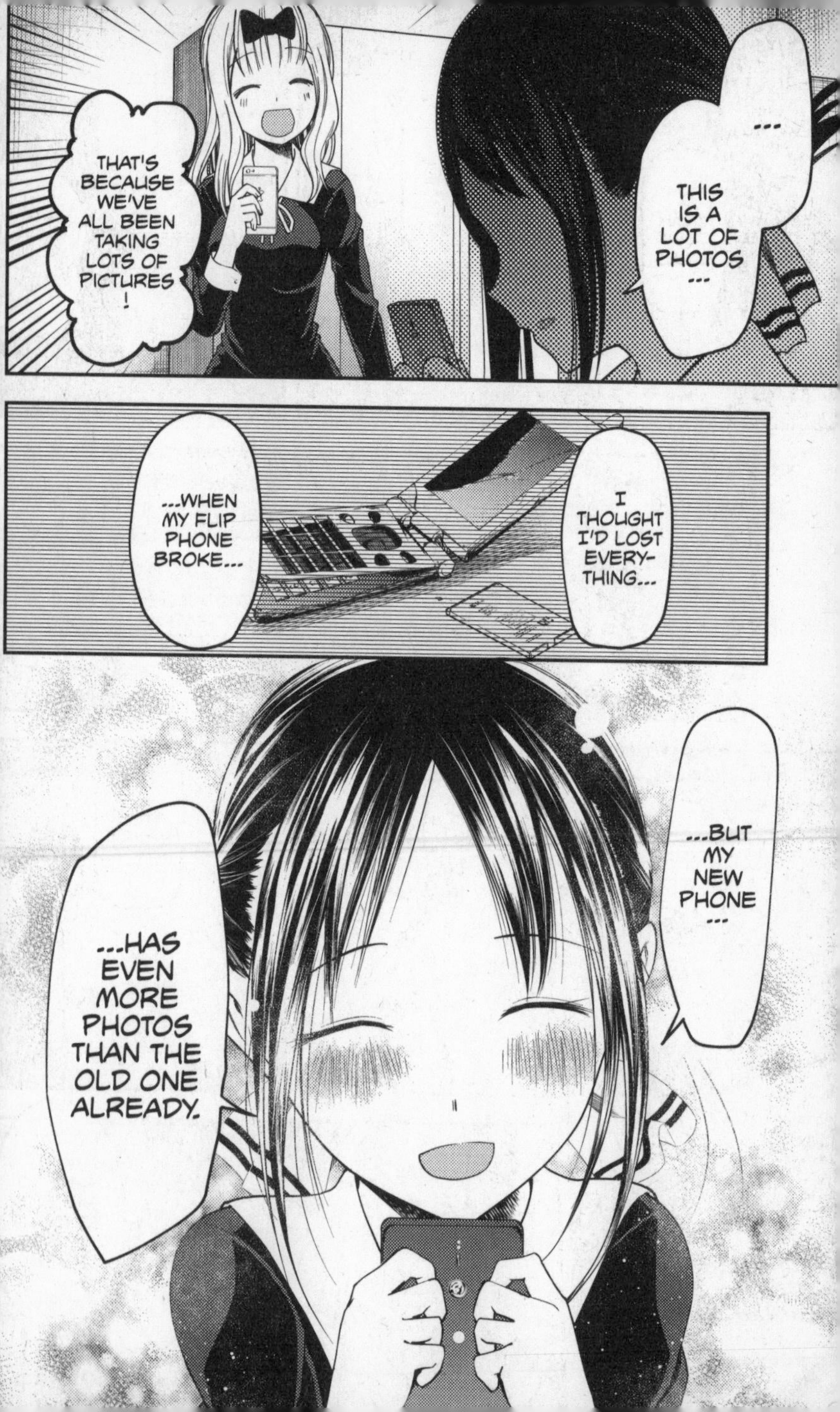
...
THIS IS A LOT OF PHOTOS...
THAT'S BECAUSE WE'VE ALL BEEN TAKING LOTS OF PICTURES!
I THOUGHT I'D LOST EVERYTHING...
...WHEN MY FLIP PHONE BROKE...
...BUT MY NEW PHONE...
...HAS EVEN MORE PHOTOS THAN THE OLD ONE ALREADY.

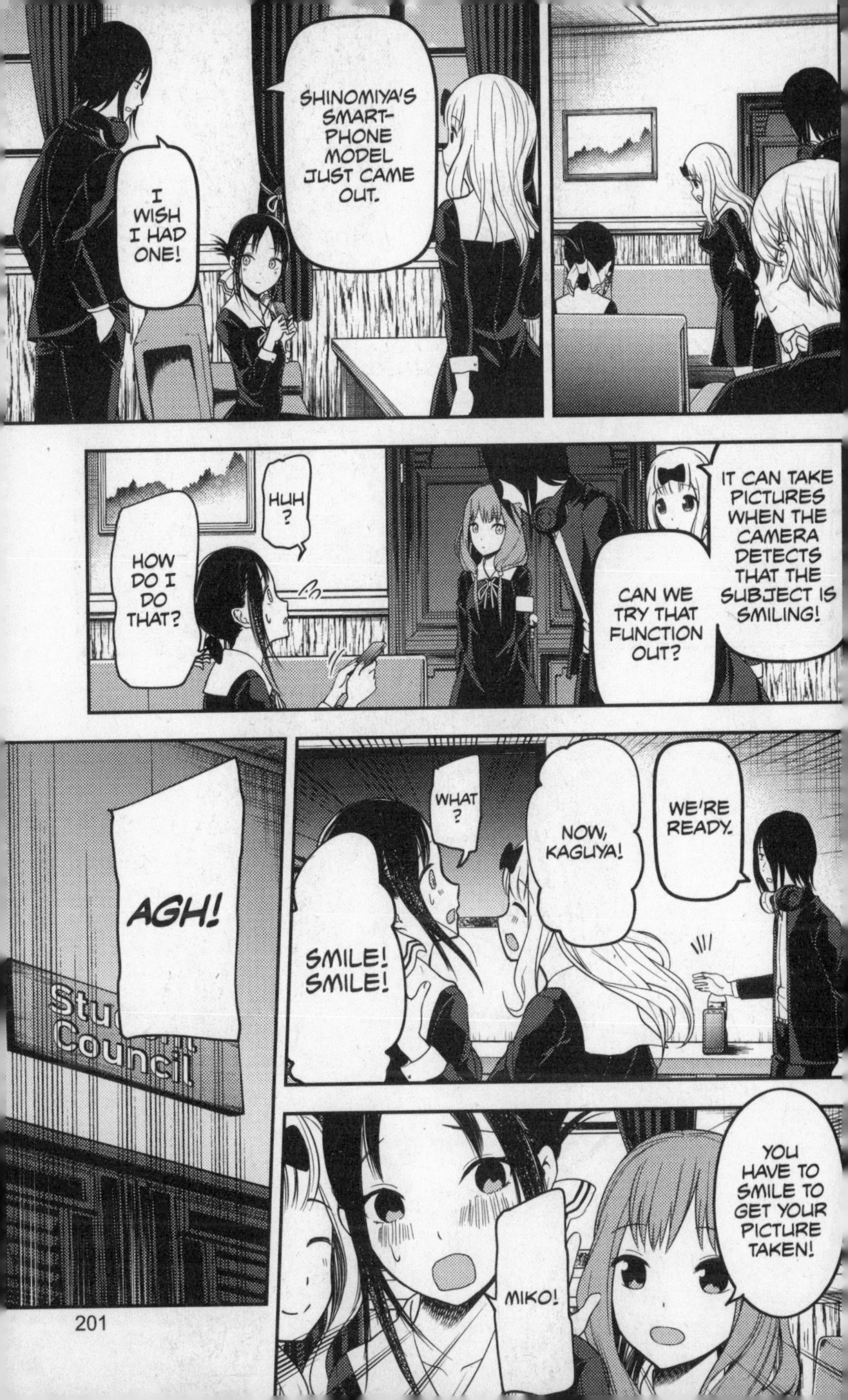

SHINOMIYA'S SMART-PHONE MODEL JUST CAME OUT.
I WISH I HAD ONE!
IT CAN TAKE PICTURES WHEN THE CAMERA DETECTS THAT THE SUBJECT IS SMILING!
CAN WE TRY THAT FUNCTION OUT?
HUH?
HOW DO I DO THAT?
WE'RE READY.
NOW, KAGUYA!
WHAT?
SMILE! SMILE!
YOU HAVE TO SMILE TO GET YOUR PICTURE TAKEN!
MIKO!
AGH!
Council

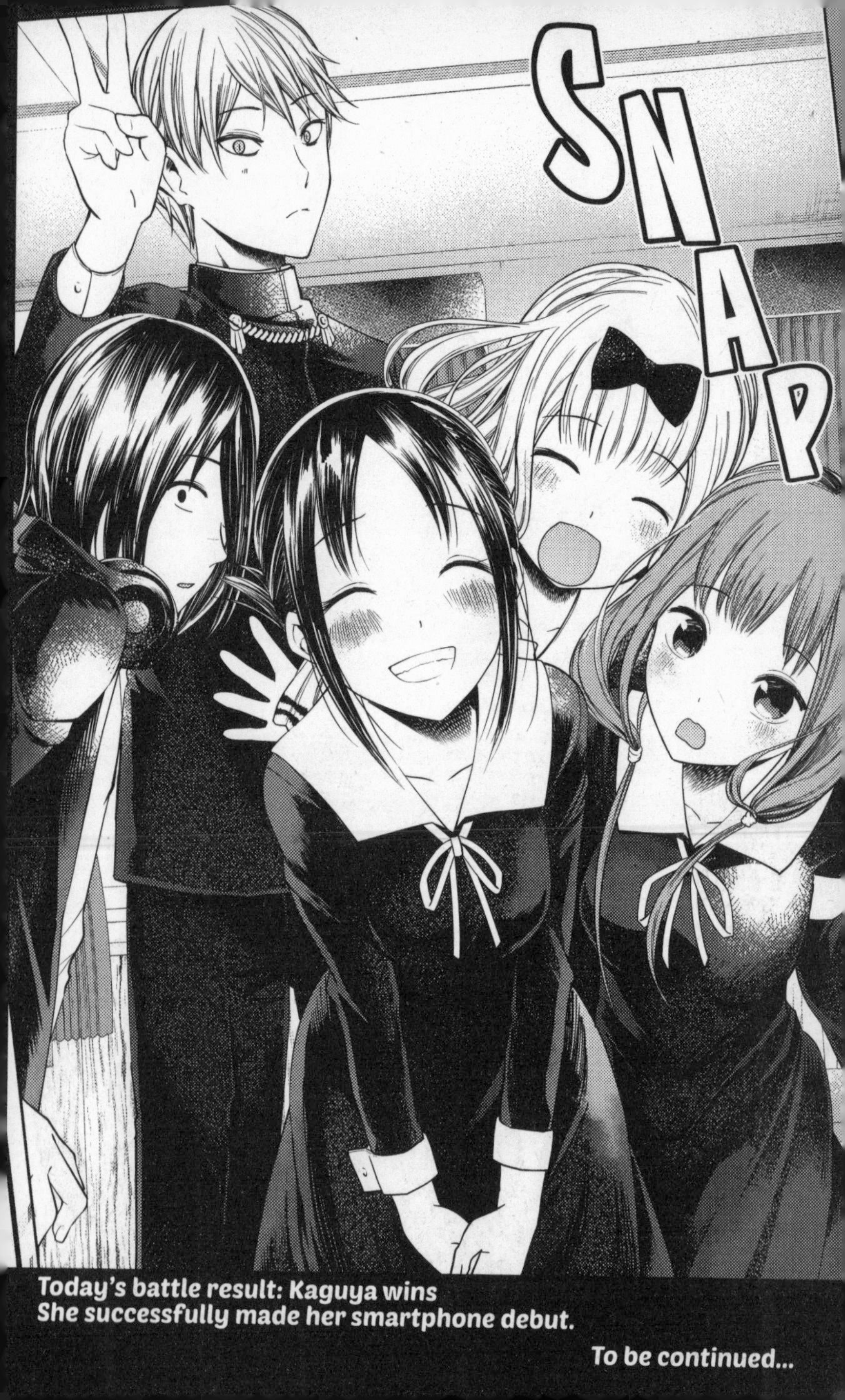
SNAP

Today's battle result: Kaguya wins
She successfully made her smartphone debut.

To be continued...

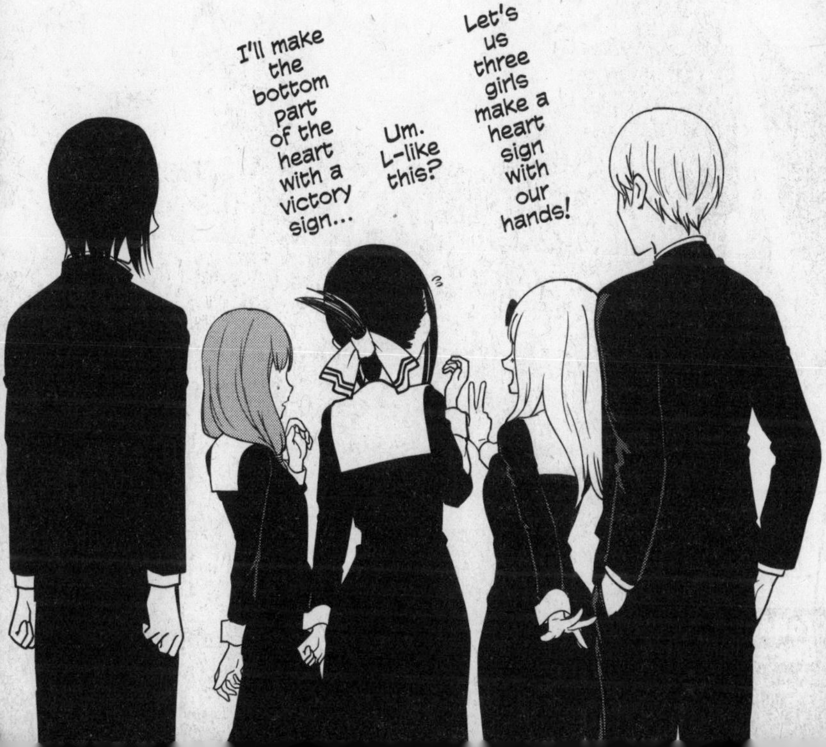
Let's us three girls make a heart sign with our hands!
Um. L-like this?
I'll make the bottom part of the heart with a victory sign...

...NEVERTHELESS, LOVE IS WHAT MAKES LIFE WORTH LIVING.

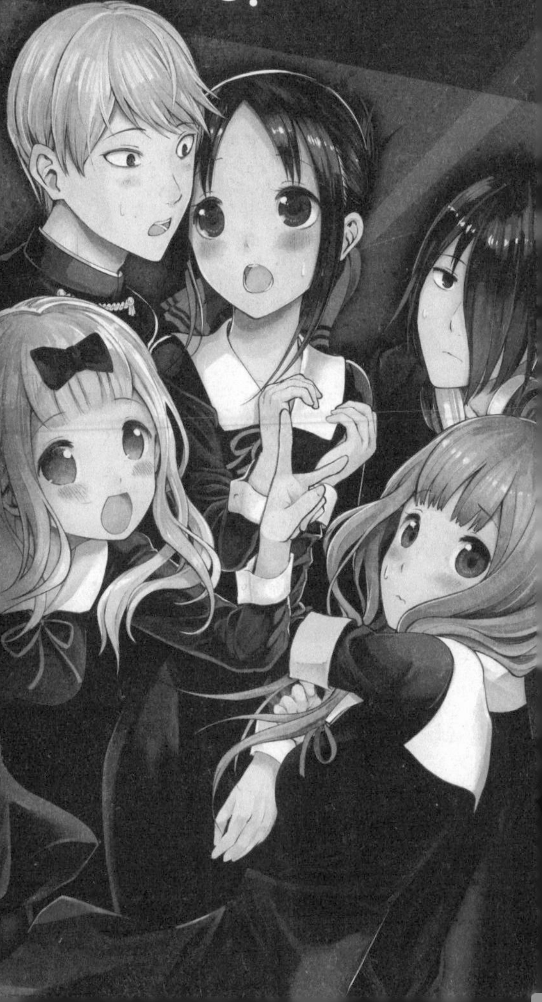

AKA AKASAKA

Aka Akasaka got his start as an assistant to Jinsei Kataoka and Kazuma Kondou, the creators of *Deadman Wonderland*. His first serialized manga was an adaptation of the light novel series *Sayonara Piano Sonata*, published by Kadokawa in 2011. *Kaguya-sama: Love Is War* began serialization in *Miracle Jump* in 2015 but was later moved to *Weekly Young Jump* in 2016 due to its popularity.

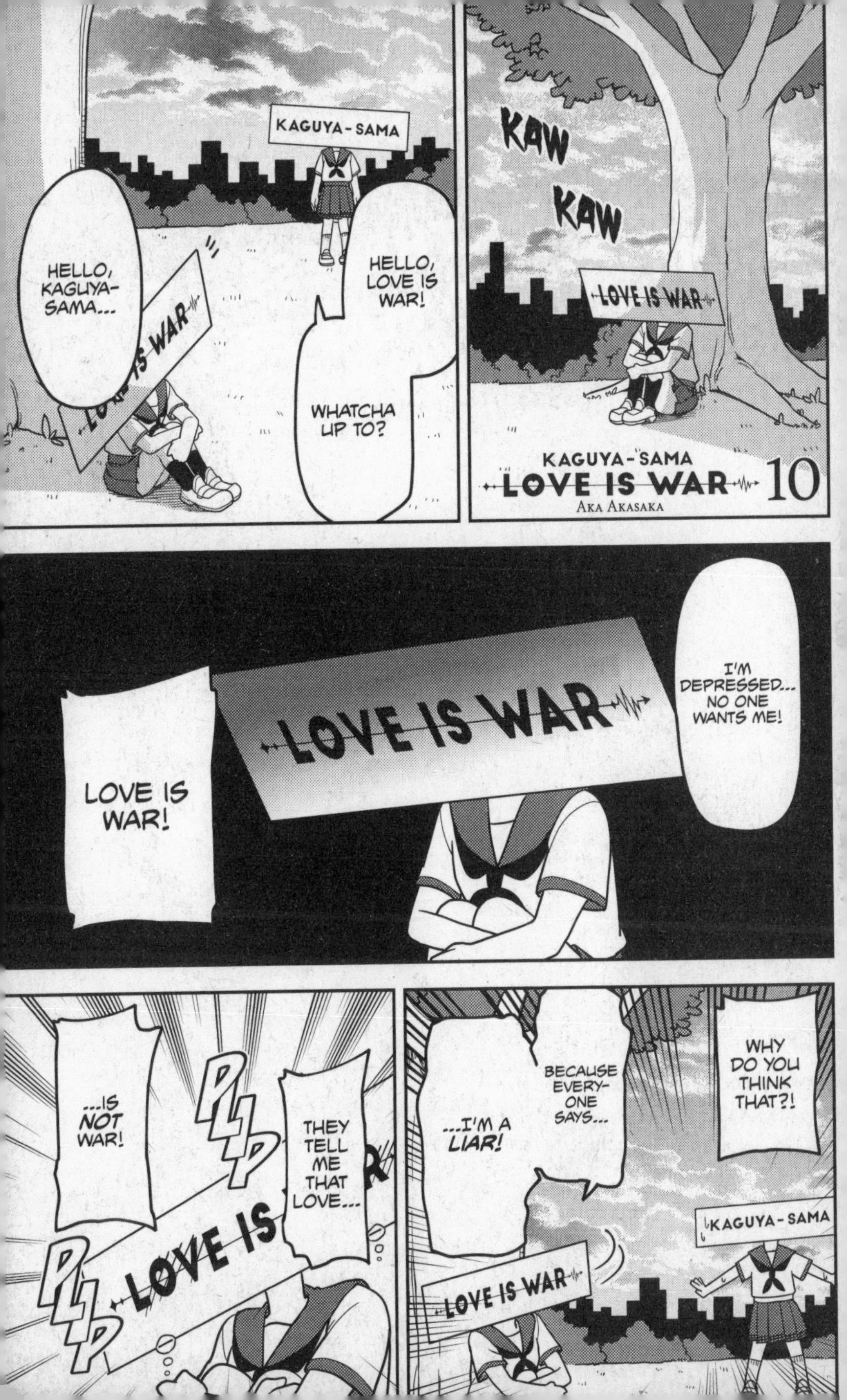

KAW
KAW
LOVE IS WAR
KAGUYA-SAMA
LOVE IS WAR 10
AKA AKASAKA
KAGUYA-SAMA
HELLO, LOVE IS WAR!
WHATCHA UP TO?
HELLO, KAGUYA-SAMA...
LOVE IS WAR
I'M DEPRESSED... NO ONE WANTS ME!
LOVE IS WAR
LOVE IS WAR!
WHY DO YOU THINK THAT?!
KAGUYA-SAMA
BECAUSE EVERY-ONE SAYS...
...I'M A *LIAR!*
LOVE IS WAR
THEY TELL ME THAT LOVE...
PLIP
PLIP
...IS *NOT* WAR!
LOVE IS

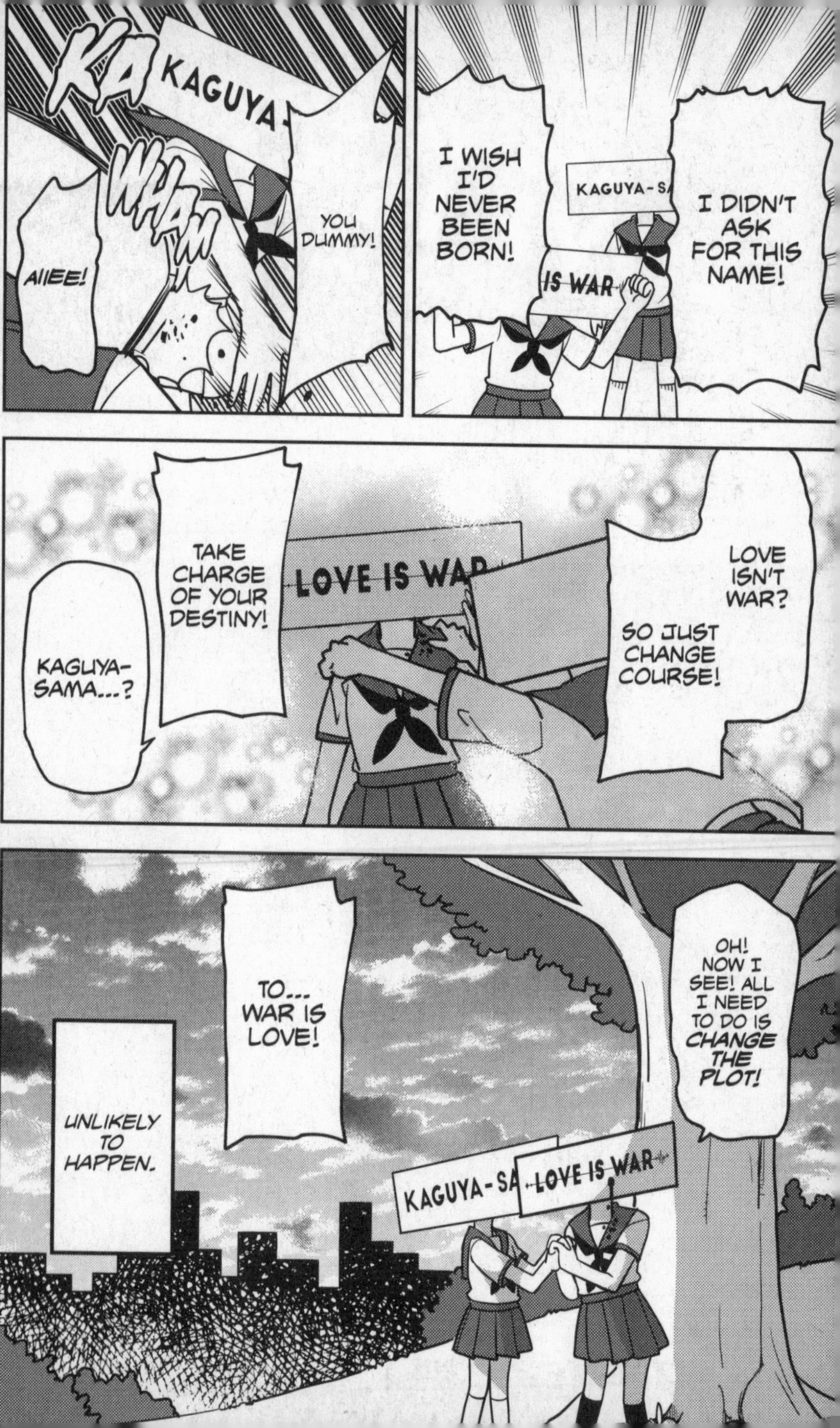
I DIDN'T ASK FOR THIS NAME!
KAGUYA-SA
I WISH I'D NEVER BEEN BORN!
IS WAR
KAGUYA-
KA
YOU DUMMY!
WHAM
AIIEE!
LOVE ISN'T WAR?
SO JUST CHANGE COURSE!
LOVE IS WAR
TAKE CHARGE OF YOUR DESTINY!
KAGUYA-SAMA...?
OH! NOW I SEE! ALL I NEED TO DO IS *CHANGE THE PLOT!*
LOVE IS WAR
KAGUYA-SA
TO... WAR IS LOVE!
UNLIKELY TO HAPPEN.

KAGUYA-SAMA
LOVE IS WAR

SHONEN JUMP MANGA EDITION

10

STORY AND ART BY
AKA AKASAKA

Translation/Tomoko Kimura
English Adaptation/Annette Roman
Touch-Up Art & Lettering/Stephen Dutro
Cover & Interior Design/Alice Lewis
Editor/Annette Roman

KAGUYA-SAMA WA KOKURASETAI~TENSAITACHI NO REN'AI ZUNO SEN~
© 2015 by Aka Akasaka
All rights reserved.
First published in Japan in 2015 by SHUEISHA Inc., Tokyo.
English translation rights arranged by SHUEISHA Inc.

Printed in Canada

Published by VIZ Media, LLC
P.O. Box 77010
San Francisco, CA 94107

10 9 8 7 6 5 4 3 2 1
First printing, September 2019

COMING NEXT VOLUME

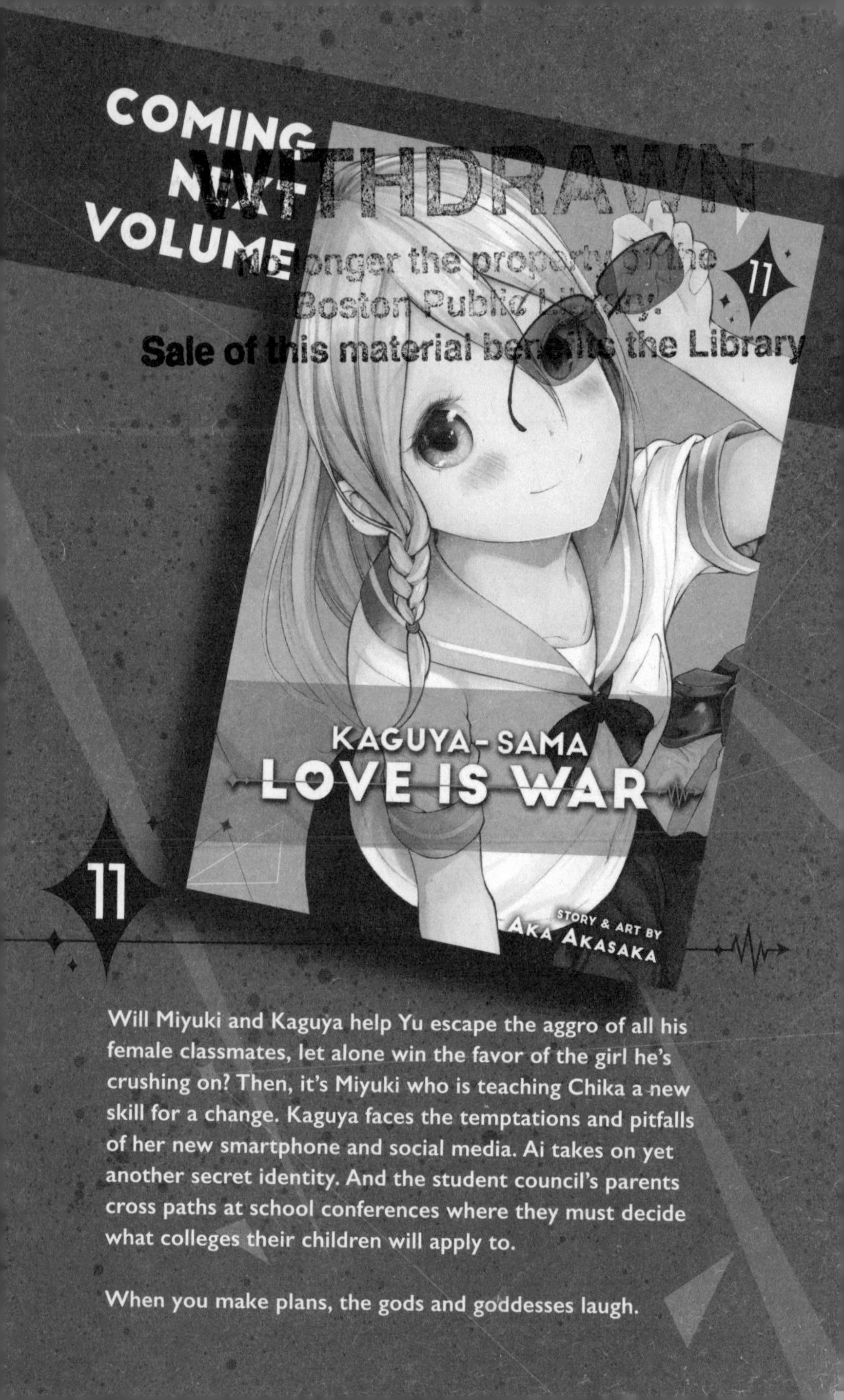
11
KAGUYA-SAMA
LOVE IS WAR
STORY & ART BY
AKA AKASAKA

Will Miyuki and Kaguya help Yu escape the aggro of all his female classmates, let alone win the favor of the girl he's crushing on? Then, it's Miyuki who is teaching Chika a new skill for a change. Kaguya faces the temptations and pitfalls of her new smartphone and social media. Ai takes on yet another secret identity. And the student council's parents cross paths at school conferences where they must decide what colleges their children will apply to.

When you make plans, the gods and goddesses laugh.